The Political Dimensions
of Religion

SUNY Series in Near Eastern Studies
Said Amir Arjomand, Editor

THE POLITICAL
DIMENSIONS
of RELIGION

Edited by

Said Amir Arjomand

STATE UNIVERSITY OF NEW YORK PRESS

Published by
State University of New York Press, Albany

Printed in the United States of America

For information, address State University of New York Press,
State University Plaza, Albany, N.Y., 12246

Production by Cathleen Collins
Marketing by Theresa A. Swierzowsky

Library of Congress Cataloging in Publication Data

The Political dimensions of religion / edited by Said Amir Arjomand.
    p.   cm. — (SUNY series in Near Eastern studies)
    Includes bibliographical references and index.
    ISBN 0-7914-1557-0. — ISBN 0-7914-1558-9 (pbk.)
    1. Religion and politics. 2. Religion and state.   I. Arjomand,
Said Amir. II. Series.
BL65.P7P635 1993
291.1'77—dc20   92-28757
                                              CIP

10 9 8 7 6 5 4 3 2 1

To my new friend, Manuel Sarkisyanz, a kindred spirit, on the occasion of his seventieth birthday, and in recognition and admiration of his work.

Contents

Contributors

Said Amir Arjomand is Professor of Sociology at the State University of New York at Stony Brook. His books include *The Shadow of God and the Hidden Imam* (University of Chicago Press, 1984) and *The Turban for the Crown* (Oxford University Press, 1988).

José Casanova is Assistant Professor of Sociology at the Graduate Faculty of the New School for Social Research. He is presently working on comparative Studies of democratization in Eastern Europe, Southern Europe and Latin America. Among his forthcoming works are *Public Religions in the Modern World* (University of Chicago Press) and *The Opus Dei Ethic and the Modernidation of Spain.*

Javier Diaz-Albertini is an Associate Professor at the University of Lima in Peru, and a Ph.D. candidate at the State University of New York at Stony Brook. He is the author of *La Promoción urbana: balance y desafíos* (Lima, 1989), and the co-editor of *Estrategias de vida en el sector urbano popular* (Lima, 1987).

S. N. Eisenstadt is Professor of Sociology at the Hebrew University of Jerusalem, Foreign Honorary Fellow of the American Academy of Arts and Sciences, and the recipient of the Balzan Prize for Sociology in 1988. His many books include *The Political Systems of Empires* (Free Press, 1963), *Revolutions and the Transformation of Societies* (Free Press, 1978), and the edited volume, *Origins and Diversity of Axial Age Civilizations* (State University of New York Press, 1986).

Karen E. Fields teaches at the Frederick Douglass Institute for African and African-American Studies of the University of Rochester.

She is the author of *Revival and Rebellion in Colonial Central Africa* (Princeton University Press, 1985), and the co-author, with Mamie Garvin Fields, of *Lemon Swamp and Other Places: A Carolina Memoir* (Free Press, 1983).

Martin Riesebrodt is Associate Professor of Sociology and in the Divinity School of the University of Chicago. His main interests are in classical social theory, especially the work of Max Weber, and in comparative and historical sociology. He is the author of *Pious Passion: The Emergence of Modern Fundamentalism in the United States and Iran* (University of California Press, 1993).

Manuel Sarkisyanz is Professor of Political Science of Southeast Asia at the University of Heidelberg. His extensive publications include *Rußland und der Messianismus des Orients* (Tübingen: Mohr, 1955), *Buddhist Backgrounds of the Burmese Revolution* (The Hague: Nijhoff, 1965) and *Vom Wirken und Sterben des Felipe Carrillo Puerto, des "Roten" Apostels der Maya-Indianer* (Heidelberg: Winter, 1991).

Steven M. Tipton teaches sociology and ethics at Emory University and its Candler School of Theology. He is co-author of *Habits of the Heart* (University of California Press, 1985) and *The Good Society* (Knopf, 1991), and author of *Getting Saved from the Sixties* (University of California Press, 1982).

Preface

When the president of the American Sociological Association, William Julius Wilson, asked me to organize a thematic session on religion and politics for the 1990 annual convention of the association, the thought occurred to me that the theme of religion and politics had been globally topical for over a decade, and yet there were no compelling analytical statements on it. In the hope of stimulating such statements, I organized a small gathering of experts with a broad conception of the field on August 12, 1990, in Washington, D.C., immediately following the ASA thematic session. This volume grew out of the lively discussion at that gathering, which indicated that the intricate relationship between religion and politics was nevertheless analytically tractable. I wish to express my gratitude to those who participated in that gathering, and to R. Scott Appleby, associate director of the Fundamentalism Project of the American Academy of Arts and Sciences, for hosting it.

I am also grateful to the editor of the *Journal of Asian History* for his permission to reporduce, in modified form in Chapter 8, the article of M. Sarkisyanz, "On the Place of Caodaism, Culturally and Politically," published in that journal, vol. 18 (1984); and to the editors of the *International Political Science Review* for their permission to include in Chapter 9 material previously published in my article "History, Structure and Revolution in the Shi'ite Tradition in Contemporary Iran," in vol. 10, no. 2 (1989) of their journal. Finally, I wish to thank the chair of the Department of Sociology at the State University of New York at Stony Brook, Professor Andrea Tyree, for covering the cost of the index.

Pfaffenweiler, Baden
Stony Brook, Long Island

xi

Introduction

Definition and Mutual Delimitation of Religion and Politics

Religion, the conscious reflection of the constitution of order in nature and society, is one of the oldest institutions of humankind. Politics, the art and science of government, has a narrower scope and is not of the same antiquity. At the most fundamental level, politics subsists in religion. The reflection of the act of foundation of political order in consciousness is pure religion; and political action merges with religion to the extent that it approaches the foundation of order.

A useful distinction has recently been made between "absolute" politics and routine politics. Absolute politics has been defined as the state of affairs where no boundaries are set to political will, and everything social is seen as transformable by politics.[1] It is the refusal to accept the extablished order and to recognize any of its boundaries that gives absolute politics ultimacy, and hence a religious character. The possibility of absolute politics also points to potential tension between religion and politics. The symbolization of order and the normative governance of action are central to both these human ventures. This makes them, in Field's words, "dynamic claimants to the fundamental organizatin of collective life."[2]

The coexistence of religious and secular normative orders, the differentiation of the religious and the political spheres, and the international interpenetration of diverse traditions, make the relationship between religion and politics highly complex. For one thing, it is necessary to distinguish between different kinds of politics and different senses of religion. The distinction between absolute and routine politics has already been mentioned. An

1

analogous distinction between two meanings of religion must also be maintained. In Chapter 1, S. N. Eisenstadt thus posits a fundamental distinction between religion in the broad sense of the basic premises of social order, and religion as devotional and ritual beliefs and practices in the narrow modern sense. This corresponds to Steven M. Tipton's distinction, in Chapter 11, between the "civic" and the "liberal" construals of religious freedom as defined by the American Constitution. Cross-cutting this general distinction are the culturally specific differences among the historical religions concerning the symbolization of order.

The distinction between the religious and the political vanishes when the fundamental premises of the established order are actively challenged. This point is central to Karen E. Fields' analysis of the shift from order to millennial action in Chapter 7. The same fusion of the political into the religious dimension is found in Manuel Sarkisyanz's chapter (5) on millennial myths, and my own analysis of Shi'ite millennialism in Chapter 9.

Under routine circumstances, however, the diversity of normative orders implies distinction and differentiation between the religious and the political spheres. Needless to say, this differentiation is a matter of degree. As these spheres overlap, a phenomenon may have a primary religious and a secondary political aspect, or vice versa. It is therefore important to determine, in each concrete event and movement, which of our two categories makes up the cake and which the icing. Taking "political action" and "religious action" for limited instances of complete mutual independence, implying disjunction of the religious and the political spheres, I have proposed the terms *politically relevant religious action, religiously conditioned political action, religiously relevant political action*, and *politically conditioned religious action* to capture the range of varying relationships in what is ambiguously described as religiopolitical.[3] More challenging than such scholastic categorization, however, is substantive analysis of the relationship between religion and politics in concrete historical cases, which is the subject matter of the essays offered in this volume.

Order and action constitute the modalities of political life; religion is closely related to the foundations of political order, and to a variety of forms of political action. The focus of the essays in Part I is on the political order, while the ones in Part II focus on political action. Part III, finally, deals with the normative contentions that inevitably stem from the diversity of competing orders in the contemporary world. In what follows, I will briefly introduce each essay individually, leaving the discussion of the surprising connection between normative order and millennial utopia, and of the broader implications of these chapters for our theme of diversity of moral orders for a more systematic treatment in Chapter 2.

Religion, Order, and Pluralism

Although a most ancient institution, religion was not destined to maintain its dominion over the symbolization of order unchallenged. With the institutionalization of transcendence in the world religions of salvation and in philosophy, it became possible to distinguish between the actual and the ideal order, and established religions were forced to combat and/or accommodate competing normative orders. In Chapter 1, Eisenstadt offers a historical panorama of cultural diversity across the world religions and civilizations. He assesses the importance of heterodoxies and sects as forces of social transformation in the "Axial Age civilizations." These heterodoxies and sectarian movements arise from within the world religions but nevertheless offer alternative normative orders on the basis of reinterpretation of fundamental values of their respective traditions. Conflicts between orthodoxy and heterodoxies, between the establishment and sectarianism, result in cultural-political reconstruction and thus in the transformation of civilizations. Normative pluralism is thus built into the civilizational dynamics of the world religions.

In Chapter 2, I try to separate what is general from what is culturally specific in the relationship between religion and political order. The general element is the cosmological myth: society as the analogue of the cosmos. As a component of the cosmological myth, sacral kingship can be seen as symbolization of the principle of sociocosmic unity (and *not* as the justification of personal, arbitrary exercise of power, or attribution of personal charisma to the king). I underline the astonishing ability of the cosmological myth to survive the onslaught of the world religions of salvation, and to persist in the modified form of a variety of civil theologies in all major civilizations. In addition, two sets of culturally specific patterns of diversity are identified. The first set is due to the fact that supreme religious authority can supply the model for supreme political authority, and that notions of religious authority differ among the world religions of salvation. Second, there is one particular cultural pattern that is central to our issue—the Greek conception of the political order as a self-contained sphere for the realization of transcendent truth, the truth, this time, not of revelation but of reason. This pattern was destined to spread throughout the world; and its differential accommodation/reception in different religio-cultural traditions account for the second—and more consequential—culturally specific variation in normative patterns, or political ethics. In the second half of the chapter, I turn to the analysis of millennial beliefs only to discover an unexpected connection between order and utopia, between sacral kingship and millennial soteriology.

The world religions have had to face the competition not only of philosophy but also of the survivals of pre-Axial Age normative orders. These competing "secular" normative orders progressively narrowed the sphere of religion in the course of history. This process of secularization has gone furthest in the West, and has resulted in considerable "privatization" of religion. But it would be a grave mistake to assume, as is commonly done, that the pluralism of normative orders is the exclusive characteristic of the modern West. Normative pluralism, albeit of varying degree, is in fact a distinctive mark of historical civilizations that are presented in Chapter 2 as products of the commingling of diverse cultural traditions. These traditions contain multiple truths that make normative diversity their distinct, albeit unacknowledged feature. Not only do our political cultures contain both general elements and those based on culturally specific ideas of transcendence, but the public representation of transcendent truth itself is a matter of contention within each religiocultural tradition. The very fact of this normative pluralism itself, I argue, has normative consequences. Modernity, I contend, should consist in the explicit acknowledgment of the diversity of moral orders and its elevation to a normative principle.

Constitutions are considered the foundations of political order in the modern world. In Chapter 3, I examine two important stages in the reception of constitutionalism in the Islamic world by comparing constitution-making in an old monarchy, Iran, in 1906–1907, and in the new state of Pakistan in the late 1940s and early 1950s. The study compares Western Christianity as the original matrix of constitutionalism with contemporary Islam as its receptacle, and serves as an illustration of the diversification of political ethics and the normative order through the transmission of an international political tradition.

Political order consists not only in the regulation of political authority, but also in the constitution of the political community. In this connection, it should be pointed out that the world religions generally allowed for political integration, irrespective of their specific political ethics. Eisenstadt notes this consequence with respect to Japanese Buddhism in Chapter 1. In Japan, as another observer put it,"whereas Shinto was related to the authority structure of the clan, Buddhism helped turn the attention of the people toward the capital and the imperial court."[4] Similarly, when a Polish state was resuscitated in 1918 in a country divided among Russia, Prussia, and Austria in the eighteenth century, the nationwide organization and supraethnic and supralocal orientation of the Catholic Church enabled it to act as an agent of national integration.[5] G. M. Thomas has underlined the importance of religious revivalism in nineteenth-century America for nation-building in the absence of a centralized state.[6] In Chapter 4, José Casanova, by contrast, traces the important contribution of the Catholic Church to nation-building in competition with a hostile, atheistic, centralized state.

Traditionally, the study of the relation between religion and the state has focused on the interface between the church and the state, and has largely been the domain of the historians. While by no means neglecting the importance of the state, Casanova additionally brings into focus the church's interface with the nation and with civil society. Although concretely overlapping, these notions are analytically distinct; and Casanova demonstrates the utility of keeping them separate. He compares the historical patterns of church-state, church-nation, and church-civil society relations in Spain and Poland. The lasting consequences of specific historical contingencies within the same branch of Christianity stand out with particular clarity. Casanova shows how these historical contingencies have led to the predominant orientation of the church toward civil society in Spain, with greater consequent privatization of religion, in contrast to the more emphatically national orientation of the Catholic Church in Poland.

Religion and Political Action

In Part II, we move from the constitution of order to the motivation of action. Religion can, in a variety of ways and under various circumstances, provide a source of normative guidance for political action. Millennialism is perhaps the most dramatic instance of the religious motivation of revolutionary action, and one of the oldest forms of absolute politics. Millennial beliefs motivate political action by upholding utopia, ideal order to be realized by revolutionary action.

In Chapter 5, Sarkisyanz describes the Andean cosmogonic myth of eternal return and its combination with Christian apocalyptic expectations in Peru, and documents its resurfacing in the twentieth century. He then takes us to the other side of the Pacific to survey the more Catholic type of millennialism in the Philippines in the nineteenth and twentieth centuries which, nonetheless, draws on the same general archetype of lost primeval bliss as a utopia to guide political action. Chapter 6 by Javier Diaz-Albertini serves as a supplement to Chapter 5 by covering the apocalyptic cult of violence in Peru's Shining Path.

In her noted study of millenarianism three decades ago, Y. Talmon stated: "Perhaps the most important thing about millenarism is its *attitude towards time*. . . . It is a sudden and revolutionary leap onto a totally different level of existence."[7] In Chapter 7, Fields turns to this crucial issue and, drawing on her work on Central Africa, analyzes the political consequences of the millennial conception of time. In Central Africa in the present century, we find a correlation between the loss of chiefly authority and the rise of messianic prophetism in the 1920s,[8] which is reminiscent of the parallel correlation in ancient Judaism between the crisis of monarchy and demise of the northern kingdom (Israel) and the flourishing of canonical prophecy.[9] Millenarianism, Fields argues, intensifies the sense of historical movement toward a goal, or indeed the very goal-directedness denoted by our sociological concept of "action," and does so in defiance of the established order, which is embodied in our sociological notion of "structure." It should be noted further that the millenarian denial of structure does not stop at the level of social order but descends to the cosmological level.[10] In the apocalyptic literature, no distinction is made between revolution in nature and revolution in society. Fields shows how metaphors about time order and structure attitudes and action. The political order is premised on a cyclical understanding of time, which is rejected by the millenarian. The cyclical time metaphor of orthodox theology, which corresponds to the sociological concept of structure, induces obedience to worldly law and authority, while the millenarian metaphor, by accentuating the present in the light of a transcendent vision, stimulated goal-directed antinomian action now or soon!

It should be noted that despite their essentially liminal character underlined by Fields, millennial patterns are also culturally specific. Millenarian movements, even when they present themselves as revolutionary, "remain attached to the very tradition they want to break."[11] Culturally specific millennial patterns and their transformations are the subject of the remaining chapters in Part II. In Chapter 8, Sarkisyanz shows how the millenarian yearning can be harnessed by a colonized people in its search for authenticity in order to produce alternative normative orders in response to alien cultural domination. He explains how the cultural crisis of the

Vietnamese urban elite, produced by French domination and the threat of social dissolution it posed, stimulated Caodàism, the movement of the Great Way of the Third Epoch of Salvation. Caodàism, founded in 1926, was a major movement in the Vietnamese revolution. Its students have generated one of the liveliest current debates in the social sciences in the United States, namely, the controversy between the respective proponents of "rational choice" and "normal economy."[12] In view of the fact that these two approaches, despite their value, are reductionist, it is refreshing to be reminded of the religious integrity and the cultural dimensions of this major Vietnamese social movement.[13]

The compatibility and interchangeability of religion and revolution, which is touched upon by Sarkisyanz, are the subjects of the subsequent chapter by myself. In modern societies where a plurality of indigenous and imported normative orders prevail, albeit inconsistently, millennialism is unlikely to unfold in massive revolutionary action without modification, and without subserving a variety of structural factors. In Chapter 6, Diaz-Albertini describes the modernization of the Andean millennial belief through their amalgamation with Maoist Marxism in contemporary Peru. In Chapter 9, I compare the pure Shi'ite millenarianism of the Babi movement in the mid-nineteenth century with the transmutation of the millenarian motif into the myth of revolution in twentieth-century Iran.

The contribution of transformed millennial beliefs to the Islamic revolution of 1979 is then put alongside other normative and structural factors, most notably the structure of religious authority. The outcome of the conflict between the Shi'ite hierocracy and the Iranian state is as dramatic as that of the much more prolonged investiture contest between the popes and the emperors in Western Christendom. In line with our general theme of normative diversity, I conclude that the paradoxical result of the Islamic revolution has been increased normative pluralism in the Shi'ite tradition as a consequence of the absorption of the legal underpinnings of the modern state.

Normative Contentions

Normative pluralism, documented for all major religiocultural traditions in Part I, makes contrary normative contentions, and conflicts arising therefrom, endemic. The two essays in Part III explore some of these contentions in the contemporary world.

The subject of Chapter 10 by Martin Riesebrodt is the normative contentions of the fundamentalists concerning the role of women in society. He draws our attention to two paradoxes: that in "patriarchal fundamentalism," as instanced by Shi'ite fundamentalism in Iran and Protestant fundamentalism in the United States, women are mobilized to advocate what to Western observers seems to be their own repression; and that they are mobilized in the public sphere to assure that their role remains a private one. We are dealing here with the unintended consequences of religiously motivated action that inevitably takes place in a political, secular environment. The greater autonomy of women's organizations and women's greater participation in higher education are adduced as the two factors likely to subvert the goal of retraditionalization of women's roles in the United States in comparison to Iran. Riesebrodt's explanation of the different outcomes of the two cases of mobilization also hinges on the relations of power between the fundamentalists and their political environment, or more precisely, on the nonhegemonic position of the Protestant fundamentalists in the United States as compared to the hegemonic position of the Shi'ite traditionalists in Iran. These differences notwithstanding, Riesebrodt concludes that monistic thrust of religious fundamentalism is likely to miscarry in a pluralistic modern world with powerful secular trends. Referring to the well-known sociological categories of "church," "sect," and "denomination," he suggests a "denominational"—that is, optional—model of gender relations as the most appropriate to a culture of pluralism.

If I have been right in stressing the diversity and multiplicity of political ethics throughout the world, the ambiguity of the American polity, which is the subject of Chapter 11 by Tipton, is not atypical. In determining the place of religion in American public life, Tipton shows how both the liberal social philosophers and their communitarian critics err in assuming a value-consensus in American society. The thrust of his own argument is that it is possible to have a moral community without consensus.[14] The number of normative political traditions shown by Tipton to be currently in contention and dialogue in America may be larger than in premodern times, but the fact of diversity and pluralism itself is not exceptional. On the contrary, his analysis of normative pluralism in the contemporary American polity is an apt conclusion to our theme of the intra- and cross-cultural diversity of the political dimensions of religion.

Notes

1. A. Pizzorno, "Politics Unbounded," in C. S. Maier, ed., *Changing Boundaries of the Political* (Cambridge: Cambridge University Press, 1987), p. 27.
2. See Chapter 7, below.
3. S. A. Arjomand, *The Shadow of God and the Hidden Imam: Religion, Political Order and Societal Change in Shi'ite Iran from the Beginning to 1890* (Chicago: University of Chicago Press, 1984), pp. 18–19.
4. R. Bendix, *Kings or People: Power and the Mandate to Rule* (Berkeley and Los Angeles: University of California Press, 1978), p. 68.
5. M. Osa, "Resistance, Persistence and Change: The Transformation of the Catholic Church in Poland," *Eastern European Politics and Society* 3, no. 2 (1989): 268–299.
6. G. M. Thomas, "Revivalism, Nation-Building and Institutional Change," in G. M. Thomas et al., *Institutional Structure* (London: Sage, 1987), pp. 308–309.
7. Y. Talmon, "The Pursuit of the Millennium: The Relation Between Religion and Social Change," reprinted from the *European Journal of Sociology*, 3 (1962), in N. Birnbaum and G. Lenzer, eds., *Sociology of Religion* (Englewood Cliffs, N. J.: Prentice-Hall, 1969), p. 240.
8. J. M. Janzen, "Deep Thought: Structure and Intention in Kongo Prophetism, 1910–1921," *Social Research* (1979): 106–136.
9. According to MacGaffey, the messianic crisis was in part produced by the refusal of the European administrators to be cast in the chiefly role. See W. MacGaffey, *Custom and Government in the Lower Congo* (Berkeley and Los Angeles: University of California Press, 1970).
10. See Chapter 2, below.
11. M. I. Pereira de Queiroz, *Réformes et révolutions dans les sociétés traditionnelles: histoire et ethnologie des mouvements messianiques* (Paris: Anthropos, 1968), p. 166.
12. S. L. Popkin, *The Rational Peasant: The Political Economy of Rural Society in Vietnam* (Berkeley and Los Angeles: University of California Press, 1979); cf. J. C. Scott, *The Moral Economy of Peasant Rebellions and Subsistence in Southeast Asia* (New Haven: Yale University Press, 1976).
13. It is equally salubrious as a corrective to some current views on "peasant revolutions" to be reminded of the urban provenience of the movement.
14. Those interested in sociological theory will note here that Simmel scores a point against Durkheim.

Part I

Religion and the Institution of Order

1

Religion and the Civilizational Dimensions of Politics

S. N. Eisenstadt

Introduction

It has long been recognized that religious groups and organizations have played a very important role in the political process in most societies, especially in the more developed ones, such as the great empires in which they constituted relatively autonomous social organizations and political actions. It has also been recognized that under some conditions, groups, expecially heterodoxies can be a major factor of social change. This was, of course, the leitmotif of Weber's comparative sociology of the world religions.

What has been less recognized or fully confronted are some other implications of Weber's analysis—namely, that at least in the historical civilizations, religions provided some components of the broader civilizational premises and frameworks, and this partly determined the ways in which religious activities and organizations became related to political processes.

The fact that in most historical civilizations the basic premises were couched in religious terms made it difficult to distinguish between the two analytical aspects of the world religions: those aspects that constituted components of the basic cultural or civilizational frameworks of their societies, and, on the other hand, those aspects that, from a later "secular" perspective, could be designated as specifically religious—above all patterns of belief, ritual and worship. This chapter illustrates the importance of this analytical distinction by focusing on a central problem of classical sociology of religion—namely, the relation between sectarian groups with potentially heterodox orientations and the processes of social change in different societies.

Heterodoxies in Axial Civilizations

Axial Age civilizations[1] (to use Karl Jasper's nomenclature) are those civilizations that crystallized during the millennium after 500 B.C., when new types of ontological visions, of conceptions of a basic tension between the transcendental and mundane orders emerged and were institutionalized in many parts of the world—in ancient Israel, in second commonwealth Judaism, and in Christianity; in ancient Greece; in Zoroastrian Iran; in early imperial China; in Hinduism and Buddhism; and, beyond the Axial Age proper, in Islam.

The crystallization of these civilizations can be seen as a series of revolutionary breakthroughs in the history of humankind, which changed the course of human history. The central aspect of these revolutions was the emergence and institutionalization of new basic ontological conceptions of a chasm between the transcendental and mundane orders. These conceptions, which first developed among small groups of autonomous, relatively unattached "intellectuals," were ultimately transformed into the basic "hegemonic" premises of their respective civilizations, that is, they became institutionalized. They became the predominant orientations of both the ruling as well as of many secondary elites, fully embodied in their respective centers or subcenters.

The development and institutionalization of such conceptions of a basic tension and chasm between the transcendental and the mundane orders, gave rise in all these civilizations to attempt to reconstruct the mundane world—human personality and the sociopolitical and economic order according to the appropriate transcendental vision and the principles of the higher ontological or ethical order.

The given mundane order was perceived in these civilizations as incomplete, inferior, bad, or polluted—at least in some of its parts—and in need of being reconstructed. This reconstruction would take place by bridging the chasm between the transcendental and the mundane orders, according to the precepts of the higher ethical or metaphysical order. In Weberian terms, the goal of "salvation" (basically a Christian term, some equivalents of which are to be found in all Axial civilizations) made the world an arena for the implementation of a transcendental vision.

The political order as the central locus, or one of the central loci of the mundane order, was usually conceived as lower than the transcendental one and accordingly had to be restructured according to the precepts of the latter.

With such restructuring, the nature of the rulers became greatly transformed. The king-god, the embodiment of the cosmic and earthly orders alike, disappeared, and a secular ruler—even if with sacral attributes—who was in principle accountable to some higher order, appeared. Thus there emerged the conception of the accountability of the rulers and of the community to a higher authority (God, Divine Law, the Mandate of Heaven, and the like). Accordingly, the possibility of calling a ruler to judgment appeared. The first most dramatic appearance of this conception was in ancient Israel, in the priestly and prophetic pronouncements. A different "secular" conception of such accountability to the community and its laws appeared in ancient Greece.

Concomitantly with the emergence of conceptions of accountability of rulers there began to develop autonomous spheres of law as somewhat distinct from ascriptively binding customs and purely customary law. Such developments could also entail some beginnings of conception of rights. The scope of these spheres of law and rights varied greatly from society to society but they were all established according to some distinct and autonomous criteria.

These new modes of continuous reconstruction of the social and civilizational orders gave rise to continuous tensions in their very premises. The root of such tensions lies in the fact the very institutionalization of the perception of the tension between the transcendental and the mundane orders and of the quest to overcome this tension, generates an awareness of a great range of possibilities or visions of the very definition of such tensions; of the proper mode of their resolution as well as an awareness of the partiality or incompleteness of any given problem of institutionalization of such vision. Moreover such institutionalization was never a simple, peaceful process; it has been usually connected with a continuous struggle and competition among many groups and among their respective visions.

It is this very multiplicity of alternative visions that gave rise in all these civilizations to an awareness of the uncertainty of different roads to salvation, of alternative conceptions of social and cultural order, and of the seeming arbitrariness of any single solution. Such awareness has become a constituent element of the consciousness of these civilizations, especially among the carriers of their great traditions. This was closely related to the development of a high degree of "second-order" thinking, of reflexivity turning on the basic premises of the social and cultural order.

Out of these tensions there emerged another element common to all these civilizations—that of the utopian vision or visions, the visions of an alternative cultural and social order beyond any given place or time. Such visions contain many of the millenarian and revivalist elements that can be found also in pre-Axial or non-Axial "pagan" religions, but they go beyond them by combining these elements with a vision based on the emphasis on necessity to construct the mundane order according to the precepts of the higher one, with the search for an alternative "better" order beyond any given time and place.[2]

The development and institutionalization of the perception of the basic tension between the transcendental and the mundane orders were closely connected with the emergence of a new social element, of a new type of elites, of carriers of models of cultural and social order, of autonomous intellectuals—such as the Jewish prophets and priests, the Greek philosophers and Sophists, the Chinese literati, the Hindu Brahmins, the Buddhist sangha, and the Islamic ulema.

Once such a conception of a tension between the transcendental and mundane orders became institutionalized, it was also associated with the transformation of political elites, and turned the new scholar class into relatively autonomous partners in the major ruling coalitions and protest movements. The new elites, intellectuals, and clerics were recruited and legitimized according to distinct, autonomous criteria, and were organized in autonomous settings, potentially independent of other categories of elites and social groups. But at the same time they competed strongly with them, especially for the production and control of symbols and media communications.

The nonpolitical cultural elites and the political elites each saw themselves as the autonomous articulators of the new order, with the other type potentially inferior and accountable to themselves. Moreover, each of these groups of elites was not homogeneous; and there developed a multiplicity of secondary cultural, political, and educational elites. These different elites in general and the intellectuals in particular constituted also the most active element in the movements of protest and processes of change that developed in these societies, and above all in the construction of a new type of such movements—sects and heterodoxies that upheld different conceptions of the resolution of the tension between the transcendental and mundane orders, and of the proper way of the institutionalization of such concepts, of various alternative conceptions of the social and cultural order.[3]

The transformation of such alternative conceptions into heterodoxies was effected by their confrontation with some institutionalized orthodoxy. The continuous confrontations between orthodoxy and antinomian heterodoxy have thus become crucial components in the history of humankind.

There emerged in these civilizations the possibility of structural and ideological linkages between different movements of protest and foci of political conflict, and above all among rebellions, central political struggle, and religious or intellectual heterodoxies. These linkages were effected by different coalitions of different secondary elites and different religious and intellectual sects and heterodoxies. Accordingly, there developed the possibility of the greater impingement of all such movements, especially of sects and heterodoxies, on the center or centers of the society.

Thus, there developed a new type of civilizational dynamics. It transformed group conflicts into potential class and ideological dynamics. It transformed group conflicts into potential class and ideological conflicts, cult conflicts into struggles between the orthodox and the heterodox. Conflicts between tribes and societies became missionary crusades for the transformation of civilizations. The zeal for reorganization informed by each society's concept of salvation made the whole world at least potentially subject to cultural-political reconstructin, and in all these new developments the different sectarian movements and movements of heterodoxy played, because of the reasons outlined above, a central role.

Varieties of Sectarianism and of Heterodoxies and Their Institutional Impact

Beyond all these characteristics common to all the Axial Age civilizations, there developed among them far-reaching differences in the structuring of sects and heterodoxies and in their overall civilizational impact.[4] The most crucial difference is, of course, between those civilizations to which it is legitimate to apply the term *heterodoxy* and those in which it is more appropriate to talk only about sects and sectarianism. The term *heterodoxy* is applicable only to cases when one can talk about orthodoxy. This term, in its turn, implies a certain type of both organizational and cognitive doctrinal structures.

With respect to both the organizational and the doctrinal aspects, the major difference among the Axial Age civilizations is that between on the one hand the monotheistic civilizations and Christianity[5] and, on the other hand, Hinduism and Buddhism[6] with Confucian China constituting a sort of in between.[7]

It is within Christianity that these organizational and doctrinal aspects of orthodoxy developed in the fullest way. Thus, it was in Christianity that there developed full-fledged churches that constituted potentially active and autonomous partners of the ruling coalitions. In Judaism and Islam there developed powerful, but not always as fully organized and autonomous organizations of clerics. But of no lesser importance is the fact that in Christianity and to a smaller, but yet not insignificant, degree also in Judaism and Islam, there developed strong tendencies to structure relatively clear cognitive doctrinal boundaries.

This tendency was rooted first of all in the prevalence, within the monotheistic civilizations in general and within Christianity with its stronger connections to the Greek philosophical heritage in particular, of strong orientations first of all to the cognitive elaboration of the relations among God, man and the world. Second, this tendency was rooted in the fact that, in all these montheistic religions, with their other-worldly orientation, the mundane world was seen—even if in different degrees—as at least one focus of other-worldly salvation, and hence the proper designation of such activity became a focus of central concern and of contention between the ruling orthodoxies and the numerous heterodoxies that developed within them.[8]

The importance of the struggle between orthodoxies and heterodoxies, of the structuring of such cognitive boundaries, of the elaboration of visions, of the reconstruction of the mundane world according to transcendental other-worldly vision, is best seen—in a negative way—in the case of Hinduism and Buddhism.

In both these cases we find, despite a very strong transcendental and other-worldly orientation, that the structuring of cognitive doctrines (as distinct from ritual) and above all, of their applicability to mundane matters, did not constitute a central aspect or premise of these religions or civilizations. Hence even when, as in Buddhism, it is not impossible to talk about something akin to church—albeit a much more loosely organized one—it is very difficult to talk about heterodoxy. At the same time sectarianism abounds—Buddhism itself being in a sense a sect developing out of Hinduism.

These differences between sects and heterodoxies are not just matters of scholarly classification. They are closely related to the impact of these sects or orthodoxies on the dynamics of their respective civilizations. it would not be correct to state (in misreading Weber) that it was only in Christianity (or perhaps, stretching it, in the monotheistic civilizations) that sects and heterodoxies had far-reaching consequences on the structure of mundane fields.

Given the strong other-worldly orientation, Buddhist sects were not oriented—as was the case in Islam or in the other monotheistic civilizations—to the reconstruction of the political centers of their respective societies.[9] Nevertheless, the various Hinduist sects, and Buddhism itself, did indeed have a far-reaching impact on the structuring of the mundane spheres of their respective civilidations.[10] First, they extended the scope of the different national and political communities and imbued them with new symbolic dimensions.[11] Second, they changed some of the bases and criteria of participation in the civilizational communities, as was the case in Jainism,[12] in the Bhakti movement, and, of course, above all, in Buddhism when an entirely new civilizational framework was constructed.

Buddhism also introduced new elements into the political scene, above all that special way in which the sangha, usually politically a very compliant group, could in some cases, as Paul Mus[13] has shown, become a sort of moral conscience of the community, calling the rulers to some accountability.

This impact was of a different nature from that of the struggles between the reigning orthodoxies and the numerous heterodoxies that developed within the monotheistic civilizations of Judaism, Christianity, and Islam. While the reconstruction of political centers was not the major orientation of Buddist sects, yet even in these societies there did develop a mode of involvement in the political arena with potentially subversive challenges to the authorities. Above all Buddhist (and Hindu) sects had a great impact on the construction of the boundaries of the respective national collectivities.

From all these points of view Confucian China constitutes a rather mixed case, paradoxically somewhat nearer to the monotheistic than to the other Axial civilizations.[14] There did not develop in China an elaborate religious doctrine, as distinct from the "secular" precepts of Confucianism. These precepts—in which there was almost no reference to God or to other-worldly concerns—did, however, entail very strong transcendental albeit this-worldly orientations with a very explicitly cognitive elaboration of the

precepts according to which the mundane world had to be constructed. Similarly, while there did not exist in China any official
church, the stratum of literati and the bureaucracy, in coalition with
the emperor, exercised not only strong political control, but also
control over the communication of the major symbolic reference
orientations, over official rituals, and over the major channels of
education.

The mode of the involvement of the Confucian elites in the
political centers in China, Korea, and Vietnam developed in a rather
different direction from that of the Buddhist sangha, and was in
many ways closer to the sectarian activities in the montheistic
civilizations. Confucianism was indeed very strongly oriented to the
political centers. Given the strong, almost exclusively this-worldly
orientation of Confucianism, however, the potentially heterodox
groups of literati rarely challenged the political center and order.
They were, however, as we shall see, politically very active, and often
engaged in intensive discourse and moral criticism of the rulers.[15]

As in all other Axial Age civlizations, there did develop in China
numerous secondary "religions" (like Buddhism and Taoism) with
strong other-worldly orientations, as well as numerous schools from
within the central Confucian fold. As the official Confucian
"orthodoxy" was not greatly concerned with their other-worldly
orientations or pure speculation, these sects never developed into
heterodoxy in the doctrinal sense, and so long as they did not
impinge on the basic institutional implications of the imperial order
with the political-cultural predominance of the literati and
bureaucracy, they were more or less left alone. But once some of
these sects did attempt—as was the case with the Buddhists under
the Tang—to impinge on these premises of the Confucian order to
construct the world according to their own premises, the Confucian
literati and bureaucracy behaved just as any other "monotheistic"
orthodoxy, engaging in fierce political struggle and far-reaching
persecutions.[16]

Moreover, throughout the various periods of Chinese history
there have been continuous attempts by the ruling literati to define
the limits of Confucian orthodoxy. Such attempts were often related
to a reaction to many important attempts at reform grounded in
Confucian and neo-Confucian visions that abounded in China,
especially from the Sung period onward, and which were greatly
influenced by Buddhism and in some ways constituted a response
to it. Neo-Confucian groups were closely concerned with the reconstruction of the imperial order, in accordance with the metaphysical
and moral visions they articulated, and they had far-reaching impact

on some aspects of policy (land allotment and taxation) and to some extent also on some of the details of the examination system itself.[17] They were continually politically active, and often critically engaged in the political discourse. Unlike the Islamic sects or heterodoxies or those of other monotheistic civilizations, however, the Confucian literati have but rarely challenged the basic political premises of the regimes, the very foundatin of the imperial order. This was probably to no small extent due to the fact that they conceived the political arena or political-cultural arenas, as the main, possibly only, institutional arena (as distinct from the more private, contemplative one) for implementing the Confucian transcendental vision.

The differences between sects, sectarian organizations, and heterodoxies, and their impact on their broader social settings as they developed in different ways in these civilizations are rooted not only in their respective belief systems or in the concrete power relations between them and the political powers. They are rooted also—and perhaps above all—in the different ways in which various components of religious beliefs became incorporated into basic premises of these respective civilizations and influenced their basic institutional derivatives.

The Expansion of Islam

The importance of "civilizational" factors in the structuring of the political impact of religious sects and heterodoxies can be best seen in the analysis of the expansion of religions in selected Axial civilizations. Within all these great religions there developed strong tendencies to expansion—tendencies that were rooted in their universalistic and potentially missionary orientations. The story of such expansions is too well known to need documentation or exposition here. Here we shall provide only some illustrations that will indicate how such processes of expansion underline the difference between, on the one hand, the spread or expansion of religious belief and patterns of worship and of religious behavior, and on the other hand, their acting as components of transformation of the basic ontological vision and premises of the social order—or in other words, of the premises of the respective civilizations or societies into which they have expanded.

The first case we shall analyze will deal with the expansion of Islam. We shall examine the differences between the mode of such expansion in Central and East Asia (India, Indonesia, Malaysia) up to the end of the nineteenth century and the beginning of the twentieth century with that of expansion of Islam in the classical period of Islam, as well as the different modes of spread of Islam in Sub-Saharan Africa.[18]

In a very broad and simplified way it can be said that, while in classical Islam from the seventh to the tenth centuries, and later in some African societies, it was the civilizational component of Islam that was here predominant, while in Eastern Asian and South African societies it expanded mostly as a system of belief and worship without greatly affecting the civilizational frame of these societies, even when it was adopted by the rulers as their official religion.

In the classical period of expansion of Islam, especially in the transition from the Umayyad to the 'Abbasid caliphs in the mid-eighth century, whatever the degree of adherence of different sectors of the conquered populations, or for that matter of some of the conquerors, to the beliefs and patterns of worship of Islam, Islam created a new civilization with very distinct premises. It generated new institutional formations to a large extent shaped by the basic ontological vision, cultural orientations, and societal premises of "classical" Islam, as well as new specific dynamics of religious organizations in general and of sects in particular.

Among the basic ontological conceptions that crystallized in the Islamic realm, the following were the most important for the shaping of the institutional formations: the strong distinction or tension between the cosmic transcendental realm and the mundane one; the emphasis on overcoming this tension by total submission to God and by this-worldly above all, politicomilitary activity; the strong universalistic element in the definition of the Islamic community; the ideal of the *umma*, the politicoreligious community of all believers, distinct from any ascriptive, primordial collectivity; the principled autonomous access of all members of the community to the attributes of the transcendental order, to salvation, through submission to God; and the closely connected emphasis on the principled political equality of all believers.

This ideology entailed a complete fusion of politicoreligious collectivities, collective identity, and elites. The original vision of the *umma* assumed complete convergence between the socio-political and religious communities. Many of the later caliphs (such as the 'Abbasids and Fatimids) and other Muslim rulers came to power on the crest of religious movements that upheld this ideal, and legitimized themselves in such religicopolitical terms. They sought to retain popular support by stressing the religious aspect of the authority and by courting the religious leaders and religious sentiments of the community. Concomitantly, political problems were central to the development of Islamic theology.

In the implementation of all these orientations, Islam evinced the characteristics of a "totalitarian movement," or as Maxime Rodinson has put it, of a revolutionary political party strongly oriented to the reconstruction of the world and very militant in this pursuit.[19]

This emphasis on the reconstruction of a combined politico-religious collectivity was connected with the development of a strong ideological negation of any primordial element within this sacred politicoreligious identity. Among all the Axial Age civilizations, especially the monotheistic ones, Islam was ideologically the most extreme in its denial of the legitimacy of primordial dimensions in the structure of the Islamic community—although in practice, as Bernard Lewis has shown, the story was often markedly different.[20]

Given the basic premises of Islam, Islamic civilization had a very strong tendency to develop imperial regimes with very distinct institutional patterns—new centers permeating the periphery, autonomous political and religious elites and institutions, and specifically Islamic patterns of urban life.[21]

Yet it was only in the 'Abbasid Empire, in such regimes as the Fatimid and later in the Ottoman, that the imperial pattern became relatively predominant. In most other cases there developed mostly sultanic, patrimonial regimes with less autonomous religious elites and less religiously committed political elites, such as military slaves, an institution unique to Islam. In other parts of the Islamic world, such as in North Africa and Central Asia, it was seemingly, as was shown already by Ibn Khaldun,[22] tribal regimes often moving into a sultanic direction that became the most prevalent ones.[23]

It is a rather paradoxical but central fact of Islamic history that the final crystallization of this universalistic ideology and institutional format took place with the so-called 'Abbasid revolution,[24] involving a shift in the legitimation of rulers in Sunni Islam from direct descent from the Prophet and consensus of the community to seniority and ultimately the fulfillment of the Prophet's will. It also spawned in close relation to the institutionalization of this universalistic vision, a de facto separation between the political and religious leadership.[25] It was also at the end of the 'Abbasid period that military rulers and a caste of military slaves started to become predominant[26]—and it was after that period that patrimonial of tribal regimes became relatively predominant in the realm of Islam.

Yet all of these seemingly patrimonial or tribal regimes evinced some very distinct characteristics that distinguished them from other such regimes, be they those of the ancient Near East, or of ancient Southeast or Central Asia, or Mesoamerica.

The most important distinctive feature of these regimes was the nature of political dynamics that developed within them—and above all the place of sectarian activities in the political process. These political dynamics were indeed rooted in the basic ontological-social vision of Islam, above all in the undying vision of a unified political religious community, the *umma*. Yet there was the failure, going back to the very first stages of Islam, to implement that view.[27]

It was the combination of the de facto impossibility of institutionalizing the *umma* with the strong latent religioideological orientation toward such unification, the fusion of religious and political spheres and elites, and the reconstruction of a union between them, that was at the core of many of the political and religious developments of Islam—and it was manifest above all in the nature of Islamic sects and in the central role played by these sects in the potentially strong "semirevolutionary" sectarian activities, in the expansion of Islam, and in the political dynamics of different Islamic regimes.

At the core of these special traits of the basic religious orientations of the Islamic sects was the importance of the political dimension. The emphasis on this dimension could be oriented toward active participation in the center, its destruction or transformation; or toward a conscious withdrawal from it—a withdrawal that, as in the case of Sufism and Shi'ism, often harbored potential political reactivation. But whatever its concrete manifestations, the political orientation was potentially inherent in any Islamic religious setting, and generated some of the major movements, political divisions, and problems in Islam, starting with the Shi'a.[28] In appropriate historical circumstances it could be activated by new and dynamic political elements. One distinctive characteristic of Islamic societies was that the internal sectarian political impact was often connected with the problem of the expansion of Islam and especially with the continuous impingement of tribal elements as the carriers of the original idea of Islam and hence, also to some degree, of the pristine Islamic polity and vision.

True, Islam never developed a concept of revolution.[29] But at the same time, as Ernest Gellner has shown in his interpretation of Ibn Khaldun's work, a less direct yet very forceful pattern of accountability of rulers arose, manifest in the possibility of rulers being disposed by the combination of sectarian groups with the resurgence of tribal revival against corrupt or weak regimes.[30] Such possible subsequent regeneration out of new tribal elements, either from within Arabia itself, or from new elements converted to Islam in Central Asia or in North Africa.

It was this specific dynamic element that distinguished the Islamic regimes from other patrimonial or tirbal ones, and the Islamic sects or orders from those of other religions, however much they may seem to have in common.

It was exactly this element of the active transformation of the religious beliefs into components of an ever-reaching hegemonic ontological vision of civilizational premises that was for a long time lacking or at most very weak in Southeast Asian Islam.[31] Even when Islam was adopted by the rulers, not only did it often develop in a rather syncretic mode, but—above all—it did not, for a very long time, give rise to a restructuring of the basic ideological and institutional premises of these civilizations.

The acceptance of Islam by the rulers did not give rise here to reconstruction of the political arena, of the traditional, pre-Islamic, patrimonial patterns in the political realm. Such acceptance did not give rise to a new pattern of accountability of rulers and to the emergence of a new autonomous political elite. The Islamic teachers became mostly religious specialists at the courts of the rulers or in other sectors of the society, but did not develop as an autonomous political elits. Nor did the Islamic merchants who were amoung the main carriers of the expansion of Islam in those societies. The original Islamic ontology and conception of political and social order never became culturally hegemonic. The various Islamic religious organizations or groups tended on the whole, to be mostly confined in the context of these civilizations to what may be called the "private" religious sphere. Sects or sectarian tendencies were relatively few. At the same time there arose numerous individuals with some semisectarian, especially mystical orientations and tendencies, but they were on the whole politically passive and basically not oriented to the political arena.[32]

This weakness of such political sectarian dynamic in these countries at least up until the end of the nineteenth century attests to the fact that such sectarian dynamics were much more attached to its specific patterns of belief, ritual, and worship than to the overall civilizational vision of Islam. Later in the eighteenth and nineteenth centuries, and above all in the post-World War II period, these orientations were greatly transformed. Such transformation took place when there developed new types of elites who aimed at creating overall Islamic civilizational patterns.

A rather similar distinction can be identified in the expansion of Islam in Africa. The difference between the expansion of Islam as a system of belief and worship and as a civilization can be perhaps even more clearly identified in the modes of Islamization of various African societies.[33]

These different patterns of expansion of political dynamics in Islam were closely related to very important differences in the composition and characteristics of the Islamic carriers and elites.

Insofar as merchants and rather dispersed clerics and religious specialists constituted the major carriers of expansion of Islam, Islam tended to expand as a system of beliefs and worship while the expansion of Islam as a civilization has been usually predicated on the activities of highly organized and cohesive religious elites or orders in close cooperation with new types of political elites. It is such religious and political elites that often exhibited very strong sectarian tendencies.

But it is not just the "occupational" composition of the carriers of Islam that is of crucial importance, but their internal structure as well as their place in the ruling coalitions of their societies. Thus, for instance, in the indigenous African Islamic states (and in the parallel cases in Southeast Asia) the Islamic elites were nonautonomous, secondary partners in existing "traditional" coalitions, highly embedded in the ascriptive communities of their societies, while in the Jihad states they were highly autonomous, independent partners in coalitions of relatively autonomous elites, very often generating new types of such political elites.

It is these different types of elites that generated different modes of sectarian activities and dynamics. In the indigenous African states there developed few full-fledged sectarian activities, certainly almost none with any strong political orientations—even less than in Southeast Asia. The Jihad states on the other hand were essentially created by tribal elements that had developed very intensive sectarian-like orientations and activities, promulgating the pristine Islamic civilization model.

The Expansion of Confucianism and Buddhism

Parallel—although obviously not identical—differences between the "religious" and civilizational components can be identified with respect to the expansion of Confucianism, as well as of Buddhism, in Asia.

The crucial difference is between the impact of expansion of Confucianism on the respective institutional and ideological formats of Korea and Vietnam on the one hand, and on Japan's on the other.

The institutionalization of Confucianism first of all in China itself and then in Korea and Vietnam has transformed the basic institutional premises of the social and political order in these societies, in the structure of their centers and their ruling strata in comparison with perceding periods of regimes.[34] This was not the case, however, in Japan.

In both Korea and North Vietnam there have developed new regimes as a result of expansion or adoption of imperial Confucianism, of centers, the like of which persisted in South Vietnam, even if not as fully articulated as in China, as well as new types of structure of the ruling elites and the systems of stratification.[35] This change was effected by the transformation of "feudal" or rather feudal-patrimonial ruling groups into something similar to the Chinese literati, to an autonomous bureaucratic-cultural elite, recruited according to distinct, independent criteria and organized in relatively autonomous frameworks.

It is true that in Korea the elite have never achieved tht degree of autonomy and independence that characterized the Chinese Empire, and the aristocratic and patrimonial tendencies were here indeed strong. In Korea the Confucians encountered very strong Buddhist opposition in alliance with large parts of the older aristocracy and some of the rulers.[36] Once, however, the Confucian institutions and elites became predominant, even the aristocracy became "Confucianized." It is also true that aristocratic families and lineages continued to be much more important in Korea than in post-Tang China. Their importance, however, was manifest in the success in monopolizing or at least in semimonopolizing the Confucian bureaucratic literati positions or in reverting to a distinct "semifeudal" aristocratic type of polity. In other words they played already on the Confucian playgrounds, according to Confucian rules, even if they manipulated those rules to their advantage. In North Vietnam the Confucian state was even more coercive than in Korea and in some ways more analyzed than the Chinese one.[37]

The story of Confucianism and Buddhism in Japan is radically different. True enough, both Confucianism and Buddhism have greatly influenced the entire cultural and social ambiance of Japanese society. Their influence was indeed very far-reaching and it is, as well known, impossible to understand the history of Japanese society and culture without taking this influence into account. Confucianism and Buddhism were also very important in generating many arenas of cultural creativity as well as in the constitution of the realm of private meaning of many sectors of Japanese society. They have greatly contributed to the cultural and religiocultic life in Japan, have greatly influenced the pattern of creativity in these areas, and were also of great importance in transforming the general cultural ambiance and climate.[38]

Institutionally, however, neither Confucianism nor Buddhism has changed the structure of the center, or of the ruling elites. In Japan, the "importation" of Confucianism did not develop those central institutional aspects that shaped the Confucian regimes in China, Korea, and Vietnam—the examination system and the crystallization through this system of the stratum of the literati and of the imperial bureaucracy.

Buddhism too in Japan developed some very distinct characteristics that distinguished it from those of Buddhist communities in India, China, and Southeast Asia. The most important of these characteristics was the development of very strong this-worldly orientations and a very sectarian familistic organizational structure of Buddhist groups or sects. On the organizational level, Buddhist sects developed in highly personalized and familistic directions. Buddhist sectarianism in Japan was rooted not in a strong transcendental orientation but in its having become embedded in the strong emphasis on personal "enlightenment" on the one hand and on concrete social nexus, on "groupism" with tendencies to hereditary transmission of leadership roles on the other.[39]

In close relation to such far-reaching institutional changes some of the major premises or concepts of Confucianism and Buddhism were also transformed in Japan. We have noticed already above all how Buddhist orientations become transformed in a highly this-worldly direction. The ontological conceptions that stressed (as in all Axial civilizations) the chasm between the transcendental and mundane orders, between "culture" and "nature," went in a more "immanentist" direction,[40] with a much stronger emphasis on the mutual embeddedness of the cultural and natural orders and on nature as given.

It is, however, probably with respect to the conception of the national collectivity and its relation to the broader Confucian and Buddhist civilizations as well as with respect to conceptions of authority, especially imperial authority, that the ideological transformation of Buddhism and Confucianism is most fully manifest. The crux of this transformation was the redirection of the universalistic orientations of Buddhism and Confucianism into a more particularistic primordial direction.

Buddhism, as well as Confucianism, had indeed a powerful impact on the definition of the overall "national" Japanese community and on the basic conceptions or premises of authority in

Japan (the strong emphasis on commitment to center, hierarchy, and group solidarity). Confucianism and Buddhism imbued these definitions with a very strong moral or metaphysical dimension. But the impact of Buddhism and Confucianism did not change the basic institutionalized patterns. Above al, it did not change the strong sacral particularistic components of Japanese collective self-definition and of the system of legitimation of authority within it—contrary to the case in Vietnam and Korea, not to speak of China itself. If anything it has strengthened these definitions and the legitimation of the social and political order in such sacral-primordial ties by combining them with strong ethical dimensions.[41]

True enough, the encounter with Confucianism and Buddhism did give rise to continuous reformulations and reconstructions of the definitions and symbols of the Japanese collectivity, but such reformulations have never changed the basic ontological and social import of these symbols. The first encounter of Japan with Buddhism transformed the older sacred kingship into a sacred liturgical particularistic community, rooted in the older "Shinto" conception; all the subsequent formulations of the nature of this community have only strengthened this conception.[42] At the same time, however, the strong universalistic orientation inherent in Buddhism, and more latent in Confucianism, was subdued and "nativized' in Japan.[43] Japan was defined as a divine nation—a nation protected by the gods, a chosen people in some sence, but not a nation carrying God's universal mission.[44]

Parallel developments took place with respect to the basic conception of political authority and accountability of rulers. These conceptions were also greatly transformed from the original Chinese-Confucian conceptions prevalent in China, Korea, and Vietnam.

Unlike in China (and Korea and Vietnam),[45] where in principle the emperor, even if a sacral figure, was "under" the mandate of heaven, in Japan he was sacred and seen as the embodiment of the gods and was accountable to nobody. Only the shoguns and other officials—in ways not clearly specified and only in periods of crises, as for instance at the end of the Tokugawa regime—could be held accountable.

The difference between the modes of expansion of Confucianism and the impact of such expansion on institutional structures in China, Korea, and Vietnam, and of Buddhism in different countries of mainland Asia, on the one hand, and of both Confucianism and Buddhism in Japan, on the other hand, are closely related to differences in the structure and composition of their respective elites, as well as of the orientations and activities of their respective sects. These differences are very close to those we have identified in the Islamic case, to differences in the structure, especially of the relative autonomy, of the "cultural" elites, their relation to the ruling elites, and their place in the ruling coalitions.

On mainland Asia, the Confucian and Buddhist elites were highly autonomous. The Confucian elites constituted a new, distinct, autonomous politicocultural stratum that was, in principle if not always in practice, recruited through the examination system.[46] The Buddhists, at least in the religious arena, were also highly aautonomous and not in the existing structures of power or family.

In contrast to this in Japan both the Confucian scholars and the Buddhist sects were highly embedded in the existing power, kinship, and family settings. Yet while the Confucian academies in Japan were often relatively independent institutions, they were highly dependent on the rulers for any offices.[47] The Confucian scholars served in Japan at the courts of the rulers according to the criteria set up by the rulers, and they served at the ruler's will. The Buddhist sects became, as we have seen, strongly embedded in the familistic setting predominant in most sectors of Japanese society.

The different modes of expansion of Confucianism in different societies had some very important repercussions on the nature of the sectarian activities that developed within them. In many ways this was also parallel to the developments in Islam analyzed above. It is true that, from the very beginning, the entire development of sectarianism in Confucianism and Buddhism differed greatly from that of other monotheistic civilizations, including Islam. But both Buddhist sects and groups of Confucian (especially neo-Confucian) literati participated in mainland Asia in the political arena, constituting at least potentially, a challenge to the existing political regimes—even if in modes that differed greatly from the Islamic patterns.

It was indeed this strong, often critical political involvement, with political challenges to the regime, which disappeared almost entirely in Japan. Here most Buddhist sects and Confucian schools became either supporters of the existing political orders, performing religious or cultural functions for the powers that be, imbuing the political process with proper Buddhist (or Confucian) ethical values and orientations, or politically passive.

The major new sectarian orientations that have developed in Japanese Buddhism most clearly manifest in the Pure Land sect were, in principle, oriented to the perfection of the individual, seemingly without any direct political orientation—certainly without attempts to change the premises of the political realm. Insofar as they had any orientations they were also very strongly oriented to the strengthening of the national community, but they could, contrary to the Confucian teaching, be political passive or withdraw.[48]

The Religious-Civilizational Framework of the Great Revolutions

We shall conclude with an analysis of the religious-civilizational frameworks of the "great revolutions" that ushered in the modern era in Europe and in the world: the Great Rebellion in England, the American and French revolutions, and the later revolutions in China and Russia. The Turkish and Vietnamese revolutions can probably also be included in this category.[49]

The analysis of revolutions has become in the last decade or so a very important focus of research in the social sciences, especially in political and historical sociology. Most of these studies were very closely connected with the emphasis on the growing recognition of the autonomy and distinctiveness of the state. This growing recognition of the autonomy and distinctiveness of politics and the state developed in several directions, such as, for instance, the emphasis on the autonomy of political agents and especially civil sevants in the formulation and execution of policy,[50] in the development of corporative practices,[51] or in the various "objectives" (especially structural) characteristics of the state, particularly its relation to other social groups and the ways in which these characteristics and relations tend to influence the development of different modes of economic conflict,[52] class formation and social movement (especially revolutions),[53] or in the analysis of different forms of modern states, defined not in constitutional terms but in terms of their strength and modes of activity, both in Europe and beyond.[54] Yet another approach, of special interest from the point of view of our analysis, represented above all in the work of John Meyer and his colleagues,[55] saw the modern state as an autonomous ideological and institutional entity, continuously expanding the scope of its activities, both internally and in the international nexus.

These works have indeed provided a more extensive analysis of the relations between political control and manifold types of social processes, and also of the formation of economic and social policies, the structure of social movements of classes, modes of conflict resolutions, and the like. Yet the tendency to the reification of the state led to a rather limited conception of the political process, which was seen chiefly in terms of a struggle among real actors over distributive resources, with scant attention paid either to the symbolic and ideological dimension of this process or to the framework of rules within which such struggle takes place.

At the same time, the basic conception of the state, especially the modern state, predominant in many of these works, was couched in terms of the European experience; the structural characteristics of this experience were taken as common to all states. Thus, for instance, the variations among different states were often conceived (to use M. Mann's experession)[56] in terms of the relations between state and civil society, and were expressed in terms based at least implicitly on this historical experience. This combination of the reification of the state with the predominance of the European model of the state was connected with a failure to consider the importance of the cultural dimension in the political process and in the formation of the state. Even when the importance of the cultural dimension began to be recognized (e.g., by John Meyer and his collaborators), the emphasis was more on the specific ideological dimension of the modern state system as it developed in the West and expanded throughout the world. Even these important suggestions about the importance of the specific ideological dimension of the modern state have not been fully explored—in analytic and comparative terms—in most works that emphasize the autonomy of the state.

This impoverished conception of the political process can perhaps best be seen in the analysis of one central aspect of this process, emphasized by many of these scholars: protest. Most of these analyses focus on protest and on patterns of distribution and allocation of resources, but pay little attention to the symbolism of protest as a relatively autonomous dimension of such movements, or to the possibility that such symbolism may be important in the impact of such movements on the political process, particularly in democratic societies—chiefly by effecting changes in the basic rules that regulate political struggle and conflict.

The same neglect can be found in many recent works in comparative historical sociology, such as, for instance, those of John Hall, Michael Mann, and Jean Baechler,[57] which have taken up again the problem of the origins of the West in a broad comparative framework. Most of these works analyze, often in a very sophisticated way, various structural factors such as power relations among different groups, various politicoecological conditions, and above all intersocietal relations.

They have, however, almost entirely neglected to analyze the influence of one type of social group—heterodoxies, so strongly stressed by Weber and to some extent also by Marx and some of the early Marxists—on the political dynamics of civilizations.[58]

The analysis of the religious-civilizational frameworks of the great revolutions that will be presented in the next section will, by emphasizing the religious and civilizational frameworks of these revolutions, connect with our preceding analysis and will also attempt to correct the neglect in recent literature in political sociology, of the civilizational component in the crystallization of institutional formations and dynamics.

On the ideological level, these revolutions were characterized by the intensification, transformation, and combination of several ideologies found separately in most Axial Age civilizations. The most important of these are a highly articulated ideology of social protest, especially in a utopian emancipatory vein, based on symbols of equality, progress, and freedom, presumably leading to the creation of a better social order; a strong emphasis on violence, novelty, and totality of change; and a strong universalistic missionary zeal oriented to the creation of a new type of man and ushering in a new historical era.

Similarly, on the organizational level they were characterized by bringing together several components of social movements and political struggle articulated and organized by counterelites, central political struggle, and religious (or intellectual) heterodoxies. While the tendency to such combinations of different symbolic and organizational components, as well as of these two sets of components can be found in all Axial Age civilizations, only in these revolutions was this potential fully actualized.

The ideological and organizational aspects of these revolutions shaped their outcomes and distinguished them from other changes of regimes in the history of mankind. They interwove "cultural" and institutional dimensions in a way not found in other processes of change, generating a simultaneous change in central aspects of the ontological conceptions prevalent in a civilization alongside changes in the basic rules regulating the political arena and the center.

These revolutions were characterized by the overthrow of existing political regimes and changes in their basic premises and constitutional arrangements and in the bases of symbols of their legitimation; by a radical break with the past; by the displacement of the incumbent political elite of ruling class in favor of another one; and by the concomitant development of significant changes in all major institutional spheres of society—above all in economic and class relations.

How can these revolutions be explained? This question seemingly refers to the problem of the "causes" of revolutions. Here, in broad terms, two types of explanations have been predominant in the literature—one dealing with different types of structural conditions and the other with specific historical circumstances.

Among the structural conditions singled out in the literature one can find interelite struggles in combination with other forces, such as class struggle; the dislocation, social mobilization, and political articulation of broader and newly emerging social groups; and the weakening of the state, often under the impact of international forces. Yet a closer look at the historical evidence reveals that most of these conditions could also be found historical evidence reveals that most of these conditions could also be found in many human societies, especially in the more differentiated ones, in other types of regimes within both Axial Age and non-Axial Age civilizations.

It may of course be claimed that these revolutions occurred only in special historical conditions of crucial importance, and that such historical conditions can be seen as necessary, if not sufficient, causes of revolutions. The most important condition singled out in the literature involves the relatively early states of transition of modern settings in which three major aspects of the breakthrough from a "traditional" to a modern setting occur together.

While there is not doubt that these revolutions occurred only in such historical conditions, there remains a crucial problem for comparative analysis: How can we explain that such relations did not occur in all societies where the types of conflict analyzed above could be identified, or in all societies making this transition to modernity (e.g., Japan and India)?

Our analysis begins with a simple yet basic historical fact: The first revolutions (in Europe and America) occurred in the decentralized setting of Europe, in imperial-feudal societies, while the later revolutions occurred in centralized imperial societies. No such revolutions have occurred in patrimonial societies, whether centralized or decentralized—India, Buddhist societies (Southeast Asia), Islamic countries (with the partial exception of the Ottoman Empire and much later in Iran)—or in centralized feudal-patrimonial ones like Japan. Thus, it was only in some special types of societies that these different movements, conflicts, and protest movements came together and coalesced. The difference between the imperial and the imperial-feudal societies, on the one hand, and various patrimonial regimes, on the other, cannot be explained in terms of the variables often stressed in recent sociological literature or in the literature of the state referred to above—such as the types of social division of labor, degree of economic development, and the like— which have been heavily stressed in those approaches that tend to reify the concept of the state or of social structure.

Most of the imperial and imperial-feudal societies developed within the framework of some great civilizations or traditions of the Axial Age civilizations, and shared some of the basic cultural orientations and institutional premises that developed in these civilizations. These characteristics included a highly distinct center perceived as an autonomous symbolic and organizational entity, and continuous interaction between center and periphery. Another characteristic important for our present discussion is the development of distinct collectivities—especially cultural or religious—with a very high symbolic component in their construction as well as ideological structuring of social hierarchies. A third characteristic is the development of relatively autonomous primary and secondary elites, especially cultural-intellectual religious ones, which continuously struggled with one another and with the political elites.

These elites, particularly the religious and intellectual, many of whom are also carriers of strong utopian visions with universalistic orientations, constituted the crucial element in the development of heterodoxies and in activating the connection between them and different arenas of political struggles and protest movements.

Common to all the civilizations within which great revolutions occurred—imperial and imperial-feudal regimes, as distinct from other Axial Age civilizations—was the perception of the this-worldly arenas in general, and the political one in particular, as the major arenas in which the attempt to bridge the transcendental and mundane, in which salvation could be achieved, could be institutionalized.

The combination of all these characteristics gave rise in the imperial and imperial-feudal premises to a tendency toward a high degree of coalescence among protest movements, institution-building, levels of articulation, and ideologization of the political struggle; and a tendency toward a process of change in the political system containing at least some kernels of the revolutionary process analyzed above.

The basic cultural orientations and civilizational premises inspired visions of new social orders with strong utopian and universalistic orientations, which the organizational and structural characteristics provided the framework to institutionalize some aspect of these visions. The two were combined by the activities of the different types of elites analyzed above.

When these characteristics were not present, the transition to modernity, however far-reaching, tended to develop in different and nonrevolutionary patterns. In Japan, an imperial-feudal regime that did not experience an Axial Age breakthrough, the "transcendental" dimensions and utopian orientations were very weak, as were autonomous intellectual and religious heterodoxies. Many of the structural outcomes of the Meiji restoration most closely related to the process of modernization seemed comparable to those of the great revolutions, and in some aspects even more far-reaching.

Yet the symbolism of the Meiji restoration was quite different from that of the great revolutions. True, the Meiji restoration "restored" a regime that had not previously existed. Yet, the very definition of the change as a restoration underlined its emphasis on the crystallization of a neo-traditional polity that seemingly emphasizes the ultimate nonaccountability of the new rulers to the population, and the legitimation of the new regime in terms of the inviolable emperor. In parallel, this ideology did not contain universalistic missionary orientations, but rather emphasized the reconstruction—albeit in seemingly modern terms—of the specifically Japanese collectivity.

The characteristics of the outcome of the Meiji revolution were closely related to one basic trait of the revolutionary process itself, which distinguished it from the great revolutions—namely, the absence of autonomous religious or intellectual elements or heterodoxies. Similarly, the processes of change in India and in Buddhist countries, especially after the onset of modernization— and, in a different vein, in most Latin American countries, where other-worldly premises were predominant or very strong—were also different from those of the great revolutions.

Thus it was in Western and Central Europe—and later in Russia and China, and to a smaller extent in the Ottoman Empire—that the development of sects and heterodoxies and their combination with secondary political elites proved to have the most far-reaching impact on the restructuring of conceptions of ontological reality, as well as on the major ground rules regulating the major arenas of social life and cultural creativity. We encounter here a rather interesting parallel, or even continuity, with the analysis of the development of sectarian activities in different civilizations.

The combination of civilizational and structural conditions and historical contingencies that generated the great revolutions has been rather rare in the history of mankind. In many ways, their occurrence and the later institutionalization of postrevolutionary regimes are similar to the crystallization of revolutionary regimes.

But however rare such occurrences may be, they may still recur in "propitious" circumstances, albeit in a different format from the two types of revolution discussed here.

Perhaps the closest approximation to such an occurrence has been the Iranian revolution led by the Ayatollah Khomeini. Here also, as many scholars have shown, the disenchantment with an autocratic modernizing regime and the attack on it by a combination of religious, intellectual, and popular elites with a strong missionary and universalistic semiutopian vision were of crucial importance in spawning this revolution. Needless to say, the basic cosmology of this revolution differed radically from the antitraditionalistic cosmology of earlier revolutions. In many ways, this cosmology was oriented against the premises for the earlier ones, against the premises of modernity, but it was also a univeralistic-missionary one, albeit in an Islamic vein. It constituted the central symbolic element in this revolution, while the intellectual elites that carried and articulated it constituted a central organizational element in it.

Concluding Remarks

The preceding analyses alert us first of all to the great impact of religions on the political process in various societies. Second, they indicate that the importance of this impact can be best understood not in terms of the direct impact of religious beliefs or patterns of worship on politics, but rather through the mediation of the civilizational premises of which religious belief constitutes an important component.

Notes

The research on which this chapter is based was supported by the World Society Foundation.

1. S. N. Eisenstadt, "The Axial Age: The Emergence of Transcendental Visions and the Rise of Clerics," *European Journal of Sociology* 23, no. 2 (1982): 294–314; idem, "Macrosociology and Sociological Theory: Some New Directions," *Contemporary Sociology* 16, no. 5 (1987): 602–609.

2. G. Kaleb, *Utopia and its Enemies* (New York: Free Press, 1963); *Eranos Jahrbuch, Vom Sinn der Utopie: A Collection of Essays* (Zurich: Rhien Verlag, 1964); A. B. Seligman, *Order and Transcendence: The Role of Utopias and the Dynamics of Civilizations* (Leiden: E. J. Brill, 1989).

3. S. N. Eisenstadt, "Heterodoxies, Sectarianism and Dynamics of Civilizations," *Diogenes* 120 (1982): 3–25.
4. Ibid.
5. J. Le Goff, ed., *Hérésies et sociétés dans l'Europe pré-industrielle* (Paris: La Haye, 1968).
6. J. C. Heesterman, *The Inner Conflict of Tradition* (Chicago: University of Chicago Press, 1986). R. Thapar, *Ancient Indian Social History* (London: Orient Longman, 1978); idem, *Asoka and the Decline of the Mauryas* (London: Longman, 1971). W. T. DeBary, ed., *Sources of Indian Tradition* (New York: Columbia University Press, 1958); S. Tambiah, *World Conqueror and World Renouncer: A Study of Buddhism and Polity in Thailant Against a Historical Background* (Cambridge: Cambridge University Press, 1976).
7. J. K. Fairbank, ed., *Chinese Thought and Institutions* (Chicago: University of Chicago Press, 1957); A. Wright, *Buddhism in Chinese History* (Stanford: Stanford University Press, 1959); A, Wright and D. Nivison, eds., *Confucianism in Action* (Stanford: Stanford University Press, 1959).
8. Le Goff, *Hérésies*; H. Laoust, *Les schismes dans l'Islam* (Paris: Payot, 1965).
9. I. F. Silber, "Opting Out in Theravada Buddhism and in Medieval Christianity—A Comparative Study of Monasticism as Alternative Structure," *Religion* 15, no. 3 (1985).
10. S. C. Malik, ed., *Dissent, Protest and Reform in Indian Civilization* (Simia: Indian Institute of Advanced Study, 1973); M. S. A. Rao, ed., *Social Movements in India* (New Delhi: Mahonar, 1982).
11. Tambiah, *World Conqueror.*
12. C. Gaillat, "Jainism," in *The Encyclopedia of Religion* (New York: Macmillan and Free Press, 1987) 7: 507–514; J. B. Carman and F. A. Marglin, eds., *Purity and Auspiciousness in Indian Society* (Leiden: E. J. Brill, 1985); J. B. Carman, "Bhakti," *The Encyclopedia of Religion* 2: 130–134, J. Lele, ed., *Tradition and Modernity in Bhakti Movements* (Leiden: E. J. Brill, 1981).
13. Paul Mus, "La sociologie de George Gurvitch et l'Asie," *Cahiers internationaux de sociologie* 43 (1967): 1–21; idem, "Traditions anciennes et bouddhisme moderne," *Eranos Jahrbuch* 32 (1968): 161–275.
14. Wright, *Buddhism*; Fairbank, *Chinese Thought.*
15. T. A. Metzger, *Escape from Predicamant—Neo-Confucianism and China's Evolving Political Culture* (New York: Columbia University Press, 1977).
16. E. Zurcher, *The Buddhist Conquest of China* (Leiden: E. J. Brill, 1959); Wright, *Buddhism.*
17. Metzger, *Escape*; DeBary, *Sources.*
18. M. G. S. Hodgson, *The Venture of Islam: Conscience and History in a World Civilization* (Chicago: University of Chicago Press, 1974);

I. M. Lapidus and E. Burke, eds., *Islamic Politics and Social Movements* (Berkeley: University of California Press, 1988); I. M. Lapidus, *A History of Hislamic Societies* (Cambridge: Cambridge University Press, 1988); B. Lewis, *Islam in History* (London: Alcove Press, 1973)
19. Maxime Rodinson, *Mohamed* (London: Penquin Press, 1971).
20. Lewis, *Islam*.
21. E. Ashtor, "Republiques urbaines dans le Proche-Orient a l'époque des Croisades,—*Cahiers des civilizations médiévales*, 18, no. 2 (1975) 117–131; C. Cahen, "The Body Politic," in *Unity and Variety in Muslim Civilization*, G. E. von Grunebaum, ed., (Chicago: University of Chicago Press, 1955), pp. 132–167; H. A. R. Gibb, *Studies on the Civilization of Islam* (Boston: Beacon Press, 1962); I. Lapidus, *Muslim Cities in the Later Middle Ages* (Cambridge: Harvard University Press, 1967); idem, "Muslim Cities and Islamic Societies," in I. Lapidus *Middle Eastern Cities* (Berkeley: University of California Press, 1969), pp. 47–79; S. N. Eisenstadt and A. Schachar, *Society, Culture and Urbanization* (Beverly Hills and London: Sage, 1986); M. A. Shaban, *The Abbasid Revolution* (Cambridge: Cambridge University Press, 1970).
22. A. Ibn Khaldun, *The Muqaddimah* (London: Routledge and Kegan Paul, 1958); M. Mahdi, *Ibn Khaldun's Philosophy of History* (London: Allen and Unwin, 1957).
23. B. S. Turner, *Weber on Islam* (London: Routledge and Kegan Paul, 1974); E. Gellner, "Rulers and Tribesmen," in E. Gellner, ed., *Muslim Society* (Cambridge: Cambridge University Press, 1981), pp. 221–230.
24. Shaban, *Abbasid Revolution*.
25. Gibb, *Studies*; I. Lapidus, "The Separation of the State and Religion in the Development of Early Islamic Society," *International Journal of Middle Eastern Studies* 6, no. 4 (1975: 363–385.
26. D. Ayalon, *L'esclavage du Mamelouk* (Jerusalem: Israel Oriental Society, 1951); idem, "Mamluk," *The Encyclopedia of Islam* vol. 6 (Leiden: E. H. Brill, 1991). pp. 314–321; D. Pipes, *Slave Soldiers and Islam* (New Haven: Yale University Press, 1981).
27. S. A. Arjomand, *The Shadow of God and the Hidden Imam: Religion, Political Order and Societal Change in Shi'ite Iran from the Beginning to 1890* (Chicago: University of Chicago Press, 1984); M. Djait, *La Grande discorde—Religion et politique dans l'Islam des origines* (Paris: Gallimard, 1989).
28. Arjomand, *Shadow of God*.
29. Lewis, *Islam*.
30. A. S. Ahmed, *Millennium and Charisma among the Pathans* (London: Routledge and Kegan Paul, 1979); E. Gellner, *Muslim Society* (Cambridge: Cambridge University Press, 1984).
31. H. J. De Graaf, "South East Asia until the Eighteenth Century," in *The Cambridge History of Islam*, P. M. Holt, B. Lewis, and A. K. S. Lambton, eds., (Cambridge: Cambridge University Press, 1970), 2: 139–154;

G. W. J. Drewes, "Indonesia—Mysticism and Activism," in G. E. von Grunebaum *Unity and Variety in Muslim Civilization* (Chicago: University of Chicago Press, 1955), pp. 284–311; M. Hodgson, *The Venture of Islam* (Chicago: University of Chicago Press, 1974); C. A. O. van Nieuwenhuize, "Indonesia," in J. Schacht with C. E. Bosworth, *The Legacy of Islam*, 2d ed. (Oxford: Clarendon Press, 1974), pp. 144–156; M. C. Rickfels, "Six Centuries of Islamicization in Java," in N. Levtzion, ed., *Conversion to Islam* (New York: Holmes and Meier, 1979), pp. 100–120; W. R. Roff, "South East Asia in the Nineteenth Century," in P. M. Holt, B. Lewis, and A. K. S. Lambton, eds., *The Cambridge History of Islam* (Cambridge: Cambridge University Press, 1970). 1: 155–181; idem, "Islamic Movements: One or Many?" in W. R. Roff *Islam, the Political Economy of Meaning* (Berkeley: University of California Press, 1986).

32. Van Nieuwenhuize, "Indonesia"; Roff, "South East Asia"; idem, "Islamic Movements."

33. N. Levtzion, "Islam and State Formation in West Africa," in S. N. Eisenstadt, M. Arbitol, and N. Chazan, eds., *The Early State in African Perspective* (Leiden: E. J. Brill, 1986), pp. 98–109.

34. M. Weber, *The Religion of China* (New York: Free Press, 1951, 1964); S. N. Eisenstadt, "Innerweltlich Transzendenz und die Strukturierung des Welt. Max Webers Studie über China und die Gestalt des chinesischen Zivilisation," in W. Schluchter, ed., *Max Weber's Studie uber Konfuzianismus und Taoismus: Interpretation und Kritiks* (Frankfurt am main: Suhrkamp, 1983), pp. 363–412.

35. J. B. Palais, *Politics and Policy in Traditional Korea* (Cambridge: Harvard University Press, 1975); A. Schonberg, *Social Structure and Political Order in Traditional Vietnam* (London and Beverly Hills: Sage, 1970); A. Woodside, "History, Structure and Revolution in Vietnam," *International Political Science Review* 10, no. 2 (1989): 143–159.

36. Palais, *Politics.*

37. Woodside, "History"; Nguen Hyes and Ta Van Tai, *The Le Code—Law in Traditional Vietnam* (Athens, Ohio: Ohio University Press, 1982).

38. E. O. Reischauer and J. F. Fairbank, *A History of East Asian Civilization*, vol. 1, *East Asia: The Great Tradition* (Boston: Houghton Mifflin, 1960); H. P. Varley, *Japanese Culture, a Short History* (Tokyo: Tuttle, 1973).

39. J. Kitagawa, *On Understanding Japanese Religion* (Princeton: Princeton University Press, 1987); Shigeru Matsumoto, *Motoori Norinaga—1730–1801*, Harvard East Asian Series, no. 44 (Cambridge: Harvard University Press, 1970).

40. See, for instance, T. Umehara, "Shinto and Buddhism in Japanese Culture," *Japanese Foundation Newsletter* 15, no. 2 (1987): 1–7; and H. Nakamura, *The Ways of Thinking of Eastern People: India—China—Tibet—Japan* (Honolulu: East-West Center Press, 1964), pp. 345–588.

41. J. Kitagawa, "The Japanese Kokutai (National Community)—History and Myth," *History of Religions* 13, no. 3 (1974): 214–225.
42. M. Wahida, "Sacred Kinship in Early Japan: A Historical Introduction," *History of Religions* 4, no. 4 (1976): 335–340.
43. Kitagawa, *Japanese Religion*, pp. ii, iii, iv.
44. Minoru Sonoda, "The Religious Situation in Japan in Relation to Shinto," *Acta Asiatica* 51 (1987): 1–21; Shoji Okada, "The Development of State Ritual in Ancient Japan," *Acta Asiatica* (1987): 22–41; C. Blacker, "Two Shinto Myths: The Golden Age and the Chosen People," *Themes and Theories in Japanese History—Essays in Memory of Richard Story* (Princeton: Princeton University Press, 1987).
45. W. T. DeBary, ed., *The Rise of Neo Confucianism in Korea* (New York: Columbia University Press, 1985).
46. Wright and Nivison, *Confucianism*; Wright, *Buddhism*.
47. P. Nosco, ed., *Confucianism and Tokugawa Culture* (Princeton: Princeton University Press, 1984).
48. Kitagawa, *Japanese Religion*.
49. This analysis follows S. N. Eisenstadt, *Revolutions and the Transformation of Societies* (New York: Free Press, 1978); idem, "Frameworks of the Great Revolutions: Culture, Social Structure, History and Human Agency," *International Social Science Journal* 133 (1992).
50. B. Nordlinger, *On the Autonomy of the Democratic State* (Cambridge: Harvard University Press, 1981).
51. G. Lehmbruch and P. C. Schmitter, eds., *Trends Towards Corporatist Intermediation* (Beverly Hills and London: Sage, 1981).
52. T. Skocpol, *States of Social Revolutions: A Comparative Analysis of France, Russia and China* (Cambridge: Cambridge University Press, 1979); P. B. Evans, D. Rueschemeyer, T. Skocpol, eds., *Bringing the State Back In* (Cambridge: Cambridge University Press, 1985).
53. B. Badie and O. Birnbaum, *The Sociology of the State* (Chicago: University of Chicago Press, 1983).
54. A. Stepan, ed., *Authoritarian Brazil* (New Haven: Yale University Press, 1973); idem, *The State and Society Peru in Comparative Perspective* (Princeton: Princeton University Press, 1978).
55. J. M. Meyer, "The World Polity and the Authority of the Nation-State," in J. M. Meyer et al., eds., *Institutional Structure—Constitutional State, Society and the Individual* (Beverly Hills and London: Sage, 1987).
56. M. Mann, "States, Ancient and Modern," *Archives européennes de sociologie* 18, no. 2 (1977): 262–298.
57. J. Baechler, "Aux origines de la modernite: castes et féodalités (Europe, Inde, Japon)," *Archives européennes de sociologie* 27, no. 1 (1986): 31–57; J. A. Hall, *Powers and Liberties* (Berkeley: University of California Press, 1985); M. Mann, *The Source of Social Power*, vol. 1 (Cambridge: Cambridge University Press, 1986).
58. See S. N. Eisenstadt, "Macrosociology and Sociological Theory: Some New Directions," *Contemporary Sociology* 16, no. 5 (1987): 602–609.

2

Religion and the Diversity of Normative Orders

Said Amir Arjomand

The relationship between religion and political order is both intimate and complex. Certain elements in this relationship are phenomenal and general, others culturally specific. Let us begin our enquiry by separating the general from the culturally specific.

Order, Transcendence and Normative Pluralism

The creators of the early historical empires in Mesopotamia and China could allow no differentiation between the "religious" and the "political." As E. Voegelin puts it, "to establish a government is an essay in world creation. When man creates the cosmion of political order, he analogically repeats the divine creation of the cosmos."[1] This statement points to a general element in the relationship between religion and political order: the conception of society as an analogue of the cosmos, of the social order as modeled on the order of the cosmos. Sacral kingship is rooted in this analogy: The king as the lord of the four quarters symbolizes the principle of sociocosmic unity.

It is true, as S. N. Eisenstadt emphasizes in Chapter 1, that during the Axial Age, transcendence drove a wedge into the homology/harmony between the cosmic and the social orders. But the cosmological myth is not thereby eliminated, and subsists, in modified forms, in political cultures despite the superimposition of the world religions of salvation upon it. It survives Babylonia in the Hellenistic idea of the cosmos as a polis,[2] and beyond the Hellenistic age in a variety of national religions and civil theologies. Max Muller (1860) coined the term *henotheism* for social monotheism in the form of belief in a single tribal or national god, the latest transformation of which is modern nationalism. H. R. Niebuhr rightly extends the notion of henotheism as "unity of a socially organized loyalty" to communism and fascism.[3] As for civil theologies, perhaps the oldest of these is found in Varro's *Antiquities* (47 B.C.); and of its modern forms, two in particular are worth mentioning, one political, the other sociological. In the *Social Contract* (1762), Rousseau defined civil religion as "a form of theocracy, in which there can be no pontiff save the prince, and no priests save the magistrates," asserting that it would make "country the object of the citizens' adoration."[4] A century and a half later, in the *Elementary Forms of Religious Life* (1912), Durkheim would consider God society divinized. Indeed, if T. Parsons is right about the centrality of the problem of order in classical sociology, at least some elements of civil theology have been incorporated into modern sociological theory.[5]

Beyond the shared general substratum of the cosmological myth, in due course modernized as civic religion,[6] the culturally specific elements of our political ethics can be grouped into two basic categories. The first derives from revelation, the second, from philosophy; the first from the Asian and Near Eastern religions of salvation, the second, from the Greek science of politics.

The wedge driven between the cosmic and the political orders by the emergence and institutionalization of transcendance, wherever it occurs, results in the differentiation of the religious and the political. Hinduism provides us with the clearest case of such differentiation. The clarity of this differentiation is in no small measure due to the absence of a prior tradition of sacral kingship. During the formative period of Brahminical Hinduism, India was ruled by a large number of princes and kings with no single sovereign over them. Consequently, no monarch could claim religious authority over the Brahmins. The Brahmins, on the other hand, willingly acknowledged the independent authority of the rulers.[7] By arranging occupational functions, as castes, in hierarchical order in accordance with their respective distance from the supreme transcendental value, and by instituting a specific ethical code (*dharma*) for each caste, kingship was delineated as temporal authority—that is, authority pertaining to the political domain and subject to its own rules. In *Arthašastra* (ca. 300 B.C.), Kautilya could use the notions of *danda* (punishment) and *artha* (material advantage) as cornerstones of an autonomous art of government, conceived as "the exercise of force for the pursuit of interest and the maintenance of order."[8]

The articulation and coordination of the two differentiated spheres of life, the religious and the political, represent the starting point of variation and diversity in different civilizations that are shaped by the world religions. Perhaps the most important aspect of this articulation is the religious legitimation of political power. This legitimation can be both general and culturally specific. As a rule, both layers are found in the post-Axial Age political cultures. The former layer ultimately derives from the pre-world-religion, undifferentiated cosmological myth, and represents residues of the compactness found in the notions of sacral kingship. The ability of the cosmological myth to withstand the impact of the world religions is strikingly manifest in the case of Buddhism, where transcendence took the form of the categorical rejection of the reality of established order. Sacral kingship not only survived in the symbolism of the four quarters and Hindu incarnationist beliefs concerning the king,[9] but also acquired distinctly Buddhist form, as the pivotal human element in the Buddhist conception of the cosmic order as process, comprehending the political order as a "Commonwealth of Trans-migration."[10] The survival of the cosmological myth is equally striking at the other end of the spectrum—that is, in the case of Islam, the last of the world religions that is sometimes misleadingly characterized as a theocracy. There, too, we find the persistence of a political culture independent of the Islamic religion, and with roots in the pre-Islamic ideas of universal monarchy and sacral kingship that embody the cosmological myth.[11] Like the *Arthašastra*, the autonomous art or craft of government in medieval Islam rested on punishment and the use of force to maintain order, the very word for "politics" being none other than *siyāsat* (punishment).[12]

The culturally specific layer in theories of legitimacy of authority presupposes the differentiation introduced by the world religions, and makes the superior religious authority the model of, and the basis for, political authority. What E. H. Kantorowicz called the "royal christology" of the early Middle Ages,[13] the Islamic idea of the caliphate as successorship of the Prophet in Sunni Islam, and the Buddhist idea of the Chakkavatti as reincarnation of the Buddha and the universal savior-king can be given as examples. The notions of king as *Christus*,[14] the Chakkavatti,[15] and the caliph[16] are all culturally specific and idiosyncratic in comparison to a variety of subsisting notions of the king as the Animate Law, or the king as

God's image or shadow on earth,[17] in all of which the monarch symbolizes the social order.

It is interesting to note that in medieval Russia, the Christ-like notion of the saintly prince, ideally a passion-sufferer (*strastoterpets*), persisted much longer than in the West. According to Cherniavsky, it was not until the reign of Ivan IV the Terrible (1533-1585), after Byzantium had fallen and Moscow claimed to have become the Third Rome, that the imperial notion of the tsar (Caesar) became primary in the Russian royal ideology. This clearly entailed "a certain distanciation between Christ and the prince."[18] Nevertheless, the older christological and kenotic features remained attached to the notion of "the pious tsar," and "the most-gentle tsar."[19]

Philosophy and the world religions can be compared as comprehensive solutions to the problem of meaning. What best differentiates the two, is the Greek view of the political order as a self-contained sphere for the realization of transcendent truth based on reason. The ultimacy of meaning attached to the political community and its organization in this view is unique. The paradigms for the political order developed by Plato and Aristotle were fundamentally different from the symbolization of political order by cosmic analogies found in the early empires. Far from conceiving the social order as a part of the cosmic constitution, they were developed in opposition to the established order and, furthermore, "never formed the institutional order of any concrete society."[20] With them, the anthropological principle replaces the cosmological analogy. The political society is conceived as the field for the actualization of human nature. To understand the constitution of the polis, we need to understand human nature.[21]

The dislodging of the cosmological myth by revelation follows a very different path. As Eisenstadt shows in Chapter One with respect to Buddhism, Confucianism and Islam, even within the same tradition, different paths are followed depending on varying sociopolitical structural conditions. In the case of Japan, the cosmological myth is not dislodged but fully accommodated. As the transcendental elements in both Buddhism and Confucianism were subdued by the Japanese immanentist theology, the royal cosmogonic myth[22] could survive unscathed to be made the basis of the Meiji Restoration. Furthermore, it has even survived the impact of modern constitutionalism, as was demonstrated in November 1990 when the new emperor, Akihito, performed the Shinto rite of *Daijosai*, the Great Rice Offering to the sun-goddess, Amaterasu.[23]

The accommodation of the cosmological myth in Indic Southeast Asia was almost as complete. In Bali, to take Clifford Geertz's paradigm of "the doctrine of the exemplary center,"[24] the differentiation of the religious and political functions distinctive of Hinduism lapsed in confrontation with the notion of kingship as "the model-and-copy conception of order."[25] Political order, embodied in the Balinese king and the court around him, was the facsimile of cosmic order: The king was "the numinous center of the world," and the palace, the seat of the king, was its axis.[26]

The best-studied case of the dislodging of the cosmological myth, in Western Christianity, merits attention both on comparative grounds and because of its special significance in world history.[27] By postulating a transcendent divine reality, and by institutionalizing religious authority, all world religions desacralize the political order in principle, and thus introduce an element of duality into the normative order. The dualism of spiritual and temporal authority established by the papal revolution in the medieval West was but one particular resolution of the fundamental tension between religion and politics, which had deep roots in the Old Testament and was to resurface in Islam. Yahweh's begrudging consent to the decision of His people to have a king like their neighbors[28] instituted a fundamental tension between kingship and prophecy. Although Yahweh's covenant with David legitimated the kings as His Anointed, it did not supersede the prior Sinaitic covenant. The latter more fundamental covenant gave the prophets direct and unmediated authority to criticize the Anointed of Yahweh.[29]

In Western Christianity, however, normative dualism went the furthest. In Voegelin's words, in the final version of the orthodox political theology, "the spiritual destiny of man in the Christian sense cannot be represented on earth by the power organization of the political society; it can be represented only by the church. The sphere of power is radically de-divinized; it has become temporal."[30] Hence, the "double representation of man in society through church and empire [that] lasted through the Middle Ages."

Normative pluralism in Western medieval culture was even more far-reaching. The successful introduction of Aristotelianism to Western Christianity produced, in Aquinas, a far more radical differentiation between religion and politics than the one implied by the doctrine of the two swords and described by Voegelin. It established the distinction between the natural (political) and the spiritual man, thus differentiating between the citizen and the Christian, or rather between the *humanitas* and the *christianitas* of the individual.[31] Aquinas's treatment of the distinction between nature and grace, his argument for the divine emanation of the law of nature and its accessibility to human reason, coupled with the direct adaptation, from Aristotle, of public welfare as the supreme goal of the political order, made possible the development of an autonomous political science (*scientia politica*), a term, incidentally, coined by Aquinas himself.[32] Henceforth, two types of truth would have to exist together; and the tension between them would be a permanent feature of the Christian civilization.[33] With one further step, Dante would cross the threshold to humanistic secularism, shattering the Thomist unity of temporal in the spiritual, and substituting the notion of "mankind" for the church's ideal of universal Christendom.[34]

Normative dualism is by no means absent in medieval Islam, which is usually characterized as monistic in contrast to medieval Christianity. The Koran[35] seeks to resolve the tension between kingship and prophecy by assigning kingship to God, but this solution is never institutionalized. In *Kutadgu Bilig*, the first extant Turko-Islamic mirror for princes, written in 1069 or 1070, the king (Rising Sun), as the representative of Justice, is confronted with the Sufi ascetic (Wide Awake) who represents the End; and the author can exhort the prince: "Here is the path of Religion *and* the path of the World. Stray not from the path or you will howl in hell."[36] It is no accident that the representative of the transcendent truth of religion against the immanent truth of order is the figure of the Sufi. Sufism represented a very important mode of institutionalization of transcendence in medieval Islam. Although world-renouncing and apolitical, early Sufism had momentous political implications: It amplified normative pluralism and enhanced the duality of religious and political authority.

The famous Muslim theologian, al-Ghazzālī (d. 1111), expresses this same duality:

> Know and understand that God has chosen two categories among mankind, and placed them above all others: the prophets, and the kings. He has sent the prophets to His creatures to lead them to him; and he chose [variant, sent] the kings to protect men from one another, making the common weal dependent on them . . . ."The ruler is the shadow of God on earth." [Prophetic Tradition][37]

This highly significant passage represents the reconciliation of the pre-Islamic Persian idea of kingship with the Islamic doctrine of prophecy. The terminology of the Islamic doctrine of prophecy is used to establish the unmediated divine sanctioning of temporal rule: God chooses/sends kings to maintain order as He chooses/sends prophets to rectify religion.

In an interesting stylistic reversal a century later, Najm al-Dīn Rāzī employs the terminology of royal ideology to establish the same dichotomy of religious and political authority:

> There are two classes of kings: Kings of the world and kings of religion. Those who are kings of the world are the form for God's attributes of favor and wrath, but they are imprisoned within their form and unable to recognize their attributes. . . . As for those who are the kings of religion, they are both the manifestation of the divine attributes of favor and wrath and the recipients of that manifestation . . . . They have penetrated to the mystery of the treasure of "he who knows himself, knows too his Lord," (Qur'an 76:20) and have mounted as rightful owners the throne of eternal kingship and abiding monarchy.[38]

It is obvious, however, that the terminology of sacral kingship is appropriated only to effect its spiritual transposition. Earthly kingship is radically devalued as "borrowed and transient kingship" in contrast to the true and eternal kingship of religion.[39]

For comparative purposes, it is important to note, however, that there was no parallel to the absorption of Aristotelianism and accommodation of politics by the orthodoxy in medieval Islam and Judaism. In both cases, there were important Aristotelian trends, but these were defeated by the traditionalists. In Islamic political thought, the Greek philosophical trend never displaced the traditional ideas of monarchy and statecraft, and remained subservient to it even at its height in the Middle Ages.[40] It would not be an exaggeration to say that the contemporary clerical constitution-makers of Iran are the first established Muslim authorities to feel the urgent need to reconcile the fundamental concepts of the Greek science of politics with the Islamic sacred law (*sharīʿa*) as the public representation of transcendent justice in Islam.[41]

The impact of Christianity on medieval Europe was much greater than that of Buddhism on medieval Japan. The politically fragmented feudal Europe was juridically integrated by the church, which was doctrinally conceptualized as the *corpus Christi mysticum*. With the help of Aristotle through Thomism, this idea was transformed into the *corpus reipublicae mysticum*, with the king as its head and in conjunction with the independent, secular notion of *patria*, the forerunner of our idea of the nation.[42] The authority and privileges of the church could henceforth be challenged in the name of the common weal (*salus rei publicae*).[43] More crucially, the king's body politic could be separated from his body natural; and even more abstract notions of the state could develop in early modern times. The notion of the political community was disengaged both from the cosmological myth and from Christology, and resumed the character of the commonwealth, the *res publica*, the common thing. It was thus detached from both its royal and its religious symbol, and secularized. This manner of secularization meant the multiplication of the idea of community. The old notion of the church persisted while the newer notions of the state and the nation were superimposed upon it. To these, the Enlightenment added the notion of civil society, which implied the recognition of the ligitimacy of private interests as autonomous, as independent of the public authority of the state. The normative pluralism of modern societies is inherent in the coexistence of these overlapping orders.

In the present century, the modern ideas of the state and the nation as legally constituted orders, together with the republican form of government, were imported into the Islamic world. There, the notion of political community had been that of the subjects (*re'āyā*) of the king, and the notion of religious community, the *umma*, had undergone none of the secularizing and pluralizing transformations of the *corpus mysticum*. The consequences of the reception of constitutionalism in the Islamic world have entailed the diversification of political ethics and the normative order through the transmission of international political culture.[44] The paradoxical consequences of the more recent fundamentalist attempt to reject normative pluralism in the Islamic Republic of Iran are touched upon in Chapter 9. Constitution-making under Khomeini shows the impact of a militant religion that enters the revolutionary ideological politics, and appropriates the modern state and its legal framework. It is not the differentiated religion of the kind that deabsolutized the political order, but a monistic religion donning the garb of the secular political ideologies of the twentieth century. The result is a radical modification of the traditional Shi'ite dualism of authority in the monistic direction typical of Sunni Islam.[45] The state thus "Shi'itized," however, imposes its own (secularizing) normative logic on its clerical masters.[46]

Modern Catholicism has faced increasing normative pluralism differently. The interface of the Catholic Church and political order in modern times can be conceived of as three sets of relationships: those with the state, the nation, and civil society. In the era of secularization through the state, it is natural for the church, whose independent authority is progressively restricted and weakened, to orient itself toward society. This reorientation explains the early twentieth-century Catholic conception of civil society as fundamentally apolitical,[47] and thus the attempt by the Catholic Action movement to consolidate and mobilize Catholic society "apolitically." As José Casanova shows in Chapter 4, there had been an unmistakable shift in the orientation of the Catholic Church in Poland and Spain in the last decades—away from the state and in the direction of the political community, variously and simultaneously conceived as the nation and/or civil society. This dissociation of the church from authoritarian states in both countries enabled it to play a significant role in the transition to democracy, and in furthering political pluralism.

The contemporary American polity arguably enjoys the highest degree of normative pluralism, not only because of the greater ethnic and religious heterogeneity of its population but also because of the relative vigor of both traditional and civic religious sentiment. This is not to say that the Protestant Christianity of the formative period of nation-building has had no lasting effect. In passing, Steven M. Tipton makes the interesting point that the political and denominational alignments in American society do not overlap significantly.[48] The same point has recently been made with respect to the political and religious alignments within evangelical Protestantism.[49] The implication is clear: There is no distinctive Christian politics in the United States, not even a distinctive fundamentalist Protestant politics. Therefore, the political divisions among American Christians take the shape of the contour of the larger political society. Here, a comparative perspective points to the ethics of Christianity—and more specifically to the tenet on the separation of church and state—as the best explanatory factor.

Nevertheless, there can be little doubt concerning the prevalence of multiple moral traditions within the American political culture as highlighted by Tipton in Chapter 11 of this book. He urges us to discard the oversimplified model of American culture, and to think, instead, about the ongoing and fertile, if painful, cultural conversation between the multiple moral traditions. If there is a common culture, or rather cultural matrix, it is not uniform and homogeneous, but woven of contrasting moral traditions. In addition to civic republicanism and utilitarian individualism, we have a variety of public theologies that include not only Protestant fundamentalism but also such latter-day offshoots of the Greek science of politics as feminism and liberationism. It should be pointed out that the diversity of contemporary American political culture goes even further. In addition to "civil religion" and "public theology," covered by Tipton, the principles of legitmacy in the American political culture also include a number of amoral and areligious legitimatory factors such as utilitarianism and efficiency.[50]

The de facto pluralism of the normative orders crystallized around the world religions, although often taken for granted by people of learning in traditional societies, was seldom explicitly endorsed by them. Furthermore, this de facto pluralism has throughout history stimulated a variety of reactive monistic counter-claims to possession of truth. Most recent among such monistic counterclaims are the nontheistic political religions of the twentieth century, notably communism and fascism. Until the collapse of communism in 1989, our age could aptly be characterized as "the age par excellence of political faiths, of secular salvations offered on a national or universal scale."[51]

Under Robespierre, Rousseau's civil religion was translated into reality as the first modern political religion: the cult of the Supreme Being whose priests were the magistrates and whose rites were the patriotic festivals.[52] The political religion of the French Revolution, however, was ideologically underdeveloped. This deficiency was rectified by the political religions of the twentieth century. As Voegelin persuasively argues, these modern political religions are premised on the transposition of the salvational dimension of transcendence into history: "The death of the spirit is the price of progress."[53] With the spirit dies the transcendent idea of truth, paving the way for the effacement of the distinction between truth and political "rightness."[54] The religious sphere is swallowed by the political sphere and thereby obliterated. The result is the reinstitu-tion of immanent political monism in the form of totalitarian ideology. In a manner evocative of the Zoroastrian notion of the Lie (pseudo-order in opposition to Truth/Order),[55] Ciliga (in 1930), Orwell (in 1949), and following them Kolakowski, see the totalitarian ideology as amounting to the abrogation of "the very idea of truth," and its replacement by "organized mendacity."[56] Furthermore, "The ideology is total in a much stronger sense. . . than any religious faith has ever achieved. . . . [It] annihilates the personal form of life. This is much more than any religion has ever prescribed."[57] This funda-mental disregard of the private, and the obverse sacralization of the public, make modern political religions distinct from the world religions of salvation. In fact, they hark back to the ancient "political religion Christianity tore up by the roots"[58]—namely, the Roman civic religion whose restriction of sacrality to the public sphere elicited Tertullian's protest that "nothing is more alien to us [Christians] than public life."[59]

The pretension of the political creeds of the twentieth century to take the place of religion was apparent to the educated Muslims from the beginning. An Iranian observer of the rise of Bolshevism and fascism viewed these political creeds (*maslak* in the singular) as substitutes for religion when Europe had entered "the stony path of materialism."[60] More recently, the blind Egyptian fundamentalist preacher, Shaykh Kishk, found it natural to narrate: "And socialism then was a religion which the Ruler without God[61] [i.e., Nasser] adopted."[62] The sharper observers in the Islamic world have not failed to note that various secular substitutes for religion in our days have become "deities in their own right, one-eyed superbeings."[63] But many of their fellow Muslims have succumbed to the fascination of political religions, and have sought to recast traditional Islam in their frame.[64] For this reason, the Islamic revolution in Iran is interesting in displaying the amalgamation of the millennial beliefs of the world religions with an Islamic political ideology constructed in imitation of the nontheistic political religions.

Millennial Transposition of the Idea of Order

The enterprise of symbolization of order, which is central to religion, gives it the power of both social construction and social destruction. Religion does construct normative order. By rearranging the positive and negative elements in the symbolism of order, however, it can also uphold a utopia premised on the cataclysmic destruction of the prevailing evil order. From the perspective of symbolization of order, the "conservative" and "revolutionary" aspects of religion, far from constituting the insoluble paradox of the sociology of religion, can in fact be seen as two sides of the same coin. This can be demonstrated by considering millennialism from the perspective of symbolization of order.

If the Mesopotamian cosmological myth captured the general relationship between religion and political order, millennial myths based on the notion of a lost Golden Age, an archetype of cosmic regeneration,[65] give us the general archetype of religious utopia of restored primeval order as a vision that can motivate "absolute" political action.[66] The Andean cosmogony of eternal return, described by Manuel Sarkisyanz in Chapter 5, belongs to this category. The utopia is set in the mythic past, as the Golden Age, but time being cyclical, it supplies the archetype of "re-volutionary renovation" following periodic cataclysm. Apocalyptic destruction of evil order is the inevitable prelude to the restoration of true, primal order. As with order, so with chaos, no distinction is made between nature and society in the archetype. Accordingly, in all apocalyptic writings natural, moral, and political catastrophes occur together in the days preceding the end of time and the restoration of eternal order.[67]

Upon the general archetype of cosmic regeneration, world religions of salvation can impose culturally specific millennial notions. This archetypal substratum can be found in the Old Testament,[68] and much more clearly in Buddhism. But the Abrahamic religions[69] and Buddhism[70] imposed fundamentally different millennial notions upon this common substratum.

When the articulation of religion and politics is primarily in terms of theodicy, the differentiation of the religious and political spheres remains labile, problematic, and contestable. In this respect, Judaism and Islam stand in sharp contrast to Hinduism. The sacred laws of these monotheistic religions are monumental attempts to translate theodicy into minute regulation of social life according to God's commandments; but they cannot eliminate the contestational and antinomial potential of theodicy. The potential for contestation becomes especially intense when the problem of theodicy is solved by an eschatological distinction between an evil present and the approaching breakthrough of the millennium of bliss.

As Weber remarked in his prefatory note to *Ancient Judaism*, "the social order of the world was conceived to have been turned into the opposite of that promised for the future, but in the future it was to be overturned. . . .The whole attitude toward life of ancient Jewery was determined by this conception of a future God-guided political and social revolution."[71]

The problem of theodicy, absent from the "naive" monotheism of the Elohistic and Yahwistic collections, only arose with "the decline of the national state." It was only with the crisis and collapse of monarchy that the idea of compensation became "particularly indispensable for political theodicy; . . .God was to be a god of just compensation."[72] Then the exile "produced the most radical . . . theodicy of ancient Jewry," namely, the Second Isaiah's "theodicy of Israel's suffering in the universal perspective of a wise and divine world government."[73] The completely this-worldly horizon of the pre-exilic prophecy underwent a radical change with the soteriology of the Second Isaiah,[74] and the subsequent development of apocalyptic messianism. In this juncture, Persian Zoroastrian influences during the latter part of the Babylonian exile seem quite probable.[75] After all, in the Second Isaiah we have the beginning of a sharp eschatological distinction between things past and things to come that was distinctive of Zoroastrianism, and thereby the decisive move beyond the preexilic conception of the day of the Lord as one of unmitigated doom.[76] The Second Isaiah couples the historical deliverance of Israel with "a glorious transformation of the natural order (43:19, 51:16, 55:12–13).[77] Persian influences, especially the Zoroastrian doctrine of the transfiguration of the world (*frašo.kereti*), are discernible in this development. In the next two centuries, under the Achaemenid Empire, Zoroastrian ideas spread throughout the Middle East, and the classical apocalyptic writings of the Hellenistic era, as we shall see presently, bear an even clearer mark of their influence.[78] Such historical connections notwithstanding, and apart from the fact that Zarathustra (1400–1200 B.C. according to Boyce; 1000–600 according to Widengren) is the oldest known millenarian prophet, the development of millennial soteriology in Zoroastrianism merits our attention for the light it throws on the unexpectedly intimate relation between the religious conceptions of order and utopia.

The following prayer of Zarathustra is preserved in the Gathas (the capitalized terms are hypostasized deities): When, Mazda (Wisdom), shall Devotion come with Order (*aša*), having good dwellings, having pasturage through Dominion? Who will stop cruelty by bloodthirsty, wicked men? To whom will come the teaching of Good Purpose? They truly shall be 'saoshyants' (the beneficent ones) of the land who follow knowledge of Thy teaching, Mazda."[79]

The Zoroastrian savior, the Saoshyant ("He who will bring benefit"), predicted by Zarathustra as the one "greater than good" to come after him (Yasnā 43.3),[80] will come when the transfiguration of the world (*frašo.kereti*) is at hand. There is evidence that at some stage Zarathustra believed that he himself would experience the end of time and the final annihilation of the Lie by the forces of Truth. He accordingly enjoined his followers to be prepared to destroy the enemy with weapons in the great final battle between the forces of good and evil. Zarathustra himself is thus a saoshyant. His millennium is, however, to be followed by those of two other saviors before the coming of the last millennium.[81] The eschatological savior of this final millennium is named Astvat-ereta. He will be born of a virgin mother and the seeds of Zarathustra preserved at the bottom of a lake she bathes in. He comes out from Lake Kansaoya, "brandishing the victorious weapon that . . . King Vishtaspa bore to avenge Order/Truth (*aša*) upon the enemy host; then he will drive the Lie (Drug) from the world of Order/Truth (*aša*).[82]

The philogical evidence from these texts throws considerable light on our central issue, namely, the relation among order, utopia, and soteriology. The name of the savior, Astvat-ereta, a western Iranian dialectal variant of Astvat-aša, means "He who embodies Order (=Truth),"[83] deriving from another prayer of Zarathustra's:

> May Order/Truth be embodied, strong with life.
> May Devotion dwell in the sun-beholding kingship
> (khšathra).[84]

The savior, then, is but the agent of transfiguration of a world overwhelmed by the Lie/pseudo-order into Truth/righteous Order. The poetic beauty and terrible simplicity of this millennial solution to the problem of theodicy make the image of order a potent tool for revolution. This clash of Order/Truth with the existing pseudo-order makes millennialism one of the oldest forms of absolute politics.

The adduced philological evidence is not merely accidental but rather reveals a phenomenal connection between order and utopia. This same phenomenal connection explains the widespread parallelisms between sacral kingship and soteriology, between royal and messianic symbolism. The divine charisma of the Zoroastrian savior, for instance, is none other than the royal charisma (khvarenah).[85] The key soteriological notions in the Bible were also originally political terms. Not only the term *Messiah* (māšîaḥ, Anointed) but also the Hebrew and Greek terms for savior—môšîa' and sōtēr, respectively—were originally political terms associated with the idea of kingship. Hammurabi was the "saving shepherd" (re'u mušallimu) of his people.[86] Gideon had saved his people from the power of Midian;[87] and during the reign of Jehoahaz (814–798 B.C.), Yahweh gave Israel a savior (môšîa') to free them from the grip of Aram.[88] Kings were saviors/helpers of their people; the formula for paying homage to the king was "save, king!" (hôšî'â hammelek).[89] Like the Saoshyant who "brings benefits," the king in the Old Testament saves by bringing salvation (yĕšâ') (width, spaciousness—i.e., well-being).[90] The royal messianism of the "Book of Immanuel"[91] and Jeremiah (23:5) is therefore by no means accidental. Nor, for that matter, is the Buddhist notion of savior-king described above.

The Second Isaiah's picture of Cyrus as Yahweh's shepherd and his Anointed (Messiah) follows the Near Eastern paradigm closely; and it can plausibly be said that his depiction of the Suffering Servant (esp. 53:2) is a deliberate contrast to the royal picture of

Cyrus, and resulted from the prophet's disappointment with the latter.[92] Needless to say, the Messiah ("the Anointed one") remained king, albeit "humble and mounted on an ass."[93]

Meanwhile, as long as the house of David reigned, albeit in a shrunken Judah and with Israel (the northen kingdom) divided into administrative units of the Assyrian Empire, the imagery of the king as the Anointed, the shadow of God and the people's shield and protector persisted.[94] Thus Isaiah 32:1-2:

> Behold, a king shall reign in righteousness
> and his princes rule with justice, . . .
> like the shadow of a great rock in a thirsty land.

With the destruction of Jerusalem by the Babylonians, however,

> The breath of our nostrils, the Messiah of Yahweh,
> was caught in their pits,
> of whom we had said, "In his shadow
> we shall live among the nations."[95]

Under Babylonian and especially Hellenistic domination, the messianic transportation of the cosmological myth of sacral kingship became complete. The savior of the world took the place of the king of the four quarters. As S. Mowickel put it, "The Messiah is the future eschatological realization of the ideal of kingship."[96]

Millenarian utopianism juxtaposes the normative idea of order to the fact of an existing order based on falsehood and destined for destruction at the appointed hour. Apocalytic millenarianism was Zarathustra's means of transcendentalizing order, as it was Jesus Christ's centuries later. The same is true of Muhammad, as evidenced by the early apocalyptic Meccan verses of the Koran. Apocalypticism is therefore a powerful means for introducing transcendence independently of political considerations. One set of political circumstances is particularly important in stimulating apocalyptic yearnings, however. When the established order is based upon alien political and cultural domination or penetration, the utopian counterclaim is more likely to rouse apocalyptic images of destruction. Indeed, the apocalyptic destruction of the established order in millenarianism can be considered an archetypal reaction to foreign domination. The hated present order is to be destroyed in apocalyptic chaos to pave the ground for the establishment of the envisioned authentic order. Zephaniah's protomillennial proclamation (1:7-8) under Assyrian hegemony, that "the day of the Lord is near," begins with the dire threat to "punish the royal house and its chief officers and all who ape outlandish fashions." Above all, the Hellenistic domination of the Near East gave currency to a rich apocalyptic literature in Zoroastrian Iran, and thence in intertesta- mental Judaism and Christianity.[97]

After the overthrow of the Achaemenid Empire by Alexander and in reaction to Hellenistic rule, Iranian apocalyptic beliefs increasingly assumed the form of political restoration. This restora- tion consisted in the establishment of the fifth monarchy—a notion passed on from the *Bahman Yasht* to the Book of Daniel, probably around 250 B.C.[98] The Oracle of Hystaspes, which replicates many of the essential details of the Iranian apocalyptic literature of this period,[99] also records the belief that the agent of this restoration is the Great King, who will be sent from the heavens by God to save the besieged righteous in response to their loud cry for heavenly help. The Great King was considered the reincarnation of Mithra, the sun-god.[100]

This restorative royal apocalypticism in reaction to Hellenistic domination has an Egyptian parallel in the anti-Hellenistic Oracle of the Potter, which foretells that "Egypt shall be made to flourish when the king. . .comes from the Sun-god as a bestower of blessings." This prophecy finds an unmistakable echo in the Third Sibylline Oracle: "And then from the Sun-god will God send a king who will keep the whole earth from evil war."[101]

In the second century B.C., Iranian apocalyptic notions became absorbed into the Jewish apocalyptic tradition, alongside Satan and his armies. "The Old of Days" of the Book of Daniel and "the Head [chief] of Days" of the Book of Enoch are none other than the Iranian god of time, Zervan ("old age," etymoligically).[102] The sections of the Book of Daniel that bear the imprint of the Iranian apocalyp- ticism were written about 165 B.C., and are the oldest part of the Bible where a current political struggle—that between Egypt and Syria—is seen apocalyptically. There, for the first time, we have "that apocalyptic interpretation of contemporary political struggles which was to become an ordinary feature of later rebellions of the Jews against foreign rule."[103]

Once millenarian tenets become doctrinally established in a religious tradition, they can be endemically activated under a wide variety of circumstances. Even so, alien political and cultural domination provides a specially powerful stimulus for the activation of millenarian tenets. The threat from an alien culture need not involve foreign political domination. The threat to Orthodox Christianity posed by the Westernization of Russia that began by

Peter the Great stimulated the apocalyptic messianism of the Old Believers. Peter's Westernization meant that the Third Rome had fallen; and, as a fourth Rome there could not be, Antichrist reigned. To the Old Believers, Peter was thus Antichrist whose reigned continued under his successors.[104] During the second quarter of the nineteenth century, in the fertile grounds of Theravada Buddhism in Burma,[105] of Zaydi Shi'ism in the Yemen,[106] and, to a lesser extent, of Twelver Shi'ism in Iran,[107] colonialist intrusion was evoking millennial responses. In our days, millennialism resurfaces under the garb of Maoist Marxism among the Peruvian *mestizos* of the Shining Path who are seeking to overthrow the heirs of the Spanish *conquistadores.*[108]

The utopian crystallization of transcendence, first effected in the oral tradition of Zoroastrianism, was given scriptural embodiment in the Judeo-Christian tradition and transmitted to Islam. In Theravada Buddhism, it is *political* authority, the authority of the monarch that rests on the preemption of millennialism through the idea of the Chakkavatti, the universal savior-king.[109] In rabbinical Judaism, Western Christianity, and Shi'ite Islam, by contrast, the containment of millennialism serves as the precondition for the institutionalization of *hierocratic* authority. Rabbinical authority rests on the containment of apocalyptic messianism,[110] buttressed by the prohibition of calculating the arrival of the messianic age and ideas such as the occultation of the Messiah born on the day of the destruction of the temple.[111] As Voegelin points out, religious authority in Christianity, especially since the time of St. Augustine, rests on the suppression of the millenarian tenet.[112] The same is true of Islam,[113] especially Shi'ite Islam, where the institutionalization of clerical authority went hand in hand with the containment of millennialism in the form of the belief in the return of the Mahdi by means of the doctrine of the occultation of the Twelfth Imam.[114] The inclusion of the millennial tenet in the Jewish, Christian, and Shi'ite scriptures, however, makes the activation of the utopian potential of transcendence a recurrent possibility.

Like so many other phenomena represented by god Janus, millennialism has two faces. With one face it looks in fury at the established order, with the other at all normative pluralism. The millenarian, like the prophet and the philosopher, is the representative of a new truth that is in rivalry with the established truth of society. One consequence of this refusal to accept the established truth of society, however, is great condensation of reality. The result is a (re)fusion of the religious and the political spheres, and thus a reduction of normative pluralism, a result that is due to the utopian hypostatization of transcendence. For this reason, millennialism invites comparison with the modern political religions, which project the undifferentiated sacral myth of society into the future as the perfect society to be realized by revolutionary action. From this point of view, the latter appear as a secularized equivalent of the former, as has been demonstrated by the studies of Bolshevism as political messianism.[115]

In short, millennialism and political religions are alike in that they both entail denial of normative pluralism. But whereas the political religions are immanentist and historicist, the millennial hypostatization is inherently utopian, and as a consequence, millennialism remains inevitably liminal.

Pluralism and Normative Contention

At the close of a century marked by the clash of rival Christian creeds that had produced the wars of religion in Europe and the Puritan revolution in England, Locke deduced "the duty of toleration" from the normative distinction between the business of civil government and the concern of religion with the salvation of the soul.[116] Lock qualifies the duty of toleration with a proviso: "if they do not tend to establish dominion over others, or civil impunity [for their] church."[117] This big *if* points to the limits of toleration in Lock's times as in ours. The clash of rival creeds in the century now coming to a close has been more global, and has drawn into conflict a far broader variety of political religions and religious fundamentalisms. The clash of contemporary monisms makes Locke's principle of tolerance all but nugatory. Yet, never before has the world been as unified as it is at present; and never before has the need for the recognition of the moral implications of normative pluralism been as great. To avoid the "sacrifice of the intellect,"[118] we must make of the de facto normative pluralism of the historical civilizations an explicit ethical principle. Only by acknowledging the diversity of normative orders, and the coexistence of conflicting worldviews "among which in the end one has to make a choice,"[119] can politics be made morally responsible, or in other words, become an autonomous vocation in Weber's sense.

In Weber's view, under the impact of modern scientific rationalism, "many old gods ascend from their graves; they are disenchanted and hence take the form of impersonal forces." Life is again treated as immanent and interpreted in its own terms, as it had been before the rise of the world religions of salvation.

Therefore, "it knows only of an unceasing struggle of these gods with one another."[120] This view overestimates the normative impact of modern science in a typically Victorian fashion. It is true that the pantheon of our diverse normative cosmos is rent by constant struggle. Yet the struggle is not so much among the resuscitated and disenchanted immanent gods as among two other groups of deities: the surviving, although disenchanted god of order, and the surviving transcendental truths of revelation and philosophy. The last group, at any rate, remains unscathed by the "disenchantment of the world." Not only has the cosmological myth once more risen from its grave with the rise of modern nationalism and statism, as one state after another is Asia and Africa "promotes a political metaphysic in place of religion,"[121] but the truths of the Greek science of politics are upheld with more conviction than ever and the truths of revelation have retained much of their vigor in the Islamic world, and are probably reemerging from their long eclipse in Eastern and Western Europe. Tolerance is an insufficient normative principle, and may prove an unaffordable luxury, but moral responsibility can nevertheless to freely exercised. The condition for the free exercise of moral responsibility in the modern world is the recognition of pluralism as the normative principle of politics. Given this diversity of normative orders, political freedom and politics as a vocation must be premised on the inevitable necessity of choice among the agonistic gods of the modern political arena.

Notes

1. E. Voegelin, *Order and History* (Baton Rouge: Louisiana State University Press, 1956), 1: 16.
2. Ibid., p. 45.
3. H. R. Niebuhr, *Radical Monotheism and Western Culture* (New York: Harper Torchbooks, 1960), p. 25.
4. J.-J. Rousseau, *The Social Contract and Discourses*, trans. G. D. H. Cole (New York: Dutton, 1973 [1762]), pp. 272–273.
5. T. Parsons, *The Structure of Social Action*, 2 vols. (New York: McGraw-Hill, 1937).
6. R. N. Bellah, "Civil Religion in America," *Daedalus* 96 (1967): 1–21.
7. M. Weber, *Religion of India: The Sociology of Hinduism and Buddhism*, ed. and trans. H. H. Gerth and D. Martindale (New York: Free Press, 1958), pp. 141–145; E. Shils, "Some Observations on the Place of Intellectuals in Max Weber's Sociology, with Special Reference to Hinduism," in S. N. Eisenstadt, ed., *The Origins and Diversity of Axial Age Civilizations* (Albany: State University of New York Press, 1986), pp. 447–448.

8. L. Dumont, *Religion, Politics and History in India* (The Hague/Paris: Mouton, 1970), pp. 68, 80, 86. Furthermore, the Indian legal system was pervasively pluralistic. Patrimonial adjudication as an aspect of the art of government apart, the Hindu sacred law coexisted side by side with particular laws of occupational groups and castes; and consociations, especially castes, had autonomy in the administration of justice and arbitration. See M. Weber, *Economy and Society*, ed. G. Roth and C. Wittich (Berkeley: University of Californai Press, 1978), 2: 816–817.

9. See J. M. van der Kroef, "Kingship and Political Legitimacy in Southeast Asia: Patterns of an Enduring Traditin," *Asiatische Studien* 22 (1968), esp. pp. 70, 76.

10. P. Mus, "Thousand-Armed Kannon: A Mystery or a Problem?" *Journal of Indian and Buddhist Studies* (1964): 1–33.

11. See S. A. Arjomand, *The Shadow of God and the Hidden Imam: Religion, Political Order and Societal Change in Shi'ite Iran from the Beginning to 1890* (Chicago: University of Chicago Press, 1984).

12. Ibid., p. 100.

13. E. H. Kantorowicz, *The King's Two Bodies: A Study in Medieval Political Theology* (Princeton: Princeton University Press, 1957), Chapter 3.

14. The Carolingian Empire introduced the christological conception of kingship, which was unknown to previous Christianized barbarian kingdoms. The new Carolingian rites of anointing and crowning referred directly to the Bible: "the ruler as the Lord's Anointed and therefore another Christ or partaking in Christ's rule, the crown as the crown of Life, *corona vitae*, but also the sign for co-reigning with Christ" (L. Ejerfeldt, "Myth of the State in the West European Middle Ages," in H. Biezais, ed., *The Myth of the State* ([Stockholm: Almqvist and Wiksell, 1972], p. 165).

    This curious retransposition of the Lord's Anointed (Messiah) into its original political meaning was not to hold, owing to the entrenched normative dualism that became definitively institutionalized with the papal revolution of the eleventh and twelfth centuries.

15. In the case of the notion of the Chakkavatti, the idiosyncracy consists in the accretion of the soteriological feature to the earlier general features that derive from the integration of the political order into the cosmic process. See S. Tambiah, *World Conqueror and World Renouncer: A Study of Buddhism and Polity in Thailand Against a Historical Background* (Cambridge: Cambridge University Press, 1976), Chapters 2, 4–6; and B. L. Smith, "The Ideal Social Order as Portrayed in the Chronicles of Ceylon," in B. L. Smith, ed., *Religion and Legitimation of Power in Sri Lanka* (Chambersburg, Pa.: Anima Books, 1978), pp. 63–67; idem, "Kingship, the Sangha, and the Process of Legitimation in Anuradhapura Ceylon," in B. L. Smith, ed., *Religion and Legitimation of Power in Sri Lanka* (Chambersburg, Pa.: Anima Books, 1978), pp. 74, 78.

16. The caliph was the successor/deputy (*khalīfa* of the Prophet of God. His legitimacy derived from the direct continuation of Muhammad's rule over the community of believers.
17. See H. Frankfort, *Kingship and the Gods* (Chicago: University of Chicago Press, 1948); A. M. Hocart, *Kings and Councillors: An Essay in Comparative Anatomy of Human Society*, ed. R. Needham (Chicago; University of Chicago Press, 1970); Arjomand, *Shadow of God*, Chapter 3.
18. M. Cherniavsky, *Tsar and People: Studies in Russian Myths* (New York, Random House, 1969), p. 64.
19. Ibid., p. 71: "The myth of the pious ruler drew its strength from the eschatology of Russian political theory. From its beginning around 1500, the Third Rome, Moscow, was the chief fact in the economy of salvation. Upon the orthodoxy and personal piety of the tsar depended the salvation of Russia as a state and thereby the salvation of the whole world. As the saintly-prince insured the individual salvation of his people, so the pious tsar guaranteed the salvation of . . . the State."
20. Voegelin, *Order and History*, 2: 28.
21. Voegelin, *Order and History*, 3: 355.
22. H. P. Varley, trans., *A Chronicle of Gods and Sovereigns: Jinnō Shōtōki of Kitabatake Chikafusa* (New York: Columbia University Press, 1980).
23. The critics, however, pointed out that Akihito was being enthroned not as a god-king but as a symbol of national sovereignty, and that the performance of the rite violated the constitutional separation of state and religion (*International Herald Tribune*, Nov. 23, 1990).
24. C. Geertz, *Negara: The Theatre State in Nineteenth-Century Bali* (Princeton: Princeton University Press, 1980), p. 13.
25. Ibid., p. 124.
26. Ibid., pp. 109, 126.
27. To recognize this world historical significance is not, needless to say, to subscribe to such paraochialism as betrayed by Pizzorno's statement that the "politics of transcendence" first arose in Western Christianity and was "a style of politics, unique to the West, whose potentiality was then implanted in the European political institutions" (A. Pizzorno, "Politics Unbounded," in C. S. Maier, ed., *Changing Boundaries of the Political* [Cambridge: Cambridge University Press, 1987], p. 49).
28. Deut. 17:14–20.
29. J. Pedersen, *Israel: Its Life and Culture* (Copenhagen: P. Branner, 1940), III: 95–101; B. Albrektson, "Prophecy and Politics in the Old Testament," in H. Biezais, ed., *The Myth of the State* (Stockholm: Almqvist and Wiksell, 1972), p. 47.
30. E. Voegelin, *The New Science of Politics* (Chicago: University of Chicago Press, 1952), p. 106.
31. W. Ullmann, *Law and Politics in the Middle Ages* (London: Sources of History, 1975), pp. 270–272.

32. Ibid., p. 283.
33. Voegelin, *New Science*, p. 158.
34. Kantorowicz, *King's Two Bodies*, pp. 464, 471.
35. Verses 3:189, 4:19–20, 42:49, 64:1, and elsewhere.
36. R. Dankoff, ed. and trans., *Wisdom of Royal Glory (Kutadgu Bilig): A Turko-Islamic Mirror for Princes* by Yusuf Khass Hajib (Chicago: University of Chicago Press, 1983), p. 252; emphasis added.
37. Gazālī, *Naṣīḥat al-Mulūk* ed. J. Homā'ī, 4th printing, (Tehran: Hōmā, 1367/1988), p. 81. The same idea of the two powers was stated earlier by the Persian historian and proponent of the royal political tradition, Bayhaqi (d. 1077): "Know that the Lord Most High has given one power to the prophets and another power to kings; and He has made it incumbent upon the people of the earth that they should submit themselves to the two powers and should acknowledge the true way laid down by God" (cited in translation by B. Lewis, *The Political Language of Islam* [Chicago: University of Chicago Press, 1988], p. 134, n. 8).
38. Najm al-Dīn Rāzī, *The Path of God's Bondsmen from Origin to Return*, trans. H. Algar (Delmar, N. Y.: Caravan Books, 1982), p. 396.
39. Ibid., p. 397.
40. This trend arguably reaches its highest point in the political theories of Aquinas's Persian contemporary, Naṣīr al-Dīn Ṭūsī (d. 1274), but declines sharply thereafter.
41. S. A. Arjomand, "Shi'ite Jurisprudence and Constitution-Making in the Islamic Republic of Iran," in M. Marty and R. S. Appleby, eds., *Fundamentalisms and the State: Remaking Polities, Economies, and Militance* (Chicago: University of Chicago Press, 1992).
42. Kantorowicz, *King's Two Bodies*, Chapter 5; J.-P. Royer, *L'Église et le royaume de France au XIVe siècle d'après le "Songe du Vergier" et la jurisprudence du parlement* (Paris: Librarie Générale de Droit et Jurisprudence, 1969). pp. 55, 207.
43. Ibid., pp. 51, 54, 314.
44. See Chapter 3, below.
45. Arjomand, "Shi'ite Jurisprudence."
46. See Chapter 9, below.
47. S. Berger, "Religious Transformation and the Future of Politics," in C. S. Maier, ed., *Changing Boundaries of the Political* (Cambridge: Cambridge University Press, 1987), pp. 127–129.
48. See Chapter 11, below.
49. J. D. Hunter, *Evangelicalism: The Coming Generation* (Chicago: University of Chicago Press, 1987), pp. 141, 147, 152–153.
50. R. Wuthnow, *The Restructuring of the American Religion* (Princeton: Princeton University Press, 1988).
51. E. B. Koenker, *Secular Salvations: The Rites and Symbols of Political Religions* (Philadelphia: Fortress Press, 1965), p. vii.
52. Ibid., pp. 86–88.

53. Voegelin, *New Science*, p. 131.
54. L. Kolakowski, "Totalitarianism and the Virtue of the Lie," in I. Howe, ed., *1984 Revisited: Totalitarianism in Our Century* (New York: Harper and Row, 1983), p. 131.
55. See the following.
56. Kolakowski, "Totalitarianism," pp. 127, 135.
57. Ibid., p. 126.
58. A. von Harnack, cited in C.-M. Edsman, "The Myth of the State or the State's Religious Legitimation," in H. Biezais, ed., *The Myth of the State* (Stockholm: Almqvist and Wiksell, 1972), p. 172; order transposed.
59. Cited in B. Gustaffson, "Durkheim on Power and Holiness," in H. Biezais, ed., *The Myth of the State* (Stockholm: Almqvist and Wiksell, 1972), p. 23.
60. M. Q. Hedāyat, Mokhber al-Salṭana, *Khāṭerāt va Khaṭarāt* (Tehran: Zavvār 1344/1965), pp. 299, 307.
61. *Al-ḥākim min dūn Allāh*, a play on the regnal title of al-Hakim, the megalomaniac Fatimid ruler of Egypt in the early eleventh century: Ruler by the Order of God (*al-ḥākim bi-amr Allāh*).
62. Cited in F. Malti-Douglas, "A Literature of Islamic Revival?: The Autobiography of Shaykh Kishk," in S. Mardin, ed., *Cultural Transitions in the Middle East* (Leiden: E. J. Brill, forthcoming).
63. Cited in L. Sanneh, "Religion and Politics: Third World Perspectives on a Comparative Religious Theme," *Daedalus* 120, no. 3 (1991): 210; see also A. Shari'ati, *Marxism and Other Western Fallacies: An Islamic Critique*, trans. R. Campbell (Berkeley: Mizan Press, 1980).
64. See S. A. Arjomand, "The Emergence of Islamic Political Ideologies," in James A. Beckford and Thomas Luckmann, eds., *The Changing Face of Religion* (London: Sage, 1989).
65. M. Eliade, "'Cargo Cults' and Cosmic Regeneration," in S. L. Thrupp, ed., *Millennial Dreams in Action* (New York: Schocken Books, 1970).
66. See the Introduction for the definition of "absolute politics."
67. The Zoroastrian apocalyptic literature, the earliest in the Axial Age, records droughts, earthquakes, famine, and other natural disasters accompanying the disintegration of society and the family, international disorder and wars among nations (invasions of Gog and Magog in the later literature), and thus the spread of injustice, evil, and tyranny throughout the world.
68. A. R. Johnson, *Sacral Kingship in Ancient Israel*, 2d ed. (Cardiff: University of Wales Press, 1967), Sections 4–6, esp. pp. 101–103.
69. N. Cohn, "Medieval Millenarism: Its Bearing on the Comparative Study of Millenarian Movements," in S. L. Thrupp, ed., *Millennial Dreams in Action* (New York: Schocken Books, 1970), p. 41.
70. E. Sarkisyanz, *The Buddhist Backgrounds of Burmese Socialism* (The Hague M. Nÿhoff, 1965), pp. 43–48, 88–90; C. F. Keyes, "Millennialism, Theravada Buddhism, and Thai Society," *Journal of Asian Studies* 36, no. 2 (1977).

71. M. Weber, *Ancient Judaism*, trans. and ed. H. H. Gerth and D. Martindale (New York: Free Press, 1952), p. 4.
72. Ibid., pp. 207, 216.
73. Ibid., pp. 369, 375.
74. According to Mowinckel, the Second Isaiah "lifts the whole conception of restoration into the supra-terrestrial sphere, representing it as a drama of cosmic dimensions" (S. Mowinckel, *He That Cometh*, trans. G. W. Anderson [New York: Abingdon Press, 1954], p. 138.)
75. M. Boyce, *A History of Zoroastrianism* (Leiden: E. J. Brill, 1982), 2: 193–194.
76. Amos 5:18–20; Isa. 2:12–22; Zeph. 1:12–18.
77. G. W. Anderson, *The History and Religion of Israel* (Oxford: Oxford University Press, 1966), p. 153: see also Mowinckel, *He That Cometh*, pp. 145–147.
78. See G. Widgren, *Die Religionen Irans* (Stuttgart: W. Kohlhammer, 1965) [French trans., *Les religions de l'Iran*, Paris: Payot, 1968], Chapter VI.4; M. Boyce, "Apocalyptic. In Zoroastrianism," in *Encyclopaedia Iranica* (London: Routledge & Kegan Paul, 1987), 155–257.
79. Yasnā 48:11–12; English translation in M. Boyce, *Zoroastrianism: Textual Sources* (Totowa, N. J.: Barnes and Noble, 1984), p. 39. Boyce's translation has been slightly modified here and in the subsequent passages in light of our own terminology.
80. Boyce, *History of Zoroastrianism*, 1: 282.
81. G. Widengren, "Leitende Ideen und Quellen der iranische Apokalyptik," in D. Hellholm, ed., *Apocalypticism in the Mediterranean World and the Near East*, 2d ed. (Tübingen: J. C. B. Mohr, 1989), pp. 77–86.
82. Yasht 19:92–93; Boyce, *Zoroastrianism* p. 90.
83. J. Kellens, "Saošiiant," *Studia Iranica* 3 (1974): 209; Boyce, *History of Zoroastrianism*, 1: 293; idem, "Astvat-Ereta," in *Encyclopaedia Iranica*, 2: 871–873.
84. Yasnā 43:16.
85. Yasht 19:89–90.
86. Mowinckel, *He That Cometh*, p. 47.
87. Judg. 6:14; 8:22.
88. 2 Kings 13:5.
89. 2 Sam. 14:4; 2 Kings 6:26.
90. Pedersen, *Israel* p. 81; Mowinckel, *He That Cometh*, pp. 69, 177. The term *ṣĕdāqâ* (rendered "vindication" or "righteousness") has the same original suggestion of good fortune and well-being (ibid., pp. 177–179).
91. Isa. 6–11.
92. Anderson, *Israel* pp. 150–151.
93. Zech. 9:9.
94. Psa. 84:9; Johnson, *Sacral Kingship*, p. 105.
95. Lam. 4:20.
96. Mowinckel, *He That Cometh*, p. 156.
97. See R. Otto, *The Kingdom of God and the Son of Man: A Study in the History of Religion*, rev. ed., trans. F. V. Filson and B. Lee-Woolf,

(London: Lutterworth Press, 1943), pp. 97–107; Mowinckel, *He That Cometh*, pp. 270–284; S. K. Eddy, *The King Is Dead: Studies in the Near Eastern Resistance to Hellenism, 334–31 B.C.*, (Linclon: University of Nebraska Press, 1961); G. Widengren, "Iran and Israel in Parthian Times with Special Regard to the Ethiopic Book of Enich," *Temenos* 2 (1966): 139–177; J. R. Hinnells, "Zoroastrian Influences on the Judaeo-Christian Tradition," *Journal of the K. R. Cama Oriental Institute* 45 (1976): 1–23; S. S. Hartman, "Datierung der jungavestischen Apokalyptik," in D. Hellholm, ed., *Apocalypticism in the Mediterranean World and the Near East*, 2d ed. (Tübingen: J. C. B. Mohr, 1989), p. 73.

98. Eddy, *King Is Dead*, p. 32.

99. E. Benvéniste, "Une apocalypse pehlévi: le Zāmāsp-Nāmak," *Revue de l'histoire des religions*, 106 (1932): 373–380; Widengren, "Leitende Ideen," pp. 119–127.

100. Widengren, "Iran and Israel," p. 144.

101. Cited in J. Gwyn Griffiths, "Apocalyptic in the Hellenistic Era," in D. Hellholm, ed., *Apocalypticism in the Mediterranean World and the Near East*, 2d ed. (Tübingen: J. C. B. Mohr, 1989), p. 407.

102. Widengren, "Iran and Israel," pp. 154–158. Zervanism had been prevalent in northwestern Iran, and produced a distinctive apocalyptic current that was absorbed into Zoroastrianism "Leitende Ideen," pp. 101–140. Theopompus's account of the Iranian apocalypticism in its Zervanite version, written about 330 B.C., agrees astonishingly with the Pahlavi texts. See A. Hultgård, "Forms and Origins of Iranian Apocalypticism," in D. Hellholm, ed., *Apocalypticism in the Mediterranean World and the Near East*, 2d ed. (Tübingen: J. C. B. Mohr, 1989), p. 407.

103. A. Momigliano, *Alien Wisdom: The Limits of Hellenization* (Cambridge: Cambridge University Press, 1975), p. 112.

104. According to a late eighteenth-century formulation, "the Beast of the Apocalypse...was imperial power as such; the 'icon' (or image) of the Beast was all civil authority; its body, spiritual authority." (M. Cherniavsky, "The Old Believers and the New Religion," *Slavic Review*, 25 (1966), p. 23)

105. Sarkisyanz, *Buddhist Backgrounds*, p. 90.

106. B.-Z. E. Klorman, "Jewish and Muslim Messianism in Yemen," *International Journal of Middle East Studies*, 22, no. 2 (1990) 201–228.

107. A. Amanat, *Resurrection and Renewal: The Making of the Babi Movement in Iran, 1844–1850* (Ithaca and London: Cornell University Press, 1989).

108. See Chapter 6, below.

109. Van de Kroef, "*Kingship*," p. 75; Keyes "Millennialism," p. 288.

110. G. Scholem, *The Messinanic Idea in Judaism and Other Essays in Jewish Spirituality* (New York: Schocken Books, 1971); A. Funkenstein,

"Maimonides: Political Theory and Realistic Messianism," *Miscellanea Medievalia*, 2 (1977): 81–103. With the historical disappearance of "the crown of kingship," and "the crown of priesthood," the messianic challenge was the only remaining threat to the authority of the spokesmen for "the crown of the Torah" in Rabbinical Judaism. See S. A. Cohen, "The Concept of the Three *Ketarim*: Its Place in Jewish Political Thought and its Implications for Jewish Constitutional History," *A. J. S. Review* 9, no. 1 (1984), pp. 27–54.

111. Scholem *Messianic Idea*, pp. 11–12.
112. Voegelin, *New Science*, pp. 108–111.
113. Y. Friedmann, *Prophecy Continuous: Aspects of Ahmadi Religious Thought and Its Medieval Background* (Berkely and Los Angeles: University of California Press, 1989), pp. 95–99, 107–111.
114. E. Kohlberg, "From Imāmīyya to Ithnā-'Asharīyya," *Bulletin of the School of Oriental and African Studies* 39 (1976) pp. 521–534; Arjomand, *Shadow of God*, pp. 160–163.
115. N. A. Berdiaev, *The Russian Revolutin* (Ann Arbor: University of Michigan Press, 1961); E. Sarkisyanz, *Rußland und der Messianismus des Orients* (Tübingen: J. C. B. Mohr, 1955).
116. J. Locke, *A Letter Concerning Toleration* ed. P. Romanell (New York: Liberal Arts Press, 1955 [1689]), p. 23. It is interesting to note that Locke includes the religions considered idolatrous, but excludes atheism from the privilege of toleration, as "the taking away of God, though but even in thought, dissolves all."
117. Ibid., p. 52.
118. M. Weber, *From Max Weber: Essays in Sociology*, trans. and ed. H. H. Gerth and C. Wright Mills (London: Routledge and Kegan Paul, 1948), p. 154.
119. Ibid., p. 117.
120. Ibid., pp. 149–152.
121. Sanneh, *"Religion and Politics,"* p. 207.

3

Religion and Constitutionalism in Western History and in Modern Iran and Pakistan

Said Amir Arjomand

When Khomeini was persuaded in 1979 to use the modern device of a written constitution as the foundation for the theocratic government he had advocated, two radically different legal traditions were brought together and forced into rapid symbiosis. This process of symbiosis has been treated elsewhere, without, however, being put in a historical or comparative perspective.[1] The purpose of this chapter is to supply at least a partial historical perspective on the emergence of the political tradition of constitutionalism, and on its accommodation into the normative order of Islamic polities. Its historical coverage is partial, being restricted to the role played by religion in the formation of the tradition of constitutionalism in Western Christianity, and its reconciliation with Islam in Iran after the revolution of 1906, and in Pakistan after its creation in 1947. The first chapter in the reception of constitutionalism in the Islamic world, which began with grants of constitution by rulers of Tunisia and Egypt and culminated in the Ottoman Constitution of 1876, is excluded because no serious confrontation between constitutionalism and Islam had yet taken place. On the other hand, the two important instances of confrontation of constitutionalism and Islam in Iran and Pakistan are put in a comparative perspective. Three sets of comparisons are used to throw light on the role of religion in the reconstruction of political order: comparisons between

Western Christianity and Islam, between the predominantly Sunni Islam in the Indian subcontinent and Shi'ite Islam in Iran, and between the processes of constitution-making and the Islamic provisions in the Iranian Fundamental Laws of 1906 and 1907 and the constitutions of the Islamic Republic of Pakistan (1956, 1962, and 1973).

Religion, Law, and Constitutionalism

The Conception of constitution as the foundation of political order and the term itself have secular origins. They are contributions of ancient Rome to legal history.[2] From our point of view, three elements in the heritage of Roman law can be underlined: the idea of legislation, or the creation of man-made law (*lex*) proposed by the magistrates and approved by the popular assemblies, the fundamental distinction between public and private law, and the idea of the political order as *res publica* (the public thing).

The contribution of the world religions to legal history was of a very different nature. With the rise of rabbinical Judaism, Christianity, and Islam in the Middle East, the idea of the sacred law, an eternal law based on the transcendent justice of God, replaced the charismatic revelation of law through the law prophets and oracles. A new kind of sacred law thus came into being. Transcendent justice was equated with divine commandments. As the sacred law was in principle eternal and unchanging and the explicit divine commandments were few, however, the problem was finding what the law was in particular instances. The determination of legal norms thus took the form of law-finding rather than law-making. There was a parallel to this situation in Roman history too, where *lex* as enacted law coexisted with the more fundamental *jus* as transcendent law and where jurisprudence by private jurists developed as the science of law-finding.

The establishment of the sacred laws of the world religions nevertheless had a profound effect on the conceptions of law and the political order. As justice was in principle a divine order transcending any earthly commonwealth, it was independent of and superior to the laws and requirements of the thus deabsolutized political order. Laws governing the political order, therefore, could claim legitimacy only if they could be shown to conform to transcendent justice.

The church played the decisive role in the transmission of Roman law, the medieval church borrowed the term *constitution* and applied it to ecclesiastical regulations concerning the church and the monastic orders. The term also became used for documents regulating the relations between church and state, as in the Constitutions of Clarendon enacted by Henry II and his council of the realm in 1164 in England.[3] The contribution of canon law to constitutionalism was very considerable. As Weber points out, canon law of Western Christendom was unique among the sacred laws of the world religions in traveling the path from law-finding to law-making, from being a jurists' law, consisting of compilations and interpretation of traditions and of *responsa*, to "legislation by rational enactment." This was due partly to the unparalleled importance of the church councils in Christian history, but mainly to the "unique organization of the Catholic Church as a rational institution," whose functionaries held "rationally defined bureaucratic offices."[4] In the Islamic tradition, the two activities remain separate: finding the sacred law (*sharī'a*) remains the province of the religious jurisprudence while the law of the state (*qānūn*) is made by the ruler's decrees. This historical difference merits close examination.

Law-making and law-finding already coexisted in ancient Rome, where *lex* as enacted law was distinct from *jus* as transcendent law, and where jurisprudence by private jurists developed the prototypical "jurists' law" that existed side by side with the legislated law of the state. The four old sources of Roman law consisted of custom (unwritten law), legislation by the popular assemblies, edicts of the magistrates, and *auctoritas prudentium* as embodied in the *responsa* of the jurists. By the end of the classical period (mid-third century A.D.), two new sources had been added to these: the resolutions of the senate and the constitutions of the emperor.[5] The jurists' law that developed in Rome as the exercise of *auctoritas prudentium* by private jurists in their answers to legal questions and commentaries on *jus civile* was an integral component of Roman law. In fact, "in the creative period of early classical times the development of new law by *interpretatio* far exceeded in bulk and in significance the new law provided by statute."[6] It is important to note that the jurists completely dominated the Roman private law but paid little or no attention to the public and other fields of law. Consequently, the bulk of the Roman private law consisted of the legal norms and principles of the jurists' law.[7]

The equal authority of the eminent Roman jurists produced a pluralism that could be mitigated only through state intervention. The fact that the authoritative private jurists could have different opinions on the same question required the intervention of the magistrate (*praetor*) or the emperor. The emperor often settled the controversal issue by rescript. Roman emperors were thus drawn into the jurisprudential process and would give free legal advice in response to a *libellus* (written petition) from a private citizen, and their legal service soon developed into the office *a libellis*. The records from the late second and third centuries show that this rescript office was manned by professional jurists who issued *responsa* in the emperor's name, whose perspective was that of private lawyers, and whose emphasis was on private law.[8]

The medieval church resembled the Roman Empire in many of its features. This resemblance was fostered by the canonists' use of the Justinian Code.[9] In particular, they applied to the pope whatever had been said of the *princeps*. In this fashion, the legislative power of the emperor was transferred to the pope: "The Pope is the *princeps* of the church. *Quod principi placuit legis habet vigorem.*"[10] The pope also assumed the emperor's function of issuing rescripts. These rescripts, the decretals, were the means of converting law-finding to law-making. A decretal was not necessarily or usually a decision on a concrete case, but rather an abstract answer to an abstract question like the one posed to and answered by the Islamic jurisconsults (*muftīs*) But as the questions were submitted by the bishops to the pope, the answering *epistolae* would be declaring the common law (*jus commune*) of Christendom, the law of the universal chruch. Thus, by the thirteenth century, the popes had gradually converted the power of finding and declaring the law into the power of making law. The decretals, representing papal legislation, could be collected as the law of the church. The publication of the collection of decretals by Pope Gregory IX in 1234 ushered in the age of papal legislation that lasted until the publication of the Clementines in 1317.[11]

The canonists' conception of the corporation also played an important role in the law of the monastic orders. As the orders became organized in the thirteenth century, canon law treated them both as universities and as hierarchical dependencies of the pope. In former capacity, they acquired a considerable measure of administrative and legal autonomy. In the latter capacity, they were the subject of papal legislation. By the mid-thirteenth century, the basic statutes concerning the organization of the monastic orders were referred to as the constitutions of the Roman pontiffs.[12] It was Thomas Aquinas, the great monk of the Dominican Order, a model order with its constitutions and electorate,[13] whose seminal ideas, as we shall see presently, paved the way for the use of natural law as the transcendental basis of modern constitutions.

In Western Christianity, canon law was a crucial factor in the emergence of constitutionalism. Modern constitutionalism emerged from the late medieval system of estate representation (*Ständesstaat*) in Europe. This system came into being, alongside feudalism, during the centuries of intensified contention between the papacy and the temporal rulers. During the investiture contest in the eleventh and twelfth centuries, "the popes chose to emphasize the principle of elective monarchy," and the office of the Holy Roman Emperor was eventually made elective.[14] As O. Hintze emphasizes, it was not feudalism but the church state dualism in the medieval West that crucially contributed to the development of estate representation.[15] It was in this system that the idea of representation was taken from ecclesiastical assemblies, extended to the body politic, and institutionalized in parliaments.[16]

It is not often remembered that the parliaments were courts of law. As such, the *parlement* of Paris played an important role in the appropriation of an integrated ecclesiastical jurisprudence for the king's nascent territorial state from the second half of the thirteenth century onward. Montesquieu acutely perceived "the flux and reflux of ecclesiastical and temporal jurisdiction" in this era: The fragmentation of civil jurisdiction in feudal Europe had facilitated the continuous extension of ecclesiastical jurisdiction, which created a unified legal system only to be taken over by the nascent royal state.[17] The *parlement* now became the court of last resort in all the affairs of the kingdom,[18] and with remarkable suppleness, used the canon law as a tool for the unification of jurisprudence and establishment of legal uniformity in France.[19] At the same time, the *parlement* recognized the jurisdiction of ecclesiastical authorities over the members of the clerical estate in a gradually decreasing number of mixed and spiritual matters. In this manner, parliamentary jurisprudence also contributed significantly to the institutionalization of the division of religious and temporal powers.

The impact of Thomism on the political theory that took shape in the context of estate representation deserves special attention. To Aquinas is due the fundamental intellectual breakthrough that made possible the emergence of a distinctively modern transcendental basis for the legitimacy of human laws, and thus for the foundations of the political order. In line with his fundamental distinction between nature and grace, Aquinas recognized the eternal, the natural, and the human law in descending order. He also adopted the Stoic idea of natural law, and established the divine emanation of the law of nature and its accessibility to human reason.[20] With the triumph of Thomism, Western Christianity

accepted human reason as the agency for the determination of
transcendent justice in matters political and secular. Natural law
was henceforth not only independent of and superior to positive law,
but the very source of legitimation of positive law. The revolutionary
potential of this conception was demonstrated during the Reformation, and natural law was to become the transcendent basis legitimating the revolutionary constitutions of the eighteenth century.

Institutionalization of Juristic Authority in Three Muslim Empires

There was no trend comparable to the growth of papal authority
in medieval Islam, where legal pluralism remained a prominent
feature. The ruler appointed official jurisconsults (*muftīs*) whose
function was to produce legal *responsa* upon demand, but there is
no evidence of jurisprudential hierarchy and centralization. It was
only in the Ottoman Empire and in the sixteenth century that the
issue of disagreement among authoritative jurisconsults was
resolved along the lines of the Roman, and presumably Byzantine,
rescript office. The sultan appointed *muftīs* who were subordinates
of the chief jurisconsult, the Shaykh al-Islam, whose advice they
could request in writing when necessary. A centralized office for
issuing injunctions performed a similar function to the rescript office
of the Roman emperors.[21]
      There was no parallel development in Shi'ite Iran. Down to the
present century, the Shi'ite sacred law remained very much a jurists'
law. It never made the transition to law-making that sets the canon
law of Western Christianity apart from the other sacred laws. During
the centuries that followed the establishment of Shi'ism as the state
religion of Iran in 1501, the Shi'ite ulema gradually created a
powerful and autonomous hierocracy.[22] The Shi'ite hierocracy,
however, lacked the centralized organization of the Catholic Church,
and the Shi'ite religious jurists engaged exclusively in law-finding,
experiencing that last spurt of its jurisprudential creativity as late
as the nineteenth century. The fact that the Shi'ite sacred law was
a jurists' law also had important implications for the institutionalization of authority in Shi'ism: it produced the pluralism of
religious authority at the highest level. The lay believer would choose
a jurist whose rulings in the sacred law he or she would follow. This
practice of the voluntary choice of a religious jurist, known as
"imitation" (*taqlīd*), resulted in pluralism and the equal authority

of the preeminent jurists with a large following who were referred to as the "sources of imitations" (*marāji'-e taqlīd*). This is not to say juristic authority was not institutionalized, only that it was not centralized. In fact, the institutionalization of juristic authority of the ulema in Shi'ite Iran was very impressive in comparison to the Moghul Empire in India. According to a recent study, the Indian ulema remained a relatively unimportant element in the polity.[23] They never secceeded becoming fully distinct from the Sufis, and in terminating the control of the latter over popular religion, as did the Shi'ite ulema in Safavid Iran.[24] According to one interpretation, consequently, the neo-Hanbalite Islamic fundamentalism that spread in India after 1818 posed a serious challenge both to their exclusive juristic authority and to their popular influence.[25] British rule, finally, also deprived them of the patronage of the state and institutionalized integration into the structure of authority.

Secularization of Public Law in the West

At the close of the seventeenth century, Domat would still begin his treatise on *Public Law* with revelation, however legally perfunctory his invocations of God may have been. Not so with Montesquieu's *Spirit of the Laws*, published in 1748.[26] Montesquieu was appreciative of the fact that sacred laws prevented arbitrariness by creating a measure of pluralism of authority,[27] argued for the acceptance of the established religion on purely pragmatic grounds,[28] and deduced religious tolerance from the rights of the citizens.[29] Religion, however, had no significant role in his system, in which reason replaced revelation as the foundation of human laws. In fact, he characterized the papal decretals as "a bad kind of legislation," owing to their manner of amalgamation of particular cases, and extended the criticism to their progenitor, the Roman rescripts, disparaging Justinian for having codified them.[30] Nor did he think highly of Roman law.[31] For Montesquieu, public law had a rational basis: the natural law. Natural law, according to Weber, is the only consistent principle of legitimacy of a legal order that can remain once religious revelation and the authoritarian sacredness of a tradition and its bearers have lost their force.[32] Natural law had thus been the specific form of legitimacy of a new order created by a revolution. The written constitutions of the eighteenth century, which provide the model for the rest of the world, all drew on the philosophy of natural rights and its offshoot, theories of social contract.

The constitutionalism that was imported into the Islamic world in this century was also the product of other complex legal developments that have been summarized elsewhere.[33] Here, it suffices to point out that by the end of the eighteenth century, the principle of national sovereignty was firmly established. With it, democracy was taking the place of the rule of law as the first principle of political organization. While the rule of law was not inconsistent with the prevalence of a transcendent sacred law, national sovereignty as the sole legitimate source of all legislative power was. Religion was henceforth dependent on the grace of the nation for whatever safeguards granted to it in man-made constitutions.

As the notion of the state as a service-rendering organization for the promotion of the economic and social rights of its citizens and the welfare and development of the nation gained influence in the latter part of the nineteenth and through most of the twentieth centuries,[34] there was a gradual shift in the balance of power and right that enhanced the authority of the state at the expense of the civil rights of the individual. This development further reduced the salience of religion, as no significant responsibilities for national education, provision of welfare services, modernization, and economic development were assigned to religious institutions.

The present century has witnessed the spread of constitution-making throughout the world. Whereas in 1870 only thirty nine of the forty seven nations possessed written constitutions, today nearly all of the over 150 independent nations have them.[35] With continuous accretions to the international repertoire of political culture, selective appropriation of its various elements becomes possible and likely. Furthermore, increasing syncretism becomes not only possible but also attractive. Appeals can be made to more than one principle. Religion, in particular, can be added to natural rights, in order to provide transcendental justification and legitimacy of the political order. This last possibility is, in fact, highly pertinent to constitution-making throughout the world. The constitution-makers of most countries frequently resort to religion to reinforce the transcendental authority of their products. Their invocations of religion "serve to suggest some bedrock upon which political order rests that is beyond the authority of the framers to negotiate.[36] This is especially true of the Islamic world, with the exception of the Turkish Republic.

Shi'ite Islam and the Iranian Fundamental Laws of 1906-1907

The first modern Asian revolution occurred in Iran in 1906, and has been labeled the constitutional revolution (*enqelāb-e mashrūṭiyyat*) in view of its primary objectives of establishing limited government (*mashrūṭiyyat*) and framing the foundations of the new order in a written constitution. Limited government meant subjecting absolute monarchy to the rule of law and the establishment of a parliament (*Majles*).

The ideas and terminology of constitutionalism traveled from western Europe to Iran through the Ottoman Empire and into the twentieth century.[37] The term for constitution in the Ottoman Empire and Iran, *qānūn-e asāsī*, is indicative of its mode of accommodation in the Islamic legal universe. The word *qānūn* had entered into Arabic in the early Middle Ages. It retained its original Greek fiscal connotations as regulation of land taxes, but also acquired the more general sense of state law. It came to mean financial and administrative regulations laid down by the ruler independently of the sacred law. From the beginning of modernization, *qānūn*, as state law, constituted the precedent for the adoption of European legal codes. In Iran as in the rest of the Middle East, *qānūn* came to refer to the codes inspired by European ligislation and introduced by the state, and the constitution, as the foundation of public law, was naturally regarded as "the fundamental *qānūn*." The term, however, became established in Iran after a short and interesting struggle over terminology.

In August 1906, the ruling monarch ordered the elections for a parliament, for which a charter was subsequently drawn up and ratified at the end of December. It is interesting to note that during the three months of negotiation over the draft, the charter was referred to as the fundamental charter (*neẓām-nāma-ye asāsī*). It was only in the ensuing months that the terms *fundamental law* (*qānūn-e asāsī*) and *constitutional* (*mashrūṭa*; literally conditional) *government*, both emanating from the Ottoman Empire, became established. The fundamental charter was not a systematic legal text, but rather a hasty document largely concerned with the constitution and functions of the parliamentary assemblies. Its inadequacy as a constitution prompted the setting up of a new committee to draft a supplement to it. Using the Belgian Constitution of 1831 as its basic text, but also consulting the Bulgarian Constitution of 1879, the committee produced a draft supplement that referred to the fundamental charter as the fundamental law.

The designation became definitive when the final draft of the supplement was eventually ratified by the *Majles*, and signed by the king. The constitution of Iran came to consist of the Fundamental Law of December 30, 1906, and its Supplement of October 8, 1907.

The bearers of constitutionalism in Iran in the early years of the century were the merchants and the enlightened bureaucrats. They succeeded in obtaining the grant of a constitution from the monarch only by enlisting the support of the prominent religious leaders, the highest ranking ulema, who in fact appear as leaders of the constitutional movement. Although some of them accepted the arguments of the constitutionalists, they had no special program or interest to be served by the adoption of a constitution. They were willing to support the idea because they assumed that the limitation of the power of government would enhance hierocratic power. But once they came to realize the secularizing potential of parliamentary legislation, they insisted on safeguarding their institutional interests. As a result, the final version of the Supplementary Fundamental Law of 1907 goes to considerable length to accommodate Shi'ite Islam as the established religion.

Most of the provisions in this regard were original, and were added to the draft supplement as a result of the pressure exerted by the traditionalist clerical leader, Shaykh Fazl Allāh Nūrī, during the months following the completion of the committee's work. The committee consisted of a handful of reformist bureaucrats, merchants and an energetic secularist Democrat, Sayyed Ḥasan Taqīzāda. When the committee had been selected at his urging in January 1907, Sa'd al-Dawla, a reformist bureaucrat who chaired it, had made the perfunctory remark that the supplement would be consistent with "the laws of constitutional monarchy and also the law of *sharī'a*."[38] The ulema, however, were not invited to join the committee, nor were they consulted. Shaykh Fazl Allāh Nūrī, who was one of the three prominents religious leaders who had pressured the shah to grant a constitution initially, did not trust the Westernizers in the committe and proposed, in an autographed circular dated April 20, 1907/7 Rabī' I, 1325, the inclusion of an article requiring the approval of all legislation "in every age," by a council of "*mojtaheds* (religious jurists) of the first rank and pious jurisconsults."[39] The Majles was responsive, and set up a special committee of ulema to consider Nūrī's proposal and to examine the draft supplement generally from the viewpoint of Islam. Nūrī participated in the deliberations of this second committee, and was also invited to attend some of the sessions of the Majles. The committee completed its work on May 29, 1907/16 Rabī' II, 1325, adopting Nūrī's proposal and a number of other amendments.[40] Taqīzāda and his fellow Democrats were alarmed by these amendments. Taqīzāda opposed Nūrī's proposed article, arguing sophistically that it would restrict the general right of all ulema to a particular committee.[41] His ally, Mīrzā 'Alī Tabrīzī put forward the more cogent argument that the religious jurists determined the general norms of the sacred law, but the determination of subjects or cases to which they were applicable (*tashkhīṣ-e mauẓū'āt*) was with the laity (*ahl-e 'orf*). Another speaker added that, if the amendment was accepted, there should be a qualification that the ulema have no right to interfere with customary laws (*aḥkām-e 'orfiyya*).[42] But the constitutionalists who were willing to speak out against the Islamic amendments were very few. Nūrī knew many constitutionalists did not like his proposaal but few would dare reject it openly.[43] He was proved right; on June 14, 1907/ 3 Jumādā I, 1325, the Majles passed his proposed article, as amended by the committee of ulema, with an overwhelming majority (58 in favor, 3 against with 28 abstentions).[44]

Outside the Majles, the Democrats and other radicals demanded Nūrī's banishment, and organized gatherings to intimidate him. A week after the passage of his article, Nūrī left Tehran to take refuge (*bast*) in the shrine of 'Abd al-'Aẓīm, where he remained until mid-September. During these months, Shaykh Faẓl Allāh launched a massive campaign against the imatative constitution-making of the Westernizers in Iran and the Shi'ite holy cities in Iraq. In this campaign, he formulated the ulema's hitherto incoherent objections to parliamentarianism into a consistent Islamic traditionalist ideology, and succeeded in mobilizing a considerable segment of the Iranian population that had not yet been drawn into constitutional politics.[45] Nūrī did not relent his agitation against parliamentarism and support the shah's attempt to restore autocracy in 1908. After the bombardment of the Majles in June 1908, Nūrī referred contemptuously to "the accursed constitution called the fundamental law,"[46] and argued that parliamentary legislation implied the denial of the perfection and full adequacy of Muhammad's revelation and sacred law for all times and all places, and was therefore contrary to Islam.[47] When the constitutionalists recaptured Tehran at the end of July 1909, Nūrī was hanged. The religious leaders who had remained in the constitutionalist camp, and the larger number who returned to it after the failure to restore autocracy, were satisfied with the Islamic provisions that had been added to the draft supplement by the special committee of ulema and approved by the Majles as the Supplementary Fundamental Law.

Article 1 of the Supplementary Fundamental Law affirmed that
the official religion of Iran is Shi'ite Islam. Article 2 referred to the
monarch as the "Shāhanshāh of Islam" and declared: "At no time
must any legal enactments of the National Consultative Assembly. . .
be at variance with the sacred principles of Islam." Furthermore,
"in every age, a committee of no less than five *mojtaheds* and pious
jurisconsults," to be chosen by the Majles "unanimously or by lot"
from a list of twenty ulema nominated by the sources of imitation,
was given the power to "reject, repudiate, wholly or in part, any
proposal which is a t variance with the sacred laws of Islam . . . .
In such matters the dicision of this committee of ulema shall be
followed and obeyed, and this article shall continue unchanged until
the appearance of His Holiness the Proof of the Age [i.e., the Hidden
Imam]." The duality of the traditional legal system was recognized
and endorsed, with the ulema retaining their authority over the
religious courts. Article 27 made the validity of all legal enactments
conditional upon their conformity with the standards of the sacred
law, and further stated that the judiciary power "belongs to the
shar'ī courts in matters pertaining to the sacred law (*shar'iyyāt*)
and to civil courts in matters pertaining to customary law
(*'orfiyyāt*)." Article 71 made the administration of justice in matters
of the sacred law (*omūr shar'iyya*) the prerogative of the "just
mojtaheds," and Article required the approval of the hierocratic
judge (*ḥākim-e shar'*) (*sic*) for the appointment of the prosecutor
general by the king. Nor did the Supplementary Fundamental Law
recognize the principle of secularism in its bill of rights. The freedom
to publish ideas, to learn and teach sciences and crafts (Article 18),
and to form associations (Article 21) were made contingent on
conformity with the interest of the establishment religion.

On one important point, however, the Islamic traditionalists
failed to obtain any concessions from the constitutionalists. The
religious leaders vehemently opposed the principle of equality of
all citizens before the law (Article 8 of the Supplementary Fundamental Law), which they correctly perceived as contradictory to the
provisions of the *sharī'a*. Even Mirza Ḥosayn Nā'īnī, the jurist
(*mojtahed*) who wrote a tract to justify constitutional government
in Shi'ite terms, would restrict the principle of equality before the
law to man-made laws (*qavānīn maużū'a*). But in the end, the Shi'ite
religious leaders had to give in, reportedly because of both personal
threats of violence and the restlessness of the Armenian minority.[48]
The legal implications of Article 8 were far-reaching. By declaring
all citizens equal before the law, it established public law, the state
law, as the general law of the land, and overrode the typical legal

particularism of the *sharī'a* concerning the legally autonomous Muslim and non-Muslim religious minorities.

It should also be pointed out that in practice, the above-mentioned Islamic provisions of the Supplementary Fundamental Law were increasingly ignored. By far the most important of these was Article 2. The most serious attempt to implement it was made during the Second Majles (1909–1911), and ended in failure. Once the Second Majles was in session (mid-November 1909), Ākhūnd Mollā Moḥammand Kāẓem Khurāsānī, and Mollā 'Abd Allāh Māzandarānī, the two sources of imitation in the Shi'ite holy cities who had consistently support the Majles, began pressing for the implementation of Article 2. But it was not until April 30, 1910/3 Jumādā I, 1328 that they submitted a list of twenty nominees from whom the Majles was to choose five.[49] Other sources of imitation (*marāji'-e taqlīd*) may have been consulted but very evidently reluctant to endorse the list. The Democrats tried to obstruct the establishment of a committee of five *mojtaheds*, but their obstruction ended promptly when Sayyed 'Abd Allāh Behbahānī, the prominent *mojtahed* of Tehran and one of the original sponsors of the constitutional movement, was assassinated and the Majles ousted Taqīzāda on grounds of the association of the assissin with the Democrats. Nevertheless, the supervisory committee of five *mojtaheds* could never be constituted, as most of the *mojtaheds* selected by the Majles refused to serve and resigned successively, and some accepted to serve but never attended the Majles.[50] In fact, except for a few days around the beginning of the year 1911/1329, when three ulema were concurrently present, only two religious jurists participated in the Majles regularly; and their input into the legislative process was extremely informal.[51]

The critical attempt to implement Article 2 in the Second Majles thus failed to resolve the following issues:

1. How were the sources of imitation as nominators of the twenty candidates for the supervisory committee to be formally recognized, and how were they to decide (unanimously, by majority vote, or otherwise) on the list of candidates to be submitted to the Majles?

2. What procedure was the Majles to follow for selecting five ulema out twenty "unanimously or by lot?" Was the pool of twenty to be replenished after the first round of selection? The question became acute with the rapid diminution of the pool for replacements as most of those selected were refusing to serve, and especially in view of the following problem.

3. There was no clarity as to how long the supervisory committee was to remain in office. Was its term to be concurrent

with the sessions of the Majles, or was the committee to be constituted once for "every age?"

4. Finally, the status of the members of the committee vis-à-vis the Mijles was never clarified. Were they to be considered members or "supervisors"?[52]

The non-hierarchical organization of the clerical estate, the pluralism of hierocratic authority in Shi'ism, and the relectance of many *mojtaheds* to become involved in parliamentary politics, among other factors, thus prevented the incorporation of Shi'ite juristic authority into Iran's new constitutional order. During Reza Khan's flirtation with the ulema in his rise to supreme power (from November 1922 to the end of 1924), a group of high-ranking ulema renewed the demand for the implementation of Article 2. It is interesting to note that one of the two clerical "supervisors" formally chosen by the Second Majles, Sayyed Ḥasan Modarres, who was then at the height of his influence in the Majles as an elected deputy, did not take up this demand which was dropped after Reza Khan became king.[53] The provision for the committee of five *mojtaheds* became a dead letter in the Pahlavi period. The duality of the judiciary power was also progressively violated in the Pahlavi reforms, and the religious courts gradually disappeared.[54]

Constitutionalism entered the normative order of Shi'ite Iran as an element of modern international politicolegal culture. The prior establishment of Shi'ism required that a number of adjustments be made to render constitutionalism consistent with Shi'ite Islam. Given the dual normative order and structure of authority in Shi'ite Iran, it is not surprising that legislated law took the place of decrees of the ruler, both being *qānūn*, while Islamic law (*sharī'a*) and hierocratic authority were in principle accommodated as limitations to its scope.

Islam and Constitution-Making in Pakistan

In Iran during the first decades of the century, we find no urge to construct an *Islamic* constitution, conceived as an Islamic counterpart to the Western principles of political organization. Such an urge first surfaced in the context of the decolonization of India, and as a result of the affirmation of the collective right of colonial peoples to cultural identity. It appeared when Islam was put forth as the raison d'être of the state created for the Muslims of the Indian subcontinent, and resulted in its eventual designation as the Islamic Republic of Pakistan. The Muslims of India who became Pakistanis after the partition in 1947 accordingly claimed to be engaged in the construction of an "ideological state" devoted to the implementation of Islam.

With the creation of the state of Pakistan in August 1947, the Constituent Assembly elected for all of India in July 1946 was split into two, and the portion representing Pakistan was empowered both to act as its legislature and to make a constitution for it. During the struggle for independence, the Muslims of India had taken the position that they were one of the two nations of the Indian subcontinent, and were therefore entitled to their own state. Islam was thus the justification for the new independent state, which was set up in two widely separated territories where at least five major languages were spoken. Islamic government, Islamic state, and Islamic constitution had gained currency as slogans in the last years of British rule and the early years of independence. But it was far from clear how Islam could supply the transcendental foundations of the new political order, or be used among the principles legitimating it. The debates over this issue, which the Pakistani politicians and ulema were alike forced to address inside and out of the Constituent Assembly, dominated the prolonged process of constitution-making from 1948 to 1953.[55]

The political elite of Pakistan had become self-consciously attached to their Muslim identity when acting as a group in Indian politics, but typically speaking, it saw little necessary connection between Islam as the common religion justifying a separate new state for the Muslims of India and the enterprise of constitution-making. When addressing the first meeting of the Constituent Assembly in August 1947, the founder of Pakistan, Muhammand 'Ali Jinnah, expressed his confidence that "you will find in the course of time Hindus would cease to be Hindus and Muslims would cease to be Muslims, not in the religious sense . . . but in the political sense as the citizens of the state."[56] But he would live just about long enough to discover otherwise. Once the religious identity of a people seeking to constitute a nation-state had been politicized, it was not easy to set up a secular state. In fact, by the end of January 1948, Jinnah had promised that the law of the land would be based on the *sharī'a*. Islam had become the central issue in the constitutional politics of Pakistan.

L. Binder divides the significant actors in the constitutional politics of Pakistan into four groups: the secularists, the consensus (*ijmā'*) modernists, the traditional ulema and the Islamic fundamentalists. Beyond the general agreement about reference to Islam in order to legitimate the new state, the range of opinions varied along a spectrum covering these four groups. The secularist elements in the political elite wanted Islam as mere icing; the Islamic fundamentalists wanted it to be the very cake. In between were the Islamic modernists, who saw democratic consensus as a means of updating the *shari'a* itself, and the ulema, who wanted to safeguard the *shari'a* as an unalterable component of the legal order. The fundamentalists remained outside the Constituent Assembly and exerted their influence through the ulema. Nevertheless, it was the fundamentalist Jama'at-i Islami that was the bearer of the idea of the Islamic state and thus acted as the catalyst in the process of making the Pakistani constitution Islamic.[57]

In February 1948, the leader (Amir) of the Jama'at, Abu'l-A'lā' Mawdudi, formulated "the four demands" that set the parameters for the constitutional politics of the ensuing years. He asked the Constituent Assembly to make the following unequivocal declaration:

> i) that we Pakistanis believe in the supreme sovereignty of God . . . ; ii) that the basic law of the land is the Shari'ah . . . ; iii) that all . . . laws . . . in conflict with the Shari'ah will be gradually repealed and no . . . laws . . . in conflict with the Shari'ah shall be framed . . . ; iv) that the State . . . shall have no authority to transgress the limits imposed by Islam.[58]

Mawdudi's statement is interesting not so much for its intent to preserve the supremacy of the Islamic sacred law, which is consistent with traditional Islam, but for novel and anomalous assimilation of national sovereignty to the "sovereignty" of God.

The ulema's attitude was traditionalist. They accepted the traditional duality of the legal order prevalent in the Islamic world and were naturally disposed to look at constitutional law as a modernized form of *qānūn*. Whereas the Shi'ite ulema, as established religious authorities, had been drawn into the Iranian constitutional politics of 1906–1907 by the secular constitutionalists, it was Mawdudi's fundamentalist Jama'at-i Islami who drew the Sunni ulema of Pakistan, in the same capacity as established religious authorities, into the politics of constitution-making in Pakistan. In the course of 1948, however, the ulema of Pakistan came to formulate their own position, which overlapped Mawdudi's in demanding that the laws of the state be based on the Koran and the Sunna, but went beyond it in a clericalist direction by adding that there should be a board of ulema to determine the possible "repugnancy to Islam" of all legislation. These demands provoked the secularist fears that "if Pakistan accepts an Islamic constitution, the Mullah will control the state."[59]

In October 1948, Maulana Shabbir Ahmad Usmani, who had been an important supporter of the Muslim League during the years of struggle for independence,[60] pressed the government for an Islamic constitution. Usmani was the leader of the only organized group of ulema and a member of both the Constituent Assembly and the ruling Muslim League, and had considerable influence with the ruling elite. Six months later, the government proposed an objectives resolution, which was approved on March 12, 1959, and was incorporated, with slight modification,[61] into preambles of the constitutions of 1956, 1962, and 1973. It began with the declaration: "Whereas sovereignty over the entire universe belongs to God Almighty alone, and the authority which He has delegated to the State of Pakistan through its people for being exercised within the limits prescribed by Him is a sacred trust;" it concluded the objective of setting up "the sovereign independent State of Pakistan . . . wherein [among other things] the Muslims shall be enabled to order their lives in the individual and collective spheres in accord with the teachings and requirements of Islam as set out in the Holy Quran and the Sunna [Tradition of the Prophet]."[62] In this formulation the idea behind Mawdudi's demands was accepted but stretched so as to be compatible with the modernists' conception of Islam. It should be noted in particular that the word *shari'a* is not mentioned. The omission was a concession to the modernist view that its two sources, the Koran and the Tradition of the Prophet, were accessible not only to the religious jurists but also to all literate Muslims.

A month later, a board of ulema as experts on the teachings of Islam (Board of Ta'limat-i Islamia), which included Usmani, was set up to advise the committees in charge of drafting the constitution. The views of the board, expressed in February–April 1950, were mostly drawn from the classical medieval theories of the caliphate and were mainly concerned with the qualifications of the head of the state,[63] but they included the significant recommendation that any law or ordinance repugnant to the *shari'a* be declared null and void and a committee of experts on the *shari'a* be set up to determine this.[64]

The response of the secular elite of the Muslim League was equivocal throughout the process of constitution-making. When introducing the Objectives Resolution to the Constituent Assembly, Pakistan's first prime minister, Liaqat Ali Khan (assassinated in October 1951) put forward the principles of democracy, freedom, equality, tolerance, and social justice, "as enunciated by Islam." The

fuzzy rationale for adding the last qualification, which was to be
incorporated into the preamble of the constitution, was given as
follows: "When we use the word democracy in the Islamic sense,
it pervades all aspects of our life." Predictably, the ulema were
dissatisfied with the fuss about democracy and Western concepts.
They also disliked the principle of equality of Muslims and non-
Muslims, and the delegation of power of God to the people of
Pakistan irrespective of creed.[65] This did not, however, deter the
prime minister from stretching his synthetic notion of Islam still
further. In a speech given in Lahore a few months later, Liaqat 'Ali
Khan declared: "For us there can be only one 'Ism': Islamic
socialism. This means in short: everybody in this country has the
same right to food, shelter, clothing, education and medical
facilities."[66]

The middle ground in the Pakistani constitutional politics was
occupied by the Islamic modernists who accepted Islam as the basis
of the political order, but considered Islamic laws in need of "over-
hauling" and new interpretation. The strength of the Islamic
sentiment among this group is amply demonstrated by the length
devoted to the praise of Islam in their speeches.[67] Nevertheless, their
position in substance differed little from that of the secularists
because their attachment to Islam engendered few constitutional
inferences. Their position is very interesting from our point of view
in that it presents a contrast to the clericalist demand of the Sunni
ulema of Pakistan and an even sharper one to the Shi'ite clericalism
that was to dominate Iranian constitution-making a quarter of a
century later. The Islamic modernists rejected the competence of
the religious jurists for bringing the *shari'a* up to date and adapting
it to modern needs, assigning this task to the legislative assemblies
instead. One prominent modernist considered it "obvious that the
only place where discussion can take place in connection with the
reinterpretation and reorientation of the *Shar'* is the Legislature, . . .
as the supreme representatives of the people."[68]

The interim report of the basic principles committee, presented
in September 1950, ignored the recommendations of the Board of
Ta'limat-i Islamia. The ulema began their activity outside the
Constituent Assembly by demanding the implementation of these
recommendations. A conference of ulema in January 1951 drew up
twenty two principles for an Islamic state and sent them to the
secretariat of the Constituent Assembly. Under Mawdudi's influence,
the ulema had only insisted on the consistency of all laws with the
sacred law and no demand was made for a *shari'a* committee. The
constitution-makers made some concessions to these demands in

the draft constitution, the report of the basic principles committee presented to the Constituent Assembly on December 22, 1952.

By this time, however, East Pakistan was in the midst of the anti-Ahmadi political turmoil fanned by the extremist group of Islamic militants, the Ahrar. Shortly after the passage of the Objectives Resolution, which to them implied the exclusion of non-Muslims from positions of public authority in an Islamic ideological state, the Ahrar had begun their virulent agitation against the Ahmadis in general, and Foreign Minister Zafrullah Khan in particular. The Ahmadi religious minority accepted Mirza Ghulam Ahmad of Qadian (d. 1908) as the returning Messiah, thus contradicting the Muslim dogma of the finality of prophethood with Muhammad. In May 1952, Foreign Minister Zafrullah Khan had resigned from the basic principles committee to address an Ahmadi public meeting; riots ensued. First the ulema (in June) and then Mawdudi's Jama'at (in July) joined the Ahrars, and made the latter's demand that the Ahmadis be declared a non-Muslim minority and barred from positions of public authority and policy-making their own. When the basic principles committee did not give way to this demand, which had been transmitted to them through the Board of Ta'limat-i Islamia, the discussion of the role of Islam in the new state was taken out of the board meetings into the streets.

Recognizing that the ulema constituted the only channel available for having an impact, Mawdudi and his fundamentalist group drew closest to them, while seeking to swing the anti-Ahmadi agitation behind amendments to make the constitutional proposals more Islamic. At the end of a conference in January 1953, with Mawdudi acting as their draftsman, the ulema proposed their own amendments to the report. On the issue of repugnancy to Islam they suggested that the determination of this matter be left to the supreme court, but as the training of the judges had been purely secular, for a period of transition, five ulema be appointed to the supreme court to decide, together with one other judge, to be nominated by the head of the state in consideration of his piety and knowledge of Islamic law, "whether or not the law in dispute is in conformity with Qur'an and Sunnah."[69]

The anti-Ahmadi agitation, however, could neither be rechanneled into supporting constitutional proposals nor otherwise controlled by Mawdudi and the constitutionally oriented ulema. In fact, fearing the Ahrar might monopolize anti-Ahmadi agitation, some of the ulema assumed its leadership. The result was the Punjab disturbances in early March 1953, and the complete breakdown of public authority in that province.

In the course of the discussion and amendment of the draft constitution in October 1953, the Islamic modernists accepted the idea of the jurisdiction of the supreme court over cases of repugnancy, but rejected the appointment of the ulema. As Binder notes, this granting of authority over the determination of the content of the Islamic law was a departure from the central tenet of consensus modernism.[70] Nevertheless, it was hailed by the modernist Fazlur Rahman as a step toward bringing about a revolution in Islamic law by reopening the gate of *ijtihād* (jurisprudential competence), while at the same time remedying "anarchism in *ijtihād*."[71] The head of the state was to be a Muslim, and the amendment of the ulema that the name of the state be the "Islamic Republic of Pakistan" was accepted.

The fundamentalists considered the inclusion of the repugnancy clause a victory. So did the ulema, even though it gave them no authority over the determination of the consistency of laws with Islam. Despite minor reservations, both groups considered the report of the basic principles committee as amended an Islamic constitution.[72] Disagreements over other issues, especially the issue of federation, prevented the final approval of the draft constitution, however, and the Constituent Assembly was dismissed in October 1954 without having resolved these. A new assembly was convened in July 1955, and began work on the reorganization of the judiciary in West Pakistan. A draft constitution was prepared by the government and presented on January 8, 1956. In his comments on the draft, while maintaining that giving the supreme court jurisdiction over the repugnancy of laws to Islam was still the best solution, Mawdudi now suggested that, in view of the majority opinion of the constituents, the determination of repugnancy to Islam be made by the majority of the Muslim members of the legislature.[73] The draft constitution was adopted on February 29, with only a few important amendments, and the constitution of the Islamic Republic of Pakistan finally came into force on March 2, 1956. Its preamble opened with the following declaration:

> WHEREAS sovereignty over the entire Universe belongs to Allah Almighty alone, and the authority exercised by the people of Pakistan within the limits prescribed by Him is a sacred trust; WHEREAS the Founder of Pakistan, Quaid-i Azam Mahomed Ali Jinnah, declared that Pakistan would be a democratic State based on the Islamic principles of social justice; AND WHEREAS the Constituent Assembly, representing the people of Pakistan, have resolved to frame for the sovereign independent State of Pakistan a constitution . . .

Thus, in a syncretic manner typical of late-comers into the international process of constitution-making, the constitution is grounded upon three principles of legitimacy of the political order: the sovereignty of God, the founding of the state, and the will of the people as represented by the Constituent Assembly. In addition, an appeal is made to the principles of social justice, which are now qualified as "Islamic" in attribution to the founder. This compromise formulation is problematic; behind it lurks the unresolved heterogeneity of these four principles and their potential contradiction. The Objectives Resolution, for instance, speaks of the delegation of God's (sovereign) authority to the state of Pakistan, to "exercised within the limits prescribed by Him," and refers to "the sovereign independent State of Pakistan." But a state that respects the legal limits prescribed by God cannot be described as sovereign in the sense used by modern constitutional law.[74] The question of compatibility of Islam and federalism is also sidestepped.

In fact, the constitution contained only two significant Islamic provisions. The president was instructed to establish an organization for Islamic research and instruction to assist social reconstruction on a truly Islamic basis (Article 197). The repugnancy clause was adopted, but its implementation was left to a commission that was to be appointed by the president, whose status was purely advisory and whose task was subtly shifted from the negative rejection of un-Islamic enactments to making positive recommendatins for legislative projects (Article 198). The supreme court was given no jurisdiction over the determination of the consistency of the laws with Islam.[75] In addition, the state was directed to endeavor to enable the Muslims to order their lives according to the teachings of Islam, to make the teaching of the Korna compulsory, and to organize the collection and expenditure of the charitable religious tax (*zakāt*) (Article 25). The state was also directed to endeavor to prevent the consumption of alcohol (Articel 28).

The views of the "consensus modernism" thus eventually prevailed in the constitutional law of Pakistan, with one exception. The Iranian constitution, as we have seen, had broken an important Islamic limitation to the public authority of the state by eliminating legal particularism in personal status law. The Pakistani constitution of 1956, by contrast, failed to achieve as much, despite the assiduous effort of the Islamic modernists to substitute "Koran and the Sunna" for the *sharī'a* throughout. An explanation inserted under Article 198 perpetuated legal particularism in personal law by forbidding personal laws repugnant to the Koran and Sunna as interpreted by the Muslim sects (i.e., the *sharī'a* as interpreted by different schools of jurisprudence). Surprising though it may seem, both the ulema and the fundamentalist Jama'at-i Islami were satisfied with the watered-down repugnancy clause, and accepted the constitution of 1956 as Islamic.[76]

Thus, despite much turbulence in the course of constitutional politics, and the claim to being an "ideological state" notwithstanding, the Islamicization of the constitution achieved in the end did not amount to much. As had been the case with the Iranian constitution, in the Pakistani constitution of 1956, "where Islam does appear, it appears essentially as a *limitation*, as a 'bounding' or limiting concept."[77] There is one difference, however: The appearance of Islam as a limitation is not backed by any limitation of the legislative and judiciary branches of government by the juristic/hierocratic authority of the ulema. The Islamic "clericalist" limitation of public authority in Iran had more far-reaching legal and institutional consequences than the Islamic "modernist" in Pakistan. The difference can be explained by different patterns of prior institutionalization of juristic authority in Shi'ite Iran and in the predominantly Sunni part of India that became Pakistan. The Islamic revolution necessary for the substantive legal reconstruction of the constitutional state as an Islamic theocracy required firmer institutionalization of juristic authority; it had not yet found its bearers, and would not occur in the predominantly Sunni Pakistan but in Shi'ite Iran.

The constitution of 1956 was abrogated in October 1958 by President Iskandar Mirza, who was removed from office by Field Marshall Muhammad Ayub Khan in the same year. In a stroke of modernist legislation promulgated as the Muslim Family Laws Ordinance in 1961, Ayub Khan swept aside the limitations of the *sharī'a* and legal particularism in personal law alike. A year later, the constitution of 1962 deleted the clause "within the limits prescribed by Him" from the preamble; the explanatory clause making for legal particularism under Article 198 of the old constitution was also omitted. The triumph of Islamic consensus modernism seemed complete. Not for long, however. Under the pressure of public opinion, both the above-mentioned clauses were reinserted into the constitution by the First Amendment Act of 1963, which became effective in January 1964. The Islamic provisions were also modified in the constitution of 1962. The commission to advise on the possible repugnancy of legal projects to Islam was designated the Advisory Council of Islamic Ideology (Articles 199–206); and the Islamic Research Institute recently set up for Islamic research to assist social reconstruction (in accordance with Article 197 of the old constitution) was given formal recognition as an organ of the state (Article 207).

The constitutional arrangements of 1956 and 1962, however, could not prevent civil war and the disintegration of Pakistan into its eastern and western components in 1971. Islam, after all, did not prove strong enough to hold the two geographically separated parts together. West Pakistan became the People's Republic of Bangladesh, and adopted a straightforward secular democratic constitution in 1972. East Pakistan not only assumed the designation of the Islamic Republic of Pakistan, but its constitution of 1973 in fact reinforced some of the Islamic provisions of the earlier constitution. It retained the Council of Islamic Ideology, included a new declaration of Islam as the religion of the state (Article 2), and prohibited the consumption of alcohol categorically (Article 37). It also required an oath from the president and the prime minister that included the affirmation of the finality of the prophethood of Muhammad, presumed impossible for the Ahmadis.[78] The reinforced Islamic character of the constitution prepared by Zulfikar Ali Bhutto, whose Pakistan People's Party had a safe majority, was a concession to achieve consensus. All references to his cherished "Islamic socialism" were likewise dropped from the text at the insistence of the Islamic parties in opposition. Consequently, no vote was cast against the constitution, although there were some abstentions.

The constitution of 1973, however, included liberal guarantees on religious freedom, and finally eliminated the clause that had prevented the ending, de jure, of legal particularism in personal law for the Muslim citizens.[79] Furthermore, it introduced, as an instance of Jinnah's "Islamic principles of social justice," provisions for expropriation without compensation (Article 38 of Principles of Policy; and Article 24), which, as the opposition had pointed out, are contrary to the rules of the *shari'a*.[80] The advance of socialism, however, went hand in hand with a reversal for Islamic modernism. There had been constant tension and clashes between the two institutions created by the Islamic provisions of the constitution of 1962: the Advisory Council of Islamic Ideology and the Islamic Research Institute. The former represented the traditionalist Islam while the latter, especially under the directorship of Fazlur Rahman, was modernist in orientation.[81] The Islamic Research Institute was eliminated from the new constitution, signaling a reversal for Islamic consensus modernism whose place was now taken by socialism.

The anti-Ahmadi forces were dissatisfied with the new constitution, and continued to clamor "Long live the finality of prophethood" until they secured the unanimous passage, on September 7, 1974, of a constitutional amendment declaring the Ahmadis a non-Muslim minority.[82]

Conclusion

The unwillingness of the constitutionalists in the Iranian Majles to reject Nūrī's Islamic amendment, and the broad popular support for his campaign against the Majles in 1907 were indicative of the solid attachment of the Iranians to Shi'ism. Nor can there be any doubt about the firm attachment of the people of Pakistan to their Muslim identity, and therefore to Islam.[83] The inclusion of the Objectives Resolution, as preamble, and of the "Islamic provisions" were of great symbolic value as they expressed this attachment to Islam. A questionnaire ($N=6,269$) circulated by a constitution commission appointed in February 1960 showed 96.64 percent of the respondents in favor of incorporating the preamble into the new constitution; 97.23 percent favored the bringing of existing laws into conformity with the injunctions of Islam; and 90.5 percent favored the "enabling clause," directing the state to assist the Muslims in the realization of Islamic values.[84] Furthermore, when the phrases "within the limits prescribed by Him" and "as set out in the Holy Quran and the Sunnah" were dropped from the preamble to the constitution of 1962, as was the reaffirming qualification, "Islamic" for the Republic of Pakistan in Article 1, the same public opinion, as we have seen, forced Ayub Khan's government to amend the constitution in order to reincorporate these phrases.[85]

 Nor could there be any doubt about the explosive potential of Islam for political mobilization. This point was made amply clear by Nūrī's massive anti-constitutional campaign in Iran in 1907, and by the anti-Ahmadi riots of late February–early March 1953 that resulted in "the complete breakdown of adminstrative machinery and total collapse of civil power," the capitulation of the government of Punjab to the demands of the Islamic militants, and the famous soul-searching Munir Report of 1954.[86]

The implications of the deep attachment of the peoples of Iran and Pakistan to Islam for the constitutional law of the new state, however, were far from clear. In Iran, the supervision of the ulema over legislation was never properly institutionalized and soon became a dead letter. The case of Pakistan is more instructive. The contradictory rhetoricolegal semantics of the Objectives Resolution points to the crux of the problem of translation of modern constitutional law into the Islamic normative universe. The problem is one of accommodation of two heterogeneous principles of order, one deriving from the Greco-Roman antiquity, the other from Islam as a world religion of salvation.[87]

The Iranian constitution, as we have seen, originated in a royal decree. This decree was mentioned in its brief preamble to record the legitimation of the new constitutional order by the established, traditional monarchical authority. The partial transfer of sovereignty from the monarch raised a number of problems, as it had done earlier in the West, but none that involved Islam. The Iranian constitutionalists had taken the sovereignty of the monarch for granted, and had assimilated the principles of national sovereignty to it without any conceptual difficulty. By contrast, the republican form of government raised a serious conceptual problem for the proponents of an Islamic constitution in Pakistan who had not lived under the sovereignty of a native monarch for a century. This was due to the fact that the jurists of the *sharī'a* had never endowed the community of believers with sovereignty, as had been the *res publica* in the late medieval West, nor even developed a notion corresponding to sovereignty. The compromise solution to this conceptual problem was found in the Objectives Resolution. Let us trace the logical steps required for arriving at its opening line. God is the "legislator" of the *sharī'a*. The body politic is the *umma* (community of believers). The *sharī'a* is the law of the *umma*. Sovereignty consists in the power of legislation. Therefore, sovereignty belongs to God.

The truth of the matter is otherwise. Islam did not know the idea of legislation and the conception of body politic as the republic. Mawdudi and the Islamic fundamentalists were unwilling to admit this. They made no distinction between legislation and jurisprudence, between law-finding (by the religious jurists) and law-making (by popular assemblies), and none between the Roman conception of the republic and the Islamic conception of the *umma*. The traditionalist ulema accepted these faulty conceptual translations based on confusion of heterogeneous notions. The result was what F. Rahman characterizes as the "comic" transfer of political sovereignty to God.[88]

Mawdudi had thus sought to challenge the entire Western development of the notion of sovereignty as the source of public authority: "*it is God and not Man whose Will is the Source of Law in a Muslim Society.*"[89] The law that expresses God's will is, needless to say, the *sharī'a*. This erroneous and ahistorical initial equation of public law with the *sharī'a* rather than with the *qānūn*

underlines Mawdudi's persistent and pervasive confusion between
law-finding by individual legal experts and law-making by collective
bodies, between legislation and jurisprudence (*ijtihād*).[90]
    Montesquieu's construction of public law on the premises of the
natural law was heterogeneous to Christianity and Islam alike. The
written constitutions of the late eighteenth and early nineteenth
centuries, however, accepted Montesquieu's premises. The constitutional law they created on the basis of the natural law was received
by the constitution-makers of Pakistn who were, however, unwilling
to acknowledge their heterogeneity to Islam. But this sovereignty
had no legal implications other than the limitation of the scope of
popular legislation; and the institutions set up to implement such
limitation, as we have seen, were inadequate to that prupose. The
declaration of the sovereignty of God in the constitutions of the
Islamic Republic of Pakistan, therefore, was vacuous—and necessarily so, given the articulation of public and sacred law in the
traditional Islamic order.
    Yet words inscribed in monuments, however vacuous, are never
completely devoid of consequences. Mawdudi's confusion or *sharī'a*
and *qānūn* became more persistent and widespread throughout the
Islamic world[91] until it reached a group—perhaps the only group—in
the Muslim world with the cultural and institutional assets needed
to spread the cover of the *sharī'a* over the *qānūn*. Without a doubt,
a revolution in Islam was necessary to make the sovereignty of God
a legal reality by reconstructing the constitutional state as an
Islamic theocracy.[92] It is no accident that such a revolution occurred
in Iran, where the hierocratic authority of the Shi'ite jurists had been
much more firmly institutionalized than that of their Sunni
counterparts in Pakistan and the rest of the Muslim world. Our
comparative perspective suggests that only against the background
of this firmer institutionalization of clerical authority was it possible
for the Shi'ite hierocracy to make the transition from law-finding
to legislation. This transition is in many respects comparable to that
made by the medieval papacy, even though the major impetus to
it came not from Roman law but from its latter-day successor,
Western constitutional law.

Notes

1. S. A. Arjomand, "Shi'ite Jurisprudence and Constitution-Making in
    the Islamic Republic of Iran," in M. Marty and R. S. Appleby, eds.,
    Fundamentalisms and the State: Remaking Polities, Economies, and

Militance (Chicago: University of Chicago Press, 1993); idem, "Constitution of the Islamic Republic," in *Encyclopaedia Iranica* (1993), 6: 150–158.

2. H. F. Jolowicz and B. Nicholas, *Historical Introduction to the Study of Roman Law* (Cambridge: Cambridge University Press, 1972), pp. 355, 365–373; C. H. McIlwain, *Constitutionalism: Ancient and Modern* (Ithaca and London: Cornell University Press, 1947), p. 26.

3. W. Stubbs, *Select Charters and Other Illustrations of English Constitutional History*, 8th ed., (Oxford: Clarendon Press, 1905), pp. 135–140.

4. M. Weber, *Economy and Society*, ed. G. Roth and C. Wittich (Berkeley and Los Angeles: University of California Press, 1978), pp. 828–829.

5. Jolowicz and Nicholas, *Roman Law*, Chapter 21; A. A. Schiller, "Jurists' Law," *Columbia Law Review* 58 (1958): 1230.

6. Ibid., pp. 1227–1228.

7. Ibid., pp. 1231, 1235.

8. Tony Honoré, *Emperors and Lawyers*, (London: Duckworth, 1981), esp. p. 102.

9. F. W. Maitland, *Roman Canon Law in the Church of England* (London: Methuen, 1898), pp. 100–101.

10. Ibid., p. 16.

11. Ibid., pp. 9–11, 124–127.

12. Dom J. Hourlier, *Les religieux*, being *Tome X: L'Age Classique (1140–1378)* of *Histoire du droit et des institutions de l'Égilse en Occident* (Paris: Editions Cujas, 1974), pp. 27–34, 532–537. This use of the term "constitution" for papal legislation parallels the above-mentioned use of the term for the legislative acts of the Roman emperors.

13. G. R. Galbraith, *Constitution of the Dominican Order* (Manchester: Manchester University Press, 1925).

14. R. Bendix, *Kings or People: Power and the Mandate to Rule* (Berkeley and Los Angeles: University of California Press, 1978), p. 140.

15. O. Hintze, Historical Essays of Otto Hintze, ed. F. Gilbert (New York: Oxford University Press, 1975), pp. 167–168, 171–172, 312–318, 245–351.

16. Ibid., pp. 310, 319–325; F. W. Maitland, *The Constitutional History of England* (Cambridge: Cambridge University Press, 1920 [1908]), p. 77.

17. Montesquieu, *De l'esprit des lois*, ed. V. Goldschmidt, 2 vols. (Paris: GF-Flammarion, 1979 [1748]), XXVIII.41.

18. Ibid., XXVIII.39.

19. J.-P. Royer, *L'Église et le royaume de France au XIVe siècle d'après le "Songe du Vergier" et la jurisprudence du parlement* (Paris: Librarie Générale de Droit et Jurisprudence, 1969), esp. p. 108.

20. Thomas Aquinas, *Aquinas: Selected Political Writings*, ed. A. P. d'Entreves, trans. J. G. Dawson (Oxford: Blackwell, 1965), pp. 114–131.

96 **Said Amir Arjomand**

21. H. J. Liebesny, *The Law of the Near and Middle East: Readings, Cases, and Materials* (Albany: State University of New York Press, 1975), pp. 38–41.
22. S. A. Arjomand, *The Shadow of God and the Hidden Imam: Religion, Political Order and Societal Change in Shi'ite Iran from the Beginning to 1890* (Chicago: University of Chicago Press, 1984).
23. M. Gaborieau, "Les oulémas/soufis dans l'Inde moghole: anthropologie historique de religieux musulmans," *Annales economies, sociétés, civilizations*, 5 (1989), pp. 1185–1204, esp. p. 1196.
24. S. A. Arjomand, "Religious Extremism (*Ghuluww*), Sufism and Sunnism in Safavid Iran: 1501–1722," *Journal of Asian History* 15, no. 1 (1981): 34.
25. Gaborieau, "Le oulémas/soufis."
26. The point was made in an objection and admitted by Montesquieu in his defense (*Defense de l'esprit des lois*, pt. 1, 4th obj.).
27. Ibid., XII. 29.
28. Ibid., XXV.10–11.
29. Ibid., XXV.9.
30. Ibid., XXIX.17.
31. The chapter on Justinian in his *Considérations sur les cause de la grandeur des Romains et de leur décadence* does not even mention the code. See V. Goldschmidt, "Introduction" to Montesquieu's *De l'esprit des lois* (Paris: GF-Flammarion, 1979), p. 16.
32. Weber, *Economy and Society*, p. 867.
33. See S. A. Arjomand, "Constitutions and the Struggle for Political Order: A Study in the Modernization of Political Traditions," *European Journal of Sociology* 33, no. 1 (1992): 39–82.
34. See E. Barker, *The Development of Public Services in Western Europe: 1660–1930* (Oxford: Oxford University Press, 1944); and T. H. Marshall, *Class, Citizenship and Social Development* (Garden City, N.Y.: Doubleday, 1964).
35. J. Markoff and D. Regan, "Religion, the State and Political Legitimacy in the World's Constitutions," in T. Robbins and R. Robertson, eds., *Church-State Relations: Tensions and Transitions* (New Brunswick, N.J.: Transaction Books, 1987), p. 162.
36. Ibid., p. 180; see also pp. 173, 176.
37. See S. A. Arjomand, "Constitutional Revolution. (iii) Constitution," *Encyclopaedia Iranica*, 6: 187–192.
38. *Moḏākerāt-e Majles* (Tehran: Rūznama-ye Rasmī-ye Keshvar-e Shāhanshāhī-ye Īrān, 1946–7/1325), 1: 79.
39. Reproduced in M. Torkamān, "Neẓārat-e mojtahedīn-e ṭerāz-e avval: sayr-e taṭavvor-e aṣl-e dovvom-e qānūn-e asāsī dar dawra-ye avval-e taqannīna," *Tārīkh-e Mo'āser-e Īrān* (Tehran: Mo'assesa-ye Pazhūhesh va Moṭāle'āt-e Farhangī), 1: 17–18.
40. Ibid., pp. 17–25.
41. *Moḏzākerāt-e Majles*, pp. 1: 188.

42. Torkamān, "Neẓārat," pp. 27–28.
43. Ibid., p. 24.
44. Ibid., p. 29.
45. S. A. Arjomand, "The *Ulama*'s Traditionalist Opposition to Parliamentarianism: 1907–1909," *Middle Eastern Studies,* 17.2 (1981) pp. 174–190.
46. Cited in Torkamān, "Neẓārat," p. 19.
47. F. Nūrī, "Book of Admonition to the Heedless and Guidance for the Ignorant," trans. H. Dabashi, in S. A. Arjomand, ed., *Authority and Political Culture in Shi'ism* (Albany: SUNY Press, 1988), pp. 354–370.
48. See A.-H. Hairi, *Shi'ism and Constitutionalism in Iran* (Leiden: E. J. Brill, 1977), pp. 225, 232–233.
49. M. Torkamān, "Sayr-e taṭavvor-e aṣl-e dovvom-e qānūn-e asāsī dar dawra-ye dovvom-e taqannīna," *Tārīkh-e Mo'āser-e Īrān* (Tehran: Mo'assesa-ye Pazhūhesh va Moṭāle'āt-e Farhangī, 1990/1369), 2:22–23. It is interesting to note that Ayatollahs Khurāsānī and Māzandarānī took the occasion to insist on the ulema's exclusive authority over judiciary matters. The duty of the Majles in all such matters was to refer them to an appropriate authoritative *mojtahed.* (Ibid., p. 23.)
50. *Moḍakerāt-e Majles,* 2: 362–383, 419–435, 580, 798–807, 834–844.
51. Torkamān, "Sayr," pp. 43–49.
52. Ibid., p. 43. Some deputies raised objections to calling the *mojtahed*s "supervisors" but the issue was never resolved.
53. M. Torkamān, "Neẓārat-e hey'at-e mojtahedīn," *Tārīkh-e Mo'āser-e Īrān* (1991-2/1370), 3:51–65.
54. W. Floor, "Change and Development in the Judicial System of Qajar Iran (1800–1925)," in E. Bosworth and C. Hillenbrand, eds., *Qajar Iran* (Edinburgh: Edinburgh University Press, 1983).
55. The issue of federalism, which proved more intractable in the long run, delayed the making of the constitution by three more years.
56. Cited in L. Binder, *Religion and Politics in Pakistan* (Berkeley and Los Angeles: University of California Press, 1961) p. 100.
57. Ibid., Chapter 3.
58. Cited in ibid., p. 103.
59. G. W. Choudhury, *Constitutional Developments in Pakistan* (London and New York: Longmans, Green, 1959), pp. 67–68, 76.
60. K. B. Sayeed, *Pakistan: The Formative Phase 1857–1948,* 2d ed. (London, New York, and Karachi: Oxford University Press, 1968), pp. 203–205.
61. The phrase, "the authority which He has delegated to the State of Pakistan," was omitted from the preamble of the constitution of 1962. The attempt to reintroduce it into the preamble of the constitution of 1973 failed at the last minute. See M. D. Ahmed, "The Permanent Constitution of Pakistan," *Orient* 14 (1973): 119.
62. Cited in Binder, *Pakistan,* pp. 142–143.
63. Ibid., pp. 170–177 and Appendix.

64. Ibid., p. 169.
65. Choudhury, *Pakistan*, pp. 52, 57–58.
66. *Pakistan News*, Sept. 4, 1949; cited in E. Sarkisyanz, *Rußland und der Messianismus des Orients* (Tübingen: J. C. B. Mohr, 1955), pp. 292–293.
67. Binder, *Pakistan*, p. 323.
68. I. H. Qureshi, cited in Choudhury, *Pakistan*, p. 71.
69. Cited in Binder, *Pakistan*, p. 289.
70. Ibid., pp. 338–339.
71. Ibid., p. 325.
72. Ibid., pp. 336–337.
73. A. Maududi, *Islamic Law and Constitution*, 2d ed., trans. and ed. Khurshid Ahmad (Karachi and Lahore: Islamic Publications, 1960), pp. 400–401.
74. An Islamic state, as the Munir Report pointed out, "cannot in this sense be sovereign because it will not be competent to abrogate, repeal or do away with any law in the Quran or the Sunna. Absolute restriction on the legislative power of the State is a restriction on the sovereignty of the people of that State" (cited in Ahmed, "Constitution," p. 119).
75. Demands that it should be were revived by the opposition during the debates over the constitution of 1973 but did not prevail. See D. Conrad, "Die Neubegrundung der Verfassung Pakistans," *Zeitschrift für ausländisches öffentliches Recht und Volkerrecht*, 34 (1974): 282.
76. Binder, *Pakistan*, pp. 370–373.
77. F. Rahman, "Islam and the Constitutional Problem of Pakistan," *Studia Islamica* 32, no. 4 (1970): 276.
78. Ahmed, "Constitution," p. 118.
79. F. Rahman, "Islam and the New Constitution of Pakistan," in J. H. Korson, ed., *Contemporary Problems of Pakistan* (Leiden: E. J. Brill, 1974), p. 40.
80. Conrad, "Die Neubegrundung," pp. 290–291.
81. Rahman, "New Constitution," p. 41.
82. Y. Friedmann, *Prophecy Continuous: Aspects of Ahmadi Religious Thought and Its Medieval Background* (Berkeley and Los Angeles: University of Calaifornia Press, 1989), pp. 40–45. The anti-Ahmadi Council for the Preservation of the Finality of Prophethood continued its activity as a pressure group. President Zia al-Haqq needed little persuasion to institute persecution of the Ahmadis by an ordinance promulgated on April 26, 1984. In August 1985, he promised to "persevere in our effort to ensure that the cancer of Qadianism is exterminated" (cited in ibid., p. 46).
83. This attachment was typically displayed by the Bengali deputies of the Constituent Assembly during the eventual debate on the draft constitution in October 1953. They spent an inordinate part of their time

in hailing the millennium when all the ideals of Islam would be realized through an Islamic constitution, and in praising the virtues of Islam. But when all this was said only six members specifically demanded the Head of the State be a Muslim, only two specifically demanded that Islam be declared the state religion, and only eight specifically demanded that Pakistan be declared an Islamic republic. (Binder, *Pakistan*, p. 323).

84. G. W. Choudhury, *Documents and Speeches on the Constitution of Pakistan* (Dacca: Green Book House, 1967), pp. 677, 685, 687.

85. Ibid., pp. 843–844, 862.

86. The report itself brought out further implications of the potency of Islamic symbols:

> That the demands were presented in such a plausible form that in view of the emphasis that had come to be laid on anything that could even be remotely related to Islam or Islamic State, nobody dared oppose them, not even the Central Government which . . . did not make even a single public pronouncement on the subject. (Cited in A. Ahmad, and G. E. von Grunebaum, *Muslim Self-Statement in India and Pakistan 1857–1968* [Wiesbaden: Otto Harrassowitz, 1970], p. 194).

87. See Chapter 2, above.

88. Rahman, "Constitutional Problems," p. 277.

89. Maududi, *Islamic Law*, p. 50. And further, "The philosophers have tried to place the cap of sovereignty on man—a being for whom it was never intended" (ibid., p. 178).

90. The willful confusion between the heterogeneous notions of legislation and *ijtihād* stands out with greatest clarity in a paper Mawdudi delivered on the topic in January 1958 (ibid., Chapter 2).

91. See S. A. Arjomand, "The Emergence of Islamic Political Ideologies," in J. Beckford and T. Luckmann, eds., *The Changing Face of Religion* (London: Sage, 1989).

92. See S. A. Arjomand, "The Rule of God in Iran," *Social Compass* 36, no. 4 (1989): 539–548; and idem, "Shi'ite Jurisprudence and Constitution-making in the Islamic Republic of Iran," in M. Marty and R. S. Appleby, eds., *Fundamentalisms and the State: Remaking Polities, Economies and Militance* (Chicago: University of Chicago Press, 1993).

4

Church, State, Nation, and Civil Society in Spain and Poland

José Casanova

Spain and Poland are two representative, yet markedly different Catholic countries. Historically, both have stood repeatedly at the forefront of Roman Catholic expansion or defense against other religions. In both cases, "frontier" conditions led to an early and lasting identification of religious and national-cultural identity, which often took the form of an exclusive and militant cultural Catholicism. At different periods of their histories, however, both Spain and Poland offered striking examples of religious tolerance or, at least, of coexistence between religions that were at loggerheads elsewhere. The determining factor weighing in the direction of either militancy or tolerance seems to be the nature of the relationship between church and state. Indeed, Poland's failure to develop an early modern centralized state may be the single most important factor in explaining the divergence in Spanish and Polish Catholic developments. This chapter will explore three related topics: (1) the different and historically shifting relationships among church, state, nation, and civil society in Poland and Spain; (2) the conditions that have permitted the Catholic Church in Spain and Poland to play a positive role in recent processes of democratization; and (3) the incipient trend—clear in the case of Spain, less definite in the case of Poland towards the reprivatization of Catholicism, following the transition to democracy and the institutionalization of political society.

From the early 1960s there has been a major transformation in the political orientation of the Catholic Church from a state-centered strategy to a society-centered one. In the process, Catholic churches throughout the world have dissociated themselves from and entered into conflict with authoritarian regimes that were then predominant in many Catholic countries. This "disestablishment" of Catholicism has permitted the church to play a key role in the transition to democracy in several countries. This chapter will analyze these processes in Poland and Spain. But similar analyses could be extended to other Catholic countries.

In analyzing Catholic developments one always has to keep in mind that the Catholic Church is both a transnational institution that transcends any particular national society and a national institution deeply embedded in the different histories and structures of particular countries. Looking at Catholicism globally since the early 1960s, one can observe two interrelated, apparently contradictory, processes. There is, first of all, a strengthening of the process of centralization of the Roman papacy, a long secular process that in its modern form has its origins in the Vatican's defensive response to the French Revolution and to the subsequent liberal revolutions spreading throughout Europe and Latin America. The opposition to the emergence of the modern liberal state shaped the practically uniform counterrevolutionary strategy of the church throughout the nineteenth century. Such a strategy was particularly pronounced under the papacy of Pius IX and culminated in the promulgation of the Syllabus (1864) and the proclamation of the dogma of papal infallibility (1870). The slow and winding process of Catholic adaptation to modernity began soon thereafter, under Leo XIII, and culminated in John XXIII's call to *aggiornamento*, a clearly belated recognition of Catholic "backwardness" and of the need to update its relationship to the modern world. The Second Vatican Council reinforced the centralizing trend, a trend that has become particularly prominent again under the papacy of John Paul II. Along with this process of administrative and doctrinal centralization, there has occurred a process of homogenization of Catholic culture, at least among the elites, throughout the Catholic world.

Simultaneously, however, with this process of Vatican centralization and cultural homogenization, there has taken place a second distinct process of centralization of the Catholic churches at the national level. This process of "nationalization" goes back to the emergence of different forms of Catholic Action with their shared strategy of mobilization of the Catholic laity to defend and promote the interests of the church in what was perceived as a hostile modern secular environment. The Second Vatican Council and the subsequent institutionalization of national bishops' conferences in most Catholic countries has reinforced the dynamics of this process of "nationalization." The active role of national conferences of bishops in defining particular national issues, together with the church's change of attitude towards the modern secular environment, constitute the two most important factors in the reorientation of many Catholic churches from a state-centered to a society-centered strategy.

This dynamic tension between Roman centralization and national centralization explains both, the globalization of a "Catholic" position on many issues as well as the particular refraction that the general Catholic position assumes in any given national context. In any case, the parallel processes of Roman and national centralization have been taking place at the expense of the traditional autonomy of the diocesan episcopate, which at least de jure still remains the locus of institutional power within the Catholic Church. Lately, however, the Vatican has been trying to reinforce once again diocesan episcopal autonomy in order to counter the autonomous tendencies of the national episcopal conferences and thus reassert greater Roman control.

Spain

The following schematic reconstruction is only meant to highlight those developments that seem of special relevance in unraveling the complex of church-state-society relations, leading up to the Spanish civil war and the establishment of the Franco regime.

The centuries-long Christian *reconquista* of the Iberian Peninsula from the Muslim conquerors led to an early identification of religious and national identity. It was, however, the formation of the early modern Spanish state under the Catholic kings that led to the identification of church and state and to the transformation of Spanish Christianity into the Church Militant. Religious mobilization played a crucial role in the making of the Spanish state. Indeed, the belatedly introduced Inquisition (1481) was bound to play a state-making function, becoming the first truly national, unified, and centralized state institution. The expulsion of Jews, Muslims, and "Moriscos" from Spain took place within a typical pattern of popular pressure from below and religious mobilization from above.[1]

In order to reintegrate itself with Europe, Spain shed its two unwanted religions precisely at a time when Europe itself was being cut asunder by the Protestant Reformation and the Catholic Counter-Reformation. The Counter-Reformation put an end to Spain's enthusiastic economic, political, and cultural experiments in early modernity. The Hapsburg monarchy, the Universal church, and the American colonial empire, all combined to sacrifice the incipient Spanish nation-state to the ideal and material interests of the "Universal Christian Monarchy," a historical project at odds with the emerging international system of European states.[2]

The Church Militant went on fighting Islam in the Mediterranean and in Asia, pagans in America, and heretics in Europe. Spain had turned the concept of religious crusade against Christian Europe. The defeat of Spain's quixotic imperialism led to Spain's bitter isolation from the emerging modern Europe. Crown and church together decided to preserve within the Spanish dominions the universalist and Catholic ideal of political and religious unity that they had failed to maintain by force in Europe. Unlike other European nations, Spain would not recover from the general seventeenth-century crisis.[3]

The Bourbons in the eighteenth-century began the slow process of reorientation toward Europe. But the task of "catching up" was complicated by the fact that those forces opposing the "enlightened" reforms refused to accept the view that the difference between Spain and Europe was one of quantifiable "backwardness," insisting that there was a qualitatively unbridgable cleavage between two mutually exclusive civilizations. When the typical sixteenth-century conflict between "ancients" and "moderns" reemerged in eighteenth-century Spain it began to resemble the form it would take in Eastern European countries, particularly in Russia, and in non-Western civilizations resisting Westernization.[4]

In eighteenth-century Spain the conflict first emerged within the church itself between a reformist wing led by Augustinians and enlightened clerics, protected by enlightened despotism, and a traditionalist wing led by the ultramontane Jesuits, who opposed Bourbon regalism and the puritan Jansenism of the reformers, and by the scholastic Dominicans, who opposed the introduction of modern philosophy and modern science into the Spanish universities. The expulsion of the Jesuits from the Spanish dominions in 1776, following a series of urban riots in Madrid for which the Jesuits were conveniently blamed, marked the temporary triumph of reformist Gallican caesaro papism. But the French Revolution and Napoleon's intervention in Spanish politics shattered the "enlightened" model of elite-controlled reform from above, took away the "aura" from the absolute monarchy, and brought in its place modern forms of political conflicts and collective action.[5]

The church played a crucial role in the mobilization of the Spanish people against the Napoleonic invasion. The War of Independence, at times led by guerrilla priests, was fought as a religious crusade against "the impious forces of Satan." The traditional identification of Catholic faith and Spanish nation was thereby strengthened. Meanwhile, cut off from the rest of Spain, unrepresentative political elites met in Cadiz to draft the 1812 liberal constitution. More than the measures dismantling the ancient regime, such as the abolition of seigneurial jurisdictions or the disentailment of the lands of the church, it was the abolition of the Inquisition (1813) that gave rise to the fiercest polemics between "Liberales" and "Serviles." Prominent liberal clerics led the attack on the Holy Office. Indeed, the clergy with ninety seven deputies constituted almost one-third of the Constituent Cortes. But the church hierarchy and the rural clergy reacted against the attempt to dissolve the Inquisition and were able to change the aim of their diatribes from the French invaders to the internal heretics, the liberal *afrancesados*. Catholic Spain now turned the concept of religious crusade against liberal Spain. The phenomenon of "the two Spains"—a Catholic Hispanic Spain and a liberal Europeanizing one—was born.[6]

In 1814 the people of Madrid offered an enthusiastic welcome to the restored absolutist king, shouting "Long live the fetters," thus mocking the liberal slogan "Let's break the fetters."[7] At the beginning of the nineteenth-century the church stood with the Crown and the people against the reformist liberal elites. The absolutist restoration forced the Spanish liberals into exile or underground into masonic lodges and conspiratorial secret societies. There took place the typical latin fusion between liberalism and anticlericalism as well as the typical Hispanic fusion between liberalism and Praetorian politics.[8]

The early identification of nation and religious faith that had facilitated early modern state formation and had spared Spain the religious civil wars of early modern Europe, now became an impediment to modern nation-building and transformed modern political conflicts into religious warfare. The three civil wars of modern Spain—the First Carlist War (1833–1840), the Second Carlist War (1870–1876), and the Spanish civil war (1936–1939)—all started as antimodern counterrevolutions and were sanctified by an embattled Catholic Church as religious crusades against godless liberalism or atheist communism. As a counterpart, the burning of churches and convents and the killing of clerics and nuns were to become typically recurrent features of Spain's modern political upheavals from the 1830s, when the first public outbursts of fierce anticlericalism occurred in Madrid and in other major cities, to the 1930s.[9]

In the 1830s, by embracing Carlism and rallying the peasantry of the north against the new constitutional monarchy, the church managed to alienate most social forces in the country. The state's response was to disentail the lands of the church, to abolish the tithe, and to dissolve most monastic orders. The sale of the lands of the church at auction provided the Treasury with the needed revenues to fight the Carlist insurrection, but it frustrated the liberal project of creating a land-owning peasantry loyal to the liberal regime. The properties fell into the hands of the conservative landowners who from that point on were bound by their material interests to the liberal cause. Thus, the "betrayed" liberal revolution consolidated the "latifundist" agrarian capitalism of the center and south, while the church lost its rural economic base as well as its ties with the rural proletariat that developed there.[10]

By mid-century, expropriation had left the Spanish church destitute. The closing of monasteries and the dissolution of the male religious orders had brought to an end the influence that the church had exerted through education and beneficence. Save in the north, the church found itself forsaken, divorced ftom the state and from the ruling class. The dramatic decrease in the size of the clergy, from approximately 200,000 in 1808 to 56,000 in 1860, despite Spain's sharp overall population increase, is a telling indicator of the extent to which the church had lost its presence in Spanish society.[11]

The church, however, soon began the process of reconquest of Spanish society through its alliance with the liberal oligarchic state. The 1851 concordat reestablished the alliance of church and state. Bourgeoisie and landowners, their revolution safely accomplished, found it opportune to reconcile themselves with a needy church. The new ruling class attained respectability and obtained an important ally in blocking the political demands of radical democrats and the socioconomic demands of the lower classes. The bourgeoisie rejoined the church's bosom, adopting a mainly extemal form of cultural Catholicism, while refusing to concede to the church control over the private conscience or morality. Spanish Catholicism, while maintaining its mass base in the landowning peasantry of the north, became an increasingly urban and "bourgeois" institution. Meanwhile, the growing rural and urban proletariat was becoming increasingly "de-Christianized." In its eagerness to regain the strayed sheep the church abandoned the larger flock. At the turn of the twentieth-century, in the chronic conflicts between capital and labor and between oligarchic *caciquismo* and mass democracy the Spanish church stood mostly on the side of capital and *caciquismo*.[12]

Moreover, the Spanish liberal state also had to pay dearly for the legitimation it received from the church. From now on the state would have to support the clergy economically, thus feeding lower-class resentment against the state and against a church that had become part of the state administration. But more important, the liberal state ceded to the church its control over education, thus giving up the best instrument it had to build a modern nation and to shape the mind of its citizenry. Thereby, religious, class, and ethnic-national identities became much more important than any all-Spanish national identity. Moreover, the reestablishment of the confessional state reinforced the old identification between the Spanish nation and the Catholic faith at a time when large sections of the population were abandoning the church's bosom and adopting militant atheist banners. Not surprisingly, anticlerical and antistatist ideologies grew together.[13]

The Second Spanish Republic (1930–1936) put an end to the establishment of the Catholic church. The republic instituted the separation of church and state, took over from the church the control of public education, and enforced the privatization of Catholicism and the laicization of Spanish society. When the republican leader Manuel Azana proclaimed in the republican Cortes that Spain had ceased being Catholic, he only stated polemically the new constitutional reality. But in the context of the aggressive anticlericalism and laicism of the republic, the Catholic Church understood the polemical statement as a call to arms. The church stopped short of stating publicly its unloyal opposition to the new republican order, but it became evident that the Spanish Catholic Church would not accept the liberal principles of separation of church and state, state control of public education, freedom of conscience, religious toleration, or privatization of religion. Unwilling to accept the loss of its privileges, apprehensive of the officially condoned anticlerical attacks, and fearful of the more serious threats posed by the impending socialist revolution, the Catholic Church joined enthusiastically the military uprising and sanctified the sanguinary civil war as a religious crusade of liberation. The violent and unrestrained religious persecution in the republican zone confirmed the church's worst fears about the militant atheism of the Spanish left. The church's response, however, was to condone and all too often to sanctify the even more violent and indiscriminate official repression in the nationalist zone.[14]

Victory in the civil war permitted Spanish Catholicism to become once again the official state religion. The church regained all its institutional privileges and was offered the modern administrative means to enforce its religious monopoly and to impose the unity of faith and nation. Through state coercion, Spanish society became Catholic again. Although often used as a derogatory term, *Nacional-Catolicismo* serves as an apt short-hand analytical characterization of the Franco regime. While the regime adopted many of the external manifestations of fascism in its ideology, organization, and symbolic paraphernalia, the most important structural characteristics of fascism were missing. It is no exaggeration to say that the Catholic Church constituted the main institutional and ideological "pillar" of the regime.[15]

The church offered the regime the original ideological legitimation of the civil war and its main initial source of mass popular mobilization. After the war, once the regime pursued a policy of demobilization, Catholicism became the source of its diffused legitimation and the basis for its authoritarian, "mentality." Catholic corporatism became the only slightly coherent ideological and formative principle of the regime. Catholic lay organizations, first the elitist Asociacion Catolica Nacional de Propagandistas (ACNdP) and later the even more elitist Opus Dei, provided the Francoist state with its most important administrative cadres. When the regime found itself boycotted and shunned as an international pariah following the defeat of the Axis Powers, the church through its links with the Vatican and other Catholic churches provided the regime with its first basis for international legitimation.[16]

It was at least part of the official rhetoric to portray the regime as the ideal Catholic model of church-state relations and as the exemplification of the Catholic "third way" between liberal democratic capitalism and totalitarian socialism. Franco himself in his public speeches and particularly in his writings appropriated the typical Catholic antimodern philosophy of history, declaring that the civil war had been a crusade against masonry (his personal bête noire), the French Encyclopedia, and all their modern derivations (i.e., liberalism, capitalism, and socialism). Modern liberal Spain, from the eighteenth-century Enlightenment to the Second Spanish Republic, was to be repressed and forgotten. The "New Spain" was to forsake all its ties with a decrepit modern world and, modeling itself after the great imperial age of the Catholic kings and the Counter-Reformation, it was to resume Spanish history where it was left prior to the introduction of the foreign heresies that had precipitated Spain's decline.[17]

Given this fusion of church and state, Catholicism and regime, the slow but progressive distancing of the church from the regime that began in the early 1960s, and the open conflict and final break between the two in the 1970s was an important factor in the legitimation crisis and the final dissolution of the regime.[18] A purely instrumental explanation of those changes as a conscious strategy of institutional adaptation on the part of the church would be inadequate. For even if one were to privilege such an interpretation, it would still be necessary to explain what made it possible for the Spanish church to abandon its traditional "reactive organicism" and adopt for the first time in its modern history such a rational future-oriented strategy of adaptation to changed circumstances.[19]

Processes of Change

The conjunction of three series of interrelated processes may serve to explain in part the change in orientation by the Spanish Catholic Church from a state-centered to a society-centered strategy.

THE INTERNAL TRANSFORMATION OF SPANISH CATHOLICISM

To a large extent, the massive re-Catholization of Spanish society after the war was rather superficial, as it was the result of administrative coercion and public pressure. As the coercion and pressure diminished progressively, the Catholic revival petered out. But some aspects of the revival were genuine and would have a deep effect both on the transformation of Spanish Catholicism and on the relationships of church, state, and society.[20]

Among the manifestations of the Catholic revival were:

— The emergence for the first time in modern Spanish history of groups of credible, autonomous Catholic intellectuals who played an important critical role in the otherwise extremely impoverished intellectual discourse of Franco's Spain and who served to mediate the chasm between the two Spains. Figures like Aranguren, Lain Entralgo, and Tovar are paradigmatic here. For the first time also lay Catholic intellectuals would have an impact upon the theological discourse of Spanish Catholicism.[21]

— The emergence of two modern, that is, inner-worldly Catholic religious movements that would play an important role in Franco's Spain and, moreover, also spread beyond Spain to become the first modern contributions of Spanish

Catholicism to the universal church. The *Cursillos de Cristiandad* would be the first manifestation within Spanish Catholicism of a Catholic type of evangelical revivalism and born-again Christianity. Similarly, the Opus Dei would be the first manifestation within Spanish Catholicism of a militant type of Protestant ethic. The Opus Dei was a secretive lay Catholic movement-organization that was very successful after the civil war in recruiting young upwardly mobile elites through its new message of sanctification in and through ascetic dedication to professional calling.[22]

—   The emergence, also for the first time in Spanish history, of a genuine social Catholicism springing from the Catholic Action movement. The Catholic Workers' movement (HOAC) and the Catholic Workers' Youth movement (JOC) would become radicalized in the 1950s and progressively confront both the Catholic hierarchy and the regime.[23]

STRUCTURAL TRANSFORMATIONS OF THE REGIME

In 1956 there took place a series of violent clashes between Catholic and Falange youth in Madrid University fighting for control of the student movement. Those clashes paralleled the power struggles taking place within the state administration between Catholic and Falange leaders trying to determine the direction of the new economic policies needed to overcome the economic impasse reached by the regime, due to the exhaustion of the import-substitution model of industrialization. Franco dismissed the leaders of both warring factions and invited Opus Dei members into the government. The Opus Dei "technocrats" introduced a radical change in the economic policies of the regime, by pursuing an agressive policy of export-oriented economic growth, the rationalization of the state administration, and the integration of Spain into the world capitalist system.[24]

The replacement of Catholic Action elites, close to the church hierarchy, by parvenu elites from the Opus Dei, a sectarian movement within Spanish Catholicism looked upon suspiciously by the church as well as by the economic, political, and cultural establishment, had the unintended consequence of facilitating the progressive distancing of the church and other established elites from the regime. Out of power, the displaced elites adopted a posture of semiloyal, semidemocratic opposition to the regime that progressively served as mediating link with the more radical opposition. Moreover, technocracy, development ideologies, and ideologies proclaiming "the end of ideology" came to replace Catholicism as the basis for the ideological legitimation of the regime. Some of the displaced Catholic elites now adopted genuinely Christian Democracy, establishing links with European Christian Democracy.[25]

As the social consequences of the new stabilization policies introduced by the technocrats became visible, some Catholic bishops from the south, first individually and later collectively, began to criticize openly in their pastoral letters the social policies of the regime. In this respect, although the radicalization was milder in the Spanish case, the bishops from the "latifundist" south played a similar role to the one played by the northeast bishops in the radicalization of the Brazilian church. Bishop Añoveros came to occupy within the Spanish church and in the eyes of the regime a position similar to the one occupied by Dom Helder Camara in the Brazilian church. Similarly, although less severe in the Spanish case, the state repression directed against Catholic priests and laity opposing the regime led the moderate sectors of the church to close institutional ranks and to confront openly the regime, while also protecting the new opposition movements emerging from civil society.[26]

The acute secularization of Spanish society that accompanied the rapid processes of industrialization and urbanization was viewed at first with alarm by the church's hierarchy. Slowly, however, the most conscious sectors of Spanish Catholicism began to talk of Spain no longer as an inherently Catholic nation to be reconquered, but rather as a *país de misión*. With the official adoption of the new Vatican policies, Spanish Catholicism ceased resisting for the first time modern processes of secularization and slowly learned to come to terms with them and eventually to view them as a "sign of the times."[27]

EXTERNAL TRANSFORMATIONS OF CATHOLOCISM

In the Second Vatican Council the Spanish bishops probably constituted one of the most conservative blocks of the assembled bishops. Prior to the council some sectors of the Spanish clergy and of the laity had began their own process of *aggiornamento*. But their demands had found little resonance within the hierarchy. Now the official policies coming from the Vatican gave the modern sectors of Spanish Catholicism the leverage they needed to pressure the hierarchy and to confront the regime.[28]

The promulgation of the encyclical *Pacem in Terris* (1963) marked a turning point. The Christian Democratic sector, gathered around the ex-minister of education Ruiz Giménez and their influential journal *Cuadernos para el Diálogo*, now took the lead in demanding the institutionalization of the rule of law, the transformation of the regime into an *Estado de Derecho* (*Rechtsstaat*), and the protection of the human, civil, and political rights to which the Spanish people were entitled. Ironically, some of the Catholic groups and individuals who in the 1950s had represented the regime internally and externally as a model of Catholic order now began to attack the regime as illegitimate. Moreover, the privileged exemption from state censorship that Catholic publications had gained after the war could now be used to criticize the regime and to defend the general principles of freedom of expression and freedom of the press.[29]

The transformation of Spanish Catholicism was both sudden and extensive. The change in language from Latin to the vernacular was accompanied by a more significant change in the content of Catholic discourse. Any superficial comparison of the Catholic press and publications from the 1950s to the 1960s will show the difference.[30] The training of priests in the seminaries underwent a radical overhaul. Scholasticism was abruptly dropped and replaced with modern philosophies and modern theologies. A new generation of priests embraced avidly the new direction, taking a confrontational attitude vis-à-vis their own older colleagues, their hierarchy, and their confused flocks. The clash between the young urbanized priests and the traditional Catholicism of rural Spain is well captured in the ethnography of the Spanish village of the period. Spanish popular religiosity, already weak when compared with that of Poland, was unable to survive the iconoclastic onslaught of the new liturgy and the new pastoral practices. Active Catholic cadres and some sectors of the laity, particularly among the middle classes, felt comfortable with the new *Catolicismo conciliar*, but many others were not able to make the transition and stopped practicing the faith altogether. Many young priests, and even some older ones, felt increasingly uncomfortable with their traditional roles as sacramental mediators and searched for personally and socially relevant pastoral practices, usually by adopting various forms of social and political activism. Religious vocations, a traditional avenue of social mobility, plummeted and the secularization of the regular and secular clergy increased dramatically. The number of seminarians, for example, decreased from 8,397 in 1961–1962 to 2,791 in 1972–1973; around 400 priests yearly left the clergy between 1966 and 1971; one-third of Spanish Jesuits left the order between 1966 and 1975.[31]

Throughout the 1960s the Spanish church was sharply divided along generational lines between the majority of bishops and a large minority of priests over sixty on the one hand and a minority of bishops and a majority of priests under forty on the other. The intervention of the Vatican, by changing the organizational structure and the composition of the Spanish episcopate, tipped the balance of forces in favor of the new Catholicism. By 1970 the reformers had gained control of the national conference of bishops, which had replaced the older conference of metropolitans. At first the Franco regime had presented a serious obstacle to the attempt to renovate the Spanish episcopate by refusing to give up its right of presentation of bishops. But the Vatican adopted a policy of circumventing this obstacle by forcing the older bishops to retire, who thereby lost their right to vote in the national conference, and by nominating younger auxiliary bishops with the right to vote. By nominating auxiliary bishops, the Vatican was able to exclude the regime's intervention in their nomination. In 1966 the Spanish episcopate was composed of seventy bishops. Of those, 65 percent were sixty years of age or older and only five were auxiliary bishops. By 1973 there were seventy seven bishops, seventeen of which were auxiliary bishops, while the number of bishops sixty years of age or older had decreased to 40 percent of the total.[32]

Two events mark the year 1971 as a turning point in the transformation of the Spanish church. That year, Cardinal Tarancón, who represented a majority of moderate bishops, was elected president of the national conference. From now on the church would demand openly the liberalization and democratization of the regime. Nothing perhaps captures better the dissociation of the Catholic Church from the Franco regime than the famous incident in 1973 when, in the funeral of the president of the government, Carrero Blanco, who had been killed by E.T.A., the Basque terrorist organization, the extreme right, shouted to the presiding cardinal, "Tarancón al paredón" ("up against the wall"). At the very moment when the Spanish left had abandoned its historical anticlericalism, it was being adopted by the Spanish right, resentful of the betrayal of a church, which after having been so pampered with regime favors, was abandoning the regime.[33]

The other important event in 1971 was the convention of the First Joint National Assembly of Bishops and Priests, which produced the celebrated public confession of sin for the role played by the church in the Spanish civil war. The famous text read: "We humbly recognize our sin and ask for forgiveness, for we did not know how to become true 'ministers of reconciliation' among our people, torn by a fratricidal war."[34] Indeed, this policy of reconciliation was probably the most important contribution of the Spanish Catholic Church to Spain's transition to democracy.

The Role of the Church in the Transition

If the dissociation of the church from the Franco regime contributed to the regime's crisis of legitimation, the church's support of the democratic opposition movements contributed to the strengthening of civil society. The role of the church in the process of democratization can be analyzed at three different levels.

THE MILITANCY OF CATHOLIC ACTIVISTS IN THE DEMOCRATIC OPPOSITION

From the late 1950s on, Catholics would play an active role in the emergence of the new democratic opposition movement. One finds engaged Catholics among the leadership of the whole spectrum of opposition parties, from the monarchists to the extreme left. Some developments have primarily symbolic significance. For instance, the theocratic Carlist movement, which from the 1830s to the 1930s had provided the shock troops of counterrevolutionary Catholicism in all three civil wars, became radicalized in its opposition to the regime and adopted a socialist platform. Some of the most radical underground opposition groups, like the Castroist Frente de Liberación Popular (F.L.P.) or the Trotskyist Organización Revolucionaria de Trabajadores (O.R.T.), had Catholic origins. None of these groups, however, would be able to survive the "transition." Of much greater historical relevance was the fact that for the first time Catholics would join and play an active role in the historical parties of the left, in the Socialist party (PSOE) and in the Communist party (PCE). Indeed, the fusion of the Catholic and the secular left in the underground opposition to the regime was an important factor in the disappearance of anticlericalism from Spanish politics.[35]

Worker priests and lay activists with origins in the Catholic workers' movement of the 1950s also played a central role in the emergence of the new working class movement of the 1960s and in the establishment of the new semiclandestine trade unions, Comisiones Obreras and Union Sindical Obrera (U.S.O.).

Catholic activists also played an important role in the reemergence of the Catalan and Basque nationalist movements in the 1960s. But this fact is less remarkable, since the Catholic Church historically had always supported the nationalist movements in both regions, maintaining there a close alliance with society against the centralist Castilian state.

THE CHURCH'S PROTECTION OF THE DEMOCRATIC OPPOSITION

Even in the worst periods of Francoist repression, the norms and values of civil society and the democratic traditions of liberal Spain were preserved and transmitted through family, working-class, and intellectual networks. The moment state repression eased in the early 1960s, oppositional activities against the regime poliferated throughout the country and in all spheres of society. In this respect, the democratic opposition movement in Spain emerged independently of any support from the institutional church.[36] Unlike in Poland or much of Latin America, the Spanish church did not need to become "the voice of the voiceless," nor the very promoter of the reconstitution of civil society. But the church contributed to the consolidation of the democratic opposition in two ways.

First, by offering religious legitimation for the democratic principles upon which the activities of the opposition were based (i.e., freedom of expression, freedom of association, civil and political rights), the church undermined the repressive policies of the regime and thereby strengthened the opposition. The regime's traditional portrayal of the democratic opposition as the work of an external, mainly communist conspiracy against Catholic Spain became no longer credible and, therefore, the repression now appeared simply as the expression of an illegitimate system of power based on naked force. When the regime introduced its first liberalization measures in the 1960s the opposition was emboldened and it increased its confrontational activities. When the regime tried to put a lid on oppositional activities in the late 1960s by reverting to more repressive policies, it proved no longer able to regain control of public order and in addition it lost most of the diffused legitimacy that the regime may still have had among Spain's silent majority.

By offering its churches and monasteries as relatively protected sanctuaries where interregional, interclass, and interparty sectors of the opposition could meet, the church helped to coordinate and to unite diverse sectors of the democratic opposition into a unified movement of civil society against the authoritarian state. Famous incidents in which the police entered church buildings where important clandestine meetings were held, such as national conventions of Comisiones Obreras or the Assembly of the entire democratic opposition of Catalonia only served to discredit the regime further, showing the entire population that the democratic opposition enjoyed the support of the church.

ROLE OF THE CHURCH IN NATIONAL RECONCILIATION

Much more important than its role in providing a physical space where the opposition could meet was the role of the church in providing a symbolic space for the reconciliation and dialogue among all Spaniards. The religious-secular cleavage had played a destructive role in modern Spanish politics because, by superimposing itself upon the other two major cleavages—the class conflict between capital and labor and the regional conflict between the hegemonic Castilian center and the nationalisms of the periphery—it had made all of them untractable. The Catholic Church's final acceptance of the legitimacy of the modern world and the abandonment by the Spanish left of its traditional anticlericalism put an end to the religious-secular cleavage in modern Spain, thus making the other conflicts more susceptible to politics of negotiation and compromise. Indeed, the spirit of compromise, the search for consensus, and the willingness to enter pacts were the most remarkable characteristics of the Spanish transition. Semantic connotations such as *reconciliación, concordia, tolerancia, acuerdo, pacificación, convivencia* all appeared again and again in the political discourse of the transition, in campaign speeches as well as in parliamentary debates. The immediate need to defend a transition still threatened by the danger of military coups and by the terrorism of the right and of the left partly explain the willingness to compromise on the part of most political forces. But only the more remote background of the collective memory of the experience of the civil war and of the system of exclusion that followed it, may explain the politics of consensus almost as an end in itself, which characterized the Spanish transition.[37]

The two great historical pacts of the transition reflect this politics of consensus. The Moncloa Pact (1977) was the first historical compromise between capital and labor, mediated by the main political parties. Of greater historical relevance, however, was the constitutional pact between all the main political forces one year later, which permitted for the first time in Spanish history the drafting of a constitution that was not the imposition of the will of the victors in the political struggle over the vanquished, but rather the end result of an exacting process of responsible backstage negotiation among political elites.[38]

Throughout the transition the Catholic Church played a low-key, yet positive back-stage role. Although the church was able to inscribe into the 1978 constitution a paragraph recognizing "the sociological fact" that the majority of the Spanish population was Catholic, the Spanish Catholic Church finally accepted the non-confessionality of the Spanish state, as well as the principles of separation of church and state and of religious freedom.[39] Equally important was the decision not to sponsor any "Catholic" party, nor to support directly any of the Christian Democratic parties. A genuine desire for religious peace; the realization that the Catholic community, the clergy included, had become pluralistic politically and would not support any monolithic Christian party; and the fear that such an officially sponsored party could become a minority party and thus undermine the church's claim that Catholicism was Spain's national religion, all probably contributed to the political neutrality of the church during the transition. None of the three competing Christian Democratic parties was able to survive the 1977 elections.

Ultimately the whole process amounted to the recognition of the voluntary principle of religious allegiance. The Spanish church has accepted the fact that it is no longer a church in the Weberian sense of being an obligatory monopolistic community of faith coextensive with the nation. The Catholic faith has ceased being de facto as well as in principle a national faith. Moreover, the constitutional recognition that Spain is a multinational state has in and of itself undermined the very principle of a unitary Spanish nation. The various nations making up the Spanish state have become institutions within a pluralistically organized civil society. By recognizing both the fact and the principle of a pluralistically organized civil society, the church has become a denomination, a powerful one to be sure, but a denomination nonetheless, functioning within civil society.[40]

Opinion surveys after the successful consolidation of democracy indicate that the Spanish population also has internalized these principles. In 1984, an overwhelming majority of Spaniards (86 percent) still considered themselves Catholics.[41] But the number of "practicing" Catholics is much lower, tending to be around 40 percent of the population. There seems to be, moreover, a noticeably decreasing trend in religious practice, particularly among Spanish youth. The number of youth attending Sunday mass has decreased dramatically—from 62 percent in 1975 to 35 percent in 1982.[42] It is also evident that there no longer exists a religious cleavage that may serve to polarize either the social classes or the policial electoral choices. Practicing Catholics are distributed relatively evenly throughout the Spanish population: 44 percent of the upper middle-classes, 38 percent of the lower-middle classes, 34 percent of the working class. This is probably the most dramatic change from pre-civil war trends. Similarly, the Catholic vote tends to be distributed relatively evenly along the entire Spanish electoral spectrum.[43] Among those who voted the Socialist party into power in 1982, 25 percent were practicing Catholics.[44] In this respect, there is presently no longer a Catholic vote susceptible of political mobilization by the church.

But not only can the church no longer control the public morality of the Spaniards, it also can no longer take for granted the control of the private morality of the Catholic faithful. According to a 1984 survey, 65 percent of Spaniards approve the use of contraceptives; 54 percent would accept married priests; 47 percent approve of divorce while 40 percent disapprove of it; and 45 percent approve of premarital sexual relations while 41 percent disapprove of them.[45] It is not surprising therefore that the Catholic Church failed to block or amend, either through institutional corporatist pressure or though Catholic mobilization, the new legislation introduced by the socialist government on precisely those issues that the church still considers to fall within its own particular sphere of competence, namely, religious education, divorce, and abortion. The same survey showed that a majority of Spaniards thought that the church ought not to exert influence over the government (43% versus 32%); that the church does not have adequate answers either to the needs and problems of the individual (43% versus 39%) or to the problems of family life (49% and 34%) and that the church's claim to moral authority is not based on a knowledge of reality (41% versus 27%).[46]

One may conclude, therefore, that in Spain religious faith and morality are becoming privatized. It remains to be seen whether the Catholic Church will reinforce these trends by retreating to the cure of souls and the protection of that which it considers to be its institutional corporatist interests, or whether it will be able to use its remaining institutional and moral weight to become a critical moral voice, by participating on an equal basis in Spain's public debates, thus enlivening the public sphere of Spain's civil society.

Poland

As in Spain, the "frontier" conditions of Polish Catholicism also led to an early identification of religious and national cultural identity, which has been maintained and reinforced by subsequent developments.[47] Polish Catholicism has been repeatedly at the forefront of Catholic expansion or defense against other religions in Eastern Europe, to wit, different versions of paganism, orthodoxy, Islam, Protestantism, and, finally, atheist communism. This gave Polish Catholicism also its particular "militant" character. But like Spain, *Polonia semper fidelis* served also as the setting for unique experiments in religious tolerance. The determining factor weighing in the direction of either "militancy" or "tolerance" seems to be the identification of church and state. Indeed, Poland's failure to develop an early modern centralized state may be the single most important factor in explaining the divergence in Spanish and Polish Catholic developments. In Poland the *Szlachta* democracy of the federalist republic of nobles frustrated both centralized absolutism and the identification of church and state. Early modern Poland became a haven for dissenting faiths fleeing generalized religious warfare in Europe. Even after the Counter-Reformation reasserted Catholic hegemony in Polish culture and the war with Sweden awakened a strong anti-Protestant reaction, Poland still continued to give, by Catholic standards, a striking example of religious tolerance.[48]

David Martin has observed that "where religion is imposed from above by a conqueror it is thereby weakened, whereas when it is the focus of resistance to a conqueror it is thereby strengthened."[49] Again, Poland is not unique in this respect. Catholic Ireland, as well as Croatia, Slovenia, and Slovakia in Eastern Europe, all offer examples of Catholic countries that also deviate significantly from the French-Latin pattern of secularization. Nineteenth-century Poland avoided the typical patterns of conflict between the Catholic Church and the secular liberal state, between the church and a secular humanist intelligentsia becoming increasingly anticlerical, and between the church and a socialist workers' movement turning first anticlerical and then militantly atheist. The typical positive correlations of education, industrialization, urbanization and proletarianization with secularization either did not obtain in Poland or were significantly attenuated.[50]

The formation of collective status and class identities, ideological positions, and political groups, were all refracted by the national question. Once again, given the absence of a Polish state, the crucial factor was the identification of church and nation at a time when the Catholic Church was the only institution able somewhat to cut across the partition of Prussian, Russian, and Austrian Poland. During the nineteenth-century, Catholicism, romantic nationalism, and slavic messianism fused into a new Polish civil religion. At first, this process was mainly restricted to the gentry and intelligentsia; but in the 1870s, the threat that Bismarck's *Kulturkampf* posed to the linguistic and religious identity of the Polish peasantry pushed this group also into the nationalist cause.[51] Remarkably enough, the fusion of the Polish national and Catholic identities took place even in the face of reactionary Vatican policies that consistently supported the conservative monarchies and condemned the Polish risings. The Vatican's "betrayal" was offset, however, by the dedication of the radical lower clergy, by the far-sighted leadership of a few hierarchs, and by the emergence, toward the end of the nineteenth-century, of a Polish version of "social Catholicism." When the first phase of industrialization took place, both the state and capital were mainly in foreign hands. Therefore, the church could not be perceived as legitimating either state domination or capitalist exploitation. As a result the first generation of Polish workers were neither de-Christianized nor denationalized— certainly not to the extent that was common elsewhere. On the contrary, often there was a fusion of class, religious and national identity.

Polish Independence and the End of Polish "Exceptionalism"

With the establishment of a Polish independent state after World War I, the unity of the nation against foreign enemies began to dissolve. There appeared the standard cleavages among classes, parties, and ideologies, while the chauvinism of every nationalism in power began to show its ugly face in its treatment of the Jewish and Ukrainian minorities. The unity between church and nation also began to dissolve and there appeared even splits between a conservative hierarchy and the more radical lower clergy. Moreover, although the church did not share state power and often found itself in conflict with the Polish state, its leanings toward Dmowski's nationalism of the right served to alienate the other political parties and to antagonize the religious and national minorities. Anticleri-calism, although a mild one by Latin standards, also began to emerge. It appeared in the quarrels between the nonconfessional Polish state and the church represented symbolically in the feud between Marshall Pilsudski and Metropolitan Sapieha. It appeared among large sectors of the intelligentsia that had finally incorporated the

Enlightenment critique as well as the positivist and Marxist critiques of religion. This anticlericalism was perhaps best represented by the remarkable and little known Polish school of sociology of religion. It appeared, as was to be expected, within the socialist left and even within the peasants' movement led by Vincenty Witos.[52]

Had these trends continued, they may have put an end to Polish "exceptionalism." But they were cut short by the renewed experience of partition, foreign occupation, and unified historical resistance. National solidarity was once again strengthened by the extreme ordeal and the Polish church found itself once more on the side of the nation, suffering more than its share of the brutal Nazi repression and supporting physically and spiritually the underground. Any bickering Poles may have had against their church was soon forgotten.

The Catholic Nation versus the Communist State

All attempts by the communist regime to sever the links between church and nation ended in failure. It is true that the odds were against the new regime. The church's prestige was at an all-time high and its identification with the nation was reinforced naturally by the fact that with the redrawing of new borders, almost the entire population of Poland was, at least formally and for the first time in modern Polish history, homogeneously Catholic.[53] By contrast, the prestige of the Polish Communists had never been high; the practical liquidation of the entire Communist party by Stalin did not help matters; and its replacement, the Polish Workers' party, was like the regime marked by the original sin of foreign conception.[54] Nevertheless, the regime could count on the nearly universal yearning for a clear break with the past, on the widespread acceptance of radical social reform, and on the delusions of large sectors of the intelligentsia.[55] Above all, the regime could count on power: the power to coerce, the power to suborn, the power to manipulate. Yet its project of total power was frustrated again and again by the resistance of a church that was willing to recognize the regime, to render unto Caesar what was Caesar's, even to lend it support and legitimacy for the sake of the nation and the requirements of the Polish *racja stanu*, something that was repeatedly stressed by Cardinal Wyszyński. But at the same time the church showed a dogged determination to deny Caesar what was God's. The consistently principled position of the church contrasted markedly with the utter lack of consistency in the state's policies toward the church, its strategies being marked by purely tactical considerations.[56]

The ultimate goal of the regime was clear—the complete elimi-
nation of the church and of religion from Polish life—and it never
ceased proclaiming it. But it was also understood that like the final
phase of communism, this goal was still far away and all kinds of
detours might be needed in order to reach it. All the strategies of
forced secularization from above, used relatively successfully first
in the Soviet Union and then throughout Eastern Europe, were also
variously tried in Poland albeit with little success.[57]

Neutralization and control through the official incorporation of
the church into the state failed. Unlike the Orthodox Church, the
Catholic Church proved immune to caesaropapism. Neither the
creation of "patriotic priests" nor that of "progressive Catholics,"
neither the support given to the schismatic Polish National Catholic
Church nor the attempt to deal directly with the Vatican and thus
bypass the unyielding Polish hierarchy, were able to either divide
the church or undermine its prestige.[58]

The strategy of coercion also failed. The amount of repression
needed to terrorize the whole nation would have been staggering
even by Stalinist standards. The selective repression of representative bishops, priests, and nuns only served to turn them into either
martyrs or national heroes, as attested by the triumphal popular
acclamation with which the release of Cardinal Wyszyński was
received.[59]

Socialist resocialization also failed. The attempt to establish a
new civil religion and to create a new "socialist man," an attempt
that was hardly successful elsewhere in Eastern Europe, was a total
failure in Poland. In spite of the state's control of all official means
of communication, education, and socialization, the church and the
Polish family were able to serve as effective counteragencies of
socialization, and together they defended successfully the right to
a religious education. All attempts to rewrite Polish history and to
depict the church as collaborator, as enemy of the nation, and as
enemy of the people backfired;[60] the official propaganda machine
lost all its credibility and the church became the cherished trustee
of the nation's history, culture, and traditions, and of the collective
memories of the Polish people.[61]

The marginalization of religion to a private religious sphere also
failed ultimately because neither church nor state could agree on
the boundaries or accept the set limits.[62] Neither Catholic principle
nor Polish tradition could be reconciled easily with a conception of
religiosity borrowed from bourgeois Protestantism and restricted to
the private and unmediated relationship between the individual
conscience and God, adorned at most by an Orthodox conception

of ceremonial ritual, spiritually edifying but restricted to sacred places. Neither could Soviet socialism recognize in earnest the right of an autonomous sphere to exist, where "antisocialist," that is, antisystem norms and values could develop. Such a model of autonomous differentiation of the spheres, borrowed from bourgeois modernity, implied the recognition of a pluralism of norms and values that was simply irreconcilable with "the leading role of the party."

Finally, secularist planning through economic development also failed to bring the expected results. The expressed hopes of the Gierek era that economic development, borrowed from the West materially and ideally, would have in Poland the same secularizing effects it apparently had in the West, were also disappointed.[63] It is true that the model of economic development itself failed. But even before its failure had become obvious, the evidence of progressive secularization was ambiguous at best.

Marxist sociologists of religion had been collecting every promising sign indicating that the laws of secularization were operating also in Poland.[64] But at the end of the Gierek era most indicators seemed to point rather to a reverse process of desecularization.[65]

— There was an absolute and relative increase in the number of bishops, priests, nuns, and seminarians, when compared with prewar Poland.

— There was a progressively accelerating increase in the number of parishes, churches, and Catholic periodicals and publications.

— Indicators measuring the religious beliefs of the population, which had always remained inordinately high, even showed some tendency to rise, most significantly among the young.

— The figures on religious practice were even more overwhelming since even those who did not consider themselves "believers" participated in religious ceremonies as a symbolic opposition to the regime.

Clearly the church had won the war of secularization as well as all the main battles. Every time there was a direct confrontation over the control of religious education, over the control of ecclesiastical appointments, over the curriculum in the seminaries, over the millennium celebration, even over constitutional revisions, the regime had to withdraw and the power and the prestige of the church were enhanced in the process.

Cardinal Wyszyński was, no doubt, the individual most directly responsible for the victory of the church. Traditionally, during interregna or whenever the Polish throne became vacant, the primate of Poland had served as interrex, as a symbolic regent. Unofficially for almost forty years, Cardinal Wyszyński filled symbolically the office of interrex certainly as effectively as any other primate in Polish history. In a sermon at the Warsaw Cathedral on February 7, 1974, elaborating on his conception of the relations among church, nation, and state in Poland, Cardinal Wyszyński revealed his explanation of the victory of the church, namely, the primacy of the relationship between church and nation, over that between church and state:

> From the beginning there has been true cooperation in Poland between the Church and the Nation—and often cooperation between the Church and the State as well. Of course the dimension of the increasing links between the Church and the Nation are one thing, and the cooperation between the Church and the State another. The nation, after all, is a permanent phenomenon, like the family, from which the nation is born. The proof of this permanence is the fact that, despite the persecutions and the increasing struggle it has been subjected to in defense of its independence, living on the borders of (various) cultures, languages, faiths and rites, the nation has nevertheless survived until today. The Church, supporting the Polish nation so that it would not be destroyed, has helped it to survive. . . . There have been moments when the state fell silent, and only the Christ's Church could speak out in the Polish nation. It never stopped speaking out, not even when, in the time of the partition, the state was forced into silence. . . . It is the particular merit of the Church never to have stopped working, even in the most difficult situations. We ought to realize this when we speak of establishing correct relations between the Nation and the Church, between the State and the Church in our country.[66]

The characteristic structure of beliefs and practices of Polish Catholicism was formed mainly during the Counter-Reformation and has remained largely unchanged until the present.[67] Some of the most salient characteristics are:

— The public ceremonial, highly sacromagical character of the typical Polish rituals: pilgrimages (Czestochowa), processions (Corpus Christi), passion plays (Kalwaria Zebrzydowska).[68]

— The highly centralized hierarchic structure of the church, with the primate at the top, in his unique dual role as head of the Polish church and interrex, thus symbolizing the union of church and nation.

— The prominent position of the clergy, with a prestige and influence perhaps unequaled in the Catholic world, functioning as sacerdotal and sacramental mediators between the sacred and the profane, and between God and the Polish people, but also functioning as mediators, representatives, and guides of the community in its social functions.[69]

— The Marian devotion and the two most representative Polish national cults, Czestochowa and Kalwaria. Particularly, Our Lady of Czestochowa at Jasna Gora serves as the national shrine of Polish Catholicism and as the symbolic fortress of the nation against foreign invasions. The Icon of the Black Madonna has since long been associated with historical and collective memories of national suffering, resistance and final triumph. But it was made most effectively into an impressive symbol of national and Catholic resistance to the communist regime, following the release of Cardinal Wyszyński, when he mobilized the church and the nation to implement the Marian program that he had conceived while in prison: the rededication of the nation to the Queen of Poland in 1956 at the 300th anniversary of King John Kazimierz's vows; the yearly vows of the Great Novenna culminating in the 1966 millennium celebration; the annual procession of the Black Madonna to every single town in Poland, leading up to the celebration of the ninth centenary of the martyrdom of St. Stanislaw in 1979.[70]

Every attempt by the authorities either to stop the religious manifestations or to undermine them by staging parallel secular manifestations failed. Again and again the power of mobilization of the allegedly totalitarian regime was dwarfed by the power of mobilization of the church. The Marian program was not only able to maintain mobilized the Catholic population for over twenty years around religious issues, but it also linked symbolically in a dramatic way Polish sacred and secular history, the fusion of church and nation and their ambiguous relationship to the state. Indeed it may serve to illustrate in a Durkheimian paradigmatic fashion the power of religious beliefs and rituals to serve the cause of national integration by creating and recreating the bonds of national solidarity.

The Conflict Between Church and State

Usually the conflictive relations between church and state in socialist Poland are analyzed from the perspective of institutional relations, in terms of periods of confrontation, amelioration, accommodation, mediation, and the like.[71] This essay takes a different approach, viewing those relations from the perspective of the principles of resistance that informed the church's actions. There are three such principles of resistance that correspond roughly to three different phases in church-state relations: the principle of religious resistance, the principle of national resistance, and the principle of civil resistance.

THE PRINCIPLE OF RELIGIOUS RESISTANCE

There is no doubt that from 1948 to 1956 the church was fighting for its own survival as an independent religious institution. Understandably, corporatist self-interests predominated over any other concern. Yet corporatist self-interests were transcended the moment the struggle was carried on in the name of religious freedom, a universalistic principle, against the totalitarian tendencies of an atheist yet theocratic state that wanted to impose its own secular religion upon its subjects.[72] The Polish October, when Polish workers rose up claiming "Bread and God" was the turning point in this phase. The church attained recognition and the right to autonomous existence in exchange for its support and legitimation of the embattled Gomulka government. But the struggle against the totalitarian tendencies of the state had to be renewed continuously beyond 1956, since it became clear that the state would only make concessions in times of weakness when it needed the church's support, but was not ready to institutionalize any of those concessions permanently. Indeed, the state's violation and unilateral revocation of already achieved agreements led to constant friction.

THE PRINCIPLE OF NATIONAL RESISTANCE

Having ensured its own institutional survival the church could now attend to its traditional role as the nation's keeper. The new autonomous space gained by the religious institution could be used in defense of the nation. The pulpit, the religious classroom, the seminaries, the pastoral letters, the Catholic University, the Catholic press, all became autonomous spaces where the collective national identity and the traditions and values of Polish culture could be preserved and transmitted. But the activities of the church were not restricted to this traditional "organic work" in times of partition or foreign occupation. From the very beginning, the church had played a very active role in the, "Polonization" of the Western territories, despite the Vatican's reluctance to recognize the new Polish-German boundaries. Soon the church began to challenge the state directly by reminding it repeatedly that the defense of national sovereignty is the primary duty of the state toward the nation. The clear implication was that the state was either violating or neglecting its national duties and that this was also the reason for its lack of legitimacy. The series of accusations and counteraccusations that followed was a reflection of the battle over the minds of the Poles in which both church and state were consciously engaged. The state accused the church of appropriating intolerably sovereign functions of the state in trying to represent the nation both externally (conflict over the Polish bishops' letter of reconciliation to the German bishops) and internally (conflict over the 1966 millennium celebrations). The Poles clearly decided the contest by attending the celebrations of the millennium of Polish Christianity rather than the competing celebrations of the millennium of Polish statehood.

THE PRINCIPLE OF CIVIL RESISTANCE

Having established at least its own right to defend both religious rights and the rights of the nation, the church slowly began to expand its protection into the areas of human rights, civil rights, and worker rights. Interestingly, at first those later rights were defended in connection with the rights of the nation, as if to imply that civil rights were derived from national rights or, at least, that the duty of the Polish church to protect human and civil rights was derived from its role as the nation's keeper. Progressively, however, the Polish church began to use a new language of universal rights, detached from any particular religious or national tradition. Moreover, the right and duty of the Polish church to defend those right would no longer be grounded on the national character of the Polish Catholic Church, but rather on the universal mission of the church of Christ.

The precipitating factor in steering the Polish church in the new direction was probably the "Polish December," which consolidated the typical pattern of food price increases, worker protests, and change in party leadership.[73] The episcopate's letter of December 29, 1970, addressed to "All compatriots of our common Motherland" already resembles the type of chartist manifesto that the church's public pronouncements would increasingly display from that point.

> The recent events have made it amply apparent that the nation's right to existence and independence must include: the right to freedom of conscience and freedom of religious life. . . , the right of our nation to free cultural activity. . . , the right to social justice. . . , the right to truth in social life, to truthful information and to freedom of expression. . . , the right to material conditions. . . , the right of citizens to be treated without abuse, unfair injury or persecution. Both the central authorities and the entire state administration, and especially those charged with the maintenance of order in society, are responsible for the assurance of these rights. All citizens of the state are to share in this responsibility.[74]

The church's clear call to civic responsibility materialized in 1976 in the widespread public reaction against the announced amendments to the constitution. Obviously, the authorities not only had failed to assume their responsibility in guaranteeing those rights, but actually they were planning to make their de facto violation into the law of the land. The church joined in the public reaction and protested against the attempt to link the entitlement of rights to the fulfillment of state obligations, against the attempt to limit constitutionally Polish sovereignty, and against the attempt to inscribe in the constitution the actual division between leaders and led.

This resistance against further state penetration marks the starting point of the movement for the self-defense and self-organization of society. These civic actions promoted first by intellectuals and protected and supported by the church would crystallize that same year in the foundation of the Workers Defense Committee (KOR) and would culminate in the emergence of Solidarity in its triple dimension as a national, democratic, and workers' movement.[75] The new dialogue between the church and the left, and the coming together of Catholic and secular intellectuals in KOR was to be of crucial significance for the emergence as well as for the character of Solidarity.[76]

The Normative Challenge to the Authoritarian
and Totalitarian Tendencies of the Modern State.

One could possibly view this new role of the Polish church in civil defense as a natural extension of its historical role of national defense. But it is important to stress that this extension implied a qualitative jump and was influenced by general developments in the Roman Catholic Church. Indeed, the moment one looks at the pastoral letters of the Polish episcopate from the early 1970s on and compares them with those of the Spanish or Brazilian episcopates it is striking how similar their language is.[77] Of course, the similarity in their language derives from the fact that all of them have the same common source, namely, recent papal encyclicals (*Mater et Magistra, Pacem in Terris, Populorum Progressio*) and the documents of the Second Vatican Council, particularly the Constitution of the Church in the World, *Gaudium et Spes*. It is undeniable that throughout the Catholic world, from the mid-1960s on, the church or at least some sectors of the church have been highly vocal in the defense of human, civil, and social rights against authoritarian states and economically oppressive regimes.[78]

In many Catholic countries, like Spain and Brazil, the new position entailed a radical change in church-state relations and/or in the class alliances of the church.[79] In the case of Poland the qualitative nature of the change has passed largely unnoticed since it appeared as a continuation of the established pattern of church-state conflict and church-nation alliance. The slogan was still the same ("Let Poland be Poland"), but the meaning of what Poland ought to be had changed.

In *The Church and the Left*, Michnik correctly argues that the pastoral letters of the Polish bishops and the pronouncements of the pope served to legitimate religiously the model of a modern, differentiated, pluralistic, and self-regulated society. He notes, of course, that this is also the model of society pursued by the secular left and seems to be struck by the fact that the church appears to have assumed the norms and values of modernity, of the Enlightenment, and of the French Revolution. One could add that ironically the church seems to have assumed those secular values precisely at a time when they are being abandoned for postmodern ones and the left appears to have lost its identity.

The tone of surprise in Michnik's analysis has to do with the fact that at least up to 1968, the Polish left and much of the rest of the world had regarded the Polish church as reactionary, ultraconservative, and antimodern. As in all caricatures, there was a kernel of truth behind the obvious distortion. In explaining the new dialogue between the church and the left, Michnik stresses in a characteristically self-critical fashion the process of rethinking on the part of the left, which has permitted the rediscovery of the Christian roots of modernity. Here Michnik is overtly generous with

the church, for he fails to stress the obvious fact that it has taken
the Catholic Church at least two centuries to accept the legitimacy
of modernity, or to uncover the Christian roots of many of the
modern developments it had persistendy opposed.[80] Had this been
the position of the church all along, the Enlightenment critique of
religion would have been superfluous. The process of rethinking
within the church, the *aggiornamento* that made this discovery
possible, was as drastic as the one undertaken by the Eastern
European left with respect to its Marxist creed.[81] But the reluctance
of the Catholic Church to acknowledge any fundamental change in
position and the fact that Cardinal Wyszyński remained at the helm
throughout this period have served to obscure the nature of these
changes. Undoubtedly, Michnik is correct in pointing out that even
a traditional Catholic Church has an anitotalitarian potential,
something that the "revisionists" failed to notice, at least until the
late 1960s. But a look at other Catholic churches in Eastern Europe
shows that only in Poland was this potential truly actualized.[82]

It is true that the impact of the Vatican *aggiornamento'* upon
Polish Catholicism was neither as sudden nor as radical as in Spain.
Partly this was the case because of the different nature of church-
state relations in both places and because of the embattled character
of Polish Catholicism. On the one hand, not being an established
state church, the Polish church had found it easier to unburden itself
earlier from much of the dead weight of the ancien regime. Thus,
change did not need to be as radical in Poland as in Spain. Ironically,
the Stalinist nationalization had helped to free the church from its
remaining historical ties with the conservative propertied classes.
On the other hand, being as embattled as ever, Polish Catholicism
could not afford too sudden a change and thus it maintained some
of the rigidity and conservatism that had served so well to preserve
the Polish cultural identity through the ordeal of the partitions.

But equally relevant was probably the fact that Polish Catholicism had already been undergoing its own internal process of
aggiornamento. Given the exceptional fusion of religious, class, and
national identities, modern Catholic social doctrines had found a
natural resonance in Poland.[83] For all his rigidity and conservatism,
Cardinal Wyszyński had been an outspoken defender of "social
Catholicism." Furthermore, sectors of the lay Catholic intelligentia,
organized in Catholic Clubs (KIKs) and around Catholic publications
such as *Tygodnik Powszechny, Znak,* and *Wiez,* had been receptive
to modern Catholic currents coming from abroad such as humanism
and personalism.[84] Perhaps one of the most important effects of the

Second Vatican Council was the support it gave to lay Catholic intellectuals in their traditional quest for autonomy from clerical control.

It was not by chance that Karol Wojtyła was elected pope by his peers.[85] He had a few important interventions during Vatican Council II (one of them in defense of the principle of religious freedom along with the American bishops). He was the main force behind the movement for postcouncil reform in Poland. He was probably the only bishop in the entire Catholic Church who personally undertook the task of explaining the meaning of all the council's documents to the faithful. Himself an intellectual, he found it easier than Cardinal Wyszyński to develop close ties with reform-minded Catholic intellectuals, particularly with the Znak group, who often internalized the council's message sooner and deeper than much of the Polish hierarchy. As cardinal of Cracow he had promoted the "Oasis" or "Light-Life movement," the first revivalist-evangelical movement within Polish Catholicism.[86] As pope he is the sign of the mutual influences and interdependencies between the universal church and Polish Catholicism.

At a certain level, the Catholic *aggiornamento* can be understood as a Catholic reformation, indeed as a process of Protestantification. It proclaims a soft version of the universal priesthood of all believers; it introduces a pronounced inner-worldly orientation; it emphasizes the sacrament of the word over sacramental ritual; it breaks with the scholastic metaphysical tradition and returns to the biblical origins with their historicist and eschatological spirit. But certain elements of traditional Catholicism are maintained, while other elements of Protestantism are not adopted. Catholicism finally recognizes the legitimacy of the modern age and accepts the autonomy of the secular spheres. But it does not view this autonomy as absolute. Particularly, it does not accept the claims of these spheres to have detached themselves completely from morality. Consequently, it does not accept the relegation of religion and morality to the private sphere, insisting on the links between private and public morality. It resists the radical individualization that accompanies privatization and stresses the collective and communal, that is, ecclesial character of the proclamation of faith and of religious practices, while simultaneously and paradoxically upholding also the absolute rights of the individual conscience. Thus, it affirms simultaneously dogma and freedom of conscience. It further maintains an organicist conception of society that demands that all its parts work toward the common good and be subordinated to higher moral principles. In this sense, it maintains the principle of communal ethical life.

Superficially this may appear like a reassertion of medieval Thomist organicism. The influence of Neo-Thomism on twentieth-century Catholic theology would seem to support such a view. But there is a fundamental break with Thomist organicism. The "common good" is no longer tied to a static ontological view of natural law, itself tied to a conception of a natural social order. The church's claims to be the depository of the common good is no longer tied to its expertise in a divinely prescribed natural law, but rather to its "expertise in humanity," a striking formulation that sometimes appears in pastoral letters. It is the transcendent, divinized humanity revealed in Jesus Christ that serves to ground the sacred dignity of the human person, as well as the absolute values of human life and freedom. The church escapes the nominalist critique of the traditional ontological conception of natural law by embracing the historicism implicit in the biblical message. With some lingering Neo-Thomist strains, this is the core of Karol Wojtyła's theology, equally visible in his prepapal writings as well as in his papal pronouncements. In addition, Wojtya has developed a personalist philosophical anthropology, informed by the work of Max Scheler, which is consistent with this theology but not derived from it. This permits him to maintain both the religious particularity and the anthropological universality of the Christian message.[87] Striking in his papal pronouncements, particularly in those dealing with issues of public morality, is the fact that they are not addressed to Christians as faithful members of the church, obliged to follow specific particular rules of the Catholic moral tradition. He addresses every individual qua member of humanity, challenging them to live up to universal human norms, which are derived from the universal human values of life and freedom. These absolute values serve to ground both the sacred dignity of the human person and the inalienable rights to human autonomy and self determination. The fact that the pope also ties these allegedly universal norms and values to a particular religious tradition is certainly bound to affect the reception of the universalistic claims by non-Christians. But at the same time, there where this particular religious tradition is still alive, it will probably serve to sanctify and legitimate modern norms and values as Christian ones.[88]

It is possible, of course, to see a continuity between the contemporary Catholic defense of human and civil rights against the modern authoritarian state and traditional Catholic critiques of tyranny and despotic rule. One can even view contemporary church-state conflicts as a continuation of the traditional Catholic struggle against the absolutist claims of the secular state. Against the arbitrary rule of the tyrant and against claims of raison d'état, the church has always argued that the legitimacy of the state ought to be subordinated to the common good. There is a fundamental difference, however, between the traditional opposition to immoral rule because it violates the natural social order, and opposition to modern authoritarian rule because it violates the dignity of the human person and the rights to freedom, autonomy, and self-determination. The first conception of the common good can serve to defend a traditional social order from radical social change. The second conception presents a prophetic challenge to the established authoritarian order and may serve to legitimate a modern civil society. Paradoxically, what Durkheim saw as old gods dying out are being revived today to legitimate what he anticipated would become "a new cult of man," the modern religion of humanity, "a religion in which man is at once the worshiper and the god."[89] In Poland, this new universal religion has come to reinforce an already powerful political tradition based on the defense of the traditional historical liberties of the Polish gentry and an equally powerful cultural tradition in which the martyrdom of St. Stanislaw reminds every Pole that there is a higher moral law and a higher principle of legitimation than raison d'état.

The Catholic Church and the Rise of Solidarity

Uniquely among Eastern European societies (Yugoslavia being a case apart), Poland was able to preserve two autonomous institutions that escaped the totalitarian tendency of the state: the Catholic Church and private agriculture. This was to be the most important heritage of the Polish October. Particularly, the church was to play a crucial role against state penetration in a dual sense. First, it served as a refuge against the complete Sovietization of Polish society by defending first its own institutional self-preservation as an autonomous church and then by extending its protection increasingly to other areas and sections of society: peasants and farmers, national culture and traditions, lay Catholic groups, students, workers, and intellectuals, human rights, and finally the right of society as a whole to self-organization. The second important function of the church was that of being, in Michnik's words, "the most perfect model of the coexistence of an independent social institution with state power."[90] Andrew Arato has argued rightly that Michnik's own program of democratization, spelled out in his 1976 essay "New Evolutionism," can be interpreted as the extension and generalization of the institutional model of church independence, aiming to include other groups and institutions in a dual system of autonomous societal pluralism and monolithic state power.[91]

There were other ways in which Polish Catholicism contributed to the emergence of Solidarity.[92] The striking image of the shipyard workers on their knees manifested the extent to which traditional popular Polish religiosity, with its typical undifferentiated fusion of sacred and profane time and space, has survived the thrusts of modern Polish history. Catholic intellectuals, associated with the Catholic Intellectual Clubs (KIKs), also played an important role first in the foundation of KOR and later as official and unofficial advisers to the movement. Finally there was the impact that the election and the visit of a Polish pope had on public opinion and on the Polish collective consciousness. A member of KOR recognized this influence when he said: "We would probably have had isolated strikes and maybe won some concessions from the government. But a Polish Pope united the Poles in a way I personally never imagined possible."[93]

If the role of Polish Catholicism in the emergence of Solidarity is both unquestionable and definitively positive, the role that the church and Polish Catholicism played thereafter in the martial law period, in the reemergence of Solidarity, and in the present ongoing process of democratization is much less clear and certainly more ambiguous.[94] The following concluding remarks only point to a few issues at the level of strategic institutional church influence, without entering into other levels of analysis such as normative-doctrinal issues or the role of increasingly diverse Catholic sectors of the Solidarity movement and of Polish society.

The almost natural ease with which the church, following the establishment of martial law, reverted to its traditional role of mediator between the communist state and Polish society should serve at least as a warning signal of the threat that the institutional power of the Polish church poses to a fully autonomous civil society. Since within the structure of Communist Poland the church tended to attain its greatest influence precisely at the point when both state and society needed the church's mediation, it was almost natural for the church to fall into "the mediation syndrome."[95]

Under martial law, the church intervened to protect society from state repression and to demand from the state the protection of individual human and civil rights, but it stopped short of demanding the institutionalization of full political rights. The state, in turn, needed the church's mediation in order to obtain from society at least passive compliance, so that the state of emergency could be "normalized." By working together with the state toward such a normalization, the church adopted a policy of political realism that basically implied the acceptance of the reality of the present as the point of departure for efforts to improve conditions in the future, while relegating Solidarity to the historical past.[96]

It is of course not easy to ascertain which kind of strategic considerations had a greater weight in the church's position, whether it was the consideration of institutional self-interest or rather the realistic accommodation to a lesser evil. Martial law may have been deplorable, so the official argument went, but it was necessary in order to save the Polish nation either from the threat of external aggression or from the danger of internal disintegration and civil war. Polish civil society had to be sacrificed for the sake of the Polish nation. There is no doubt that the patriotic appeal to save the Polish nation found a deep resonance in the collective conscience of the Polish church. However, it is equally evident that from the point of view of institutional self-interest, martial law was good for the church. Never had the churches in Poland, which normally are full, been so crowded as in the martial law period, for even "nonbelievers" attended mass as a symbolic act of political protest against the regime. At the same time, however, the constructive cooperation with the regime paid off. Never had it been so easy for the church to obtain the desired state permits to build new churches.

Thus, one may say that, while in the 1960s church and state had been consciously engaged in a battle over the mind of Polish society, now during the martial law period state and society were engaged in a battle over the mind of the church.[97] The Popieluszko "affair" may serve to illustrate the complex interrelations and the tug of war among the three.[98] Radical priests like Popieluszko, who had unambiguously sided with society against the state, were impeding the regime's project of "normalization." By recreating sacramentally, in the Durkheimian sense, the collective effervescence of the original experience of Solidarity, they were helping to maintain alive the movement as well as its norms and values.[99] Having failed in all its attempts to silence Popieluszko through personal threats, blackmail, and slander, the regime began to pressure the church hierarchy to restrain the radical priest, arguing that such an extremist political use of religion was impeding the normalization of state-society relations and endangering the gains already achieved in church-state relations. The church passed along the state's pressure, adding its own heavier hierarchical pressure by demanding institutional obedience over any other allegiance. Even after Popieluszko's murder by the secret police, the hierarchy went along at first with the game of normalization and tried to

arrange for a private family burial, seeking to avoid the kind of public
political manifestation of Solidarity into which the people converted
his funeral. It was the people, not the church hierarchy, which made
Popiełuszko into a Polish and Catholic martyr.[100]

Similarly, Solidarity was kept alive and reemerged politically
with the round-table talks in spite of the fact that the church, at least
the hierarchy, seemed to have accepted its relegation to the past.
Due to the extreme hierarchic centralization of the Polish church,
the kind of open internal conflicts, indeed the hegemonic struggles
among the various groups and tendencies within the episcopate,
which were so visible in Spain and in many other Catholic countries,
could neither develop fully nor manifest themselves publicly in
Poland. For the same reason, the character and personality of the
individual at the top of the hierarchy, the primate play an extraordinary role in setting the tone, as well as the direction of the
church's policies. It is pertinent to add, moreover, that in this respect
as in many others, the presence of a Polish pope in Rome compli-
cates reality as well as any simple analysis.

The electoral triumph of Solidarity and the collapse of the
communist state have opened up a completely new chapter both
in church-state and in church-society relations in Poland. There is
a whole series of new fundamental questions that will need to be
addressed and resolved constitutionally, institutionally, and
culturally.

If there emerges finally a legitimate democratic Polish state,
recognized by Polish society as its nation-state, will the church
relinquish willingly its historical role as the nation's keeper, or will
the church continue competing with the state over the symbolic
representation of the Polish nation?

Will the church accept fully the principle of separation of church
and state and will the church permit public issues to be resolved
through institutional democratic channels, such as free electoral
choice and open legislative and public debate, or will the church
try to impose the Catholic confession upon state and society, by
curtailing or bypassing those channels and by using its enormous
corporate power to restrict the electoral choices or to censor public
debates?

Which form of social integration or solidarity principle will the
church privilege, that of "civil society" or that of "nation"? Will the
church accept the principle of self-organization of an autonomous
civil society, based on the plurality and heterogeneity of norms,
values, interests, and forms of life, or will the church privilege the
principle of a homogeneous Polish Catholic national community?

It is, of course, still too early to tell, but recent interventions of the church in Polish politics have not been conducive to the establishment of an autonomous civil society within a free democratic state. The ministry of education, under obvious pressure from the church, introduced religious education back into the public schools. Such an administrative act was at least technically unconstitutional since de jure the old constitution is still in force. But, more important, it contradicted the spirit of the yet to be written democratic constitution, by removing administratively such a crucial issue from public debate.

The church's heavy pressure was equally evident in the recent passage by the Solidarity-controlled senate of a bill delegalizing, abortion. Again, most disturbing was the way in which the bill was passed, practically without debate—only one female senator dared to raise some questions and all the others virtually echoed the official Catholic position. One suspects that the fear of the electoral consequences of contradicting the church on this issue weighed heavily on the senatorial minds.

But the issue, and the questions it raises, have by no means been resolved. The often stated discrepancy between the evident strong hold that the church has over the public mind of the Poles on public collective issues and the much weaker hold it has over the conscience of individual believers on issues of private morality, clearly indicate that Polish Catholicism has served historically more as a public civil religion than as a private religion of individual salvation. The high rates of abortion in Catholic Poland indicate that, for all kinds of reasons, abortion has become a normal method of birth control. The state certainly promoted it, perhaps trying to embarrass the church by showing how weak an influence the church appeared to have over the private morality of the supposedly Catholic Poles. Given the insufficient availability of modern forms of contraception and their proscription by the church, the stage appears to be set for the emergence of conflict between church and civil society. Indeed it will be interesting to see how long long it takes for a Polish feminist movement to emerge.

If the interwar period of Polish history offers an indication of things to come, one may expect increasingly new forms of conflict between the church and the secular state as well as new forms of ideological and political polarization in Polish society along religious-secular lines. Ironically, anticlericalism may also emerge in Poland at a time when it has practically disappeared in most Catholic countries. The reemergence of the hydra of anti-Semitism and the repeated attacks on radical secular intellectuals indicate that there is still a danger that some form of Polish National Catholicism may develop that would serve as an obstacle to the institutionalization of an open pluralistic Polish civil society.

Conclusion

It may be inappropriate to attempt to draw precise generalizations about Catholicism from recent trends in Poland and Spain, two Catholic countries with such a diverse history of church-state-society relations. But looking at similar developments in many other Catholic countries from Brazil to the Philippines, one finds the Catholic Church from the early 1970s on disengaging itself from authoritarian regimes, openly confronting authoritarian states, promoting the reconstitution of civil societies, and participating actively in transitions to democracy. Such developments would seem to warrant some broad, tentative generalizations about global Catholic historical trends.

First, the Catholic Church has finally accepted the legitimacy of the modern age in the dual sense of accepting the differentiation of the secular spheres, particularly the principle of separation of church and state, as well as of upholding the modern principle of freedom of conscience and all the freedoms that derive from it.

Second, a church that accepts the dual clause of "no establishment" and "free exercise of religion" ceases for all practical purposes to be a "church" in the sense of being a territorially organized, obligatory, monopolistic community of faith; it becomes a voluntary religious association, even though in many countries most people may still be born, or rather baptized into it. As the recent papal encyclical on evangelization indicates, globally, Roman Catholicism still maintains its claim to be the One, Holy, Catholic, and Apostolic Church. But it no longer seeks to become an "established church" at the level of the nation-state. In this sense it has given up the model of "Christendom."

Third, the era of Catholic "reactive organicism," "Catholic Action," and "Christian Democracy" has come to an end. All of them were variants of a defensive reaction against what was perceived as a hostile, modern, secular environment, either within the state or within society. The church no longer seeks to reenter the state through the mobilization of the laity in order to regain control over society.

Fourth, assumedly, the Catholic Church not only will protect the right to the free exercise of religion, but most likely it will confront attempts by the modern state to abridge individual rights, human, civil, social, and political. While the church's position may not impede the recurrence of military dictatorships in Catholic countries, it will likely serve as a serious obstacle to the institutionalization of authoritarian regimes in such countries. Indeed, as Kolakowski has pointed out, "this kind of coalescence of Christianity, in its worldly aspects, with the human rights movement and democratic values has never before been achieved. It might herald dramatic changes throughout the entire Christian world."[101]

Finally, a church which no longer seeks a place or a function within the state will have to find its place within civil society. In principle, the Catholic Church faces three ideal-typical alternatives.

Privatized Catholicism is the model prescribed by theories of secularization that assume the differentiation of a privatized religious sphere.[102] The role of the church would be restricted to the salvation of individual souls and to the pastoral care of the Catholic religious community, either in a free, denominational, religious market or in a more closed, oligopolistic environment. Spain seems to have joined other Western European societies along this road. Catholic doctrine, Vatican policies, and lingering identifications of church and nation will resist this model, but well-established structural patterns and pressure from the secular state, from secular culture, and from the Catholic faithful, many of whom have internalized the model of a privatized religious sphere, will make the church's resistance largely ineffective.

The *Catholic Hegemony in Civil Society* model is particularly tempting in societies such as Poland, where a strong identification of church and nation still persists. It would mean the triumph of the principle of nation over that of civil society as a model of social integration. The identification of Catholic and national identities leads perforce to a more or less tolerant form of "national-Catholicism" that tends to exclude non-Catholic groups and elements of the national tradition as "the other" and, therefore, as "unnational." Formally, such a model of Catholic establishment in civil society could be compatible with a non-confessional state and with democratic majority rule, but it would tend to abridge the rights of secular and non-Catholic minorities and culturally it would tend to be monolithic and authoritarian. Even in Poland, however, where the hierarchic, centralized, and clericalist nature of the Catholic Church, along with traditional elements of Catholic culture, would seem to press in this direction, one also finds strong countervailing forces. Once the need for a unified societal resistance against the communist state has disappeared, Polish society has exhibited increasing pluralism of interests, norms and values, belying any notion of a homogeneous national community.[103] Any attempt to impose Catholic solutions to societal problems would open up deep religious-secular cleavages. Moreover, Polish Catholicism itself has become increasingly pluralistic internally to such an extent that the attempt to impose a Catholic solution to secular issues could lead to internal conflicts and divisions within the church.[104]

The *Catholic Pluralism in a Pluralist Civil Society* model, which recognizes the legitimacy of the modern age, presupposes that the church can no longer influence the secular spheres directly, that it can only do so indirectly through the normatively grounded conduct of the Catholic laity. But the church does not have the coercive means, nor can in principle impose its norms upon lay conduct, once it has recognized the modern principle of freedom of conscience. As in Spain, opinion surveys in Poland also indicate that large sectors of the population have internalized these principles.[105] The cleavages that became so noticeable in the 1990 electoral campaign to the presidency in Poland indicate that Polish civil society is indeed pluralistic and that the "us" versus "them" identification is no longer so easy to make. Moreover, it is equally obvious that the cleavages do not run along Catholic-secular lines, despite all the attempts to discredit the former prime minister, Mazowiezki, and other Catholic intellectuals as "crypto-Jews."

A superficial comparison of recent transitions to democracy in Catholic countries from Nicaragua to the Philippines, from Brazil to Poland shows that when the phase of consolidation begins and political society becomes institutionalized, the church has tended to withdraw from political society proper, leaving this realm to professional politicians. It shows, furthermore, that the church has avoided the attempt to either promote, sponsor, or support any "Catholic" or "Christian" party. In general, it has also avoided the partisan mobilization of the laity around Catholic issues. This partial withdrawal of the church from political society, however, does not mean that the church has accepted its relegation to a privatized religious sphere. The church has continued, and surely will continue, to speak up and take public stands on allegedly private moral issues (abortion, divorce, sexual conduct), on national issues (education, fair distribution of national resources, national economic development and government economic policies, social consequences of market allocation of resources, political corruption and lack of citizens' participation in political society), and on international issues (fair international division of labor and fair international division of power, war and peace, nuclear disarma-

ment, etc.). In this respect, the church is contributing to the constitution of a public sphere within civil society, separate and differentiated from the state and political society proper.[106] Once the
church enters this public sphere, however, while being buttressed
by whichever moral authority it sill possesses, the church's public
statements must perforce lose their hierarchic, authoritative character and be exposed to open, critical, public deliberation. The
church can still become "the voice of the voiceless," of those whose
views and interests do not find representation in political society.
But by accepting the rules of public discourse in a free, democratic
public sphere, the church also implicitly accepts the risk that its
voice will become just another cry in the cacophony of modern civil
society.

Notes

1. Brief but insightful histories of Spain are Jaime Vicens-Vives,
    Approaches to the History of Spain (Berkeley: University of California
    Press, 1970), and Pierre Vilar, *Spain, a Brief History* (Oxford: Pergamon
    Press, 1967). Standard histories of the period are J. H. Elliott, *Imperial
    Spain, 1469–1716* (New York: St. Martin's Press, 1964); Antonio
    Domínguez Ortiz, *El Antiguo Régimen: Los Reyes Católicos y los
    Austrias* (Madrid: Alianza, 1973). See also Stanley Payne, *Spanish
    Catholicism: An Historical Overview* (Madison: University of
    Wisconsin Press, 1984); Henry Kamen, *The Spanish Inquisition* (New
    York: New American Library, 1966); Américo Castro, *The Spaniards:
    An Introduction to Their History* (Princeton: Princeton University
    Press, 1971); Claudio Sánchez-Albornoz, *Spain: A Historical Enigma*
    (Madrid: Fundación Universitaria Española, 1975) : José Casanova,
    "The Spanish State and Its Relations with Society," *State, Culture,
    and Society* 1, no. 2 (1985) pp. 109–136; Fernando de los Ríos, *Religión
    y Estado en la España del Siglo XVI* (New York: Instituto de las
    Españas, 1927).
2. Fernand Braudel, *The Mediterranean and the Mediterranean World
    in the Age of Philip II*, 2 vols. (New York: Harper and Row, 1973); Perry
    Anderson, *Lineages of the Absolutist State* (London: New Left Books,
    1974); Immanuel Wallerstein, *The Modern World System* (New York:
    Academic Press, 1974); Charles Tilly, ed., *The Formation of National
    States in Western Europe* (Princeton: Princeton University Press,
    1975); Juan J. Linz, "Early State-Building and Late Peripheral
    Nationalisms Against the State," in S. N. Eisenstadt and S. Rokkan,
    eds., *Building States and Nations* (Beverly Hills: Sage, 1973).
3. C. R. Boxer, *The Church Militant and Iberian Expansion, 1440–1770*
    (Baltimore: Johns Hopkins University Press, 1978); Geoffrey Parker,

142 José Casanova

The Army of Flanders and the Spanish Road. 1567–1659 (Cambridge: Cambridge University Press, 1972); J. H. Elliott, The Revolt of the Catalans: A Study in the Decline of Spain (1598–1640) (Cambridge: Cambridge University Press, 1963); idem, "Self-Perception and Decline in Early Seventeenth-Century Spain," Past and Present 74 (1977) pp. 51–61; Vicente Palacio Atard, Derrota, Agotamiento, Decadencia en la España del Siglo XVII (Madrid: Rialp, 1949); José A. Maravall, Poder, Honor y Élites en el Siglo XVII (Madrid: Siglo XXI, 1980); H. R. Trevor-Roper, "The General Crisis of the Seventeenth Century," in Religion, the Reformation and Social Chance (London: Macmillan, 1967).

4. Luis Sánchez Agesta, España al Encuentro de Europa (Madrid: Biblioteca de Autores Cristianos, 1971); Pedro-Laín Entralgo, España como Problema (Madrid: Aguilar, 1957); Bernhardt Schmidt, El Problema Español de Quevedo a Manuel Azaña (Madrid: Edicusa, 1976); José Antonio Maravall, Antiguos y Modernos (Madrid: Sociedad de Estudios y Publicaciones, 1966); Ernesto y Enrique García Camarero, La Polémica de la Ciencia Española (Madrid: Alianza Editorial, 1970).

5. Richard Herr, The Eighteenth Century Revolution in Spain (Princeton: Princeton University Press, 1958); José A. Ferrer Benimeli, Masonería, Iglesia e Ilustración, 4 vols. (Madrid: Fundacion Universitaria Espanol 1975–1977); William J. Callahan, Church, Politics and Society in Spain, 1750–1874 (Cambridge: Harvard University Press, 1984).

6. Miguel Artola, Antiguo Régimen y Revolución Liberal (Barcelona: Ariel, 1978); José Fontana Lázaro, La Quiebra de la Monaraquía Absoluta (Barcelona: Ariel, 1971); Richard Herr, An Historical Essay on Modern Spain (Berkeley: University of California Press, 1970); Raymond Carr, Spain: 1808–1939 (Oxford: Oxford University Press, 1970); Ramón Menéndez-Pidal, The Spaniards in Their History (London: Hollis and Carter, 1950); Javier Herrero, Orígenes del Pensamiento Reaccionario Español (Madrid: Edicusa, 1973); José Manuel Cuenca, La Iglesia Española ante la Revolución Liberal (Madrid: Rialp, 1971); Emilio la Parra López, El Primer Liberalismo Español y la Iglesia: las Cortes de Cádiz (Alicante: Instituto de Estudios Juan Gil-Albert, 1985); José Pérez Vilarino, Inquisición y Constitución en España (Madrid: ZYX 1973).

7. Richard Herr, "Good, Evil and Spain's Rising Against Napoleon," in idem, ed., Ideas in History (Durham, N. C.: Duke University Press, 1965).

8. Stanley Payne, Politics and the Military in Modern Spain (Stanford: Stanford University Press, 1967); Antoni Jutglar, Ideologías y Clases en la España Contemporánea (Madrid: Edicusa, 1968).

9. Callahan, Church; Gerald Brenan, The Spanish Labyrinth (Cambridge: Cambridge University Press, 1943); Martin Blinkhorn, Carlism and Crisis in Spain. 1931–1939 (Cambridge: Cambridge University Press, 1975); José M. Sánchez, Reform and Reaction: The

Politico-Religious Background of the Spanish Civil War (Chapel Hill, N. C.: University of North Carolina Press, 1962); Joan C. Ullman, *La Semana Trágica: Estudios Sobre las Causas Socio-Económicas del Anticlericalismo en España* (Barcelona: Ariel, 1972); Julio Caro Baroja, *Introducción a una Historia Contemporánea del Anticlericalismo Español* (Madrid: Istmo, 1980).

10. Edward Malefakis, *Agrarian Reform and Peasant Revolution in Spain* (New Haven: Yale University Press, 1970); Pascual Carrión, *Los Latifundios en España* (Madrid: Gráficas Reunidas, 1932); Gabriel Jackson, "The Origins of Anarchism," *Southwestern Social Science Quarterly*, vol. 36, no. 2 (1955) pp. 135–147; Manuel Revuelta González, *La Exclaustración 1833–1840* (Madrid, 1976).

11. Antonio Ramos Oliveira, *Politics, Economics and Men of Modern Spain* (London: Victor Gollancz, 1946), p. 426; Jaime Vicens-Vives, *Historia de España y América* (Barcelona: Editorial Vicens Vives, 1961), 5: 140–141; Jutglar, *Ideologías* pp. 58, 103–104, 356, and passim; J. Sáez Marín, *Datos Sobre la Iglesia Española Contemporánea, 1768–1869* (Madrid, 1975); Payne, *Catholicism*, pp. 71–87.

12. Frances Lannon, *Privilege, Persecution, and Prophecy: The Catholic Church in Spain, 1875–1975* (Oxford: Clarendon Press, 1987); Payne, *Catholicism*; Manuel Tuñon de Lara, *La España del Siglo XIX*, 2 vols. (Barcelona: Laia, 1980); José L. López Aranguren, *Moral y Sociedad* (Madrid: Edicusa, 1974); Domingo Benavides Gómez, *El Fracaso Social del Catolicismo Español (Barcelona: Nova Terra , 1973); and idem, Democracia y Cristianismo en la España de la Restauración, 1875–1931* (Madrid: Ed. Nacional, 1978).

13. Yvonne Turin, *L'éducation et l'école en Espagne de 1874 à 1902* (Paris: Presses Univesitaires Françaises, 1959); Lannon, *Privilege*; Linz, "Early State-Building"; Ullman, *La Semana*; J. B. Trend, *The Origins of Modern Spain* (New York: Russel and Russel, 1965); Elena de la Souchere, *An Explanation of Spain* (New York: Random House, 1964); Brenan, *Spanish Labyrinth*; Herr, *Modern Spain*.

14. Sánchez, *Reform*; Payne, *Politics*; E. Allison Peers, *Spain, the Church and the Orders* (London: Eyre and Spottiswoode, 1939); Gabriel Jackson, *The Spanish Republic and the Civil War* (Princeton: Princeton University Press, 1965); Richard Gunther and Roger Blough, "Religious Conflict and Consensus in Spain: A Tale of Two Constitutions," *World Affairs* 143 (1981) pp. 366–412; Herbert R. Southworth, *El Mito de la Cruzada de Franco* (Paris: Ruedo Ibérico, 1963); A. Montero Moreno, *Historia de la Persecución Religiosa en España, 1936–1939* (Madrid: Biblioteca de Autores Cristianos, 1961); Burnett Bollotten, *The Spanish Revolution* (Chapel Hill, N. C.: University of North Carolina Press, 1979).

15. Guy Hermet, *Les Catholiques dans l'Espagne Franquiste*, 2 vols. (Paris: Presses de la Fondation Nationale de Sciences Politiques, 1980): Rafael Abella, *Por el Imperio Hacia Dios* (Barcelona: Planeta, 1978);

144   *José Casanova*

J. M. Laboa, *El Integrismo* (Madrid: Narcea, 1985); William Ebenstein, *Church and State in Franco Spain* (Princeton: Center for International Studies, 1960); Norman Cooper, *Catholicism and the Franco Regime* (Beverly Hills: Sage, 1975); Ramón Garriga, *El Cardenal Segura y el Nacional Catolicismo* (Barcelona: Planeta, 1977); Juan José Ruiz Rico, *El Papel Político de la Iglesia Católica en la España de Franco* (Madrid: Tecnos, 1977).

16. Juan J. Linz, "An Authoritarian Regime: The Case of Spain," in E. Allardt and Yrjo Littunen, eds., *Cleavages, Ideologies and Party Systems* (Helsinki: Academic Bookstore, 1964); Hermet, *Les Catholiques* vol. 1, *Les acteurs du jeu politique*; Rafael Gómez Pérez, *Política y Religión en el Régimen de Franco* (Barcelona: Dopesa, 1976); B. Oltra and A. de Miguel, "Bonapartismo catolicismo: Una hipótesis sobre los orígenes ideológicos del franquismo," *Revista de Sociología* 8 (1978): Jesús Ynfante, *La Prodigiosa Aventura del Opus Dei* (Paris: Ruedo Ibérico, 1970); A. Sáez Alba, *La Asociación Católica Nacional de Propagandistas* (Paris: Ruedo Ibérico, 1974): Daniel Artigues, *El Opus Dei en España* (Paris: Ruedo Ibérico, 1971).

17. Francisco Franco Bahamonde, *Palabras del Caudillo. 1937–1943* (Madrid: Editora Nacional, 1943); *Discursos y Mensajes del Jefe del Estado, 1955–1959* (Madrid: Editora Nacional, 1960); *Pensamiento Político de Franco* (Madrid: Ed. del Movimiento, 1975); Joachim Boor (Franco), *Masonería* (Madrid, 1952); Luis Carrero Blanco, *Discursos y Escritos, 1943–1973* (Madrid: Instituto de Estudios Públicas, 1974); Juan de la Cosa (Carrero Blanco), *Spain and the World* (Madrid: Publicaciones Españolas, 1954); *Las Modernas Torres de Babel* (Madrid: Ediciones Idea, 1956).

18. José Casanova, "Modernization and Democratization: Reflections on Spain's Transition to Democracy," *Social Research* 50, no. 4 (1983) pp. 924–973; Francisco Gil Delgado, *Conflicto Iglesia-Estado (1808–1975)* (Madrid: Sedmay, 1975).

19. On "the pattern of reactive organicism" and Spain, see David Martin, *A General Theory of Secularization* (New York: Harper and Row, 1978).

20. Aurelio Orensanz, *Religiosidad Popular Española (1940–1965)* (Madrid: Editora Nacional, 1974).

21. José L. L. Aranguren, *Catolicismo y Protestantismo como Formas de Existencia* (Madrid: Revista de Occidente, 1952); *Catolicismo Día Tras Día* (Barcelona: Noguer, 1955); *Contralectura del Catolicismo* (Barcelona: Planeta, 1978): Pedro Laín Entralgo, *El Cristiano en el Mundo* (Madrid: Propaganda Popular Católica, 1961); Federico Sopeña, *En Defensa de una Generación* (Madrid: Taurus, 1970).

22. P. Llabres i Martorell, "Cursets de Cristiandat: un moviment apostolic mallorqui pels quatre vents del mon," *Questions de Vida Cristiana* 75–76 (1975); José Casanova, "The First Secular Institute: The Opus Dei as a Religious Movement-Organization," *Annual Review of the Social Sciences of Religion* 6 (1982); idem, *The Opus Dei Ethic and the Modernization of Spain* (Ph.D. diss., New School for Social Research, (1982).

23. Hermet, *Les Catholiques.*

24. José Casanova, "The Opus Dei Ethic, the Technocrats and the Modernization of Spain," *Social Science Information* 22, no. 1 pp. 27–50 (1983).

25. Xavier Tusell, *La Oposición Democrática al Franquismo* (Barcelona: Planeta, 1977); Gonzalo Fernández de la Mora, *El Crepúsculo de las Ideologías*, 4th ed. (Buenos Aires: Ed. Andina, 1970); Laureano López Rodó, *Política y Desarrollo* (Madrid: Aguilar, 1970); "Prologo," to W. W. Rostow, *Política y Etapas de Crecimiento* (Barcelona: Dopesa, 1972).

26. J. Angulo Uribarri, *Documentos socio-políticos de obispos españoles (1968–1972)* (Madrid, 1972).

27. Alfonso C. Comín, *España, País de Misión?* (Barcelona: Salvaterra, 1966); Rogelio Duocastella et al., *Análisis Sociológico del Catolicismo Español* (Barcelona: Nova Terra, 1967); Hermet, *Les Catholiques*; Fundación Foessa, *Informe Sociológico Sobre la Situación Social de España* (Madrid: Euramérica, 1971).

28. Pierre Jobit, *L'Église d'Espagne a l'heure du concile* (Paris: Spes, 1965).

29. Javier Tusell, *Historia de la Democracia Cristiana en España*, 2 vols. (Madrid, Cuadernos para el Diálogo, 1974); Manuel Fernández Areal, *La Política Católica en España* (Barcelona: Dopesa, 1970); idem, *La Libertad de Prensa en España, 1938–1971* (Madrid: Edicusa, 1971); Rafael Gómez Pérez, *Conciencia Cristiana y Conflictos Políticos* (Barcelona: Dopesa, 1972).

30. *Ecclesia, Vida Nueva, Razón y Fe.*

31. Lannon, *Privilege*, pp. 89–115; Payne, *Catolicismo*, pp. 225–231. Víctor Pérez Díaz, *El Retorno de la Sociedad Civil* (Madrid: Instituto de Estudios Económicos, 1987), Chapter 15; Enrique Miret Magdalena, *Los Nuevos Católicos* (Barcelona, 1966); William Christian, Jr., *Person and God in a Spanish Village* (New York: Seminar Press, 1972); Joseph Aceves, *Social Change in a Spanish Village* (Cambridge, Mass.: Schenkman, 1971): Richard Barrett, *Benabarre, the Modernization of a Spanish Village* (New York: Holt, Rinehart and Winston, 1974); C. Lisón-Tolosana, *Belmonte de los Caballeros* (Oxford: Oxford University Press, 1966).

32. José M. Martín Patino, "La iglesia en la sociedad española," in Juan J. Linz, ed., *España: un presente para el futuro*, vol. 1, *La Sociedad* (Madrid: Instituto de Estudios Económicos, 1984); Ruiz Rico, *El Papel*, pp. 189, 213.

33. José L. Martín Descalzo, *Tarancón, el Cardenal del Cambio* (Barcelona: Planeta, 1982).

34. Ruiz Rico, *El Papel* p. 236.

35. Alfonso C. Comín, *Cristianos en el Partido, Comunistas en la Iglesia* (Barcelona, 1977).

36. José M. Maravall, *Dictatorship and Political Dissent: Workers and Students in Franco's Spain* (London: Tavistock, 1978).

37. Juan J. Linz, "Religion and Politics in Spain: From Conflict to Consensus above Cleavage," *Social Compass* 27, nos. 2–3 (1980): pp. 257–279; José Casanova, "Never Again! Authoritarian Regimes, Democratization and Collective Learning in Argentina and Spain" (unpublished manuscript); Rafael del Aguila y Ricardo Montero, *El Discurso Político de la Transición Española* (Madrid: Centro de Investigaciones Sociológicas, 1984).

38. Antonio Hernández Gil, *El cambio político español y la constitución* (Barcelona: Planeta, 1982); Emilio Attard, *La constitución por dentro* (Barcelona: Planeta, 1983): Joaquín Ruiz Giménez, "El papel del consenso en la constitutión del estado democrático *Sistema* 38–39 (1980) pp. 159–169.

39. Richard Gunther and Roger Blough, "Religious Conflict and Consensus in Spain: A Tale of Two Constitutions," *World Affairs* 143 (1981) pp. 366–412.

40. For a noteworthy attempt to rethink these issues theologically and systematically, see Olegario González de Cardenal, *España por Pensar: Ciudadanía Hispánica y Confesión Católica* (Salamanca: Ediciones Universidad de Salamanca, 1984).

41. Centro de Investigaciones Sociológicas (C.I.S.), "Iglesia, religión y política," *Revista Española de Investigaciones Sociologicas*, no. 27 (1984) pp. 295–328.

42. J. J. Toharia, *Los Jóvenes y la Religión* (Madrid: Fundación Santa María, 1985).

43. Martín Patino, *La iglesia*, pp. 202ff.

44. Pérez Díaz, *El Retorno*, p. 457.

45. Ibid., p. 459.

46. Ibid., p. 460.

47. Good historical surveys of Poland are Norman Davies, *God's Playground: History of Poland*, 2 vols. (New York: Columbia University Press, 1982); idem, *Heart of Europe: A Short History of Poland* (Oxford: Clarendon Press, 1984). On the church and Catholicism in Polish history, see Oscar Halecki, *Tysiaclecie Polski katolickiej* (London: Veritas, 1966); Bogdan Szajkowski, *Next to God . . . Poland* (New York: St. Martin's Press, 1983): Adam Piekarski, *The Church in Poland* (Warsaw: Interpress, 1978). On the fusion of Polish national and Catholic identities, see Konstantin Symmons-Symonolewicz, *National Consciousness in Poland* (Meadville, Pa.: Maplewood Press, 1983).

48. On religious pluralism, toleration, and conflict in early modern Poland, see Oscar Halecki, *From Florence to Brest* (Rome: Sacrum Poloniae Millennium, 1958); Ambroise Jobert, *De Luther à Mohila: La Pologne dans la crise de la chrétienté 1517–1648* (Paris: Institut d'Études Slaves, 1974); Stanislaw Kot, *Georges Niemirycz et la lutte contre l'intolérance au 17-e siécle* (The Hague: Mouton, 1960); Harry Dembkowski, *The Union of Lublin, Polish Federalism* (Boulder, Colo.: East European Monographs, 1982); Feliks Gross, "Tolerance and

Intolerance in Poland: The Two Political Traditions," *Polish Review* 20 (1975) pp. 65–69.

49. Martin, *Secularization*, p. 9.
50. Józef Majka, "The character of Polish Catholicism," *Social Compass* 15, nos. 3–4 (1968) pp. 185–208.
51. Andrzej Walicki, *Philosophy and Romantic Nationalism: The Case of Poland* (Oxford: Clarendon Press, 1982); J .L. Talmon, *Political Messianism: The Romantic Phase* (New York: Irvington, 1960); Czesław Strzeszewski et al., *Historia Katolicyzmu społecznego w Polsce 1832–1939* (Warsaw, 1981); Adam Bromke, *Poland's Politics: Idealism vs. Realism* (Cambridge: Harvard University Press, 1967); Piotr Wandycz, *The Land of Partitioned Poland: 1795–1918* (Seattle, Wash.: University of Washington Press, 1974).
52. Maciej Pomian-Srzednicki, *Religious Change in Contemporary Poland: Secularization and Politics* (London: Routledge and Kegan Paul, 1982); Georges Castellan, *Dieu garde la Pologne! Histoire du Catholicisme polonais 1795–1980* (Paris: Laffont, 1981); Olga Narkiewicz, *The Green Flag: Polish Populist Politics, 1867–1970* (London: Croom Helm, 1976).
53. While in 1931 only 65 percent of Poland's population was Catholic, by 1946 the number of Catholics had risen to 96.6 percent of the population.
54. Jan de Weydenthal, *The Communists of Poland* (Stanford, Calif., Hoover Institute, 1986); Teresa Torańska, *"Them": Stalin's Polish Puppets* (New York: Harper and Row, 1987).
55. Czesław Miłosz, *The Captive Mind* (New York: Random House, 1951).
56. Szajkowski, *Next to God*; Ronald Monticone, *The Catholic Church in Communist Poland, 1945–1985* (Boulder, Colo.; East European Monographs, 1986); Anna Kaminski, "The Polish Pope and the Polish Catholic Church," *Survey* (1979).
57. Bohdan Bociurkiw and John Strong, eds., *Religion and Atheism in the USSR and Eastern Europe* (London: Macmillan, 1975); Eric Weingartner, ed., *Church within Socialism: Church and State in East European Republics* (Rome: International Documentation and Communication Center, 1976); Jakov Jukic, "La religion et les sécularismes dans les sociétés socialistes," *Social Compass* 38, no. 1 (1981). pp. 5–24.
58. Lucjan Blit, *The Eastern Pretender* (London: Hutchinson, 1965); Andrzej Micewski, *Katolische Gruppierungen in Polen, Pax und Znak 1945–1976* (Munich: Kaiser, 1978); Dennis Dunn, *Detente and Papal-Communist Relations, 1962–1978* (Boulder, Colo.: Westview Press, 1979).
59. Andrzej Micewski, *Cardinal Wyszyński: A Biography* (New York: Harcourt: Harcourt-Brace, 1984).
60. Antoni Nowicki, *Wykłady o krytyce religii w Polsce* (Warsaw: Książka i Wiedza, 1965).

61. Karol Borowski, "Religion and Politics in Post-World War II Poland," in J. K. Hadden and A. Shupe, eds., *Prophetic Religions and Politics* (New York: Paragon House, 1986); idem, "Secular and Religious Education in Poland," *Journal of Religious Education* 70, no. 1, (1975); Ewa Morawska, "Civil Religion versus State Power in Poland," in Th. Robbins and R. Robertson. eds., *Church–State Relations* (New Brunswick, N.J.: Transaction Books, 1987); Wladyslaw Piwowarski, "Polish Catholicism as an Expression of National Identity," in L. S. Graham and M. K. Ciechocińska, *The Polish Dilemma* (Boulder, Colo.: Westview Press, 1987); Jozef Majka, "Historical and Cultural Conditions of Polish Catholicism," *The Christian in the World* 14 (1981).

62. Lucjan Blit, "The Insoluble Problem: Church and State in Poland," *Religion in Communist Lands* 1, no. 3 (1973) pp. 8–11; Wiesław Mysłek, "Państwo i Kościoł," *Nowe Drogi* 5 (1979); Zenon Rudny, "Cesarzowi-co Cesarskie, Bogu-co Boskie," *Polityka*, Oct. 24, 1983.

63. Pomian, *Religious Change*; Vincent Chrypinski, "Political Changes under Gierek," *Canadian Slavonic Papers* 15, (1973) pp. 36–51.

64. T. M. Jaroszewski, *Laicyzacja* (Warsaw: Książka i Wiedza, 1966); idem, "Practiques et conceptions religieuses en Pologne," *Recherches Internationales a la Lumière du Marxisme*, (Paris: Editions de la nouvelle critique, 1965); Edward Ciupak, *Katolicyzm ludowy w Polsce* (Warsaw: Wiedza Powszechna, 1973); Jan Jerschina, *Młodzież i procesy laicyzacji świadomości społecznej* (Warsaw, 1978); Hieronim Kubiak, *Religijność a srodowisko społeczne* (Cracow: Ossolineum, 1972).

65. Pomian, *Religious Change*; Michael D. Kennedy and Maurice D. Simon, "Church and Nation in Socialist Poland," in Peter Merkl and Ninian Smart, eds., *Religion and Politics in the Modern World* (New York: New York University Press, 1983); Wladyslaw Piwowarski, *Religijność Wiejska w Warunkach Urbanizacji* (Warsaw: Więź, 1976); Witold Zdaniewicz, *Kosciol Katolicki w Polsce* (Poznan-Warsaw: Pallotinum, 1979).

66. Micewski, *Wyszyński*, pp. 342–343. See also Stefan Wyszynski, *A Freedom Within: The Prison Notes* (New York: Harcourt-Brace, 1983); and *Kościoł w służbie Narodu* (Rome, 1981).

67. Karol Górski, "L'histoire de la spiritualité polonaise," in *Poland's Millennium of Catholicism* (Lublin: Scientific Society of the Catholic University of Lublin, 1969); Jerzy Braun, "A Thousand Years of Christianity in Poland," in *Poland in Christian Civilization* (London: Veritas, 1983); Stefan Czarnowski, "Kultura religijna wiejskiego ludu polskiego," *Dziela* (Warsaw, 1956), 1: 88–107; W. I. Thomas and F. Znaniecki, *The Polish Peasant in Europe and America* (New York: Dover, 1958); *Social Compass* 15, nos. 3–4, (1968) (special issue on Poland with essays by J. Majka, W. Zdaniewicz, and W. Piwowarski et al.).

68. Ruben Cesar Fernandez, "Images de la passion. L'Eglise Catholique au Brésil et en Pologne," *Esprit* no. 133 (1987) pp. 11–22.

69. Wladyslaw Piwowarski, "The Image of the Priest in the Eyes of Parishioners in Three Rural Parishes," *Social Compass* 15, nos. 3–4, (1968) pp. 235–249; Bogdan Cywinski, "Mysli o polskim duszpasterstwie," *Znak* 23, no. 204 (1971).

70. Micewski, *Wyszyński*.

71. Monticone, *Catholic*; Szajkowski, *Next to God*; Lawrence Biondi, *Poland's Church-State Relations* (Chicago: Loyola University Press, 1981).

72. S. Malkowski, "Kosciol a totalitaryzm," *Spotkania* 3 (1978).

73. Jakub Karpinski, *Countdown. The Polish Upheavals of 1956, 1968, 1970, 1976, 1980* (New York: Karz-Cohl, 1982); Peter Raina, *Political Opposition in Poland, 1954–1977* (London: Poet's and Painters' Press, 1978).

74. Szajkowsky, *Next to God*, p. 32.

75. Jan Lipski, *KOR* (Berkeley: University of California Press, 1985); Alain Touraine et al., *Solidarity: Poland 1980–1981* (Cambridge: Cambridge University Press, 1983); Neal Ascherson, *The Polish August* (New York: Viking Press, 1982); Timothy G. Ash, *The Polish Revolution* (New York: Scribners, 1983); Abraham Brumberg, ed., *Poland: Genesis of a Revolution* (New York: Random House, 1983); Jadwiga Staniszkis, *Poland's Self-Limiting Revolution* (Princeton: Princeton University Press, 1984); Andrew Arato, "Civil Society Against the State: Poland 1980–1981," *Telos* 47 (1981) pp. 23–47.

76. Adam Michnik, *The Church, the Left: A Dialogue* (Chicago: University of Chicago Press, 1992); Leszek Kolakowski and Jan Gross, "Church and Democracy in Poland: Two Views," *Dissent* (1980) pp. 316–322; Józef Tischner, *The Spirit of Solidarity* (New York: Harper and Row, 1984); Andrew Arato, "The Theory of the Polish Democratic Opposition: Normative Assumptions and Strategic Ambiguities," *Working Papers of the Kellogg Institute* (University of Notre Dame, 1984).

77. *Listy Pasterskie Episkopatu Polski, 1945–1974* (Paris: Editions du Dialogue, 1975); J. Iribarren, *Documentos Colectivos del Episcopado Español, 1870–1974* (Madrid, 1974); *Estudos da CNBB and Documentos da CNBB*, both series published periodically by Ediçoes Paulinas of Sao Paulo.

78. Brian Smith, "Churches and Human Rights in Latin America," *Journal of Interamerican Studies and World Affairs* 21, pp. 89–127 (1979) pp. 89–127; David Hollenbach, *Claims in Conflict: Retrieving and Renewing the Catholic Human Rights Tradition* (New York: Paulist Press, 1979).

79. On Brazil, see Scott Mainwaring, *The Catholic Church and Politics in Brazil, 1916–1985* (Stanford: Stanford University Press, 1986); Thomas C. Bruneau, *The Political Transformation of the Brazilian Catholic Church* (Cambridge: Cambridge University Press, 1974),

idem, *The Church in Brazil* (Austin: University of Texas Press, 1982); Ralph Della Cava, "The 'People's Church,' the Vatican and *Abertura*," in Alfred Stepan, ed., *Democratizing Brazil* (New York: Oxford University Press, 1989): Marcio Moreira Alves, *A Igreja e a Politica no Brasil* (Sao Paulo: Editora Brasiliense, 1979).

80. On the concept of legitimacy of secular modernity, see Hans Blumenberg, *The Legitimacy of the Modern Age* (Cambridge: MIT Press, 1983). On the church's resistance, see Owen Chadwick, *The Pope and European Revolution* (Oxford: Clarendon Press, 1981); E. E. Y. Hales, *Revolution and Papacy, 1769–1846* (London: Eyre and Spottiswoode, 1960); William McSweeney, *Roman Catholicism: The Search for Relevance* (New York: St. Martin's Press, 1980).

81. Ferenc Feher and Agnes Heller, *Eastern Left, Western Left* (Cambridge: Polity Press, 1987) : Adam Podgórecki, *The Polish Burial of Marxist Ideology* (London: Poets' and Painters' Press, 1981); Jeffrey C. Goldfarb, *Beyond Glasnost: The Post-Totalitarian Mind* (Chicago: University of Chicago Press, 1989); Andrew Arato, "Social Theory, Civil Society, and the Transformation of Authoritarian Socialism," in Ferenc Feher and Andrew Arato, eds., *Crisis and Reform in Eastern Europe* (New Brunswick, N.J.: Transaction Books, 1991).

82. Pedro Ramet, ed., *Religion and Nationalism in Soviet and East European Politics* (Durham, N.C.: Duke University Press, 1989).

83. Indeed, the three historical traditions of Catholic, nationalist, and working-class solidarity, which in most countries have remained separate, often in an antagonistic relationship, came together to constitute the uniqueness of Solidarity as a movement. This unique historical configuration offers a better explanation for the persistently egalitarian character of the values and attitudes of the Polish people than the ideological success of a socialist regime, which in every other respect was so unsuccessful ideologically. For the latter view, see Stefan Nowak, "Values and Attitudes of the Polish People," *Scientific American* 245, no. 1 (1981) pp. 45–53.

84. Micewski, *Pax und Znak*; Anton Pospieszalski, "Lay Catholic Organizations in Poland," *Survey* 24, no. 4 (1979) pp. 237–245; P. Jegliński and A. Tomsky, " 'Spotkania'—Journal of the Catholic Opposition in Poland," *Religion in Communist Lands* 7, no. 1, (1979) pp. 23–28; Andrzej Swięcicki, *Les origines institutionelles de mouvement "Znak,"* Actes de la 12ieme congress de la sociologie religieuse (CSIR) (Lille: CSIR, 1973); Bogdan Cywinski, *Doswiadczenie Polskie* (Paris: Spotkania, 1984) and *Rodowody Niepokornych* (Warsaw: Więź, 1971).

85. Mieczysław Maliński, *Pope John Paul II: The Life of Karol Wojtyła* (New York: Seabury, 1979); George Williams, *The Mind of John Paul II: Origins of His Thought and Action* (New York: Seabury Press, 1981); George Blazynski, *Pope John Paul II* (London: Weidenfeld-Nicholson, 1979).

86. Grażyna Sikorska, "The Light-Life Movement in Poland," *Religion in Communist Lands* 11 no. 1 (1983) pp. 55–66. Cardinal Wojtyła also became an early sponsor and protector of the Opus Dei within the Roman Catholic Church.

87. John Paul II, *The Acting Person* (Boston: Reidel, 1979); idem, *Toward a Philosophy of Praxis* (New York: Crossroad, 1981); *Return to Poland: The Collected Speehes of John Paul II* (London: Collins, 1979); Pope John Paul II, *Brazil: Journey in the Light of the Eucharist* (Boston: Daughters of St. Paul, 1980).

89. Michnik has captured well the tension between the particularistic and universalistic aspects of the pope's Christian message. He concludes his commentary on the Pope's 1979 visit to Poland with the words, "Let me just say that when I listened to John Paul II's homily in Cracow, I had a strange feeling. When the pope asked the faithful Catholics 'never to forsake Him,' he was also addressing me: a pagan" (Adam Michnik, *Letters from Prison and Other Essays* [Berkeley: University of California Press, 1985], p. 168).

89. Emile Durkheim, "Individualism and the Intellectuals," in Robert N. Bellah, ed., *Emile Durkheim: On Morality and Society* (Chicago, University of Chicago Press, 1973), pp. 43–57.

90. Adam Michnik, "What We Want to Do and What We Can Do," *Telos* 47 (1981): 72.

91. Andrew Arato, "Civil Society vs. the State"; Adam Michnik, "A New Evolutionism," in *Letters from Prison*.

92. Alexander Tomsky, "Poland's Church on the Road to Gdansk," *Religion in Communist Lands* vol. 9, no. 1–2 (1981) pp. 28–39.

93. Steven Stewart, *The Poles* (New York: Macmillan, 1982), p. 155; Radio Free Europe Research, "The Pope in Poland," *Spectator*, June 9 and 16, 1979; Alexander Tomsky, "John Paul II in Poland," *Religion in Communist Lands* 7, no. 3, (1979) pp. 160–165; Jerzy Turowicz, "Pięć Lat Pontyfikatu," *Tygodnik Powszechny*, Oct. 16, 1983.

94. Thomas Bird and Mieczyslaw Maneli, "The New Turn in Church-State Relations in Poland," *Journal of Church and State* 24 (1982) pp. 29–51; Vincent Chrypinsky, "Church and State in Poland after Solidarity," in, J. L. Black and J. W. Strong, eds., *Sisyphus and Poland: Reflections on Martial Law* (Winnipeg: Ronald P. Frye, 1986); Hannah Diskin, "The Pope's Pilgrimage to Jaruzelski's Poland," in Black and Strong, eds., *Sisyphus and Poland*; J. B. de Weydenthal, "The Church and the State of Emergency," *Radio Free Europe: Research* 49 (1982); Peter Raina, *Kościoł w Polsce, 1981–1984* (London: Veritas, 1985).

95. For a critical analysis of the same mediation syndrome in Pinochet's Chile, see Hugo Villela, "The Church and the Process of Democratization in Latin America," *Social Compass* 26, nos. 2–3, (1979) pp. 261–283.

96. For a critical but balanced analysis of the church's role through the 1980s, see Aleksander Smolar, "The Polish Opposition," in Ferenc

Feher and Andrew Arato, eds., *Crisis and Reform in Eastern Europe* (New Brunswick, N.J.: Transaction Books, 1991); David Ost, *Solidarity and the Politics of Anti-Politics* (Philadelphia: Temple University Press, 1990), idem, "Poland Revisited: Normalization and Opposition," *Poland Watch* 7, (1985) pp. 75–96. On the ongoing debate between "realism" and "idealism" in Polish politics, see Adam Bromke, *The Meaning and Uses of Polish History*, (Boulder, Colo., East European Monographs, 1987), *Poland's Politics: Idealism vs. Realism* (Cambridge: Harvard University Press, 1967); idem, "Poland's Idealism and Realism in Retrospect," *Canadian Slavonic Papers* 31 (1979) pp. 76–91; Michnik, *Letters from Prison.*

97. Andrzej Micewski, "Kościoł ostrzegał 'Solidarność'," *Polityka*, Nov. 14, 1987; Daniel Passent, "Miedzy Kościołem a Solidarnośćia," *Polityka*, Mar. 19, 1988; Zenon Rudny, "Cesarzowi-co Cesarskie, Bogu-co Boskie," *Polityka*, Oct. 24, 1983.

98. Patrick Michel and G. Mink, *Mort d'un frere: L'affaire Popiełuzsko* (Paris: Fayard, 1985); Grazyna Sikorska, *Jerzy Popiełuszko, A Martyr for the Truth* (Grand Rapids, Mich.: Eerdmans, 1985); John Moody, *The Priest and the Policeman* (New York: Summit Books, 1987); Paul Lewis, "Turbulent Priest: Popiełuzsko Affair," *Politics* 5, no. 2, (1985) pp. 33–39.

99. Jerzy Popiełuszko, *Kazania patriotyczne* (Paris: Libella, 1984), and *The Price of Love: The Sermons of Fr. Jerzy Popiełuszko* (London, 1985).

100. In an interview with *Famiglia Cristiana* (Nov. 27, 1985), Cardinal Glemp said: "Those who manipulated Father Popiełuszko were not the Church's people. They made him the chaplain of the opposition groups to which he felt very attached. He was definitely a victim." Quoted in Smolar, *Polish Opposition*, p. 242.

101. Kolakowski, *Church and Democracy*, p. 320.

102. For a cogent reformulation of the theory of secularization against growing criticism of the classical paradigm, see Karel Dobbelaere, *Secularization: A Multi-Dimensional Concept* (Beverly Hills: Sage, 1981); "The Secularization of Society? Some Methodological Suggestions," in Jeffrey Hadden and Anson Shupe, eds., *Secularization and Fundamentalism Reconsidered* (New York: Paragon House, 1989).

103. Smolar, "Polish Opposition."

104. This was the lesson of the Chilean experience, which forced the church to rethink its political strategy everywhere. See Brian H. Smith, *The Church and Politics in Chile* (Princeton: Princeton University Press, 1982).

105. A 1977 survey of graduating secondary students pointed out that when asked to evaluate the view that "only a Catholic can be a good Pole", 31.5 percent were very negative, 31.4 percent rather negative, 18.3 percent rather positive, and 8.7 percent very positive. Similarly, when asked whether "the church should decide what is moral and

immoral in society," 15.5 percent were very negative, 26.3 percent rather negative, 30.1 percent rather positive, and 15.9 percent very positive (in Kennedy and Simon, "Church and Nation," pp. 128–129).

106. Here I follow Alfred Stepan's conceptual differentiation of the three polity arenas: "civil society," "political society," and "state". See his *Rethinking Military Politics: Brazil and the Southern Cone* (Princeton: Princeton University Press, 1988).

Part II

Utopian Religious Beliefs and Political Action

5

Lost Primeval Bliss as Re-volutionary Expectation: Millennialism of Crisis in Peru and the Philippines

Manuel Sarkisyanz

Rußland und der Messianismus des Orients, published in 1955, maintained that in agricultural Asian societies, revolutions were seen by the peasant masses as thoroughly "conservative"; "restorative" would have been a better term. This point was little understood by conventional political science at the time, even though the etymology of the word *revolution* connotes a revolving back. The notion of revolving back to an archetypical past in fulfillment of the future parallels the existential experience in the life cycle of agriculture. Mythically, the world and society are felt to be thrown into chaos when the "natural," that is, archetypical, order is dissolving or being turned "upside down." The archetypes of agrarian societies are statically conceived, and considered subject to periodic re-volutionary renovation. The timelessness of the eternal return of the world order, with its periodic renovations through re-volutions, thus makes millenarian expectations part of the traditions of agrarian societies.[1]

Something like a reflection of the archetypical city of archaic cultures has been seen in the images of perfect societies that have been conceived at the beginnings of social thought. The archetypical City (or Realm) of the Sun does not need to confront the temporal

157

problems of historical time. Like an enchanted island, it lies miraculously hidden in the remote ocean, the materialization of a deep longing. It was in the course of secularization that the Islands of the Blessed, originally eschatological spheres in the beyond, became blessed islands—or continents—in this world. The search after such "earthly paradises" stimulated not a few geographical discoveries during the Renaissance. What was sought beyond the ocean of the fiftheenth century was—besides a "New World"—the oldest of the worlds, the Garden of Eden, the fountain of human origins in paradise, the land without original sin. Even Columbus hoped to find paradise beyond the seas. Indeed, when confronted by the new western hemisphere during his third voyage, he felt certain that earthly paradise was precisely there. Some Franciscans were enthusiastic about the natives of America, in whom they saw no greed but potential for the pristine evangelic Christianity of poverty. Geronimo de Mendieta (1525–1604) saw in Indian America the very elements of an earthly paradise, of a celestial city on earth with virtues proper to those who are to inherit the heavenly kingdom. He ascribed to a part of the Indians such purity of the soul that they would not know what it means to sin and could reach the angelic state of sinlessness. Yet, already then, visions of paradise-like existence amidst such remains of the Golden Age proved no obstacle for more sturdy material pursuits, such as extorting the maximum of gold from heavenly El Dorado. Thus Europe's attitude toward the Indoamerican New World contained from the beginning archetypical longings after man's heavenly origins—a nostalgia for a "Testament of Abel" besides the more effective ambitions of Cain to accumulate the maximum of gold. It is no accident that a tragedy of the Enlightenment period (Lefevre's *Zuma* [1776]) located the biblical murder of Abel in Peru—with a son of the Spanish conqueror Pizarro as Cain.[2] Pizarro forced Atahualpa, the last Inca ruling Peru, to redeem himself by masses of gold and then, in 1533, had him killed.

Such events meant in Incaic cosmogony the end of a world age, a periodic cataclysm, a chaos like the one that had to give place to powers of order when the Incaic Empire had been established. The opposite was the effect of these events on Renaissance Europe: Being the only still flourishing archaic universalist empire of the past encountered by early modern Europe,[3] the Incaic Empire came to contribute to the Utopian tradition of the Renaissance something of the archetypes of the streamlined order of older Bronze Age "hydraulic despotisms."

Both to the Incaic America and to the Spanish Renaissance belonged Garcilaso de la Vega, whose *Royal Commentaries* (published in 1609) became in Europe a model of social utopias and in Andean America the intellectual authority for the image of the Incaic period as the lost Golden Age, an ideological source of revolutionary visions inspired by the lost past. Garcilaso's work came to transmit an intellectual myth, creating and recreating new utopias again and again.[4] Of all the myths that are politically virulent in today's world, the both conservative and revolutionary ideological myth of the Tahuantinsuyo Empire has the greatest longevity.[5] It received additional strength from Andean cosmogony of Eternal Return combined with Christian apocalyptic expectations.

Millennial aspirations to restore Andean pre-European social relationships partly survived in oral folklore up to this point as prophecies about the restoration of a social order serving Andean Indian values, revival of the Incaic Age as the archetypical time of "Tahuantinsuyo," the realm of the four cardinal directions, and the return of the Inca[6] as archetype of the creative and ordering cosmic power. His head is believed to remain alive. While separated from the body, it is powerless and the Indians remain subjugated. When the fragments of the Inca's body rejoin each other under the earth, the earth trembles. And when his body is fully reintegrated, the Inca will return. The world is then to be reinverted. The natural order that has been upturned by the Spanish conquest is then to be restored, with the above rising again Above and the Below falling again below, with the Inca bringing about the last judgment. He is then to confront, from below the earth, the Catholic God who since the *conquista* is reigning from celestial heights. Should the Inca again succumb (and not regain the heights), then perhaps all Indians will perish.

These notions were discovered after 1955 separately in many areas of Peru. Apparently they took shape before the eighteenth century. The world is thought to have fallen into chaos ever since the natural order, with the Inca as archetype of natural humankind, was overthrown. The Andean social and cosmic order does not function until the Inca's body is recomposed. Until then the world is upside down, with the highest thrown into the lowest and the lowest raised to the highest. As cosmic summit, the head of the Inca is under the chthonic sphere, in a subterranean location. The timelessness of the eternal return with periodic renovations through the archetypical Inca (the Pachakuti) puts such folk expectations into the old "re-volutionary" tradition of agrarian societies, whose statically conceived archetypes are thought ultimately to be renewable through the course of re-volution. Thus the subjugated Indians' vision of the past is at the same time a vision of the future. The Catholic conquest is understood to have manifested the end of an age of the world that had run its course and at the same time as a symptom of the beginning of a new world period. It is seen as both a precosmogonic chaos and a prelude to a restoration of the cosmic and social order, harmoniously reintegrating the above cosmogony with Catholic eschatology. The latter came hardly without Franciscan influences of the thirteeth-century teachings of Joachim of Fiore about the three ages, that of the Father, of the Son, and of the Holy Ghost—the latter with a spiritualized humanity freed of infernal torments.[7]

Something of these folk myths had already in the 1920s been absorbed into the ideology of the intelligentsia in highland Peru, long before anthropologists recorded the "subterranean Inca Rey" beliefs: In 1927, "Storm in the Andes," the very influential essay of Luis Valcarcel (father of modern Peruvian indigenism and Peru's minister of instruction from 1945 to 1948) already gave expression to the vision of a chthonic cataclysm breaking out from the Andes, a cataclysm of apocalyptic dimension, from which a New World was to arise in the Andes, with the Andean earth renovated, with its Andean man as a new Lazarus, under a renewed harmony between man and man, between man and nature:[8]

> The Andinist doctrine is an attempt to formulate Amerindian ideology. . . .The crucified race transfigures itself. Whenever was resurrection not preceded by martyrdom and death?. . .The messengers of the happy tidings go, as the disciples of Christ, through the trials of pain. Crowded are the jails by those whom Roman justice classified as delinquents because they did not conform to society and its regulations. And in the Valley of Death there shine the limbs of the countless victims. . . .Wiracocha, god of the mountain heights and of the waters, descends again from the summit of the Andean Olymp. And along his steps men break the stones of their millennial serfdom, rising as did the biblical Lazarus. Like thunder their voice resounds in the granatic cavities. And the Earth trembles. O men of stone of our times, let us awake! There is no consciousness that is not moved by bliss and awe while a new world is being born behind the Mountains.[9]

To restore the Incaic Empire 2,000 Indians from highland Peru and Bolivia rallied in 1915 around "Rumi Maqui," the "commander of the restored Incaic Tahuantinsuyo" (probably the Peruvian army major Teodomiro Gutierrez Cuevas) on Lake Titicaca. And into the Andes vanished Rumi Maqui from which he had come. "The transformation of the major into the legendary Rumi Maqui, whether a fact or not, has been believed in the whole country: Rumi Maqui became a symbol for the restoration of Tahuantinsuyo as the Amerindian Empire of the Four Cardinal Directions, a symbol for returning the lands to the Indians."[10]

As almost all Andean Indian agrarian uprisings, it had among its driving forces messianic expectations of a Pachakuti, a turning point in the sequence of world ages that would restore the ideal archetypical society. The restoration of this Tahuantinsuyo was the intitial goal of the resistance against the loss of Indian land to the Lauramarca estate as recently as 1922, with millennial features of a restoration of the solar cults and the abjuring of Catholicism. This also applies to the highland Peruvian Indian movements of 1923 in the La Mar area with their millennialist ideology and their proclamation of an "Incaic Republic."[11]

"Operation Inca" was the code name of Peru's military revolution of 1968. The agrarian transformation of Peru under Velasco Alvarado in 1969, the most far-reching since the separation from Spain, was called a turning point in the social and psychological sphere, in which things "changed . . . without stopping to persist, a catastrophy and at the same time a renovation," a turning and termination of the cycle of time: "The agrarian reform of 1969 was for southern highland Peru . . . a genuine Pachakuti," wrote Tamayo Herrera: Pachakuti is as much "mutation of the earth as cosmic transformation of the world back to its archetype."[12]

Natural harmony, whose cosmical center is mythically conceived as the Lake Titicaca, is to be only temporarily disturbed by human intervention: On the Titicaca the long draughts are supposed to have ended under President Velasco Alvarado.[13] He received legitimation through welfare models of the Incas, "who distributed land as Christ distributed bread." A commentator named "Inti Illapa" (meaning in Quechua "Solar Angel") wrote that the revolution of 1968 effaced the torments of the last Inca so that the land regained its natural taste of milk and honey, undoing the centuries of post-Incan servitude. The Incaic Tahuantinsuyo of the past becomes indentified with the kingdom of God at the end of times. The "last Inca," Tupac Amaru (who rebelled against the colonial order in 1781), is said by Inti Illapa to have been crucified so that one day the armies of the world would end the wars among nations—amidst a humanity united in brotherhood. Past Inca rule is idealized as a government over men becoming brothers through love. The sufferings of the

people since 1532 would generate a new, an immortal Tahuantinsuyo, on a New Earth, the Indians becoming the masters of this
earth. Indian America would become the Promised Land, without
hunger, without masters and serfs.

Still in 1981–1982, a professor of economy at Lima's San Marcos
University, Virgilio Roel Pineda, is said to have demanded that Peru
be returned to the Indians. He writes:

> Cycles of darkness are followed by cycles of light. . . .With the
> foreign conquest came the age of darkness. . . .of oppression,
> though every Andean Indian village preserved the expectation
> of returning light. . . .Degeneration and crisis have hit the
> Occident itself. . . .Thus we face a new Pachakuti, a turning of
> times, a liberating Re-volution [in the sense of revolving back]
> which is to usher in the new great Age of Light. . . .The new
> bright age will bring a re-turn to Tahuantinsuyo, which, em-
> bracing mankind shall lead it to the glory of reunification with
> Mother Earth: All who are Indians are to regain communion with
> plants and waters, with deserts and mountains, with the moon
> and the butterflies. Communion with nature and the environ-
> ment makes possible spiritual purification and goodness. All in
> nature contains a spirituality which has to be discovered to lead
> to Fraternity and Peace. Ethics cannot refer to society alone but
> also to relationship with nature. To feel superior to non-human
> beings has no justification. For those who have departed from
> the primeval existential sources of their being the return to these
> leads through experiencing Indianity. For the Indians Indianity
> means self-identification. And all men, absolutely all, can become
> Indians if they follow the path to humanity's primeval sources.[14]

Less pantheistic and more Catholic is the archetype of lost
primeval bliss on the other side of the Pacific, in the Philippines.
There the pre-Catholic autochthonous culture was both less highly
developed and less preserved than in Andean Peru. Thus here the
biblical Eden, that the political mythology underlying the independence struggle envisaged as lost (together with independence), a
blessed past imagined to have existed before the Spanish conquest,
a vanished paradise, was to be recovered with the recovery of independence (*kalayan*) associated with the final redemption. Andres
Bonifacio, an initiator of the armed independence struggle of
1896–1898 against Spain, invoked a paradise lost through the
serpent-like temptation to the Spanish conquerer Legazpi (in 1571),
proclaiming that the paradise lost through this fall was to be
regained through the blood sacrificed in the independence struggle.
Tagalog Catholic folklore reveals a teleology in which the destiny

of the people is seen in terms of the loss of Eden, the recovery of which demands following the roads to Golgatha. The Calvarian *Pasyon* (Passion) of the Philippine mother country alone was to lead to rebirth of Brotherhood (*katipunan*), from darkness to light. The paradise was identified with independence and independence was meant to bring back the precolonial lost paradise.[15] This folk millennialism converged with intellectual ideologies of history, beginning with Jose Rizal (1861–1896), the Filipino national hero: In numerous respects, he considered Filipino society before the Spanish colonial rule morally superior to Europe. In it a mere promise was binding—there was no theft. "Death has. . . been the first sign of the introduction of European civilization into the Pacific," wrote Rizal,[16] before meeting his own death before a colonial Spanish firing squad. Although he is considered the greatest of the Filipino enlighteners (as medical doctor, novelist, anthropologist, and journalist), he came to be located in that very "irrational" world that his enlightenment sought to efface.[17] He came to be included in a sequence of Tagalog archetypical millennial kings: "submerged for three hundred years of sorrow and suffering" of the past—in the future to "emerge as the Rising Sun in the East"[18] (symbolized in the revolutionary flag of the Philippines[19])—after being submerged "into the depth of the Earth, into the center of the world where potency is supremely concentrated."[20] Rizal was believed to have returned to the mountain, and to be at the side of the legendary Bernardo Carpio, originally a personage from Spanish romance, Philippinized into a king of the Tagalogs. That king was thought to be imprisoned in a mountain from which he would emerge to liberate the people.[21]

From that mountain, during the independence war of 1898, superhuman armies—and also a true church—were expected to emerge to assist the patriots. In the mountain was thought to be concentrated the cosmic power; some of it was sought through pilgrimages to the heights. A volcano near Rizal's hometown is associated with a paradise to be reached through prayers of Rizal, the Tagalog Christ. Having an archetype reenacted in the Passion, the road to Golgatha, the independence struggle was understood in the language of the Holy Week. Thus the Passion of Christ came to be actualized in a sense alien to the official Catholicism of Rome. Indeed, the persecution of Christ by the Pharisees and Rome was understood to have been the archetype for the martyrdom of Rizal brought about by the Catholic Church and the Spanish state. And the Virgin Mary was felt to symbolize the mother country (and even a goddess of liberty).

A second advent of Rizal as Christ is still expected by more than 100,000 Filipinos. A "Filipino Church" with such teachings was founded in 1901 by a woman addressed in a hymn as Mother Earth. A "Rizalista Church" was established in 1918, teaching that a pre-Christian God of the Filipinos destined Rizal, his son, to redeem humankind with his life, establishing—for Filipinos only—an egalitarian Kingdom of the Mountain. "A Filipino Holy Land of Jesus" is believed in both by the church of that name (founded in 1926) and the largest Rizalista Church, the "Banner of the Nation" (Watawat ng Lahi, allegedly founded in 1940, registered in 1944). The latter associates Jerusalem with an area near a sacred volcano. It attributes to Rizal powers of the Holy Ghost (as Moses had those of the Father) and Christ, embodied in Rizal, who is to appear in a new world after the atomic global war, in the power of the Son. All those believers in Rizal deny that he is dead. They preserve or revive certain pre-Christian Filipino beliefs.[22] Intellectuals like Rafael Palma compared Rizal with Christ. Rizal has been canonized in national Filipino Catholicism of the "Aglipayan Church" (with over a million members).

An advocate of Rizal's canonization in 1900, Isabelo de los Reyes introduced socialist thought into the Philippines where it filtered through the religious idiom of Passion[23] and millennialism. Claimants to the identity and messianic mission of Rizal have appeared again and again in this century. They follow the archetype first recorded since the agrarian revolt of 1841. It had centered around the Brotherhood of Apolinario de la Cruz, who announced divine intervention and ruled a local theocracy, allegedly calling himself king of the Tagalogs. After more than 1,000 of his followers were killed, the place of his execution became a center of pilgrimage. Apolinario is not believed to be dead but to have spoken to the people through numerous subsequent martyrs, his successors. He was invoked by the secret society *Colorum* and was supposed to have reappeared in 1870, inspiring a new egalitarian brotherhood that refused taxation and labor obligations. It became a predecessor of the *Katipunan* (Brotherhood) that revolted for Filipino independence in 1896. The *Katipunan* was reestablished in 1909 in the name of a second Rizal. Previously, in 1903, a Tagalog king was believed to have risen to heaven from where he requested the Kaiser's and the Czar's armed support for a Filipino millenarian commonwealth. A "Brotherhood of the Holy Church" flourished in 1894–1910 under "Pope" Felipe Salvador, called "Jesus the Savior and King of the Philippines" with 50,000 followers. This savior preached a millennium with "Rains of Gold" and the end of the world.[24] Although hanged in 1912, after his followers had revolted in masses, many refused to believe that he is dead.[25] A reincarnation of Rizal—as sovereign of the eternal city of the righteous—emerged on the eve of the end of the world, expected in 1923. Later, the end of the world was announced for 1926 by Florencio, who, although he saw himself destined to be emperor, was thought to be insane. After a volcanic eruption he called for the establishment of the millennium by bloodshed. The American governor could prevent it by having him treated royally even in a mental institution.[26]

Not discredited by lunatic fringes, the notion that a redeemer, identified with the light of the rising sun, returns from the East, the archetype of the return of lost bliss, contributed to deprived Filipinos becoming partisans of Japan, the Empire of the Rising Sun, at the beginning of the Second World War—and of the five-pointed Red Star of communist-led revolts after its end. Yet urban Marxism could no more control religiously millennial folk Marxism than the Catholic Church could control folk Catholicism. Indeed, revolutionary folk Catholicism and folk Marxism came to blend.[27] Even in 1967, a peasant sectarian army rose in Manila under the Rizalista Valentino Santos, who came to demand the resignation of Marcos and proclaimed himself to be the savior who would kill the Antichrist.[28] The crop failure and the electoral violence of 1971 were read as portents of the approaching end of the world. The nonfulfillment of apocalyptic catastrophe—in spite of symptoms of "apocalyptic chaos"—does not end apocalyptic movements. But it ends them as *movements*; they become sects.[29] And, in terms of Filipino millennialism, as long as its archetypes remain valid while folk religiosity preserves beliefs that primeval bliss, lost through the fall, is to be regained at the end of times, the Calvary meant to lead to paradise is to be reenacted politically.

Thus the still surviving political eschatology in the Catholic Philippines strives to regain the primeval harmony felt to be lost in 1571, and in Catholic Highland Peru the Golden Age lost in 1533. For the political mythology that both lands of the Pacific have in common, the European conquest of both of them is conceived as having inverted a previously ideal order that is to be reinverted into its natural state.

For earlier ecclesiastical observers, all this has been diabolic heresy, and for enlightened priests of progress backward superstition. For ethnocentric perspectives that assume human nature to be the same everywhere (and despise preachings of hellfire and brimstone as backwoods ideas that sophisitication prides itself on having left behind, as politically irrelevant in the lands of reason, so that they cannot possibly be relevant *anywhere*) the whole topic borders on the comic. But, at present, one generation since the concept of millennialism became a stereotype of anthropology, the insight that Enlightenment contributes an ideological spark that would not have exploded into social revolution without the psychological dynamite of apocalyptic expectations, is no longer such a heresy as it used to be. These observations apply most obviously in "underdeveloped" countries for social strata disappointed in—if not outright despairing of—Progress (with the political institutions it brought). Yet these natives on both sides of the Pacific might not be called underdeveloped but rather the contrary in regard of the persistence of their belief in the indivisibility of the truly political from the ethical, a naiveté lost in the sophistication of the "models."

Notes

1. Manuel Sarkisyanz, *Rußland und der Messianismus des Orients* (Tülingen, 1955), p. 396.
2. Jean Servier, *Der Traum von der großen Harmonie. Eine Geschichte der Utopie* (München: 1971), pp. 23–24; Lewis Mumford, "Utopie, the City and the Machine," *Daedalus* (1965): 261, 283–285; Harry Levin, *The Myth of the Golden Age in the Renaissance* (Bloomington: Indian University Press, 1969) p. 42; Walter Raleigh, *The Discovery of Guinea*, ed. V. T. Harlow (London: 1928), p. 17, quoted by Levin, *Myth*, p. 64; John K. Wright, Geographical Lore of the Time of the Crusades, American Geographical Society Library Series, no. 4 (New York: 1925), pp. 71–72, 261–263, quoted by Howard Rollin Patch, *The Other World According to Descriptions in Medieval Literature* (Cambridge: Harvard University Press, 1950), p. 155; Sergio Buarque de Holanda, *Visao de Paraiso* (Rio de Janeiro: 1959), according to Levin, *Myth*, p. 184; Mircea Eliade, "Paradis et Utopie: Geographie mythique et eschatologique," in Adolf Portmann, ed., *Vom Sinn der Utopie* (Zürich: 1964), p. 213; Charles L. Sanford, *The Quest for Paradise: Europe and the American Imagination* (Urbana, Ill.: University of Illinois Press, 1961), pp. 39–40, referring to LeRoy Edwin Froom, *The Prophetic Faith of Our Fathers* (Washington, D.C.: 1948), 2:170; Levin, *Myth*, pp. 58–59, citing Christopher Columbus, *Selected Letters*, ed. R. H. Major (London: 1847), p. 145; Henry Baudet, *Paradise on Earth: Some Thoughts on the European Images of non-European Man* (New Haven: Yale University Press, 1965), p. 74; John Leddy Phelan, *The Millennial Kingdom of the Franciscans in the New World* (Berkeley and Los Angeles: University of California Press, , 1970), pp. 49, 58, 60, 66–67.; Manuel Sarkisyanz, "Politische Utopien," in Anton Peisel and Armin Mohler, eds., *Kursbuch der Weltanschauungen, Schriften der Carl*

friedrich von Siemens Stiftung (Berlin: 1981), 4:38–41; Pzvetan Teodorov, *La Conquête de l'Amerique. La question de l'autre* (Paris: 1982), pp. 23–24.

3. Rafael Karsten, *La civilisation de l'Empire Inca. Un état totalitaire du passe* (Pairs: 1983).

4. Vilma Macedo Perez, *Antologia del Pensamiento literario y social del Cusco* (Cusco: 1980), pp. 123–129.

5. Manuel Sarkisyanz, *Vom Beben in den Anden. Propheten des indianischen Aufbruchs in Peru* (Munich: Dianus-Trikont, 1985), pp. xxv–xxvii.

6. Kathleen M. Klumpp, "El retorno del Inca: Una expresion ecuatoriana de la ideologia mesianica andina," *Cuadernos de Historia y Argueologia* 16, no. 14 (1974): 99, 100; Mario Castro Arena, *La rebelión de Juan Santos* (Lima: 1973), pp. 150–151.

7. Jose Maria Arguedas, *Mitos Quechuas poshispanicos. Formación de una cultura nacional indoamericana* (Mexico City: 1977), pp. 178, 181, 182; Franklin Pease, *Los ultimos incas del Cuzco* (Lima: 1981), pp. 113–125; Mircea Eliade, *Kosmos und Geschichte. Der Mythos der Ewigen Wiederkehr* (Düsseldorf: 1966), pp. 7–28, 34, 42–45, 51, 55, 60, 63, 66f., 72–79; Ernst Benz, *Ecclesias Spirituales. Kirche, Idee und Geschichtstheologie der franziskanischen Reform* (Darmstadt: 1964); Marjorie Reeves, *Joachim Fiore and the Prophetic Future* (London: 1976); Marco Curatola, "Mito y milenarismo en los Andes: Del Taki Onqoy a Inkarry," *Allpanchis* (Cusco: 1977), 10: 67, 78, 79, 82, 83, 84.

8. Sarkisyanz, *Vom Beben in den Anden*, pp. 118–119.

9. Luis E. Valcárcel, *Tempestad en los Andes* (Lima: Editorial Universo, 1972), pp. 124–131.

10. Antonio Sengifo, "Semblanza del mayor de caballeria Teodómiro Gutierrez Cuevas, Defensor de los indios," in *Album de Oro* (Puno: 1981), 8: 54, 55, 57, 67.

11. Wilfredo Kapsoli, *Los movimientos campesinos en el Peru 1879–1965* (Lima: Delva, 1977), pp. 163, 165–170.

12. Cited in Sarkisyanz, *Vom Beben in den Anden*, p. 66.

13. Author's interview with Luis Gallegos in Puno, Oct. 3, 1982.

14. Virgilio Roel Pineda, *Raices y Vigencia de la Indianidad-Cuadernos Indios* 3 (Lima: Consejo Mundial de Pueblos Indigenas, Movimiento Indio Peruano, 1980), pp. 3–32.

15. R. Clemeña Ileto, "Rizal and the Underside of Philippine history," in David Wyatt and Alexander Woodside, eds., *Moral Order and Change: Essays on Southeast Asian Thought* (New Haven: 1982), p. 295.

16. John N. Schumacher, "The Propaganda of Reconstruction of the Philippine Past," in Anthony Reid and David Marr, eds., *Perceptions of the Past in Southeast Asia* (Singapore: Heinemann Educational Books, 1979), pp. 273, 275.

17. Ileto, "Rizal," p. 276.

18. Brian Fegan, "Light in the East: Continuity in Central Luzon Peasant Movements" (typescript), pp. 11–14.

19. Domingo Abella, *The Flag of Our Fathers* (Manila: 1977), pp. 45, 57.
20. Ileto, "Rizal," p. 317.
21. Ileto, "Tagalog Poetry and the Image of the Past during the War against Spain," in Reid and Marr, eds., *Perceptions*, p. 397. Cf. Karl Vossler, *Lope de Vega und seine Zeit* (München: Biederstein, 1947), p. 208; Ileto, "Rizal," pp. 281–286; Ileto, *Pasyon and Revolution: Popular Movements in the Philippines, 1840–1910* (Quezon City: 1979), pp. 33, 126–127.
22. Marcel A. Foronda, *Cults Honoring Rizal* (Manila: 1961), pp. 5, 7, 14, 18, 20, 22, 35f., 33–36, 70.
23. Fegan, "Light," p. 21; Foronda, *Cults*, p. 1.
24. David Sturtevant, *Popular Uprisings in the Philippines, 1840–1940* (Ithaca: Cornell University Press, 1976), pp. 83–94; Ileto, *Pasyon*, pp. 37–91.
25. Ileto, *Pasyon*, pp. 256–316, 231–236; Katherine Mayo, *The Isles of Fear: The Truth about the Philippines* (New York: Harcourt, Brace & Co., 1925), pp. 188–194; Sturtevant, *Popular Uprisings*, pp. 145–157.
26. Ibid., pp. 158–171.
27. Fegan, "Light," pp. 3, 27–28.
28. Ileto, *Pasyon*, pp. 1–2.
29. Fegan, "Light," pp. 32; Wilhelm Mühlmann, *Chiliasmus und Nativismus* (Berlin: D. Reimer, 1961), p. 275; cf. Ekkehard Hieronymus, *Der Traum von den Urkulturen. Vorgeschichte als Sinngebung der Gegenwart* (München: 1975), pp. 17, 21, 32–33, 36, 47–48.

6

Note on the Shining Path and Modernized Millennialism in Peru

Javier Diaz-Albertini

Manuel Sarkisyanz's interesting chapter on millennialism in Peru mentions some of the more important instances in which Andean society has reacted to a new coming of the Inca and the attempts to recover the primeval bliss. It is important, however, to see how these beliefs are still being recreated, transformed, and readapted to a Peru that has become increasingly urbanized. This brief chapter contends that part of the success of the extremist Maoist party Shining Path—in recruiting, battling the government, and surviving repression—has been its ability to tap into the millenarian beliefs that have permanently set the Andes against the conquering Europeans.

In the twelve years since the Shining Path (*Sendero Luminoso*)—to its militants, *the* Communist party of Peru—commenced its armed struggle, more than 25,000 people have died and approximately 20 billion in property damage has been lost. In the process, the *Sendero* has been advancing and forging an extremely orthodox communist movement in times of international setbacks for socialism, and is becoming—according to some Latin American experts—the only social utopia available in times of neoliberalism and conservative politics.

The Shining Path's capacity to swim against the political tide and maintain a steady flow of militants—despite the considerable loss in lives—partially attests to the quasi-religious character of its appeal to the approximately 15,000 militants. Some experts talk of fundamentalism[1] because of the party's obsessive insistence in following the ideology as formulated by Abimael Guzmán, always referred by his *nom de guerre* "President Gonzalo." His followers call him the "fourth sword of Marxism" (following after Marx, Lenin, and Mao) because of his supposedly transcendental contributions to communist ideology and world revolutions. Without a doubt, this view is an essential part of a personality cult and messianism. The overriding importance of ideology and the strict adherence to the correct line is reflected in the degree to which all of the main activities of the organization are governed by President Gonzalo's political thought. For example, in the first "military school" held in 1980 for eighteen days, the first twelve days were dedicated to strenuous ideological formation, long processes of criticism and self-criticism, and the negating of all possible deviations from dogma, even though those attending were a small group of militants who had already been in the party for nearly a decade.[2]

In terms of whether the *Sendero* is a millennial movement, there is much discussion among experts. Several leading researchers strongly deny it, indicating that in the *Sendero*'s discourse there is no appeal to the Indian masses and ethnic-racial categories are never mentioned. Rather, social class is the the sole variable.[3] Furthermore, Carlos Degregori stresses the fact that the militants tend to be young, higher educated mestizos, either from a rural background or the children of rural emigrants and the peasants of the Andean highlands.[4] They have supposedly broken many of the ties to their rural past and are acculturated into a secular urban world.

Yet these observations fail to consider that class categories in Peru are embedded in ethnic-racial differences: Peasants are overwhelmingly Indians and the elite bourgeoisie tends to be white-European. Thus, millennianism in the Shining Path must be understood and interpreted in terms of its particular use of Marxist paradigms, concepts, and jargon. As Said Amir Arjomand mentions in the Introduction, millennialism and messianism are not static phenomena; rather, they blend with modern forms of political expression and action. This sort of transmutation of the millennial motif is noticed in the *Sendero*'s discourse and action.

The party, for example, defines Peru as having a semifeudal and semicolonial structure, analytical categories used in the early twentieth century by Peru's foremost Marxist thinker José Carlos Mariátegui. One of Mariátegui's leading contributions to Latin American Marxism was to include the Andean Indian peasantry as part of the revolutionary class coalition and Andean communal structure as one of the foundations of the modern socialist nation. Two of his main theses were that "the demands of Peruvian Indians are absolutely revolutionary" and "the demands of these Indians form part of the purest Western tradition of demand-making and national struggle." In time, however, Peruvian Marxism understood this as equivalent to eliminating "Indian" as a political category and replacing it with "peasant," modernizing the political discourse by emphasizing relations of production and classes. In this way, ethnic-racial differences and contradictions were to practically disappear in Peru's leftist jargon, even though they were vigorous forces in reality. The *Sendero* continues to recognize this legacy of misconstrual, even though it claims to go "By Way of the *Shining Path* of Mariátegui. The same is true of many researcher[5] who deny the *Sendero*'s ethnic millenarian appeal while at the same time recognizing that the party's cohesiveness is based on an "ethnic-regional solidarity."[6] In fact the Shining Path and political violence in Peru cannot be understood except in the context of the ethnic problem.[7]

The *Sendero* is successfully unleashing an existing accumulation of ethnic animosity and racist sentiment that began with the Spanish conquest. Other Latin American countries with a majority presence of Indians and mestizos and exclusionary white-controlled political systems, such as Mexico and Bolivia, have had major revolutions with mixed results for the nonwhite groups. But at least their ethnic problems were addressed and have become an important component in their political culture. Peru is a country that still lives within the colonial cultural legacy, from the monuments to the *conquistadores* to television commercials that portray only light-skinned models.

Many changes have occurred since Mariátegui's time, especially in terms of class, demographic, and economic structure. As Sarkisyanz mentions, the reforms implemented by the military government of 1968–1975 include the most radical agrarian reform in South America, and the nationalization of the country's most important export products (petroleum, copper, fishing), financial institutions, and basic industries. The *Sendero*'s insistence on a semifeudal and semicolonial description, though, perfectly intertwines with a class analysis that—as mentioned before—sets white European institutions (feudalism and imperialism) versus the long-lost communal society of pre-Columbian Peru. It is a war against European heritage, which is also captured in the *Sendero*'s adoption of the Maoist strategy of enclosing the cities from the countryside. In Peru's highly centralized political, economic, and social system, cities, and especially Lima with 30 percent of the population, represent white European dominion over the rural areas and the oppression of Indian peasants and poor emigrants. According to Flores Galindo, a leading researcher of Andean millenarian movements, these conceptualizations and strategies clearly demonstrate the *Sendero*'s distinct pretension of turning the world "on its head";[8] and this view fits perfectly with traditional Andean patterns of thought.

It is the discourse itself, however, with its metaphors, allegories, and memorized and chanted slogans that clearly defines the millennial contents. In the closing speech of the first "military school," President Gonzalo sent off the first contingency of guerrillas, whom he addressed as the "Initiators," with a clear message that they were going to turn darkness into light: "The trumpets start to sound, the rumor of the masses grows and it will grow more, it will deafen us, it will attract us to a powerful vortex . . . and in this way it will create the great rupture and we will be the makers of the definite dawn. We will transform the black fire into red and the red into light. That we are, this is the reconstitution. Comrades, we are reconstituted!"[9] Likewise, the prophetic inevitability of the *Sendero*'s triumph is expressed by President Gonzalo as a process in the evolution of nature itself, as reflected in a document published in *El Diario*, the party's official newspaper:

> Let us remember what was proposed to us in 1979, fifteen billion years of the process of matter in movement . . . led to the unstoppable march of communism. This is reality, to learn this law and bring it forward; the goal, communism, is not an idea at the margin of the material process, it is part of it and that is its perspective. It is part of the march of this material process, it is an expression of the unrestrainable movement of matter.[10]

The *Sendero*'s discourse also has an apocalyptic character that reinforces both the unquestionable commitment of its militants in the most difficult of times, and the need for complete destruction before reconstruction. In early 1980, when Guzmán wanted a clear and unanimous decision of the central committee in favor of starting the armed struggle, besides reading classic Leninist and Maoist texts, at a critical moment he quoted passages of the life of the prophet Muhammad as a means of expressing the magnitude and sanctity of the quest.[11] The ideas of destruction, suffering, and death are not expressed in the usual Marxist apologia of a necessary evil, but as a cleansing process that will permit building anew. In a recent communique Guzmán told Peruvians that the revolution will triumph after they have "crossed the river of blood" and reached the other side.[12] In more prosaic but horrible terms, another *Sendero* leader announced that this would represent about a million deaths.

Finally, let us consider the psychology of the individuals who compose *Sendero*. As mentioned before, they are not the indigenous people that Sarkisyanz examines. They are young, higher-educated men and women from the small cities of Peru or second-generation immigrants in the larger cities. Racially, a majority are *mestizos* from the Andes.[13] Yet contrary to what Degregori[14] claims, these characteristics do not make them immune to a discourse that implicitly calls for a holy war against the established white European elite, even if it is stated in the "more modern and universal" political language of class struggle. On the contrary, they are direct victims of a social system that has first, repressed and ridiculed their Indian side, and second, failed to deliver on the promises of social mobility via education. In the words of a young *senderista*, they are fighting for a new order that will reverse a system that has only brought false promises and suffering: "We (the *Sendero*) are not after an instability within the instability that society has become, but a stability within the society that is forming.[15]

Furthermore, it could be argued that what has occurred is a transmutation of the millenarian message and that this explains the appeal felt by educated *mestizos*. The "new Inca," then, is no longer the Indian *cacique* or the warrior who would make the Andes tremble in revolt against landowners and the state. Rather, it is Abimael Guzmán, who for many years was a university professor. His image is clearly that of an intellectual. He is a aways portrayed in *Sendero* iconography with glasses, and his speeches consistently stress science and progress. These are all attractive symbols for a youth brought up with the myth of education as social progress, but who at the same time were denied access to a better life. Another important change is that the New World that will arise is not the old Incan *Tahuantinsuyo*, but what the *Sendero* terms the "Andean nation" that will unify all of Latin America.[16]

In an important study concerning violence in Peru, psycho-analyst César Rodriguez-Rabanal mentions the multiple ways mestizo immigrants are forced to negate and devalue their cultural and racial heritage.[17] This, he claims, is an important component in violence and aggression and normally has had an outlet either against the self or weaker individuals (women, children). The *Sendero*, however, is offering an alternative outlet, a distinctive and attractive world vision for an educated and unemployed youth, and the possibilities of being someone feared by the establishment, respected by peers, and part of a process that will utterly destroy the system. An apocalyptic destruction will finally turn back 500 years of conquest, and bring back the lost primeval bliss.

Notes

1. Carlos Iván Degregori, *El surgimiento de Sendero Luminoso* (Lima: Instituto de Estudios Peruanos, 1990).
2. Gustavo Gorriti Ellenbogen, *Sendero, historia de la guerra milenaria en el Perú*, (Lima: Editorial Apoyo, 1990), 1: 58–68.
3. Christine Pendzich, "Peru in Crisis—Challenges to a New Government," rapporteur's report on conference sponsored by the George Washington University Seminar on Andean Culture and Politics and the Washington Office on Latin America, 1990.
4. Degregori, *El surgimiento*.
5. For a review, see Orin Starn, "New Literature on Peru's Sendero Luminoso," *Latin American Research Review* 27, no. 2 (1992): 212–226.
6. Degregori, *El surgimiento*, p. 212.
7. Rodrigo Montoya, "Etnia y clase en el Perú," *Márgenes* 7:159.
8. Alberto Flores Galindo, *Buscando un Inca* (Lima: Horizonte, 1988).
9. Gorriti, *Sendero*, pp. 66–67; author's translation.
10. *El Diario*, no. 620, Mar. 1, 1992; author's translation.
11. Gorriti, *Sendero* pp. 54–57.
12. *La República*, Apr. 4, 1992.
13. Starn, "New Literature."
14. Degregori, *El surgimiento*.
15. Romeo Grompone, *El velero en el viento: Política y sociedad en Lima* (Lima: Instituto de Estudios Peruanos, 1991), p. 630.
16. Gabriela Tarazona-Sevillano and John B. Reuter, *Sendero Luminoso and the Threat of Narcoterrorism*, The Washington Papers, no. 144 (New York: Praeger, 1990).
17. César Rodríguez-Rabanal and Franca Casstelnuovo, "Sobre la dimensión psicosocial de la violencia en el Perú," in Felipe MacGregor, José L. Rouillón, and Marcial Rubio, eds., *Siete Ensayos sobre la violencia en el Perú* (Lima: Asociacion Peruana de Estudios para la Paz: 1987).

7

Antinomian Conduct at the Millennium: Metaphorical Conceptions of Time in Social Science and Social Life

Karen E. Fields

The condition of the world, wherein the earth will be full of the knowledge of the Lord as the waters cover the sea (Isa. 11:9), does not repeat anything that has ever been, but presents something new.
—*Gershom Scholem*[1]

This essay explores antinomianism, a mode of action that embodies the freedom, as well as the predicament, of people who seek religiously to embrace, here and now, something that "does not repeat anything that has ever been." Antinomian conduct is widely observed in the context of millenarian or messianic religious movements and is often a reason for their repression. Accordingly, the term *antinomianism* has a long history as an epithet. One ancient usage refers to the charge of St. Paul's opponents that his declaration of Christian freedom and his emphasis on grace, as opposed to the Mosaic Law, led to licentiousness.[2] Thus the very use of this term, whose dictionary definition is "rejection of the moral law," moves one toward collectively disputed territory of right belief and conduct: What is, literally, "against law" or even "lawlessness" to some, is pious rigor to others. Such normative usages are not only common in the talk of the religiously committed; they also have an interesting relationship to the cognate sociological term *anomie*, which frequently appears in discussions of millenarianism. But normative usages are avoided here, except as vivid data about disputes over belief and conduct. For the present purpose, we define "antinomianism" neutrally: as theologically principled breaking of established law.

The theological principle involved is the conclusion people draw from a colossal event that destroys for them the validity of previously binding rules and laws. Millenarian believers typically embrace antinomian conduct in conjunction with their vision of a grand interruption in the flow of the world's time.[3] That such conduct can have unavoidable political meaning gives it consequences beyond the limits of "religion," as conventionally understood in our day. Therefore, by exploring antinomianism, we also explore certain temporal underpinnings of political order. The phenomena in the particular context of colonial Central Africa have counterparts in widely disparate places and times. These phenomena reveal features of the "accentuated now" in the metaphysics of social life.

The Logic of Antinomian Conduct

According to Gershom Scholem, antinomianism follows logically from the idea of an apocalyptic moment that marks a catastropic End of Days (as set forth in Isaiah) or that of a utopian day of the Lord (as set forth in Amos).[4] Alike In their conception of radical discontinuity, he says, these two ideas tick away with an "explosive charge" in the midst of traditional patterns and expectations. Scholem characterizes the logic in this way: "[E]very acute and radical Messianism that is taken seriously tears open an abyss in which by inner necessity antinomian tendencies and libertine moral conceptions gain strength."[5] The "explosive charge" that is inherent in the ideas of catastrophe and utopia detonates when people seize the apocalyptic moment, by definition a dramatic end and beginning. Guided by their vision of radical discontinuity, believers move from one time to a qualitatively different one and in consequence from one state to a qualitatively different one.

If this vision of the inner logic is right, then antinomianism has particular sociological interest. For it means that the hallmark of miilenarian ideas is not only a dense, intense, and complex attention to time, but also—by inner necessity—a dense, intense, and complex attention to social structure. In this way, a conviction about time becomes a conviction about conduct; and this conviction exposes to actors the disorder in the apparent order of routine they previously took for granted. To explore antinomianism is thus to observe people at moments of self-consciousness about social structure and about the relationship of their own action to structure. It is to watch as structure's inextricable tie to action is analyzed into component parts, as though with a camera that registers slow motion and periodic freeze-frames. For the sociologist, therefore, the antinomian practice of millenarians offers a privileged opportunity to revisit the connections between social structure and social action, those bedrock concepts of sociology.

Still, the behavior that results is often so strange that it is necessary to tackle this strangeness head-on. The topic of millenarianism reeks of the long ago or the far away: abstruse theological mathematics; local eccentricities of belief and practice; and intensely consequent, if apparently unhinged, rationality. In short, millenarianism and its relative, messianism[6], appear to point to a "there," a "then," a "that," and a "they" so remote from general questions that their credentials for appearing elsewhere than in specialized case studies seem questionable. But, exotic as they may seem, millenarian movements possess unique credentials for inclusion in any general theoretical discussion of the relationship between religion and politics. These credentials are displayed in the familiar duplex terminology—of "politicoreligious" or "religiopolitical" movements—which is commonplace in the literature. Such compound terms are meant to do no more than indicate the fusion of apparently disparate sorts of behavior that is so often noticeable when signs of the End take hold in the imaginations of people, previously quiet, who now launch themselves militantly against a given status quo or find themselves persecuted as subversives or revolutionaries. But such terms also do more. For the idea of fusion raises, willy-nilly, the question of what "religion" and "politics" might be taken to mean separately: What, precisely is fused with what? This question stands just short of explicit formulation whenever the issue is how religion and politics, presumed to be distinct phenomena, come to be joined or to take on one another's characteristics. If it is our ambition to answer empirically, not a priori, and systematically, not ad hoc, then the exotic doings of millenarians begin to acquire general interest. For if the double designation is apt—and even if it is not—then study of what adherents do, at the level of theory and at the level of practice, should reveal much about both "religion" and "politics." Or, more precisely, such study should reveal much about the common terrain of collective action that we attempt to explore using now one, now the other designation.

In describing the "explosive charge" inherent in the ideas of catastrophe and utopia, Scholem places the common terrain of religion and politics neatly on a single map: "Once the longing for a new world and for the tree of life seizes the heart, who knows what may come next? Every utopia that is more than an abstract formula has a revolutionary sting."[7] The political credentials of religiously inspired rule-breaking are never far from the surface of events. Although, from a sociological standpoint, antinomianism can be defined neutrally as theologically principled rule- or law-breaking, as a rubric for ritual departures recorded and described by religious establishments, it scarcely lends itself to a neutral tone of voice. By its nature, antinomianism comes into view as sensational piety and as extremes of conduct that cannot leave onlookers unmoved. In one of his examples, Scholem recounts the messiah in twelfth-century Persia who made the classic proclamation that his followers, having entered the state of resurrection, were freed from the yoke of the *Shari'a*. They made themselves obnoxious by publicly violating the fast of Ramadan and drinking wine.[8] Such collective practice by a group of people setting itself apart from quotidian morality and normal demeanor seldom remains a religious matter separate from politics. Scholem's own monumental study of the seventeenth-century Jewish messiah, Sabbatai Zevi, moves across an enormous religiopolitical space.[9] At one extreme of this space stands the mystic architecture of Lurianic Kabbalah, from which Zevi's apocalyptic speculation derived; at the other stands the political architecture of the Ottoman Empire, which in the person of Sultan Mehmed IV called the messiah to account for outrageous conduct: pronouncing the ineffable Name and commanding his followers to do likewise; eating forbidden fats; singing an ancient Castilian love song while clutching the Holy Scroll in his arms; promising women that he would set them free from the curse of Eve: excommunicating rabbis; and, not least, promising to be crowned in Constantinople on June 18, 1666.

As religious vice, antinomianism often comes into view in the midst of theological disputes that can become eye-glazing to the outsider, but formulations that announce its political import come readily to hand. For example, the *Hastings Encyclopedia of Religion and Ethics* (1908) begins its article on antinomianism drily on the subject of Johannes Agricola, an early coadjutor of Luther, who disputed Luther on the relationship between the Law and the Gospel; but in the second sentence it calls antinomianism "the counterpart of modern political anarchism."[10] The African movements provoked their adversaries to make a similar leap. An Anglican eye-witness summed up the heresies of the Watchtower movement as "ecclesiastical bolshevism."[11]

Antinomian Conduct and Rebellion in Colonial Central Africa

For more than fifty years, waves of millenarian expectation periodically traversed the British colonial regimes of Central Africa and sometimes shook them. For example, between 1917 and 1919 Watchtower revival swept away the apparatus of indirect rule In the northern districts of Northern Rhodesia and forced officials to engineer its systematic reconstruction; and in 1935 a shocked officialdom widely attributed the strike by mineworkers on the Copperbelt to the activities of Watchtower preachers.[12] These regimes' African subjects received the ancient Judeo-Christian heritage of apocalyptic speculation through the medium of the Watchtower Bible and Tract Society, the life's work of the visionary Pennsylvanian Charles Taze Russell and his successors. Russell's encounter in the 1870s with the esoteric Truth of history led him to calculations that predicted that Jesus' return to earth and the end of the world would take place in 1914.[13] The African preachers his prophecies influenced (partly through missionary work but far more important through propagation of *The Watchtower* magazine) naturally understood the End to mean the end of British rule, among other things. Russell's countdown gained in import with the coming of World War I to some locales in the African colonies of the European combatants.

Preaching of the End led to antinomian conduct that placed all existing patterns in question, and all laws, not simply those in which Britons had predictable interest. Battles over predictable matters like wage labor and taxes intermingled with less predictable ones like rules of marriage and respect for the dead.[14] Much of what the regime persecuted as lawlessness originated in Watchtower adherents' assertion that the apocalyptic moment was at hand. By an "inner necessity" counterpart to the millenarians' own, the secular upholders of a secular regime brought to consciousness something they could not have predicted: their own "politicoreligious" commitment to an orthodox theology of time. It mattered to them whether a preacher taught, like their missionary compatriots, that Jesus would come again, to conquer and to rule, or whether, unlike the missionaries, the preacher insisted that Jesus would come again *soon*.[15] Two kinds of incident will illustrate. The first exhibits conduct by one convert among many villagers who between 1917 and 1919 embraced the Watchtower's conviction of the End. Although produced nonviolently, the disorder that occurred was of a scope and scale that, in the minds of officials on the spot, amounted to insurrection. The second exhibits the peculiar inquisitorial predicament about time in which secular British officials found themselves, then and later, as they tried to suppress preaching of the apocalyptic moment.

Sometime in late 1918, in the British colony of Northern Rhodesia, and amid the general shout "God is great! Pray to God alone!" a villager named Jacob Kasuya embraced the idea that the End was at hand.[16] He left worldly activities and powers behind, and, as stories that the End would come in nine days sped through the northern districts of the colony, he joined the other villagers who rushed to receive the baptism that would give them access to the bright, new, imminent world. They moved out of their homes into uninhabited places. They took up the practice of talking in unknown tongues and shouting, in imitation of the passage in St. Matthew that speaks of "a voice crying in the wilderness, saying 'Prepare ye the way of the Lord.'" Children disregarded their parents. Parents disregarded their headmen and chiefs, calling them Pharisees and Sadducees and calling the British Romans. Some villagers neglected or even uprooted their crops; some soldiers deserted their units.

In January, Kasuya joined a group of other converts who walked boldly onto hallowed and forbidden ground and kicked to pieces the ancestor shrine of Musamansi, interlocutor with the departed ancestors and political authority among the inhabitants of the village that bore his name. The rules that set apart this bit of ground and the sacred objects reposing on it no longer bound Kasuya, who dramatically escaped the supernatural punishment that was ordinarily to be expected on the spot. The lesson he and his coreligionists drew from surviving the sacrilege must surely have recapitulated the shouting of the prayer meetings: God *was* great.[17] Kasuya belonged to that numerous company of Watchtower adherents, then and later, who abrogated other rules: on sex and marriage; funerals, burials, and family observances; the veneration of sacred objects and places; and the keeping of hierarchical distinctions between young and old, men and women, commoners and hereditary betters. In 1920, an administrator in the district where Kasuya committed his sacrilege wrote a colleague about his intention not to register a Watchtower marriage defined by traditional villagers as incestuous. He was determined to let Watchtower adherents see that they were not above the law. In this intimate regard, religious antinomianism was political vice.

St. Paul defended Christians against the charge of antino-mianism; but he also attacked the conduct of some Christian converts on many grounds. Stories of licentiousness told against Watchtower adherents recall practices (and hostile rumors of practices) that Ronald Knox discussed in his delightful essay "The Corinthians' Letter to St. Paul."[18] Paul's letter said, for example, "I actually hear reports of sexual immorality among you, immorality such as even pagans do not tolerate: the union of a man with his father's wife" (I Cor. 5:1–2). Accusations of sexual license belong to the common coinage of dispute over the nature of the rules that bind; but although such accusations are often fabricated, it does not follow necessarily that all are false. Paul evidently was making a pointed case against real behavior. Although in the Central African case, some charges against Watchtower adherents may be disputed as no more than hostile rumors of practices, there is documented conduct as well. Some congregations practiced the "baptism of fire," a rite that aggravated free love with the further offense of disdain for the rules against clan incest.[19] One group advocated adultery, outraging their neighbors by reinterpreting as their precedent St. Paul's relationship with the faithful church sister Lydia (Phil. 1:3–5).[20]

In the same official records that collected evidence of this kind, we find British officials obtaining from elders the details of classi-ficatory kinship in order to learn rules governing sex that were alien to them. They took notes, preparing to add such rules to an ex-panding body of provisions that came to be ultimately enforceable by the Crown as "native law and custom."[21] We find them attending to traditional rules about ancestor observance in a similar way. We even find them riding to the rescue of good manners due from the young to their elders and from commoners to chiefs. Ritual con-tempt toward elders and chiefs, to whom ritual homage was due, was widespread and forcefully expressed. In one instance, a British judge prosecuted a group of Watchtower converts for disturbing the peace. The disturbance consisted in the converts' maintaining a pointed silence upon their chief's arrival. Ritual decorum required instead a noisy chaos of of greeting and praise. Under those circumstances, silence was rowdy.[22] In another instance, a similarly troublesome silence invaded funerals. Villages that converted en masse fell into a quiet that Britons living nearby noted with apprehension. Having gradually become acclimated to nighttime drumming and wailing at funerals as safe normality, they were inclined to read the sudden silence as a plunge in the political barometer.[23] Further, where whole villages did not convert as one, division over pious conduct gave the regime's problem of keeping order new complexity. It meant not only that indigenous authorities were losing their leverage over converted minorities, but also that factional discord might necessitate direct intervention. Either result undermined the imperial strategy of rule by collaboration with indigenous authorities.

This sort of ramifying conflict over familial norms echoes—and perhaps amplifies[24]—strains in certain biblical stories such as that of the young man who wanted to follow Jesus, but who felt obligated to hurry home first and help bury his father. Brushing aside ritual propriety and family obligation in favor of urgent priorities in an accentuated now, Jesus imperiously told him, "Let the dead bury their dead" (Luke 9:60). Other pronouncements Jesus made about the invalidity of kinship ties show how subversive his teaching must have seemed to unconverted onlookers—for example his repeated statements of this type: "I am come to set a man at variance against his father, and the daughter against her mother, and the daughter-in-law against her mother-in-law" (Matt. 10:35). Similarly, Jesus asks (Mark 3:31–35) relatives who have come to take him home, "Who are my mother and my brothers?"and then answers that his fellow converts are.[25] In the context of a Roman imperial strategy analogous in some respects to that of the British, it seems probable that Jesus' preaching in regard to kinship obligation as an aspect of established law was politically consequential in a way that his apparently apolitical attitude toward the empire could not fully undo.[26] In colonial Northern Rhodesia, although officials of the regime found scandal to the living and the dead, the stream of antinomianism did not flow into the bloody channels that they feared it might. They found no one preaching into existence an anti-European army of the Last Days, and no one calling himself the human instrument of God's terrible justice against the colonizers.[27] Although repeated alarms kept alive the fear, never realized, that such events might occur, officials prosecuted Watchtower millenarianism for more immediately practical reasons as well.

Not surprisingly, therefore, although Jacob Kasuya escaped punishment in the exotic realm of direct intervention by ancestral spirits, he received punishment in the unexotic realm of British power. He was among 119 people tried by a British court and variously sentenced to floggings, fines, and terms of imprisonment. Under the system of indirect rule, the empire was parasitic upon religious authority created and maintained in African villages and among kin; officials had to sanction customary rules of all kinds, or at least strive to do so, moving in trial-and-error fashion from one bit of local particularity to the next. Therefore, like conservative voices known to us from much closer to home, officials found themselves preaching for the integrity of church and family as the basic cells, so to speak, of broader public order. Whether sanctioning customary or missionary religion, then, secular Britons sought to deploy religion that they did not officially embrace to protect a political relation they did. There was religion by raison d'état. This deployment of religion by raison d'état created a politicoreligious architecture more like that of seventeenth- than of twentieth-century England. This architecture solved some problems but created others. P. J. Macdonnell, the High Court justice who reviewed the sentences, wrote a long opinion that explored the double predicament this architecture created: how to constrain religious expression lawfully, given the religious toleration that had been, as he put it, "the uniform course of British jurisprudence for at least 100 years";[28] and how to restrict the disorder created by Watchtower preaching, given that the colonized were many, the colonizers few, and the colonies immense. Macdonnell wrote that the law conclusively protected what he adroitly called religion "per se," the meaning of which moved across the full expanse that we routinely designate as "politics" at some times and as "religion" at others.

From the standpoint of the regime, the meaning of religion "per se" moved from the obvious to the unexpected. The obvious part meant extending a not entirely unqualified welcome to missions of various stripes. The qualified welcome excluded small, poorly financed missions (typically representing small sects) that were not able to supervise their European or African personnel closely enough to satisfy the regime that they could maintain a coherent church organization. Thus, for a time, the qualified welcome excluded missions sent by Afro-American churches, even though most were tight-collared exemplars of Booker T. Washingtonesque respectability.[29] Loose church organization, no matter how conservative in theology or intent the church might be, inevitably caused the spread of local trouble along with the spread of the gospel. Among other things, religion "per se" meant a kind of church polity and financing that ensured missions' tight control over the work of African preachers and teachers. Effective control became a requirement for religious toleration.

Specifically theological tests were uncommon but not unheard of. White missionaries of the Watchtower Bible and Tract Society were for many years excluded from Northern Rhodesia; and their admission after the mineworkers' strike of 1935 was a calculated risk, part of an attempt to rein in African preachers long independent

of any missionary control.[30] Some faith-healing pentecostal groups
were viewed with distrust. These groups' disqualification followed
from their antinomian tendency to negate the hierarchical distinctions of the world, along the lines of St. Paul's principle (Gal. 3:28):
"There is neither Jew nor Greek, there is neither bond nor free, there
is neither male nor female: for ye are all one in Jesus Christ." Such
a vision of universal Christian equality made them suspect in a place
where racial particularism was deliberately being built to perpetuate
conquest, and where the *nomos* in construction created "European"
and "native" in ever more elaborate differentiation (from sumptuary
codes to criminal law). To live out the doctrine of Christian equality
affronted public rituals on which political order partly rested. In his
classic treatise on how to run the African Empire, Lord Frederick
Lugard singled out such Christians as dangerous:

> Some few missions carry the ideal of the equality of man to a
> point which the primitive savage does not appreciate in its true
> significance. That a white man should come to Africa to do
> menial work in the furtherance of an altruistic ideal is not
> comprehensible to him, and the result is merely to destroy the
> missionary's own influence for good, and to lessen the prestige
> of Europeans, upon which the avoidance of bloodshed and the
> maintenance of law and order so largely depend in Africa.[31]

In practice, missions with altruistic ideals of this kind could be
refused recognition as missionaries, and visas. In one incident a
young South African nurse, adept of a faith-healing sect, was briskly
deported from Nyasaland—her egalitarian demeanor threatened to
ruffle the local calm.[32] Toleration of religion "per se" did not permit
trespass against the ritual processes that continually reproduced
collectivity mapped out along a color line.

Nevertheless, toleration of religion "per se" had considerable
theological scope. It meant recognizing no single established
church. Dozens of missionary societies gained admission. Scots Free
Churchmen, Methodists, and even Primitive Methodists were no less
welcome than Anglicans; and Catholics no less than these. For the
missions, being tolerated as practicing religion "per se" meant
cooperation with the regime, including acceptance of regulation,
and, in due course, acceptance of grants-in-aid in support of schools,
hospitals, and the like. In short, it meant belief and conduct that
upheld a broad range of routinized colonial relationships, both
among Africans and between Africans and Britons. Within those
constraints, the prospect that Jesus as judge would return suddenly—

but only on a vague someday—upheld routine discipline. The Watchtower preachers' doctrine of "*Soon!*" by its nature corroded all routine. But the plausibility of their claim to be Christian preachers made their repression less than a straightforward matter. The regime could not attack on theological grounds without provoking the charge of religious persecution. To evade this charge, Macdonnell and others devised technical grounds for arresting Watchtower adherents. The charge of preaching without the credentials of a duly recognized missionary society was one expedient. Selective enforcement of tax laws was another. And to uncover conduct that could be prosecuted as seditious, they launched investigative activity that extended to surreptitious scrutiny of mail and dispatching African plainclothes detectives to spy at places of worship.[33]

For months and years after Kasuya's trial, officials found themselves locked in a dispute with Watchtower converts about time, specifically about what time it was in the grand flow of history and about how people should behave once they knew. Correspondence among the regime's line officers, in their often lonely rural redoubts, shows them tensing whenever an enthusiastic preacher appeared, and arguing for preventive action lest the preacher suddenly shift from what they called "harmless" preaching to a proclamation that the Day was near. In records concerned with Watchtower outbursts, officials underlined and singled out the word *soon*, as if it were the active ingredient of otherwise harmless, indeed, dismayingly scriptural, Christian teaching.[34] By this route, officials arrived at a remarkable interest in the answers arrested Watchtower adherents gave to a theological question: whether the Second Coming of Jesus was merely inevitable, as the orthodox missionaries said; or whether his return was imminent. Detectives naturally became attuned to whether definite dates were being mentioned, and if so, what dates. Religion "per se" accepted the idea of inevitability and rejected that of imminence. Kasuya and his coreligionists embraced a heresy about time that the political establishment could not ignore.

Time in the Structure of Religious Community

Religious establishments have their own reasons for unease with a metaphorical representation of time that undoes routine. It is instructive to consider the predicament of St. Paul in the well-known passage where he admonishes the Corinthians about talking in unknown tongues (I Cor. 13). In their enthusiasm, these new

Christians were departing not only from the familial norms mentioned earlier: they were departing even from the rules that constitute the paradigmatic social bond of common language. The tongues of fire through which the Spirit gave believers strange utterance did not unify the community of faith, but divided it. "If I know not the meaning of the voice," Paul wrote, "I shall be unto him that speaketh a barbarian, and he that speaketh shall be a barbarian unto me" (I Cor. 14:11). He insisted again and again that the riot of inspired but incomprehensible utterance must give way to ordinary, and orderly, speech. "God is not the author of confusion," he said. By this route, Paul arrived at what we can call a "neonomian" admonition, addressed pointedly to women but also set within a broader conclusion about the need for stability and respectability in the new church: to "let all things be done decently and in order." But, at the apocalyptic moment, teaching about order had no place or point. Paul's predicament was not only that he could not legitimize such teaching in terms of common hopes, but that he could not do so even in terms of his own. Paul shared with the Corinthians their conviction of "*Soon!*" Like his fellow true believers, St. Paul himself expected the trumpet to sound "in a moment, in the twinkling of an eye"—and said so in the very same letter. Nearly two generations later, we find St. Luke still battling the effervescence of a community that had not fully reconciled itself to the prospect that the End and the new beginning would not come soon. The community shivered and shook as believers descried the kingdom—"Lo, here! Lo, there!" (Luke 17:21). The message of St. Luke was to stop watching and waiting: "The Kingdom of Christ is in your midst."[35] He was addressing early on the problem of the internal order of the church (and the church's relation to worldly power) that St. Augustine later addressed when he pronounced that the kingdom had already come.[36] Small-scale or large-scale, state or community of faith, no coherent group life can be sustained out on the thin edges of time.

Religions whose heartbeat is messianic hope know this problem intimately and have invented several solutions to it. The impulse of the rabbinic tradition is to restrain messianic speculation and, while acknowledging that the messiah will come, to deemphasize the utopian content of the idea. This impulse is illustrated in a story that goes this way: "If there were a plant in your hand and they should say to you, 'Look, the messiah is here!' go and plant your plant and after that go forth to receive him."[37] Maimonides, whose sensibility this story exemplifies, knew from the recent history of his own time the disruptive potential of messiahs. According to Scholem, he mistrusted but could not quite suppress those elements inherent in the messianic idea that have a revolutionary sting. What he did do, in elaborate argument, was to minimize as much as possible the discontinuity between states before and after the messiah's coming and to "suppress completely the apocalyptic moment."[38]

Another solution is to retain the apocalyptic moment but to foreclose speculation about when it will come, using the heavy guns of God's majesty and inherently unknowable plan for the world. The Koran prohibits speculation about the moment in verses such as "God alone has knowledge of the hour" (31:34) and "People will ask you about the hour. Say: Knowledge of it is only with God." (33:63).[39] This is a commanding solution but unstable for all but the most austerely pious. Accordingly, in step with the widespread anticipation of the end of the world that pervaded early Islam, numerous early teachings specified dates for the appearance of the *Mahdi* and the End that is to follow his appearance. These dates subsequently had to be moved forward, pronounced spurious, or explained away. Yohanan Friedmann writes that "the air of imminence that pervaded the earliest eschatological pronouncements gradually receded into the background, and ways were found to postpone the final cataclysm to a distant, almost unforeseeable future."[40] One of these ways was to sublimate the expectation of the End into the cyclical idea that Islam would be revitalized and renewed on the eve of every century—thereby postponing the End indefinitely, while building up the religious function of renewers or *mujaddidun*. Then, according to Friedmann, in some circumstances the role of *mujaddid* became available for ascription to scholarly claimants to authority within the religious community.

This logic of inserting ideas about the end of the world into orderiy communal life can be seen in even the most intensely expectant religious traditions. According to Abdulaziz Sachedina,[41] Twelver Shi'ism makes a greatly elaborated messianic expectation the "foundation of its entire spiritual edifice." It also greatly elaborates the idea of hiddenness. A widely quoted tradition within it explicitly prohibits speculation about the time, while various others prohibit fixing the precise moment. Nonetheless, many traditions cite the day, which according to Sachedina, is theologically less problematic than fixing the year. (The day most frequently cited is the day of 'Ashura, a year-by-year commemoration, an interesting choice in that it positions the End within the repetitive annual cycle of the religious calendar.) Operating at a distance from the prohibited territory of precise dates, there are other detailed traditions about the place and the sort of person—and, as in Judaism and Christianity, about relevant, if not unambiguous signs.

St. Augustine adduced a preemptive solution to the problem of time. Exegeting Revelation in *The City of God*, he turned abruptly aside from the logical flow of his argument in order to assert that Christ's kingdom has come and is embodied in the church.[42] By so doing, he ran the Catholic clock forward, past the apocalyptic moment, to time *after* the beginning of the millennium. "Not soon" was his answer to the question of Jesus' revival date. The church's reign was the 1,000 years referred to in Revelation. Authoritatively stating what time it was, he established as divinely authoritative the cyclical movement of time through those repetitive activities that made and expressed the community of the universal church and empire. Augustine's church could not hope to perpetuate itself if the messianic hope that was its heartbeat seemed near fulfillment. What it required was a humdrum clockwork count, not the final countdown. In the celebrated Grand Inquisitor scene of *The Brothers Karamazov*, Dostoevsky portrayed with great sociological insight the problem of containing messianic hope within a coherent group life. The inquisitor audaciously asks the returned Jesus, "Why art thou come to hinder us?" and tells him, in effect, "We cannot run a church with you around." There is a hackneyed and unexpectant Protestant sermon about day-in-day-out morals that rhetorically asks, "If Jesus came today, would you be ready?" The expected answer is a remorseful "No" from hearers burdened to repair their sinful departures from lawful conduct. The answer from millenarians out on the thin edge of time would be an unburdened and ecstatic, "Yes, hallelujah!"

In the Central African setting, the subversiveness of the doctrine that Christ would arrive on earth "*Soon!*" has a certain irony. When speculation about the apocalyptic End entered the colonies in the unrespectable dress of Watchtower literature, it was not arriving for the first time. The apocalyptic teaching of the Bible was part and parcel of the missions' message. Because Bible translation was an important part of missionary business, this teaching was available not only through the vivid interpretation of Russell and his African successors but also in technicolor detail derived from the original.[43] Moreover, mission churches preached the return of Christ continuously in catechisms, sermons, and hymns. They could no more avoid it and remain Christian than could the Roman Church that St. Augustine so usefully declared to be Christ's millennial kingdom already existent in the world. The more evangelical among the missions made the reality of Christ's Second Coming burn like fire in the minds of sinners. For example, in 1910 the inspired American preacher D. L. Moody preached a guest revival in Nyasaland, producing a luminous flame that singed not only African sinners but also sinners among the upright Scots who had invited him.[44] It emerges from between the lines of the mission reports that this American guest received a heralded welcome and a relieved adieu, the emotional immediacy of his religiously correct teaching having been more than some bargained for.

The heartbeat of even the most conservative Protestant theology, addressed not to oppression but to sin, is that Jesus is coming again—suddenly, if not soon; with cataclysmic effect, if not right away. This teaching of expectation aims partly, of course, to institute discipline through fear of final judgment, but partly as well to communicate Christian hope. Inevitably, therefore, the British officials who accepted the work of Christian missionaries at the same time accepted into the midst of their regime the "explosive charge" that ticks away at the center of the messianic idea, even when that idea appears in conservative dress. As officials struggled with the unintended consequences of the missions' teaching, the issue in dispute came to be the setting of a common clock-under circumstances in which, for political reasons, there could be no such thing as secular time.

Time, Action, Structure, and Millenarian Conduct

Millenarians take a position about the qualitative nature of time, and specifically of a sharply accentuated "now," that has often given the most other-worldly of their theologies this-worldly significance. Their qualitative position about the nature of time is practically consequential not only when they make a millitant or even a military decision to "seize the time," but also when they draw from a theological premise that "the time has come" the ritual conclusion that the law valid before no longer binds them. Intense interest in what the valid bonds do or do not consist of at the End makes antinomianism one of the hallmarks of acting within sight of an apocalyptic End, or in the presence of a messiah.

Jacob Kasuya's dramatic sacrilege can be expressed in terms of time, for it translated into action the arrival of the apocalyptic moment. When people begin to act on the idea that the End is in actuality upon them, they relate what they do in the world to what is in the world with destabilizing attention. Perhaps an analogy is climbing a rock-face while pondering the relationship of each step to the abyss—and looking straight down periodically to verify the precise details. In such circumstances, routine taking of the next step is out of the question; action becomes newly consequential. The notion of the End as imminent brings believers to such a rock-face. By contrast, routine taking of the next step implies an unaccentuated "now," quantitatively arrived at from an unaccentuated previous "now." Inherent in religious and political lawfulness is a metaphorical representation of time that works to direct people away from the rock-face and onto safer ground. In terms of the story quoted earlier: Upon hearing that the messiah has come, the man at work in his field keeps carrying a domesticated plant across a domesticated hill. He lives no accentuated "now." For him, the clock bell tolls as usual, every hour up to twelve and beginning again, like a background Muzak unlistened to and vaguely soporific. But the bell that tolls an accentuated "now" alerts.

As sociologists, we are more usually concerned with time in its literal and objective aspects than in its subjective and metaphorical ones. But if we translate Kasuya's transgression back into terms of our own concept of social structure, we readily see that this concept and the concept of social action contain within them two opposed metaphors through which human beings can conceive the nature of time: the first linear and the second cyclical. The linear metaphor represents time as unique events in irreversible succession. The cyclical one represents time as a repetitive succession of events or, equivalently, as enduring sameness, pattern, and regularity. The directionality of the linear metaphor matches that of all life and of history as modern inhabitants of the West envisage it. The saying that you cannot step into the same river twice fits it, as does narrative. This metaphor lies at the core of our workhorse concept "action." The time metaphor of action is represented in the matches people make between purposes, imagined as accomplished in future time, and the means and conditions of their fulfillment, assessed in the present. The linear and directional metaphor expresses change and novelty. "Time's arrow"[45] in the concept of action, as well as in the concept of history, is the medium in which things are made new.

The opposite time metaphor expresses the antithesis of the new. The formulation in Ecclesiastes fits it: "That which has been done is that which shall be done, and there is no new thing under the sun." Time considered as cyclical underlies—and undergirds—the assumption and the possibility of a relatively permanent and thus predictable social world: "Today is much like yesterday; tomorrow will be much like today. What I see now is an instance of what I have seen before. What I do now is what I have done before and will do again." Time considered as cyclical also undergirds every conception of lawfulness. In this vast metaphorical representation of time reposes that vast universe of rules and routine in which human beings make and remake the regularity and pattern that we sociologists study—and live. Ritual, whether annunciated in a particular sacred realm or otherwise, is no more than a particular instance of this. It not only expresses but also creates its community of participants, both over and against nonmembers and, among members, in the definite relations they have with one another. Religious ritual is only a special case of the repetitiveness that creates the everyday conditions in which social beings continuously (and more or less reliably) predict the outcomes of what they say and do. This cyclical metaphor of time lies at the core of our workhorse concept "structure." In fact, cyclical time is what we must mean by it.[46] Although the concept of structure has sometimes been mistakenly opposed to that of action, through abuse of such formulas as Durkheim's "externality" and "constraint," we readily see the relationship of action to it. As Emile Durkheim demonstrated, in the most fundamental argument of his *The Elementary Forms of the Religious Life*, social structure cannot exist if it is not done—and redone—by social beings. Nor can it exist unless social beings also expect that it will be done—and redone—that is, unless they operate with a cyclical understanding of time.

If we express Kasuya's sacrilege in terms of action, we readily see that social structure is the victim of his having switched the operating metaphor. Out on the apocalyptic edge of time, action, the medium of something new, reveals the inherent logic of undoing that routine doing conceals. Being unforeordained, the next step accentuates the concept of time inherent in action and its tension with the concept of time inherent in structure. Watching in slow motion through a millenarian's lens, we readily see that we, too, move from thinking about action to thinking about structure by shifting the time metaphor that we have in mind. Action that seems not opposed to structure, but a moment of it, is action caught within the orbit, so to speak, of cyclical time, its outward vector moving at a tangent to every point on the invisible circle. Centripetal force is provided by the actor's cyclical vision of "now" as an unaccentuated moment. Viewed in these terms, the concept of action does not carry the golden aura of voluntarism that is sometimes attributed to the role of human agency in realizing structure. In so far as structure is in fact realized, this sort of voluntarism amounts to no more than the abbreviated and interrupted potential for freedom that we find in Ecclesiastes, when the Preacher punctuates his story of striving and the results with the sigh of "vanity and vexation of spirit."

It is the qualitative trait of the apocalyptic moment to intensify the actor's attention to how he answers the questions "What now?" and "What next?" Millenarians proclaim freedom in the most rigorous way. They proclaim not only the "opening of the prison to the captive," as in Isaiah, but also—and above all—the opening of time itself, a thing that can scarcely be said at all, except with the help of poetic images such as Isaiah's quoted by Paul: "Death is swallowed up in victory." Antinomianism expresses in action the dream not only of transcending the old world but also that of stepping outside of cyclical time. The manner in which millenarians do this and, even more, what they get when they do it, turns a yellow beacon upon any sociological formulation that surrounds either concept with the golden aura of freedom. What they get derives from a fundamental feature of the human world that is impossible to transcend. They continue to exist in time.[47] And they cannot continue to exist in time, their only possible locale as living humans, without returning to cyclical time; and so antinomianism transforms itself into "neonomianism," with once inspired action congealing into the obligatory practice of groups.[48] In that light we can see the poignance of the unavoidably self-contradicting integrity of our sociologists' souls, which seek to uncover collective order and pattern as well as individuality and freedom at the same time, and in the same places.

A conception of time that supports routine is fundamental to any human lawfulness. It is the hedge that keeps unfreedom visible to the actor only intermittently. The thread that connects momentary and each-time-unique action and choice to enduring and unchosen structure binds as long as it operates in a time definable by the twinkling of an eye, yet invisible during that twinkling of an eye. In their embrace of the apocalyptic moment, millenarians train a brilliant light precisely on that twinkling of an eye, making visible as action what is normally invisible as structure. For "that which has been done is that which shall be done, and there is no new thing under the sun," they substitute "Behold, all things are new." But, for all things to be new, they have to be done new and made new.

If the logic of antinomian conduct may be understood in terms of time, so may the logic of its socioiogical cognate, anomie. The usual rendering of anomie as "normlessness" camouflages but does not do away with the metaphorical representation of time as cyclical that lies at its core. "Normlessness" is the antithesis of "lawfulness," which is another way of saying "structure"—and cyclical time. Interestingly enough, in his formulation of anomie in *Suicide*, Durkheim illustrated anomie with a dramatically accentuated "now":

the sudden cirumstance of a large-scale financial panic that is correlated with a rise in the incidence of suicide. For Durkheim, anomic suicide results from a pathological condition of social structure, which suddenly deprives the individual of his self-evidently valid map for routine doing—and as a result sets him adrift from life itself. In the normal condition of social structure, valid norms provide for individuals the map for predictable, routine doing that binds groups together and, in consequence, binds individuals to life. In other words, individuals are bound to life by moving along in the succession of unaccentuated "nows" that are the locale of routine doing. Thus, in common with every notion derived from the notion of lawfulness, anomie situates action within the orbit of cyclical time.

Being captive to the time metaphor of lawfulness, the concept of anomie cannot remain agnostic in regard to actual laws. This is not obvious at first glance. Part of a secular discipline, anomie seems a world away from its normatively loaded cognate, antinomianism, as this term is used by religious establishments. Whereas anti-nomianism as epithet refers to particular laws, for the violation of which people may legitimately be punished, anomie refers to a generalized analytical notion of lawfulness, to whose specific content the analyst is not overtly committed. (And that generalized notion of lawfulness need not be concretely defined by the participants. By contrast, those who hurl the epithet mean departures from "*the* law.") We can think of what divides them as the difference between calling alcoholism a sin, for which the actor is morally condemned, or as an impairment and dysfunction, for which he is not. With its analytical content about dysfunction, anomie seems not to share the explicitly judgmental content of antinomianism.

But since ideas of dysfunction only have meaning as departures from what is thought of as normal, the sociological concept of anomie tends to absorb the concrete content of its religious cognate. To apply it empirically at all, one must presume the validity of "lawfulness" as authoritatively defined in a given setting, for there is no other from which to depart. It makes no difference that, in place of establishments' robust charges of wrongdoing, anomie evokes a pale, clinical language about motivational and systemic impairment. The conduct in question still comes into view negatively, not as what it is but as what it is not. In addition, because actors are removed from responsibility, they come into view not in purposeful action of their own but as merely acted upon. For these reasons, when applied to the conduct of millenarians, the concept of anomie never preserves the sense of powerfully affirmative action in an accentuated "now" that is present in so much of the evidence. Instead, it suggests confusion and aimlessness, notions that muddle what must have been the exuberant certainty with which Jacob Kasuya and his coreligionists emancipated themselves from the power of the ancestor shrine by invading the shrine's forbidden midst. Suppressing these affirmative features of the evidence, the concept of anomie tends to foreclose questions about what the conduct of people like these may suggest as to the direction and substance of historical change. Its analytical feet stand resolutely in the world they seek resolutely to leave behind.

With some justice, therefore, critics have said that the failure of functionalism, the theoretical frame to which the concept of anomie belongs, is that functionalism is closed to the analysis of change, and that it has a vision of social life that lets the constructive work done by human subjects occur, so to speak, behind the theory's back. These points are well taken.[49] But it goes more to the heart of the matter to say that, in the hands of many practitioners, functionalism has been guided by only one metaphor of time: time considered as cyclical. To grasp the world of social life, the opposite metaphor is required—not instead of, but as well as. Both metaphors are indispensable, and living humans move back and forth between them. For some purposes, where they are operating within this metaphorical realm must be raised to the status of an explicit empirical question. The concept of anomie contains within it the shortcoming of its theoretical matrix so long as it is deployed without self-consciousness about what the time metaphor it contains can import into the evidence at hand.

Conclusion: Time, Religion, and Politics

If Kasuya's doing can be expressed in terms of time, so can the regime's reaction to his assault upon routine in the customary order. The British regime was parasitic not only upon the production of routine elsewhere, but, more generally upon the capacity of social arrangements to keep people's sense-making within an unaccentuated "now." The proclamation "*Soon!*" enabled preacher-organizers on the neighboring Northern Rhodesian and Congolese Copperbelts to set authoritative dates for large-scale work actions. And it denuded settlers' farms of the laborers who followed preachers off to places of baptism.[50] If acceptance of the doctrine of "*Soon!* " reopened such questions as a farm laborer's continuing under a settler's command, then acceptance of a doctrine of "*Not soon!*"

helped keep them closed. Such examples can be multiplied. But my point is not these historical particulars themselves but what they collectively exhibit about the vital interest that polities acquire in determining universally and authoritatively what time it is and, still more, what the nature and meaning of the passage of time are. British officials sought to root out a theological departure whose concept of time exposed the potential for action to "make all things new." Because heretical preaching of Christ's imminent return widened the fault line between colonizers and colonized, raison d'état called for the orthodox preaching. Thus, the colonial regime that by conquest claimed a monopoly of the legitimate use of force discovered the need to conquer as well a monopoly of the legitimate use of time. In such circumstances, there could be no such thing as secular time.

But, in so far as "secular" refers to the opening of belief to freedom and private choice, there is no such thing as secular time in social life, whatever the circumstances. In Durkheimian terms, the fundamental categories with which human beings think, among them time, are authoritatively made and made real in and through social life. They are embedded in the representations human beings make of society and, as he classically put the point, of "the obscure but intimate relations they have with it." Accordingly, these categories cannot be merely private—even if to exist at all they must also exist privately. As a public or a private matter, metaphorical representations of time are embedded in the construction of groups that are bounded (as well as bound together) by norms. This construction must constantly be redone. Because this redoing is contestable all along the way, time, which is always implicit and implicitly contestable in such construction, can itself become explicit—and explicitly contested. The outcome is never emancipation from time's public being.

What the African case material brings out specifically in regard to religion and politics is that both are dynamic claimants to the fundamental organization of collective life and, not least, to the setting of its calendar and clock. The contests we saw were over how these dynamic claimants in the definition of encompassing order could be made to operate in tandem over much of the same terrain— or how this tandem operation could be disrupted. Part of the battle was over the creation of the unaccentuated "now," the pivot of routine. The British officials tried to make religious time compatible with the sort of overall order that their state sought to impose. In this effort, they presumed as normal the particular sort of institutional map that Britain had arrived at through the turbulent history that produced the constitutional separation of church and state. Justice Macdonnell read from this map his notion of religion "per se." From his standpoint, what appeared to his opponents as religious persecution was no more than an effort to restore what he at first regarded as the inherent distinction between religion and politics. He and his compatriots gradually saw that the distinction they at first understood as natural had in fact to be engineered. This experience forced them to recapitulate some of the turbulent history—including the history of inquisition and persecution—that had preceded the institutional division they carried in their minds. But they had to fight every step of the way, picking their fights trial-and-error fashion, sometimes over ritual propriety, marriage, and sex, sometimes over noise and silence, sometimes over labor relations, sometimes over the date of Christ's return. The concepts "religion" and "politics" did not in themselves delimit inherently distinct realms of belief and conduct. But to wage a just war against a rebellious religiosity, British officials naturally proceeded as if they did.

Similarly today, if people in this country straighten into battle posture when, for example, the archbishop of New York enters the public political fray, it is not because the concepts "religion" and "politics" designate inherently distinct or internally coherent realms of conduct. It is because the archbishop reopens for contest a contingent, historically constructed border between church and state, thus, between religion and politics. The issue at stake for the archbishop and his antagonists is what will be the historically constructed *public* assignment of areas of conduct between religious and political, and between public and private realms. He and they join a noisy argument about what conduct belongs where. If issues concerning family and sex provoke some of the noisiest argument, as in the African setting, it is perhaps because they stand, materially and symbolically, at the structural pivot of any society between known orderliness in the present and its more uncertain perpetuation into the future—that is, at the structural pivot between cyclical and linear time. There is heat, as well as noise, in contests over norms, because it is the nature of norms made explicit to appear, precisely as the way things not only are by nature but should be: as structure and as (obligatory) action.

Our own society's mental map of religion represents it not only as a private affair but also as one that implicates the supernatural. But if we take for granted its other-worldly reference, this in itself is the outcome of public processes within this-worldly relationships. In one of his flourishes in *Elementary Forms*, Durkheim observed that defining religion in terms of the supernatural only became possible after science delimited a natural realm with a discoverable orderliness—and shelved the reality of a supernatural one with its principles of singular intervention. He proceeded to ground religion in a reality not excluded by science: society. It is often said that the failing of his *Elementary Forms* is precisely that it confounds religion with society, leaving no scope, so to speak, for religion "per se." But as we saw, in Macdonnell's setting, no such thing existed except as one side in a continuing contest. What is important about Durkheim's definition, and the analysis of the creative power of ritual doing it supports, is that we are led by it to look at repetitive processes in making the categories of social life, not at categories as completed things—and to see what mental maps these processes both create and require as they both make social structure and make it conceivable.

But the cyclical time that is inherent in the concepts of structure and lawfulness is not always made and remade in social life. Millenarian expectancy is one source of self-conscious shifting away from cyclical time and is a source of movement in collectivities. The significance of this shifting goes beyond millenarian movements. The way in which use of one or the other metaphor of time guides (or does not guide) actors' orientation in some given present can have great public import. Consider the consequences when large numbers of people are plunged by unprecedented events into a dramatically accentuated "now." Even in the most dramatic crisis, astute rulers strive to avoid these consequences by finding ways to make a plausible display that there is "business as usual."

Not long ago, a revolutionary example of this sequence was played out in Tienanmen Square. It was striking that, immediately on the heels of the violent attack they unleashed against the demonstrators, the Chinese rulers ordered a painstakingly minute restoration of the square to its earlier appearance—down to masons crawling on hands and knees. The most observant pedestrian was to go about his business across an unchanged square. Restoring this immense theater of the seen to a past and future permanence was one means of shifting people's attention away from the Democracy Movement's breathlessly accentuated "now," and back to a humdrum march of unaccentuated "nows." Directing actors' attention to the seemingly unproductive movement of the clock, round and round, produces nothing less than the creative but conservative information that "*this*" or "*that*" is next. In contrast to threatened rulers, astute agitators approach with exuberant certainty a fundamental order of business, against "business as usual." They make the bell toll an accentuated present with the corrosive question "*What* now, *what* next?" That freedom is the mother of invention. In the days and weeks before the final assault, all the world saw the public countdown that resulted. We watched as the students marked the square with their moment by finding ever more sensational things to do, in it and to it.

In the symbolic resonance of its methods, and in its corrosive enactment of "*Now*," the Chinese students' politically principled rule-breaking has much in common with theologically principled rule-breaking. The mechanism at work is similar in both cases. This mechanism has fundamentally to do with the ability of regimes, whether religious or political, to define that most ordinary and yet most elusive idea: the time. From defining the time much of importance follows. So it is also with time in the conceptual world of sociology, and especially the metaphorical inner world of its basic concepts. This analysis of antinomian conduct was undertaken in mental dialogue with the long tradition that anomie has in socio-logical (and anthropological) writing on millenarian movements in colonized areas. That tradition is deaf to the bell that tolls for millen-arians; it only sees the sensational doing they launch thereafter— and that seeing, to borrow one last time from St. Paul, is "through a glass darkly." We sociologists are not particularly at home with the concept of antinomianism, which we prefer to leave to the less patterned and rationalized territory patrolled by specialized scholars of religion. Recourse to the term "anomie" indicates at least that we do feel the need from time to time to enter this territory, if without proper travel documents. The phenomena denoted by the term "antinomianism" bear fundamentally upon perhaps the chief and most enduring question sociologists pose: namely, the relation of structure to action.

Notes

This paper owes much to my colleagues Barbara Fields, William Green, Emil Homerin, and J. Andrew Overman, who, more like millenarians than academics, dropped other things and read several versions of this paper: *Soon!*

1. Gershom Scholem, *The Messianic Idea in Judaism: And Other Essays on Jewish Spirituality* (New York: Schocken Books, 1971), p. 13.
2. See, for example, A. H. Newman, "Antinomianianism," Samuel Macauley Jackson in, ed., *The New Schaff-Herzog Encyclopedia of Religious Knowledge*. (New York and London: Funk and Wagnalls, 1908), p. 581.

3. A caution, however: As Ronald A. Knox has pointed out, belief in the imminent second coming of Jesus is a frequent, but not the sole, source of antinomianism. Another religious source is the consciousness that perfected beings cannot sin, no matter what the standards of the unredeemed might be. This consciousness is sometimes but not always associated with millenarian or messianic expectation. A third source, which is sometimes but not necessarily related to the first two, is the routine boundary-marking activities of sects. See his classic *Enthusiasm: A Chapter in the History of Religion* (Oxford: Oxford University Press, 1950), pp. 2–4, 14–15, 583.

4. Scholem, *Messianic Idea*, pp. 7–8.

5. Ibid., p. 164; emphasis added. If Scholem is right about this logic, we should expect to find the pattern repeated in widely disparate contexts; and we do. See, for example, Hillel Schwartz, "Millenarianism: An Overview," in Mircea Eliade, ed., *The Encyclopedia of Religion* (New York: Macmillan, 1987), 9:524.

6. The complex distinctions to be made are not necessary to the present argument. On the relationship, see Schwartz, "Millenarianism," p. 525.

7. Gershom Scholem, *Sabbatai Ẓevi: The Mystical Messiah, 1626–1676*, Bollingen Series, no. 93 (Princeton: Princeton University Press, 1973), p. 12.

8. Scholem, *Messianic Idea*, p. 164.

9. See n. 7 for full reference.

10. J. Macbride Sterrett, "Antinomianism," in *Encyclopedia of Religion and Ethics* ed., James Hastings (New York: Scribner's, 1908).

11. National Archives of Zambia (hereafter NAZ), Sec/Nat 312 (vol. 5), *Bulawayo Chronicle*, "Right About Face," Apr. 22, 1936.

12. In my study *Revival and Rebellion in Colonial Central Africa* (Princeton: Princeton University Press, 1985), I trace the longer sequence to which these spectacular large outbreaks belong. Similar events occurred in the neighboring Belgian Congo. See John E. Higginson, *A Working Class in the Making* (Madison: University of Wisconsin Press, 1989), pp. 168–177. I have used the colonial names of the countries, Northern Rhodesia (now Zambia); the Belgian Congo (now Zaire); and Nyasaland (now Malawi) because this chapter is concerned with events during the period of colonial rule.

13. See Fields, *Revival and Rebellion*, pp. 91–92.

14. See Karen E. Fields, "Christian Missionaries as Anticolonial Militants," *Theory and Society* 11 (1982): 97, which addresses the durable half-truth that Christian missions facilitated colonial rule.

15. Or worse, that the millennium had already begun: In a strange episode that lasted five years, British and Belgian authorities shared intelligence in tracking down a story that a marvelous "native with gold teeth," calling himself America, had come to earth and travelled among the people, preaching dangerously. See Fields, *Revival and Rebellion*, p. 11; also NAZ, ZA 1/10 (1924) Rex vs. Isaac Nyasulo and Rex vs.

J. B. Manda, Mar. 18, 1924. Sec/Nat 312, vol. 1, directeur d'administration to governor, Northern Rhodesia, July 18, 1929 and, vice-
gouverneur. Elizabethville, to governor, Northern Rhodesia, Sept. 9,
1929.

16. Fields, *Revival and Rebellion*, pp. 128–162, presents this episode in
     detail.

17. Kasuya joined the followers of the remarkable Shadrach Sinkala, whose
     unreconstructed militance continued through the 1920s and perhaps
     beyond. See Fields, *Revival and Rebellion*, pp. 139, 152–153, 158, 160,
     and elsewhere.

18. Knox, *Enthusiasm*, pp. 9–24.

19. Fields, *Revival and Rebellion.*, p. 245.

20. NAZ, ZA 1/10 (vol. 3), "Report on Watchtower by UMCA [Anglican]
     Teachers," 1924; *Revival and Rebellion*, p. 210. Note, however, that
     African evangelists for the Anglican mission produced this evidence
     in a hot propaganda war and addressed it to administrators who they
     quaintly imagined would smell sedition in sacrilege and therefore
     intervene.

21. One function of social anthropology was to gain accurate knowledge
     of such rules. Dame Margery Perham recounts how opponents of
     indirect rule denounced anthropology as its "evil genius." See her
     article "A Re-Statement of Indirect Rule," *Africa* 7 (1943): 323. On the
     general subject of adapting supposedly "customary" law to novel
     purposes, see "The Politics of Custom," in *Revival and Rebellion*, pp.
     61–90; and Martin Chanock, *Law, Custom, and Social Order: The
     Colonial Experience in Malawi and Zambia* (Cambridge, Cambridge
     University Press, 1985).

22. Fields, *Revival and Rebellion*, p. 244.

23. Ibid., p. 246.

24. The suggestion tentatively offered is that a comparative method that
     draws on African materials about imperial rule may be used to
     reconsider well-known themes in biblical scholarship. It may prove
     fruitful to relate Jesus' threat to dominant religious symbols—e.g., his
     threat to the temple which, in Mark, is given as the reason for his
     execution—to the threat he posed to kinship as a general principle of
     organization. (The fact that Jesus operated in an apocalyptic milieu
     alive with redeemers, whose demands on their followers were similar,
     would not alter the point.) A close analysis of how modern imperial
     regimes, about whose grassroots workings we have voluminous
     documentation, operated can probably be used deductively to frame
     hypotheses about ancient empires, about whose operation at the level
     of ordinary day-to-day life we have incomparably less direct evidence.
     The meaning of some fragments can perhaps be further reconstructed.
     In addition there is probably much to be learned in this way about
     the effects of ancient imperial rule on native religions and their leaders.
     These suggestions arise out of ongoing conversation with my colleague
     William Scott Green.

25. The question of what elements in these stories belong to the time of Jesus' own teaching (thus, to the apocalyptic moment) is a thorny one in New Testament scholarship. I am indebted to my colleague J. Andrew Overman for the information that these references to kinship obligation in Matthew and Mark are generally acknowledged to belong to the early layer of the tradition.

26. Max Weber quoted from the passage in Matthew that I quoted above, when making the point that congregational religion (as opposed to religion based on the kin group) sets the fellow believer in place of the fellow clansman. He makes an interesting further observation: "Out of all this grows the injunction of brotherly love, which is especially characteristic of congregational religions, *because it contributes very effectively to the emancipation from political organization*" (Max Weber, *The Sociology of Religion* trans., Ephraim Fischoff, [Boston: Beacon Press, 1964], p. 211; emphasis added).

27. A partial exception to this is the career of the preacher Tomo Nyirenda, whose claimed divine mission included the execution of witches, a category that so far as I know in its African manifestations excluded Europeans by definition. This complex story is told by Terence O. Ranger in "The Mwana Lesa Movement of 1925," in Terence O. Ranger and John Weller, eds., *Themes in the Christian History of Central Africa*, (Berkeley: University of California Press, 1975), and, somewhat differently, in my *Revival and Rebellion*, pp. 163–192.

28. NAZ, ZA 1/10 (1925), "Watchtower Natives—Prosecutions of, Comment and Review."

29. In addition, missions from black America labored under a negative presumption that originated in the church-based revolt in neighboring Nyasaland led by John Chilembwe, who studied for a time in the United States. See George Shepperson and Thomas Price, *Independent African: John Chilembwe and the Origins, Setting and Significance of the Nyasaland Native Rising of 1915* (Edinburgh: University Press, 1958).

30. Fields, *Revival and Rebellion*, pp. 225–236.

31. Frederick John Dealtry Lugard, *The Dual Mandate in British Tropical Africa*, 5th ed., (London: F. Cass, 1965), p. 589.

32. NAZ, ZA 1/9/158/2 chief secretary to secretary for native affairs, Apr. 20, 1933, a reference to an event that had occurred many years previously.

33. Fields, *Revival and Rebellion*, pp. 198–203.

34. Ibid., pp. 140, 150, 155, 229.

35. The King James translation, "The Kingdom of Christ is within you," is commonly agreed to be inaccurate. The papyrologist Colin H. Roberts went so far as to suggest the translation "The Kingdom of Christ is within your power." Cited in G. E. M. de Ste. Crois, "Foreward," in Dimitris J. Kyrtatas, *The Social Structure of the Early Christian Communities*, (London: Verso, 1987), p. x.

36. Hans H. Constelmann put forward the theory, still widely accepted, that Luke's two books document the response of the early Christian communities to the delay of the *parousia*. The book's English title, *The Theology of Luke*, erases the vivid time reference of the German original, *Die Mitte der Zeit*—"the middle of time." I am indebted to J. Andrew Overman for this reference and for many instructive discussions about early Christianity.

37. *The Fathers According to Rabbi Nathan*, trans. Anthony J. Saldarini, (Leiden: E. J. Brill, 1975), p. 182. I am indebted to William Green for this reference and for the other points on the sensibility of rabbinic Judaism.

38. Scholem, *Sabbatai Ẓevi*, p. 13.

39. There are traditions in Judaism and Christianity that also handle the problem of "the Hour" in this way. I thank my colleague Emil Homerin for these references and for introducing me to useful sources on messianism in Islam.

40. Yohanan Friedmann, *Prophecy Continuous: Aspects of Ahmadi Religious Thought and Its Medieval Background*, (Berkeley: University of California Press, 1989), pp. 96–97.

41. Abdulaziz Abdulhussein Sachedina, *Islamic Messianism: The Idea of the Mahdi in Twelver Shi'ism*, (Albany: State University of New York Press, 1981), pp. 9, 156–157, 172. I advance this interpretation tentatively, for I deduce from Sachedina's account of the theological problems these elaborations solved that pastoral problems of order must have accompanied them.

42. *Concerning the City of God Against the Pagans*, trans. Henry Bettenson (London: Penguin Books, 1972), pp. 915–918. Citing Heinrich Scholz, Jaroslav Pelikan points out this logical break in Augustine's argument in The *Mystery of Continuity: Time and History, Memory and Eternity in the Thought of Saint Augustine* (Charlottesville, Va.: University Press of Virginia, 1986), p. 103.

43. Perhaps with the partial exception of Catholic missions, which for a time deemphasized Bible reading, by and large, in favor of catechetical methods of teaching. A local administrator in the Lovale country of Northern Rhodesia had this to say about the Catholic outlook on Bible-reading: "I have often wondered what these phrases. . .'Black sheep,' 'Resurrection,' 'Tree of Life,' etc. . . .convey to natives when translated literally, as they are, into the native languages in gospel songs and hymns. . . .I am not a Roman Catholic myself, but was. . .brought up in a Catholic country, the West of Ireland. I believe that the Church discourages the reading of the Bible amongst its ill-educated adherents in numerous countries to prevent these very misunderstandings" (NAZ, Sec/Nat 312 [vol. 1], district commissioner [Kasempa] to chief secretary, Apr. 19, 1932).

44. National Library of Scotland, *Livingstonia News* 3 (1910).

45. This argument draws upon Stephen Jay Gould's masterly account of creative metaphors at the heart of theorizing the earth's "deep time," in *Time's Arrow, Time's Cycle: Myth and Metaphor in the Discovery of Geological Time* (Cambridge, Mass.: Harvard University Press, 1987). It is set out more fully in my paper "Time?" presented at the annual meeting of the American Sociological Association, San Francisco, Calif. August 12, 1989, unpublished typescript.

46. This is true even of "structure" formulated by Anthony Giddens as "out of time." As he points out, although structure can be described "out of time," the maintenance of its "structural identity" cannot be. See *New Rules of Sociological Method: A Positive Critique of Interpretive Sociologies* (London: Hutchinson, 1976), p. 120. I am not, however, using "structure" in the special sense Giddens has chosen to assign it: See his *The Constitution of Society: Outline of the Theory of Structuration* (Berkeley: University of California Press, 1988), pp. 18–19.

47. I pose the question, which I cannot now answer, whether this fact may lead logically, for some, to the antinomian denial of perhaps the ultimate hierarchical distinction, that between life and death—and by this route to the awesome fights to the death or to the deliberate courting of martyrdom that have often accompanied active millenarianism. Think, for example, of the movements led by Jan Bockleson, Alice Lenshina, Jim Jones—and, of course, Jesus. There have been a great many. The group to which Jacob Kasuya belonged cornered themselves in a village house and taunted police by demanding to be killed (even though ultimately they were not). See *Revival and Rebellion*, p. 153.

48. Scholem's *Messianic Idea* offers a rich museum of specimens. Cf. Max Weber's point that charismatic authority only exists *in statu nascendi*, routinization being its unexciting path of survival beyond miracles and victories. See Max Weber, *Economy and Society: An Outline of Interpretive Sociology*, ed. Guenther Roth and Claus Wittich, (Berkeley: University of California Press, 1978), p. 246.

49. Still, the case cannot rest here if we consider how much this flawed theoretical apparatus permitted researchers to learn about societies constructed differently than those in the industrialized West. Nor do the flaws of functionalism in dealing with change stand in abject contrast to impressive new theories.

50. These incidents are described in detail in *Revival and Rebellion*, pp. 198–236.

8

Culture and Politics in Vietnamese Caodàism

Manuel Sarkisyanz

Chapter 5 considered the millennialism of crisis in Peru and the Philippines. In both cases, millennialism received stimulus from alien cultural domination. In Southeast Asia, too, millennialism reached its culmination in reaction to colonial or modernizing political and cultural pressures. Javanese millennialism has been described by a number of authors from Brandes to Justus Van der Kroef.[1] It is associated with prophecies centered around the messianic figure of Ratu Adil, which have been a source of inspiration from the Java War of 1825–1830, if not earlier, to Sukarno's Pantjasila Speech of 1945.[2] In this Javanese millennialism, Islamic messianic Mahdism[3] converges with Hindu-Buddhist notions of cyclical World Ages, the culmination of decline being followed by the return to the archetypical Golden Age with its ideal society.

For a long time, millennialism was wrongly considered a phenomenon limited to Judeo-Christian-Muslim teleology; and the possibility that the archetypical Golden Age could inspire virulent revolutionary millennialism in Buddhist cultures was denied.[4] We showed, however, that in the case of Burma, a Buddhist "millennium" was expected from the advent of Setkya Min (a Burmanization of the canonic Chakkavatti) as far back as 1838, if not earlier.[5] Patricia Herbert has documented the place of this ideological factor in the Burmese Peasant War of 1930–1932.[6] Until L. E. Lomax was confronted with them in Thai politics around 1967, the existence of millenarian rebels in Thailand was unknown to American area specialists.[7] It subsequently became the subject of studies by Walter Skrobanek in Heidelberg and John Murdoch and Charles Keyes in the United States.[8] Evidence of millennialism in Cambodia against the Vietnamese in 1820, and against the order of the French Protectorate in 1866 and 1916, has been presented by David Chandler and Milton Osborne.[9] Similar evidence concerning millennialism in 1927 had been revealed by the French colonial police.[10]

In all these cases millennialism appeared as a response to crisis situations, with such typical accompanying phenomena as notions of invulnerability for the elect who were to survive the universal cataclysm.[11] Throughout the area millennialism appears as a vision of return to an ideal archetype of the social order.[12] These characteristics appear also in Vietnamese Caodàism and its antecedents. Thus the subsequent Caodàist dignitary Tu' Mǎt had been active in "messianic" peasant revolts in 1913 in the Cholon and in 1916 in the Saigon areas, which were associated with expectations of the end of the world, the opening up of the earth. The celestial powers would destroy the French fleet with "rainbows of stone"; the spirits were to assist the new emperor, "Phan, the Red Dragon," who was conspiring together with Tu' Mǎt. A great epidemic would kill millions of people, so that only his followers would survive. Another "Phan, a Red Dragon" is said to have appeared to the peasant Lê Văn Trung, one of the founders of Caodàism.[13] The developing institutions of Caodàism were to lead as an ark of salvation the young and the old, the chosen saints and the wise, from a world "turned upside down" to the (Taoist) islands of the fairies—while without it certain destruction would be the destiny of the world.[14] Perhaps already since 1919 the spirits, with whom the founders of Caodàism communicated, were dictating the song about the "Advent of the Celestial Emperor" as promise of cosmic harmony.[15]

Jayne Werner wrote in her dissertation: "In the 1920's and 1930's some Caodàist peasants were known to have joined the sect for political reasons . . . to see Vietnam independent, with the monarchy restored. Some Caodàist leaders may have been seen as messianic . . . leaders, capable of restoring the golden age of the past, in line with a millenarian expectation that Caodàism would constitute a new age of liberation and freedom from hardship."[16] An attraction of joining Caodàism was constituted by the expectation that its "Grand Day of Restoration" (*Phục Hội*) or deliverance would soon come.[17] Even still in 1933 Caodàists were reported to announce the end of the world, implying that only those joining their "rebellion" would be saved. (For this purpose magic preparations of invulnerability were being made.) Expecting the end of the world some peasants (in areas afflicted by drought) stopped working altogether.[18]

The full designation of Caođàism (*Đại-Đạo Tam-Kỳ Phổ-Độ*) means "Great Way of the Third Epoch of Salvation." The Golden Age is to follow an Age of Proselytizing through miracles (1926–1937) and an Age of Temptation (1938–1948) with its eight disasters. Caođàism was to restore the primeval fraternity in an Age of Universal *Humanitas* "in 1950–1961."[20] After a War of Eighteen Years the Golden Age was to be finally established in 1996.[21] There are Caođàist prophecies that it was to be ushered in by the advent of the ideal ruler "Minh Vu'o'ng." While he has apparently Taoist associations (with the Jade Emperor), the Caođàist teleology of world ages is Buddhist and its Golden Age shows symbolic connections with the coming Buddha Maitreya.[22] Ideological associations with him formed part of the tradition of rural rebellions in the world of Chinese culture, the best-known case being the movement of the White Lotus in China of 1796–1804.[23]

As far as parts of the Caođàist peasantry inherited such revolutionary traditions of millennialism, the following generalizations of Jayne Werner apply: "These Caođàist peasants were probably not driven to violence for economic reasons alone.. . . . Messianism and apocalyptism in Caođàism may well have provided the religious incentive to rebellion."[24] "There seems to be little question that Caođàism was a nativistic or revitalization movement." Yet the following also applies: "It would be inaccurate to *define* it as a millennial or messianic one. The millennial vision was undoubtedly present in Caođàist ideology, but it does not appear to have been *the* major factor responsible for the movement's large following"; "Revolutionary qualities present in Caođàism were not developed. Unlike the Taiping in China, the Caođàist aims did not become the overthrow of the existing political and social status quo."[25]

This was partly due to Caođàism having originated less as a reaction to economic crisis (mass misery was greater in northern Annam and parts of Tonking than in South Vietnamese areas where Caođàism spread) than in reaction to a cultural crisis. Precisely among the southern Vietnamese urban elites most affected by this crisis did Caođàism originate—before it attracted the "traditionalist" rural masses. (After allegedly converting 20,000 within two months after its foundation, it allegedly embraced two-thirds of Tây Tinh Province in 1953.[26]) Urban elite politicians, acculturated if not fully assimilated through French education, and aspiring like Nguyễn Phan Long through their "Constitutionalist party" to extend the political rights valid in France to French Cochinchina, did join and promote Caodàism. Possibly the purpose was to provide their political aspirations with a mass following that they otherwise lacked.[27] But it is also possible that the (cosmic) secret on which (according to Paul Mus[28]) French-educated Vietnamese intellectuals of the early twentieth-century suspected French superiority to be founded (doubting that what they had learned about natural sciences, their application, rational organization and utilization of natural powers etc., constituted *all* that there was behind French superiority) was sought in the new synthesis of Caodàist esoterics.

The Caodàist synthesis of the intellectually esoteric with the mythically popular, of "internationally" French-imported values with the "native" Vietnamese ones, may also have offered a solution to the acculturated Vietnamese intellectual's identity problems: identity in relation to French "metropolis"—toward which the Vietnamese acculturated intellectual minority felt inferior by virtue of not being "Europeanized" enough—and in relation to the rural majority from which it was isolated through having become too Europeanized. By "supplementing" Vietnamese additions to French values Caodàism provided Westernized urban Vietnamese with something like a cultural bridge to the premodern peasant masses. And the Caodàist universalization of the message of Vietnamese religious traditions gave South Vietnamese intellectuals, previously dependent on models from France, a mission in relation to the whole of humanity, including the West. (Just as had been the case with the intelligentsia of the Petersburg period, when the Slavophilism, Narodnik populism and Tolstoyism incorporated and universalized selections from presecular Russian rural values, both emancipating it from European dependence and providing it with some cultural links with the rural people. Similarly as had been the case with India's intelligentsia, which adopted (Gandhism, or, for example, the Peruvian intelligentsia of Cuzco of the 1920s that made glorifications of the archaically Amerindian a part of its revolutionary *Indigenismo* with a universal mission of "Incaic socialism."[29])

Thus in 1926, the year of the foundation of Caodàism, one of its "Messages from the Spirit" declared: "Humanity is killing itself off. It has not been well served by science and it provokes. . . .wars. The holy doctrine of Christianity only serves to envenom the ambition of the strong. . . . A new doctrine is needed, capable of making mankind love all creatures. Only the Annamite nation retains religiously the (millennial) cult of the dead. Although this nation has only known servitude since its creation, it will be what I desire it to be."[30] And the Cao Đài Spirit declared in the revolutionary situation of 1930: "This doctrine in this world brings heavenly peace, liberty spotted with blood, denied and withered. . . .To the peoples of the West. . .I have given the peace of soul and comfort of life. But they continue to deny the prophecy of Christ. . ."[31] And the spirit of the liberal humanist Victor Hugo proclaimed in 1930 and 1933 to the Caođàists of French Cochinchina: "The right of freedom. . .proclaimed by humanitarian France. . .has been betrayed. Her representatives, unworthy of her, dishonour her." "The world will be one, one in religion, one in government, one in the New Era, as the old social forms will be defunct."[32]

In the person of the converted French Captain Monnet, who from 1923 advocated a Vietnamization of Christianity, Caođàism allegedly found in 1926 one of its "high priests."[33] French positivism contributed to Caođàism much of its pantheon of great men: besides Victor Hugo also Jeanne d'Arc and Admiral Duclos—side by side with revolutionary contemporaries like Sun Yat Sen.[34] Precisely the lack of dogmatic exclusiveness permitted Caođàism to attract heterogeneous teachings.[35] There were "spirit-inspired" prophecies that Caođàism, as synthesis of all religions of Vietnam—and potentially contained in all religions of humankind—would not only determine Vietnam's future by becoming its national religion but also the revelation for the whole world.[36]

On the other hand, as Alexander Woodside has pointed out, Caođàism bestowed a universalist legitimization on Vietnamese Confucianism such as it had not previously possessed, thus contributing an important attempt of reintegrating Vietnamese society. As Caođàism also integrated Buddhist traditions and folk Taoism as well as (aside from one exception) the ancestor cults, it came close to preserving the homogeneousness of Vietnamese village society.[37] And precisely the Catholic-inspired "hierarchization" that Caođàism contributed (its perhaps most influential hierarch, the so-called "Pope" Phạm Công Tắc had previously been a Catholic) made it a successful rival of Catholicism.[38] Caođàism had a start over Catholicism in the race for Vietnam's emancipation: It supplied Vietnamese alternatives to Western symbols—with Vietnamese popes as alternatives to Roman ones, the Vietnamese Spirit Eye instead of the Western cross.[39] Basic values of Vietnamese traditional society were revitalized against French acculturation—and even universalized by being made an object of ecumenic revelation. Precisely the crisis of Sino-Vietnamese culture and society that followed upon the consolidation of French rule stimulated the need for a new revelation of the will of heaven. Yet, according to Woodside, this very Caođàist revelation gave transcendental sanctions for the largely irreversible breach with Vietnamese traditions—that is, for acculturation and social transformations. In 1926, at a time when cooperation of Vietnamese and French seemed more possible than ever before— or ever after—the celestial spirit Cao Dao revealed that the French and the Vietnamese were his beloved children and that he desired to unite them forever.[40] For the French-acculturated Vietnamese bureaucrats the Caodàism that emerged from their midst fulfilled a need to sanction compatibility of French instruction with Sino-Vietnamese culture (for example, through the integration of French heroes into a Taoist-led pantheon), for compatibility between loyalty to France with the whole pressure of the Vietnamese environment.[41] Such needs were fulfilled precisely through selective borrowings of French cultural elements. The, so to say, "positivistically scientific" aspect of Kardec's spiritism came in Caodàism to harmonize with Vietnamese popular animism. Thus French methodology endowed the French-acculturated founders of Caodàism with a kind of heavenly commission of a high divine authority of Taoism. (The Cao Dài Spirit was identified with the Taoist Jade Emperor.) Thus Caodàism was soon able to spread beyond the urban elements of Vietnamese employees of the colonial administration, Vietnamese students and workers, to the rural masses of southern Vietnam. Its early spiritistic seances had attracted masses of the curious. In order to attract and hold believers, the entire complex of taboos and sanctions of Vietnamese popular religiosity was subsequently integrated into the initially urban and elitist Caodàism.[42]

Thus Caodàism contained an attempt to give a new social integration to dissolving Vietnamese society" to give it back a "streamlined" version of what, I. M. de Groot had called "universism."[43] It was precisely in the directly French-administered South Vietnam, the region with the most deeply reaching dissolution of Confucian society and culture, it was in Cochinchina which through acculturation had been separated from the Confucian monarchy with its ritual function so that local animistic cults revived precisely there, that Caodàism originated.

The "unclassic" spirit cults had been traditionally as suspect to the Confucian state with its rational "utopian" ideal[44] as the (partly millenarian) secret societies that were frequently linked with them. They were targets of control if not repression measures. The notion of uncontrolled or uncontrollable cults constituting a danger to the state was inherited from Sino-Vietnamese tradition by the French colonial police, for whom fears of subversion through Vietnamese secret societies made these appear as "trouble-makers of three centuries."[45] On the other hand, as Ralph Smith pointed out, to the spirit of a leader of an anti-French rising of 1874 was attributed a message relating to Caodàism.[46] An organizer for the Vietnamese "counteremperor" Cu'ò'ng Dê and the independence fighter and ideologist Phan Bội Châu (1867–1940)—an early influence on Hồ Chí Minh—had been regional head of the Minh-su' sect to which the Spirit Cao Dài had manifested himself before Caodàism was organized.[47] The links of Caodàist origins with Vietnamese monarchical resistance against French domination extended also to revolutionary nationalism and communism. According to French police sources, the leftist nationalist and "protocommunist" Nguyễn An Ninh promoted Caodàism, one of whose spiritistic mediums worked with his revolutionary newspaper *L'Indochine*.[48] Promises of an ideal society without taxation and usury were found by Vietnamese of Cambodia in Caodàism in 1927, during the year following its foundation—precisely at the time of communist ascendancy in south Vietnam.[49] As Werner has pointed out, Caodàist peasants also participated in the 1930–1931 communist-led anti-taxation revolutionary movement, wearing as charms both the Cao Dài Eye and the Hammer and Sickle. The centers of uprisings in Cochinchina were also the areas of heavy concentration of Caodàists. In nativistic style was spread the belief that only those joining Caodàism would be saved in the impending catastrophe of revolution. Police believed that Caodàism was used to popularize the expectation of collapse of the existing order (although the opposite "functional" relationship is more likely). "The line between religion and revolution was a thin one and the conditions of peasant unrest were such that at least some peasants indiscriminately flocked to both religion and revolution."[50]

There were also numerous Caodàists on a Communist Action Committee of 1937.[51] Even the most uncompromising Communists, the Trotskyists, maintained friendly relations with the Caodàist center of Tây Ninh. Their leaders visited that "See" at the invitation of the Caodàist "Pope" Phạm Công Tắc.[52] Even in 1940 some temples of the Caodàist Tiên Thiên subsect were reported to have joined forces with Communists.[53]

The postwar expansion of Caodàism in southern Vietnam outdistanced in the years of 1946–1954 that of the communist-led Việtminh. The Caodàists constituted there the only large-scale organized noncommunist peasant groups.[54] The Caodàist communities—like the Catholic communities in Vietnam already before them—were held together by stronger ties of solidarity than those common in their environment. In addition to mutual obligations of family relationships, Caodàists were to practice denominational solidarity; assistance for the poor that did not belong to one's family was something new in Vietnam.[55] Caodàism spread also through organized mutual assistance and cooperatives that contributed to the protection of rice cultivators against the price manipulators of Saigon-Cholon during crisis situations.[56] Welfare and charity were the task of Caodàism's Third Office (Co'-quan Phuôc Thiên).[57] The Caodàist Executive (Cú'u Trùng Đài) administered through its Red ("Confucian") Branch (symbolizing authority) the personnel, through its Yellow ("Buddhist') Branch (symbolizing virtue) finances, buildings, public works, and markets, and through its Blue ("Taoist") Branch (symbolizing tolerance and peace) charities and teaching. The functioning of this differentiated and "modern" bureaucracy was (theoretically) to be ratified through messages from spirits.[59] But in the course of this very institutionalization these spiritistic experiences of messages from spirits lost importance in relationship to the Caodàist bureaucracy.[60]

Thus in the case of Caodàism—as in the case of other millenarian movements—the nonfulfillment of the millennium resulted in the transition from movements into institutions and in the strengthening of organizational features at the expense of the dynamic.[61] The organizational structure of Caodàism was much more effective than that of other "unfulfilled" millennialisms of Southeast Asia as already the pre-French Vietnamese state had been far more effectively organized than any other premodern Southeast Asian state. In this process the once—at least partially—"millennarist" Caodàism developed features otherwise associated with the "utopian" Confucian state—utopian in the sense of Wolfgang Bauer. In contrast to the millenarian finality of time, the road to which leads through the desert irrigated with the blood of the martyrs, the timeless utopia does not distinguish between the elect and the damned of this earth, preserving its permanence across time.[62] A natural order in harmony with the cosmos is the archetype of utopia, of a society releasing the individual from the burden of freedom by immuring him in the social structures sanctioned by cosmic relationships.[63] It was somehow in this sense that the old Confucian and the Caodàist society was legitimizing itself out of universal cosmic rationality, realized in the most perfect society possible, whose social harmony was to be reflecting universal harmony. In so far as utopia fulfills perfection, in so far as it represents the final harmony, it has to be a union of *all* people. By definition the perfect utopia may not tolerate differences of opinion. In the fulfilled utopia there are conspicious limits of tolerance.

Forced conversions on the part of postwar Caodàists[64] were perhaps not alien to this context, as may have been their general

political reorientations since 1946. (Caodàism was the first component of the Việtminh to break with that communist-led coalition
in 1946–1947, the first noncommunist organization under the
Saigon government to demand complete independence from France,
the main support of all South Vietnamese governments before the
Catholic dictatorship of Ngô Đinh Diệm, having provided the first
the first prime minister to serve in Saigon under the ex-emperor Bảo
Đại.[65]) Even after Caodàists became reconciled with republican
(instead of monarchical) government, the social and cultural emphasis of their most representative authority of Tây Ninh, that of
Phạm Công Tắc, was "restorative" in an almost Confucian sense.[66]
But, contrary to circumstantial political appearances, when he had
demanded the restoration of monarchy in 1947, he was proclaiming
monarchist demands attributed to him by French intelligence
already in the revolutionary year 1930–1931.[67] Already the announce-
ment about the foundation of Caodàism sent to the French governor
of Cochinchina in 1926 had proclaimed prototypes of an idealized
past models for the future, declaring:

> During former times the people were so carefree that they could
> sleep without closing their doors. . . .This beautiful time no
> longer exists for the following reasons: . . .The practioners of [the
> three] religions. . .have distorted the significance of saintly
> doctrines. The Annamese at present have completely abandoned
> their good morals and traditions of former times. . . .The aim
> pursued by the undersigned is to bring back the peace and
> harmony of the former times to the people. We will thus be
> leading towards a new era.[68]

And in 1948, in spite of the main pragmatic transformations of
Caodàist political positions, Phạm Công Tắc reiterated that filial
piety was the basis of social ethics, through which, according to him,
Vietnam had been superior even to China:

> China had a similar civilization to ours, but to a lesser degree.

> The duty of the first notable was to protect the life of the people
> so that the national land could be re-distributed as communal
> land. In former times the common land. . .was plentiful because
> the people did not follow a capitalist mode of prouction. Villagers
> were asked to labor. . .the common land.

> Our society can no longer be the father and mother of the
> people. . . .The behavior of the father to the son had to be

duplicated in the behavior of the lord to the villager. If we had
been able to preserve the organization handed down by our
forefathers, then we would never have had the evil we have today
or the suffering or the confusion brought about by the under-
mining of morality.. . .The Caodàist religion can restore society
to its former state.[69]

Thus the restorative demands of the most representative Caodàist
authority actually reiterated amidst the conservative reaction of
postwar Vietnamese politics what Caodàism had announced already
at the time of its foundation, when it had been attributed revolutionary aspirations.

Attempts to classify Caodàism in terms of the stereotypes of
"traditional" or "modern" have not been very illuminating.[70] Nor
is our understanding of the phenomenon furthered by choosing
between the "moral economy" and "rational choice" approaches.[71]
Caodàism, rather, belongs to the category of millennially tinged
traditions of agrarian societies. Like other such traditions considered
in Chapter 5, millenarian expectations are among its essential
ingredients, owing to the timelessness of the eternal return of the
world order with its periodic renovation through re-volutions.

Notes

In the transcription of Vietnamese names I was kindly helped by my
research assistant Dr. J. Unselt of Heidelberg.

1. J. Brandes, "Iets over een ouderen Dipanegara in verband met een
    prototype van de voorspellingen van Jajabaya," *Tijdschrift voor
    Indische Taal-, Land en Volkenkunde* 32 (1889); Justus van der Kroef,
    "Javanese Messianic Expectations: Their Origin and Cultural Context,"
    Comparative Studies in Society and History 1, no. 4 (1959); 229–323.
2. *Lahirnja Pantjasila (The Birth of Pantjasila). President Soekarno's
    Speech of 1 June, 1945.* Issued by the Ministry of the Republic of
    Indonesia. Cf. Manuel Sarkisyanz, *Südostasien seit 1945* (München,
    1961), p. 144.
3. Sarkisyanz, *Rußland und der Messianismus des Orients* (Tübingen:
    Mohr, 1955), pp. 223–307.
4. W. Mühlmann, *Chiliasmus und Nativismus. Studien zur Psychologie,
    Soziologie und historischen Kasuistik der Umsturzbewegungen*
    (Berlin: D. Reimer, 1961), pp. 367–375; Ernst Benz, *Buddhas
    Wiederkehr und die Zukunft Asiens* (München, 1963), pp. 15–16.
5. Sarkisyanz, *Buddhist Backgrounds of the Burmese Revolution* (The
    Hague: M. Nijhoff, 1965).

6. Patricia Herbert, *The Hsaya San Rebellion (1930–1932) Reappraised*, Monash University Centre of Southeast Asian Studies, *Working Papers*, no. 27.
7. L. E. Lomax, *Thailand, the War That Is, the War That Will Be* (New York: Random House, 1967), pp. 65, 70–71; Sarkisyanz, "Die Religionen . . .Thailands," in Christel Matthias Schröder, *Religionen der Menschheit* (Stuttgart, 1975), 23:490–493, 533.
8. John B. Murdoch, "The 1901–1902 Holy Men's Rebellion," *Journal of the Siam Society* (1974): 47–66; Charles F. Keyes, "Millenianism, Theravâda Buddhism and Thai Society," *Journal of Asian Studies* 36, no. 2 (1977): 283–302; Walter Skrobanek, *Buddhistische Politik in Thailand mit besonderer Berücksichtigung des heterdoxen Messianismus* (Wiesbaden, 1976).
9. David P. Chandler. "An Anti-Vietnamese Rebellion in Early Nineteenth century Cambodia: Pre-colonial Imperialism and a Pre-nationalist Response," *Journal of Southeast Asian Studies* 6, no. 1 (1975): 18, 22f.; Milton Osborne, "Peasant Politics in Cambodia: The 1916 Affair," *Modern Asian Studies* 12, no. 2 (1975): 228, 231.
10. Gouvernement Général de l'Indochine. Direction de la Sûreté, *Le Caodaisme* (Hanoi, 1934), pp. 35–38, 95–96, 100.
11. Kenelm Burridge, *New Heaven, New Earth: A Study of Millenarian Activities* (New York: Schocken, 1969); Bryan R. Wilson, *Magic and the Millennium: A Sociological Study of Religious Movements of Protest among Tribal and Third-World Peoples* (New York: Harper and Row, 1973); Michael Barkun, *Disaster and the Millennium* (New Haven: Yale University Press, 1974); V. Lanternari, *Religions of the Oppressed: A Study of Modern Messianic Cults* (New York: Knopf, 1963); A. G. Schutte, *Die nationalistischen Bewegungen als Handelnsabläufe* (n.p., 1969); Michael Adas, *Prophets of Rebellion: Millenarian Protest Movements Against European Colonial Order* (Chapel Hill, University of North Carolina Press, 1979).
12. Mircea Eliade, *Kosmos und Geschichte. Der Mythos von der ewigen Wiederkehr* (Düsseldorf, 1966), pp. 10–15, 20–28, 55–79.
13. Jayne Werner, *The Cao Đài: Politics of a Vietnamese Syncretic Religious Movement* (Thesis, Cornell University, 1976: University Microfilms, 76–21, 143), pp. 55, 125, 131, 133; Gouvernement de la Cochinchine, "*Réquisitoire de l'affaire du complot Saigon-Cholon*," by G. Michel (Saigon, 1915); Sûreté Générale, "La propagande anti-française dans les milieux religieuses de la Cochinchine," p. 29; *L'Opinion* (Saigon), May 29, 1928; G. Coulet, *Secret Societies in Annam* (1952), pp. 204–205.
14. Phan Truong Manh, *Qu'est ce que le Caodaisme?* (Saigon, 1949), pp. 17, 31, 204.
15. Alexander Woodside, *Community and Revolution in Modern Vietnam* (Boston: Houghton Mifflin, 1976), p. 186.
16. Werner: Houghton Mifflin, *Cao Đài*, p. 497.

216 **Manuel Sarkisyanz**

17. Ibid., p. 116: *L'Opinion* (Saigon), May 29, 1928.
18. Werner, *Cao Đài*, p. 132: Political Reports of the Troisième Bureau, n.d.; monthly report of the Tây Ninh province chief, Nov. 1931; *Le Courier de Saigon*, July 18, 1933.
19. Ralph Smith, "Introduction to Caodaism," *Bulletin of the London School of Oriental and African Studies* 33 (1970).
20. Phan Truong Manh, *Qu'est ce que le Caodaisme?* p. 204: Quoting *Review Caodaïque*, Dec. 1950, pp. 91–92.
21. Smith, "Introduction," p. 581; Louis Bezacier, "Der Caodaismus," in: Chr. M. Schröder, ed., *Religionen der Menschheit* (Stuttgart, 1975), 23:352.
22. A. M. Savani, *Visage et images du Sud-Viet-Nam* (Saigon, 1955), p. 91; Smith, "Introduction," pp. 580–581.
23. E. P. Poršneva, *Učenie "Belogo Lotosa"—Ideologija narodnogo vosstanija*, [The Teaching of the "White Lotus"—Ideology of the People's Uprising]. (Moscow, 1972), pp. 37–68.
24. Werner, *Cao Đài*, p. 140.
25. Ibid., pp. 522, 531, 532; emphasis added.
26. Ibid., p. 34: Tô Vân Quá, "Rapport militaire sur la province de Tây Ninh," in Trân Huy Liệu, ed., Tài-Liệu Tham-Khảo, Cách-Mạng Tháng Tam [Research Documentation to the August Revolution of 1945 (Materials)], (Hanoi, 1960), 2: 365; Gabriel Gobron, *History and Philosophy of Caodaism* (Saigon, 1950).
27. Werner, *Cao Đài*, pp. 66, 506.
28. Paul Mus, *Sociologie d'une guerre* (Paris, 1952) p. 133.
29. Sarkisyanz, *Rußland* pp. 84–196; José Tamayo Herrera, *Historia del indigenismo cuzqueño* (Lima, 1980), pp. 25, 352–360, 362–363.
30. Spiritistic seance at Tây Ninh on Oct. 1, 1926: Werner, *Cao Đài*, p. 593.
31. Spiritistic seance on Feb. 16, 1930: Werner, *Cao Đài*, p. 598.
32. Seances on Dec. 11, 1930, and Aug. 15, 1933: Werner, *Cao Đài*, pp. 590, 599.
33. Gobron, *Caodaism*, p. 28; Sûreté, "La propagande," pp. 22–24.
34. Gobron, *Caodaism*, p. 73; Victor Oliver, *Caodai Spiritism* (Leiden: Brill, 1976), p. 1; Bezacier, "Der Caodaismus," p. 352–353.
35. Oliver, *Caodai Spiritism*, p. 85.
36. Gobron, *Caodaism*, p. 47; Savani, *Visage*, p. 99.
37. Woodside, *Community*, pp. 47, 186; cf. Gerald Hickey, *Village in Vietnam* (New Haven: Yale University Press, 1964), p. 277.
38. Nguyên Trân Huân "Histoire d'une secte religieuse au Vietnam: Le Caodaisme," in Jean Chesneaux, ed., *Tradition et révolution au Vietnam*, (Paris, 1971), p. 202.
39. Ibid., p. 202; Woodside, *Community*, p. 186.
40. Oliver, *Caodai Spiritism*, p. 44.
41. Woodside, *Community*, p. 186; Dennis Duncancon, *Government and Revolution in Vietnam*, (London, 1968), p. 125.
42. Allan Kardec, *Das Buch der Medien* (Wiesbaden, 1977), pp. 25–142; Huân, "Histoire," pp. 197, 202; Hickey, *Village*, pp. 290–291; Oliver, *Caodai Spiritism*, p. 45.

43. J. M. de Groot, *Universismus, Grundlage der Religion und Ethik Chinas* (Berlin, 1918), pp. 303–384.
44. Wolfgang Bauer, *China und die Hoffnung auf Glück. Paradiese, Utopien, Idealvorstellungen in der Geistesgeschichte Chinas* (München, 1974).
45. Sûreté, "La propagande," p. 101, 103.
46. Smith, "Introduction," p. 348.
47. Werner, *Cao Đài*, p. 133: Government de la Cochinchine, "Réquisition de l'affaire du complot Saigon-Cholon," G. Michel, Saigon, C. Ardin, 1975; Oliver, *Caodai Spiritism*, pp. 28–29, Smith, "Introduction," p. 340.
48. Werner, *Cao Đài*, pp. 68, 87: Trần Huy Liệu, Đáng Thanh-Niên [Youth Party], Hanoi: N. X. B. Sú Học, 1961; Office of the 'Ministère des Colonies', "Note sur l'activité des partis d'opposition antifrançais en Indochine," Winter–Spring, 1928.
49. Sûreté, "La propagande," p. 96.
50. Werner, *Cao Đài*, pp. 74–75: Office of the 'Ministère des Colonies', "Note sur l'activité des partis d'opposition antifrançais en Indochine," Winter–Spring, 1928; Governor Krautheimer, "Les incidents en Cochinchine," May–June 1931; Summary of Nguyễn An Ninh's view by Trần Văn Giàu, interview, Jan. 10, 1974.
51. Werner, *Cao Đài*, p. 177: "*La Lutte*" (Saigon), Mar. 25, 1937, in D. Hémery, "Révolutionnaires légaux et pouvoir colonial à Saigon de 1932 à 1937" (Thèse, Université de Paris VII, 1974) p. 342.
52. Werner, *Cao Đài*, p. 194: Governor Pagès, monthly report to the Governor General, Dec. 1936, Pagès Papers.
53. Werner, *Cao Đài*, p. 200: Sûreté, "La propagande, p. 45.
54. Werner, *Cao Đài*, pp. 503, 509.
55. *Area Handbook for South Vietnam*, by H. H. Smith, D. W. Bernier, F. M. Bunge, F. C. Rintz, Rinn-Sup Shin, and S. Teleki (Washington, 1967), p. 185.
56. Woodside, *Community*, p. 187; Hickey, *Village*, pp. 98, 143.
57. *Handbook*, p. 185.
58. Gorbron, *Caodaism*, p. 130; Oliver, *Caodai Spiritism*, pp. 50, 60.
59. Ibid., pp. 31, 76, 126.
60. Ibid., p. 55.
61. Mühlmann, *Chiliasmus*, p. 275.
62. Sarkisyanz, *Die Kulturen Kontinental-Südostasiens* (Wiesbaden, 1979), p. 120; Sarkisyanz, "Politische Utopien," in A. Peisi and Armin Mohler, eds., *Kursbuch der Weltanschauungen* (Berlin, 1981), pp. 35, 70.
63. Jean Servier, *Der Traum von der großen Harmonie* (München, 1971), p. 357.
64. Werner, *Cao Đài*, p. 346; L. Bodard, *La Guerre d'Indochine* (Paris: Editions Gallimard, 1963–1965), pp. 124–138.

65. Cf. Sarkisyanz, "Caodaismus," in *Theologische Realenzyklopädie,* 7:633–636.

66. Werner, *Cao Đài,* p. 298: Đại-Đạo Tam-Kỳ Phô-Độ Tòa-Thánh Tây Ninh [The Holy See of the "Great Way of the Third Epoch" (Cao-Dai) in Tây-Ninh], Lò'i Thuyêt-Đạo cūa Đū'c Hộ-Pháp [The Teaching of the Holy Protector of the Faith] (1948). 1:41.

67. Werner, *Cao Đài,* p. 128: Nguyễn Công Bình, "Việt-Nam Chống Chu Nghĩa Thụ'c Dân, nhū'ng suy nghĩ độc lập cúa nhà sử học Mỹ David B. Marr" [Anti-Colonialist Viet-Nam, the Independent Reflections of the American Historian David G. Marr], *Nghiên-Cú'u Lịch-Sỉl* [Historical Research] 144 (1974): 43–53.

68. Werner, *Cao Đài,* pp. 629–630.

69. Werner, *Cao Đài,* pp. 651, 659, 663–664. (appendix K): Đại-Đạo Tam-Kỳ Phô-Độ, Tòa-Thánh Tây-Ninh, *Lời Thuyêt Đạo* cú'a Dức Hộ-Pháp, Năm Mậu-Tý (1948) [Sermons of the Venerable *Hộ-Pháp* 1948] (Tây-Ninh: Holy See Printing House, 1973) [Selections of sermons delivered by *Hộ-Pháp* Phạm Công Tắc at the Great Divine Temple Cao Đài Holy See, Tây Ninh Province 1948].

70. It is no wonder that political science dependent on such "models" does not lead very far concerning this topic. See Frances R. Hill, "Millenarian Machines in South Vietnam," *Comparative Studies in Society and History* 13 (1971): 325–326.

71. See the Introduction.

9

Millennial Beliefs, Hierocratic Authority, and Revolution in Shi'ite Iran

Said Amir Arjomand

The emotive force of the modern myth of revolution derives at least as much from the underlying religious apocalyptic imagery as from any secular philosophy of history. It is therefore not surprising that religion and the cultural tradition it creates can play an important role in political revolutions,[1] as in social transformation more generally.[2] Religious factors can significantly affect both the causes and the consequences of revolutions: they can provide motives for revolutionary action, as well as the actors' idiom for understanding their own action, and can provide the repertory of the value-ideas that are selectively institutionalized by revolutions. Indeed, the emergence of an autonomous cultural tradition, created by the world religions and resting on the institutionalization of the tension between the transcendental and the mundane in the post-Axial Age civilizations can be considered the fundamental precondition of teleological or directional sociopolitical change set in motion by ideological politics and political revolutions of modern times.[3]

Shi'ite religious beliefs, and institutional structures historically shaped by them, have been crucial in the motivation and determination of revolutionary action in the history of Iran. The present account will focus primarily on the revolutionary potential of millennial beliefs. But the institutional structure will also be considered briefly.[4]

The Institutionalization of Hierocratic Authority and Societal Change in Shi'ite Iran

The seeds of the present revolutionary transformation of Iran were contained in the Shi'ite tradition. In Chapter 1, S. N. Eisenstadt has drawn our attention to the neglected importance of heterodoxies in the historical dynamics of the world religions. Shi'ism, the "heterodox" branch of Islam, in fact, evolved side by side with "orthodox" Sunnism. Their mutually oriented doctrinal articulation and self-definition occurred concomitantly in the formative period of development of Islamic institutions.[5] They therefore represent the two main coeval variants of Islam as a world religion of salvation.

Shi'ite Islam as a world religion of salvation has had considerable transformative potential. This potential in fact acted upon the structure of the Iranian polity once Twelver Shi'ism was declared the state religion of the rising Safavid Empire in 1501. Norms of authority in the world religions of salvation can contain significant implications not only for religious ranking but also for political stratification. Shi'ite Islam contains several norms of authority that have such implications. The first derives from the Shi'ite millenarian belief in the return of the Hidden Imam as the Mahdi at the end of time. The Mahdistic tenet contains the norm of charismatic authority in which religious and political authority are fused in the person of the supreme leader. As we shall see, this norm was activated directly by the founder of the Safavid Empire and indirectly by Khomeini and his followers.

A second historically important norm of authority in Shi'ism can be found in the *Akhbārī* (Traditionalist) tendency in Shi'ism, and concedes only de facto religious authority to the compilers of the Traditions of the Prophet and the Imams. The *Akhbārī* tendency, which was dominant in much of the seventeenth and eighteenth centuries, indirectly encouraged the fusion of religious and political authority, and directly militated against the consolidation of differentiated religiopolitical authority.[6]

Lastly, we have the Shi'ite norm of the juristic authority of the specialists in religious learning. By the early nineteenth century, the institutionalization of this norm resulted in the independence of the hierocracy from the state, which was enhanced by the evolution of the juristic norm of authority throughout the nineteenth century to become the distinctive feature of Shi'ite Islam in contrast to Sunnism. In contradistinction to the previous two norms, the juristic principle established differentiated religious authority de jure and thus created a basis on which hierocratic authority could be consolidated alongside political authority *and independent of it*. The establishment of Shi'ism thus transformed the societal structure of domination in Iran. By the early nineteenth century, the typical Islamic "caesaropapist" political order of the late Middle Ages had given way to a dual structure of domination in which an autonomous hierocracy—the Shi'ite ulema—exercised religiolegal authority as "general vicegerency" (*niyābat 'āmma*) of the Hidden Imam, independently of the ruler and the state.[7]

From one point of view, the establishment of an Islamic theocracy ruled by the ulema can be regarded as the last stage of the evolution of clerical authority in Shi'ite Islam, an evolution that was checked but not reversed by the centralization and modernization of the state in the twentieth century. By the early decades of the Qajar period (1785–1925), the Shi'ite hierocracy had freed itself from the tutelage of political authority characteristic of the Safavid era (1501–1722) and secured its autonomy. The next logical possibility was to assert the *superiority* of the hierocracy over the state by extending clerical authority to the political sphere. This logical possibility was explored and actualized when Ayatollah Khomeini transformed a sizable section of the Shi'ite hierocracy into a revolutionary political party. The projected final stage of the growth of Shi'ite clerical authority then became the blueprint of the militant clerics who overthrew the shah.

The Shi'ite Millenarian Tenet and the Religious Motivation of Revolutionary Action

The idea of the Mahdi, "the rightly guided one," as the expected restorer of true religion and redresser of injustices, entered the history of Islam in general and of Shi'ism in particular during the second civil war in the 680s. The term *mahdī* is a derivative of the root *h-d-y* which denotes divine guidance—a Koranic notion as central to Islam as salvation is to Christianity—but, unlike 'savior', it is not an active but a passive participle. Indeed, its first attested usages are non-messianic. Millennial connotations were present, however, when al-Mukhtār al-Thaqafī presented himself to the people of Kufa as the representative of the Mahdi, Muhammad ibn al-Hanafiyya, with authority for restoring the health of the body politic and for the "removal of the covering," in 683–4/64.[8] During Mukhtār's rebellion in the following years, these millennial connotations were greatly augmented under the influence of Mukhtār's large following of Persian clients (*mawālī*) led by client Kaysān Abū

'Amrah. When Mukhtār's rebellion collapsed, after carrying out the bloody revenge against those responsible for the martyrdom of the Prophet's grandson, al-Ḥusayn, in Karbalā in 680/61, and the Mahdi failed to fulfil his followers' expectations, the millennial connotations of the idea of Mahdihood were reinforced and became definitive. A group of Muḥammad ibn al-Ḥanafiyya's followers denied his death, maintaining instead that he was in occultation, and awaited his second coming. It is very probably in connection with the expectation of the return of this Mahdi from occultation that the term *al-Qā'im* (Riser; probably deriving from the Aramaic Samaritan *qā'em*, "the living one") became an ingredient of the Shi'ite idea of Mahdihood.[9]

The millennial belief in the Mahdi became a distinctive feature of the radical Shi'ite sects. During the last decades of the ninth century, the most notable of these radical sects, the Ismā'īlīs, organized a widespread revolutionary movement on the basis of the millennial belief in the return from occultation of Muḥammad ibn Ismā'īl who would bring justice to the world as the Mahdi, and then preside over the end of the world and the last judgement as the *Qā'im al-qiyāma* (Riser of the Resurrection).[10] In the tenth century, the moderate Shi'ite sect, the Imāmīs or Twelvers, incorporated the millennial notion of Mahdihood into the Twelver Shi'ite doctrine as a part of the doctrinal effort to solve the prolonged crisis of succession to the eleventh Imam. The twelfth Imam was said to be in occultation until the end of time when he would reappear as the Mahdi and the Riser. The Mahdi was thus identified with the Hidden Imam, and its otherworldly eschatological features became more pronounced during the ensuing centuries of political quietism.

The rise of the Safavids can be considered the first successful Shi'ite revolution in Iran. The movement arose among the Turkman tribes from the last wave of migration in northwestern Iran (Azerbaijan) and eastern Anatolia. These tribes had been recently converted to Islam and retained many of their central Asiatic beliefs, most notably in metempsychosis. The leader of the Safavid movement, Shāh Ismā'īl I (1501–1524), claimed to be the Mahdi, and was worshipped by his Turkman followers as the reincarnation of 'Alī and the other Imams—indeed as the incarnation of God. His millenarian movement turned the Turkman tribesmen into a zealous fighting force for the conquest of Iran and its subsequent conversion to Shi'ism. Once in power, the Safavid rulers modified their millenarian claims to being the lieutenants of the Hidden Imam, and their reign was said to continue until his reappearance as the Mahdi.[11] Shi'ism spread in Iran by the ulema under the patronage of the Safavid ruler was more quietistic than the extremist faith of the conquering Turkmans. It did contain millenarianism, emphasizing that the Hidden Imam would remain in hiding and yet fulfill the functions of Imamate, but could not eradicate it. The belief in the Mahdi remained inescapably chiliastic, and would from time to time be activated, the most notable instance being the rise of the Bāb and the Bābī rebellions in the mid-nineteenth century. The " 'Alī-worshiping" Ahl-e Ḥaqq communities of northeastern Iran, among whom many of the extremist beliefs of the early Safavids had survived, were among the enthusiatic converts to Babism. The same ideas were to be successfully exploited by the Bolsheviks in our century. According to one report, the Lenin legends were spread by the propagandists of Moscow, and "enriched by native agents" of the Asian countries. In "the Persian Lenin legend. . . Lenin is simply the reincarnation of holy 'Alī, who is the Messiah."[12]

Unlike the Safavid revolution, the Bābī rebellion failed, having no transformative impact on Iran's social order. Nevertheless, the rich historical documentation of this pre-modern manifestation of Mahdism, occurring as it did literally at a Shi'ite millennium, offers us an opportunity to examine its anatomy selectively from the viewpoint of the religious motivation of revolutionary action. Our brief account will focus on the process of activation of the Mahdistic tenet, and will seek an explanation for the Bābī uprising in terms of the unfolding of a common Shi'ite millenarian belief rather than any charismatic and extraordinary qualities of the individual who led it.

Sayyed 'Alī Moḥammad of Shīrāz, known as the Bāb for his initial, more publicized—and more modest—claim to be the Bāb (Gate) to the Hidden Imam in occultation, was a young merchant who was nurtured in a religious culture permeated by Sufi mysticism, and by millenarian expectations cultivated by the *Akhbārī* and Shaykhī theosophical trends in Shi'ism. In 1844/1260, at the age of twenty-five, he claimed to be the Mahdi, the Hidden Imam returning from 1,000 years of occultation. The Shaykhī theosophical doctrines of nonmaterial resurrection (*ma'ād*) and the inner-worldly presence of the Imam, and especially the cultivation of intense expectancy of the millennium by the Shaykhī leader, Sayyed Kāẓem Rashtī (d. 1844), had paved the way for the claimant who was indeed discovered by a party of Shaykhī seminarians traveling from the Shi'ite holy lands (*'atabāt*) to Shīrāz in search of the expected Mahdi. The declaration of the Manifestation (*ẓohūr*) was planned in detail in accordance with Shi'ite traditions (*aḥādīth*), and the Bāb was to proclaim his Mahdihood in Mecca and proceed to the holy lands.

But his emissary to the holy lands was arrested, tried by a joint gathering of the Shi'ite and Sunni ulema of Iraq, and eventually sent off to Istanbul to die in a labor camp. The Bab arrived in Mecca in December 1844 after an arduous sea voyage, but his proclamation fell pathetically flat. He cancelled the journey to the holy lands, and returned to Shīrāz, now termed the "city of safety," on the same boat. But things did not turn out much better in Shīrāz, where he was forced to make public and written recantations in June 1845.[13] Despite these inauspicious beginnings and serious setbacks, the Bābī movement spread very rapidly through the rest of the decade.

A. Amanat offers us fascinating details on the process of radicalization in this millenarian movement. These strongly suggest that the movement stemmed not from the personal charisma of its leader but rather from the Shi'ite messianic belief in the coming of the Mahdi. Messianic expectancy was endemic to popular Shi'ism, especially among the heterodox groups, and a number of individuals had claimed Mahdihood in the decades preceding the Bāb.[14] What is more telling on this point is that Qorrat al-'Ayn, the Bābī heroine who played the most important role in the movement other than the Bāb himself, never met him in person. Furthermore, from the beginning, the Bāb appears to have been much more cautious than his radical disciples. In 1844, while claiming to be the "great remembrance," "true guardian," and the "measure of cognition" in line with the Shaykhī theosophy, the Bāb recommended dissimulation (*taqiyya*) to his followers. In the following year, he recanted in public in Shīrāz; and in 1847, he rejected an offer of rescue by the Bābīs of Zanjān en route to imprisonment in the fortress of Mākū. The Bāb did endorse the radical moves, both in doctrine—the escalated claim to being the Mahdi as the Riser of the Resurrection—and in action—revolutionary militancy and the call to arms from Khurāsān, but he did not initiate them. These moves were initiated by his followers, especially by Qorrat al-'Ayn. It was she who acted as the spearhead of doctrinal radicalism by advocating the termination of the Islamic law (*sharī'a*) in 1847, and forced the Bāb's hand. The latter, now in captivity, decided to endorse his most radical disciple "perhaps for the first time."[16] Somewhat later, the Bāb disseminated a sermon abrogating the law of Islam and declaring himself to be the Riser, "who by God's benevolence has now manifested himself": "I am the divine fire which God kindles on the Day of Resurrection" (*qiyāmat*)." Some of the more moderate Bābīs who would have preferred to remain within the parameters of Shaykhī theosophy balked at the escalation of the Bāb's claim and left the Bābī ranks; others, who found the millenarian claim appealing, joined the movement.

In 1847, drawing on the rich cabalistic and numerological symbolism of Shi'ite millennial sects since the Ismāʻīlīs, the Bāb designated a unit consisting of himself and eighteen of his disciples as the Letters of the Living (*horūf-e hayy*), corresponding to the nineteen Arabic letters of *bismillāh al-rahmān al-rahīm* (in the name of God, the merciful, the compassionate). They were equated with "His [God's] face" (*vajhahu*) numerologically], and pantheistically taken to be representatives of all things (*kullu shay'*) [= 361 = 19x19], in reference to the Koran (28:88): "All things perish except His face." These disciples were soon to be regarded as reincarnations of the sacred figures of the earlier prophetic cycles such as Muhammad and 'Alī. The Bāb also made references to the heavenly Father, and comparisons between himself and his disciples and Christ and his. All this came into full play during the millennial uprisings of the Bābī saints in 1848. In preparation for battle at Tabarsī in 1848, the Bābī leader, Mollā Mohammad 'Alī Bārforūshī, was recognized as the "Spirit of the Messiah."[18]

Qorrat al-'Ayn's radicalism extended from theology into the realm of social and political action. She had arrived in the holy land to reside in the house of her deceased teacher and Shaykhī herald of the millennium, Sayyed Kāzem Rashtī, and had acquired a following. It was not until 1846 that there was a definitive confluence of her millenarian expectations and the Bāb's ideas that resulted in her acknowledgment of the latter's claims. Qorrat al-'Ayn was surrounded by a small circle of literate women, but her audience was, as one would expect, predominantly male. At first, she spoke to large audiences from behind a curtain. In December 1845, on the Bāb's birthday, she appeared unveiled at a gathering of the Bābīs. Her final and dramatic act of defiance came in the summer of 1848, when she removed her veil in the middle of a speech at the congress of eighty-one Bābīs in Badasht, proclaiming that she was the word of the Riser, "the word that shall put to flight the chiefs and nobles of the earth."[19] Qorrat al-'Ayn was thus decisive in assuring the final victory of revolutionary millenarianism and the call to arms. By then, political militancy and resort to physical violence at the Bābī grass roots, which had begun with the assassination of Qorrat al-'Ayn's uncle, an influential orthodox jurist, was well under way and the Bābīs were arming themselves in Khurāsān in northeastern Iran.

A series of millenarian uprisings followed Qorrat al-'Ayn's sounding of the trumpet, first in Tabarsī, the spectacular scene of millennial reenactment of sacred history, then in Nayrīz, and finally in Zanjān. In this last uprising, which began in May 1850, coins were struck bearing the inscriptions of "Riser" on one side and "O Lord of Time! " (*yā ṣāḥib al-zamān*) on the other.[20] It should also be noted that the Bābī millenarians preached common ownership of porperty. In Bārforūshī's words,

> The bounty of God's creation, which he had destined for the enjoyment of men, has been stolen from them and must be reconquered, so that the believers may everywhere . . . enjoy the gifts of God.[21]

The Bābī uprisings were put down by government troops, and the Bāb himself was executed in July 1850. The Bābīs were ferociously persecuted after an unsuccessful attempt on the shah's life in 1852. After the collapse of their millennial reign of saints on earth, the surviving prominent Bābīs scattered into exile in the Ottoman Empire, and were split into two groups under the leadership of two rival brothers: Mīrzā Ḥosayn 'Alī and Mīrzā Yaḥyā Nūrī. The first, assuming the title of Bahā' Allāh (the Splendor of God), claiming to be the one to come predicted by the Bāb, set out to eradicate millennial attitudes, by an ethical and emphatically apolitical orientation, and under increasing exposure to international trends, transformed the main branch of Babism into the Baha'i religion. The second, assuming the title of Sobḥ-e Azal (the Dawn of Eternity) remained close to the original Bābī millennial orientation.

Revolution and the Activation of the Shi'ite Millennial Tenet

If the Mahdistic millennial tenet could motivate revolutionary political action, it is no less true that a revolutionary political situation could activate millennial beliefs. The Russian revolutions of 1905 and 1917 occurred in an atmosphere charged with apocalyptic yearning, and in turn further activated chiliastic beliefs of Russian Christianity.[22] So did Iran's two revolutions in the twentieth century.

The Bābī Azalīs played a very prominent role in Iran's constitutional revolution of 1906–1911, and supplied a disproportionately large number of constitutionalist revolutionary leaders. These included the leader of the Azalī Bābīs in Iran, Mīrzā Yaḥyā Dawlatābādī (named after Mīrzā Yaḥyā Sobḥ-e Azal), the orators Malek al-Motakallemīn and Sayyed Jamāl, and the journalist Mīrzā Jahāngīr Khān, nicknamed Ṣūr-e Isrāfīl (the trumpet of Israfil [which summons humankind to resurrection]) after his newspaper. With these cultivated Azalīs, we witness the substitution of the modern political myth of revolution for the Shi'ite millennial myth. As one prominent Azalī admitted to Edward Browne, the ideal of a national democratic Iran to be created by that revolution "seems to have inspired in the minds of no few Azalīs the same fiery enthusiasm as did the idea of the reign of the saints on earth in the case of the early Bābīs."[23] It is interesting to note that, nearly half a century later, a prominent Egyptain socialist would report a parallel substitution of Marxist ideas for his earlier belief in the appearance of the Mahdi's army against the British.[24]

The political revolution in 1906–1911 kindled millennial yearings among groups other than the Azalī Bābīs. In 1911, the noted hisortian of the constitutional revolution, Nāẓem al-Eslām Kermānī, published a book entitled *The Signs of Manifestation*, in which he presented the establishment of constitutional government in Iran as an indubitable sign of the imminent manifestation of the Hidden Imam as the Mahdi: "After obtaining the constitution (*mashrūṭiyyat*), [the Iranians] cannot be deprived of it again until they hand it to the Lord of Command (*ṣāḥib al-amr*; i.e., the Mahdi); and every Muslim killed in obtaining the Constitution is a martyr."[25] Kermānī sought to establish correspondence between recent events in Iran and those predicted in the Shi'ite apocalyptic traditions in great detail. The entry of women into social life figures prominently among the signs of the end of time, which also include the appearance of the necktie.[26] It is evident from Kermānī's account that millennial speculations were common among clerics and laymen, revolutionaries and reactionaries alike,[27] and there are cryptic intimations of claim to rule by Sayyed Rayḥān Allāh, a *mojtahed* who, however, belonged to a prominent Shaykhī clerical family, and whose brother had led the Bābī millenarian uprising in Nayrīz sixty years earlier.[28] He also reports hearing at the house of the clerical constitutionalist leader, Sayyed Moḥammad Ṭabāṭabā'ī, of a twenty-year-old youth in Syria who "has ten thousand horsemen and is ready for uprising."[29]

During the 1960s in Iran, there were indications of increased millennial yearning among the population. The prayer of supplication for the return of the Mahdi (*nodba*) appeared to enjoy wide popularity, and special groups for its recitation were formed.[30] This practice drew criticism from the Islamic modernists but was defended by the traditionalist Ayatollahs.[31] Meanwhile, the modernization of Iran and secularization of its educational system and literate culture in the twentieth century had eroded the plausibility of the literal reappearance of the Hidden Imam as the Mahdi among educated classes. The Mahdistic tenet was in need of a modernized interpre-

tation. With the emergence of an Islamic revolutionary movement
in the late 1960s, the lay Islamic ideologue, 'Alī Sharī'atī, interpreted
the belief in the return of the Hidden Imam as the allegory of the
imminent revolution of the oppressed masses of the Third World:
"The belief that the final Savior of human history is the continuation
of the Shi'ite Imams and the Twelfth Imam means that the world
revolution and the final victory is the continuation and result of a
great movement [i.e., Shi'ism] for seeking justice against tyranny
in the world."[32] The one-eyed Dajjāl (Antichrist) of the Shi'ite
apocalyptic literature was the product of the evil dominant world
order, the prerevolutionary one-dimensional man of Herbert Marcuse.[33]
In this assimilation of the modern political myth of revolution to the
Mahdistic tenet, we have a striking parallel to the assimilation of
the Russian revolution to the millennial beliefs of the Asiatic
peoples.[34]

     By the 1970s, the rational plausibility of the belief in the return
of the Hidden Imam as the Mahdi after 1,100 years of concealment
was seriously undermined among the educated individuals, even
though it must have retained some of its subconscious emotional
potency. It is interesting to note that in this period, the late Ayatollah
Moṭahharī, one of the chief intellectual figures of the Islamic revolution, rejected Sharī'atī's politicized interpretation of the Mahdistic
tenet as the coming revolution, but nevertheless offered an alle-
gorical interpretation of his own: The idea of the Mahdi as restorer
of justice and true religion contained the utopia of the perfect society
to be gradually approximated and realized only at the end of the
process of human evolution.[35] Latent popular millennial dispositions, however, are not as easily undermined by considerations of
rational plausibility.

     During the Islamic revolution, Sharī'atī's interpretation of the
Mahdistic tenet as the Shi'ite version of the modern myth of social
revolution was taken over by the Islamic radicals, the Muslim
People's Mujāhedīn. In a lecture delivered at the Polytechnic of
Tehran on the eve of the birthday of the Hidden Imam (July 10, 1979),
one of the leaders of the Mujāhedīn, Mahdī Abrīshamchī, hailed the
Imam of the Age as "the great leader of the classless, monistic
(*tawḥīdī*) society," and the restorer of the pristine egalitarian society
that has been perverted by exploitation, oppression and monopolistic
acquisitiveness of dominant classes. After stressing the importance
of the correct understanding of religious beliefs within the framework of an ideology, he accordingly construed the beliefs in resurrection (*qiyāmat*) as "an existential and ontological response" to
the freedom of the human will. In the same vein, the revolutionary

and monistic ideological "understanding of the Imam of the Age within a monistic worldview" was said to amount to a "philosophy of hope." The belief in him thus requires "combat with the great idol of our time, which is imperialism," and entails "the belief in the hope, indeed certainty, of the victory of the masses."[36]

Khomeini's own political attitude must have been influenced by Shi'ite millennial dispositions. As a young man in his twenties (most probably in 1924), Khomeini was moved by the coincidence of the Persian new year (which begins at the vernal equinox) and the birthday of the Hidden Imam to compose a long poem that offers a glimpse of the apocalyptic battlefield:

> From the shelling of [his] army blood will pour on the
> darkened earth
> With pierced hearts and falling upon the plain
> Two hundred million will be felled from chariots upon the
> darkened earth
> Caesar's gut will split; Napoleon's heart will burst
> Yet from that bombardment (*sic*) the world will become the
> eternal paradise.

In a manner somewhat reminiscent of the extremist beliefs of the early Safavid milieu, our young poet presents the Mahdi as the reembodiment of the attributes of the Prophet and the other eleven Imams, indeed as "a manifestation of the Lord of the Universe," whose return as the king of the end of time is thus implored:

> O King! The predicament of Islam and of the Muslim are
> desparate
> On such a day of festivity when everyone should be chanting
> I see a heart-broken person weeping on every side
> Rise, O Chosroe, and help the faithful.[37]

Khomeini's interest in theosophy (*'erfān*) made him a very atypical Shi'ite jurist. Throughout his life, he was deeply influenced by the inner-worldly transposition of Mahdism in that tradition transmitted by the eighteenth-century thinker, Āqā Moḥammad Bīdābādī[38] and toward the very end, in 1988, he sought to appropriate the theosophical notion of the Absolute Mandate (*velāyat-e moṭlaqa*)[39] for the Jurist (*faqīh*) as the leader of the Islamic Republic.[40]

Given the climate of educated opinion and the general antimillenarian attitude of the Shi'ite hierocracy, it is not surprising that Khomeini did not make any explicit millenarian claims. Without claiming to be the returning Mahdi, however, he ingeniously exploited the Shi'ite messianic yearning by encouraging his accla- mation as the Imam from about 1970 onward. Never since the majority of them had become Shi'ite in the sixteenth century had the Iranians called any living person Imam. An unmistakably apocalyptic mood was observable during the fateful month of Moharram 1399 (December 1978) among the masses in Tehran. Furthermore, with the fourteenth Islamic century about to expire and a new one to begin, the quasi-millennial charisma of the man they called Imam was compounded for the young militant clerics by his image as the Renewer (*mujaddid*) of the century. The idea of renewal (*tajdīd*), it should be pointed out, represented a centennial transformation of the Shi'ite millennial belief.[41] Khomeini's face was allegedly seen on the moon in several cities, and those who had been privileged to see it proceeded to sacrifice lambs. Intense discussions were reported as to whether or not Khomeini was the Imam of the Age and the Lord of Time. Those who answered in the affirmative were undoubtedly among the millions who massed in the streets of Tehran to welcome the returning Ayatollah in February 1979, and whose frenzy was to be televised across the globe. But even many of those who answered in the negative were ready to accept Khomeini as the precursor of the Mahdi.[42]

The success of the Islamic revolution in 1979 seemed incredible enough to at least some of the revolutionaries themselves to generate millenarian expectations and restore the plausibility of the Mahdistic tenet. On the birthday of the Hidden Imam in June 1981, the prosecutor general of the Revolutionary Courts for the Army and the future minister of intelligence, Hojjat al-Islam Mohammadī Rayshahrī, published a pamphlet entitled *The Continuation of the Islamic Revolution of Iran until the Global Revolution of the Mahdi*, which was reissued with an added chapter exactly a year later.[43] It expounded the emerging belief in the continuation of the Islamic revolution until the coming of the Mahdi. This belief bears a striking similarity to the claim that the Safavid rule would continue until the advent of the Hidden Imam. It gained additional impetus from Iran's successes in the war with Iraq during the summer of 1982. In a speech to the Majles (Iranian parliament) in September 1982, Hojjat al-Islam Rezvānī, the clerical representative of Fīrūzābād, predicted the defeat of Iraq as a prelude to marching on Jerusalem. Adducing a number of traditions relating to the Mahdi, he added that the purpose of the march on Jerusalem would be to acclaim the reappearance of the Hidden Imam as the Mahdi, and to witness the reappearance of Jesus Christ and his final conversion to Islam by the Mahdi.[44] In November 1982, *Sorūsh*, the intellectual journal of the Islamic radicals, published an article on the "Connenctedness of the Two Movements" (those of Khomeini and the Mahdi), in which the slogan "O God, O God, keep Khomeini until the Revolution of the Mahdi" was recommended to the reader as a constant prayer. The article referred to an earlier interview in which a wounded man reported having met the Mahdi on the front and been told by him that the above prayer had expedited his return by a few hundred years.[45]

Hierocratic Authority and the Structural Determination of the Islamic Revolution

We can now turn to the crucial importance of the dual societal structure of domination that became established in Iran at the beginning of the nineteenth century. This dual structure of authority explains the prominence of the Shi'ite religious leaders in the forefront of the popular agitation in 1906. As we have seen in Chapter 3, the constitutionalists of the first decade of the century succeeded in obtaining the grant of a constitution from the monarch only by enlisting the support of the Shi'ite hierocracy. Far from determining the direction of the revolution, however, the Shi'ite ulema split once the secularizing implications of parliamentary legislation and its threat to their judiciary authority became clear. It is interesting to note in this juncture that the clerical author of the above-mentioned *Signs of Manifestation* voices the opinion that the apocalyptic council of the lowly (*ruwaybiḍa*), one of the signs of the approaching Mahdistic age, may be the judiciary council soon to be formed to interfere in the "general matters" (*omūr 'āmma*)— matters subject to the "general vicegerency"—which is the prerogative of the ulema and the *mojtaheds*."[46]

In fact, the subsequent modernization of the state did entail a drastic diminution of the institutional prerogatives and social power of the hierocracy. It did not impair the legitimacy of the exclusive hierocratic authority of the ulema, however, which assured the continued financial independence of the hierocracy. The autonomy of the Shi'ite hierocracy, institutionalized in the late eighteenth and early nineteenth centuries, thus assured its survival despite the relentless pressure from the state in the twentieth century. Consequently, it not only survived but also withstood the Pahlavi state's challenge to its virtually exclusive control over religious learning and over the authoritative interpretation of Shi'ite Islam.

The creation of centralized bureaucratic states has been identified as a fundamental precondition of modern revolutions.[47] It requires the concentration of coercive, material, and cultural resources and thus entails dispossession of some privileged strata. Such dispossessed strata are prominently represented among revolutionary leaders throughout history. In Iran, state-building made a serious headway only under the Pahlavīs (1921–1979). In this period of centralization and modernization, the state initiated a series of reforms that seriously undermined the foundations of religious authority and curbed its cultural influence.

The erosion of clerical control over education had begun earlier, even before the constitutional revolution of 1906–1911. But it culminated in the creation of a secular, national educational system under Reza Shah in the 1920s and 1930s. Control over education was the least defensible of clerical prerogatives as it was a contingent fact, lacking any doctrinal basis. More defensible citadels also fell under the attack of the centralizing state. The major defeat of the hierocracy was in the legal sphere, where clerical domination rested on a firm doctrinal basis. Under Reza Shah, the judiciary was secularized and centralized as a branch of the state. Finally, the Endowment Act of 1934 established centralized supervision over religious endowments throughout Iran that had largely been under direct or delegated control of the ulema.[48] Although less important in its consequences than his father's policies, Mohammad Reza Shah's land reform of the 1960s resulted in the redistribution of land owned by mosques, seminaries, and individual clerics. The hierocracy's remaining links to the state through the supervision of the religious endowments were virtually broken. Religious institutions became totally independent of the state; and this independence was sustained by the one last source of income that was inevitably immune from state encroachment: the voluntary payment of religious taxes to the leaders of the Shi'ite hierocracy as the vicegerents of the Hidden Imam.

These developments seriously weakened the hierocracy. But they also had another important consequence: The differentiation and separation of religious and political powers became complete. The loss of judicial and educational functions on the one hand, and the loss of control of religious endowment and land ownership on the other, meant that the Shi'ite hierocracy became largely "disembedded" from the Pahlavī regime. This economic and political disengagement of the hierocracy was strongly complemented by their social "disembeddedness." There had always been a tendency for the upper echelons of the hierocracy to intermarry, forming a highly endogamous group, the entry into which by bright young men was often accompanied by marriage to daughters or close relatives of their teachers. This tendency was accentuated by the ulema's loss of social prestige, which greatly reduced the frequency of intermarriage between them and the increasingly secularized social and political elites.

Eisenstadt has emphasized the importance of the autonomy and disembeddedness of a leading social stratum for the generation of revolutionary social change.[49] A. Oberschall demonstrated the importance of the "segmentation" of a solidary communal group from the ruling strata as a condition favorable to political mobilization, Tilly that of group solidarity, resting on common identity and a network of organized interaction, as a mobilizational asset for political contenders.[50] In the light of these considerations, it is not difficult to see the disengagement of the Shi'ite ulema from the Pahlavi regime as a crucial factor in the causation of the first traditionalist revolution in modern history, and their solidarity as a tightly knit status group in control of autonomous religious institutions, in its success.

Consequences of the Islamic Revolution: Continuity and Change in the Political Order

Nothing within the Shi'ite tradition and institutions can explain the internal crumbling and paralysis of the Pahlavī state that caused the revolution of 1979. The Shi'ite cultural tradition and institutional structures, however, had everything to do with the consequences of that revolution. The autonomous structure of hierocratic authority in Shi'ism enabled Khomeini and the militant clerics to win the revolutionary power struggle, and the Shi'ite cultural tradition crucially influenced the teleology of the Islamic revolution and the shape of the postrevolutionary regime.

Khomeini led the revolutionary movement against the shah to restore and preserve a Shi'ite tradition threatened by modernization and Westernization. The Islamic revolution is undoubtedly a traditionalist revolution. Yet the restoration of a tradition in practice always entails its transformation. In fact, the traditionalist revolution of 1979 has brought about a revolution *in* Shi'ism.[51] The distinctive institutions of the Islamic Republic of Iran that represent the unfolding of the distinctively Shi'ite teleology of the Islamic revolution have been treated in detail elsewhere.[52] The cultural and institutional changes in postrevolution Shi'ism bear the imprint of the historical contingencies that produced them. We consequently see both continuity and change between the pre- and postrevolution Shi'ism, and between the pre- and postrevolution societal structure of domination in Iran.

One of the unintended consequences of the direct takeover of the state by the clerical elite in 1980 has been the extension of the principle of bureaucratic organization from the state to the hitherto organizationally amorphous Shi'ite hierocracy itself. Nevertheless, these changes are also distinctively Shi'ite in that they are modifications and extensions of elements of prerevolution Shi'ism. Most notable among these is the sweeping extension of hierocratic authority. This and other modifications and extensions are both stimulated and delimited by the logical possibilities of the original traditional elements. The latter therefore partly determine the direction of the contemporary sociopolitical transformation of Shi'ism. This transformation, consequently, represents a pattern of social change that is culturally specific.

If the structure of hierocratic domination in postrevolution Iran is marked by continuity as well as change, so is the structure of political domination. Theocratic rule—the replacement of the post-Safavid dual structure of authority by theocratic monism—and the sacralization of political authority represent the most important aspects of revolutionary change. Elements of continuity between pre- and postrevolution structures of political domination are equally striking, however. Despite the intention of Khomeini and the militant Ayatollahs to shrink the state to a modest size, the growth of the bureaucratic state has not been checked. In fact, the Iranian state now employs over twice as many people as it did on the eve of the Islamic revolution.[53]

Finally, continuity and change in the legal sphere require a brief discussion. Already before the revolution, Khomeini had sought to make the Shi'ite law more practical and accommodating of some modern conditions in his manual of practical jurisprudence. For example, he had given "the knowledge of the judge" based on written and other modern forms of evidence preponderance over the unpractical traditional rules of evidence. Much more important, the Islamic revolution has transformed the Shi'ite sacred law from a "jurists' law" to an increasingly codified public law of the Iranian state.[54] Alongside this revolutionary transformation of Shi'ite law, there is considerable continuity between pre- and postrevolution legal systems. Despite the Islamicization of the legal system there has been considerable continuity as regards the legislative function of the *Majles*, the substance of the laws, and the administration of justice. Khomeini and the militant clerics preserved the *Majles*, the heritage of the constitutional revolution of 1906. Although its legislation is subject to the approval of the clerical jurists of a Council of the Guardians, it has shown great vigor and has enacted an impressive body of laws. These include the revision of the commercial, civil and other codes of the Pahlavī era. The revised codes now appear Islamicized by bearing the approval of the clerical jurists of the Council of Guardians. In this fashion, an enormous amount of legal material from the European-based laws of the Pahlavī era has been incorporated into the laws of the Islamic Republic of Iran. Similarly, the hierarchical organization of courts in the Ministry of Justice set up under Reza Shah, which was modeled on the continental European judiciary systems, has been taken over by the Islamic regime, with many of its secular judges continuing to serve.

The leaders of the Islamic revolution in Iran recognize this borrowing, even though they would rather not talk about it. In an outburst against the recalcitrant traditionalists who considered taxation at variance with the Islamic sacred law in December 1984, the shrewd *Majles* speaker (later president of the Islamic Republic), Hojjat al-Islam Hāshemī-Rafsanjānī, remarked:

> Is whatever occurs in the Western world contrary to the Sacred Law? . . .You are sitting in Parliament. Where is the precedent for parliament in Islamic history? . . . [or for] a president, cabinet of ministers, prime minister and the like? . . .You say that no *fatvās* [injunctions] were issued [in support of] taxes. No *fatvās* were issued for a great many things. In fact, we lack *fatvās* in Islam for 80 per cent of the things on which today we base Islamic government.[55]

Concluding Theoretical Note

The Islamic revolution in Iran has set in motion a culturally specific pattern of social change that is distinctively Shi'ite. At the same time, however, it has reinforced some global trends, the most important being the growth of the bureaucratic state and the rationalization of the legal order.

The contemporary transformation of Shi'ism produced by this revolution compels us to discard the simple models of unilineal evolution in favor of a model of culturally specific social change. If this position is accepted, cyclical and linear trends in social change can be seen to intersect at the starting point of the revolution.

"Dedifferentiation"[56] in the form of charismatic fundamentalism occurs as a result of the reactivation of millennial beliefs. The basic values of a world religion can be seen to "take on less differentiated and flexible form in order to revitalize utterly key principles of a tradition, but thereby retract legitimation from many practically important institutions."[57] As this outbreak of charismatic fundamentalism is followed by routinization, linear trends in institutionalization and rationalization set in. The similarities between modern political revolutions and traditional millenarian uprisings of the post-Axial Age cease to seem paradoxical. Finally, there would not be any paradox in saying that the Islamic revolution in Iran represents both the traditionalization of a modernizing nation-state and the modernization of the Shi'ite tradition, a tradition endowed with the usual transformative potential of the world religions of salvation.

Notes

1. See G. Lewy, *Religion and Revolution* (New York: Oxford University Press, 1974).
2. See Chapter 1, above.
3. See E. Shils, *The Intellectuals and the Powers and Other Essays* (Chicago: The University of Chicago Press, 1972), p. 30; S. N. Eisenstadt, "Cultural Traditions and Political Dynamics: The Origins and Modes of Ideological Politics," *British Journal of Sociology* 32, no. 2 (1981): 155–181; and idem., "Introduction: The Axial Age Breakthroughs—Their Characteristics and Origins," in S. N. Eisenstadt, ed., *The Origins and Diversity of Axial Age Civilizations* (Albany: State University of New York Press, 1986).
4. For a fuller account of the hierocracy-state conflict, see S. A. Arjomand, *The Turban for the Crown: The Islamic Revolution in Iran* (New York: Oxford University Press, 1988), Chapter 4.
5. M. G. S. Hodgson, *The Venture of Islam* (Chicago: University of Chicago Press, 1974), vol. 1.
6. S. A. Arjomand, *The Shadow of God and the Hidden Imam: Religion, Political Order and Societal Change in Shi'ite Iran from the Beginning to 1890* (Chicago: University of Chicago Press, 1984), Chapter 5.
7. Ibid., Chapter 10.
8. Muḥammad d. Jarīr al-Ṭabarī, *The History of al-Ṭabarī*, vol. 20, G. R. Hawting, trans. (Albany: State University New York Press, 1989), p. 120.
9. See W. Madelung, "MAHDĪ," in *The Encyclopedia of Islam*, 2d ed. (Leiden: E. J. Brill, 1986), 4: 1230–1238, esp. p. 1235.

10. F. Daftari, *The Isma'ilis: Their history and doctrines* (Cambridge: Cambridge University Press, 1990), p. 140.
11. Arjomand, *Shadow of God*, esp. p. 182.
12. Anglo-Russian News, no. 188; cited in E. Sarkisyanz, *Rußland und der Messianismus des Orients* (Tübingen: J. C. B. Mohr, 1955), p. 272.
13. A. Amanat, *Resurrection and Renewal: The Making of the Babi Movement in Iran, 1844-1850* (Ithaca and London: Cornell University Press, 1989), p. 255.
14. Ibid., p. 86.
15. E. G. Browne, "Personal Reminiscences of the Babi Insurrection at Zanjan in 1850, written in Persian by Āqā 'Abdu'l-Aḥad-i Zanjānī," *Journal of the Royal Asiatic Society* (1987): 775–777.
16. Amanat, *Resurrection*, p. 307.
17. Cited in ibid., p. 374.
18. Ibid., pp. 187–198.
19. Cited in ibid., p. 326.
20. Browne, "Reminiscences," p. 769.
21. Cited in Sarkisyanz, *Rußland*, p. 247.
22. Sarkisyanz, *Rußland*, pp. 95–106, 145–148, 195–196; S. D. Cioran, *The Apocalyptic Symbolism of Andrej Belyj* (The Hague and Paris, 1973), chapter 1.
23. E. G. Browne, *Materials for the Study of the Babi Religion* (Cambridge: Cambridge University Press, 1918), p. xix.
24. Sarkisyanz, *Rubbland*, p. 258,
25. Mīrzā Moḥammad Nāẓem al-Eslām Kermānī, *'Alā'em al-Ẓohūr* (Tehran, 1329/1911), pp. 76–77.
26. Ibid., pp. 101–107, 156–162, 194–195.
27. Ibid., pp. 99–100.
28. Ibid., pp. 193–194.
29. Ibid., pp. 129–130.
30. 'A. Sharī'atī *Enteẓār, Madhhab-e E'terāḍ* (Tehran: Abu Dharr, 1350/1971), p. 11, n. 1.
31. [Ayaollāh Sayyed Ḥasan] Ḥojjat, *Valāyat va 'Elm-e Emām* (Tehran: Javīdān, 1355/1976), pp. 338–342.
32. Sharī'atī, *Enteẓar*, p. 47.
33. Ibid., p. 49.
34. Sarkisyanz, *Rußland*, Part 2.
35. M. Moṭahharī, *Qīyām va Enqelāb-e Mahdī* (Tehran: Mash'al-e Āzādī, 1354/1975).
36. "Falsafa–ye Emām-e Zamān," transcript duplicated by the Association of Muslim Students, New York, pp. 4, 16, 19, 23–24, 29–30, 36.
37. S. H. Rūḥānī [Zīyāratī], *Barrasi va Taḥlīlī az Nahḍat-e Emām Khomeinī* (Tehran: Rāh-e Emām, 1360/1981), pp. 55–59.
38. Arjomand, *Shadow of God*, pp. 163, 269.
39. M. H. Fakhr al-Muḥaqqeqin, *Tajalli-ye Velāyat* (Shiraz: Aḥmadī, 1352/1973), pp. 19–22, 266–267.

40. S. A. Arjomand, "The Rule of God in Iran," *Social Compass* 36, no. 4 (1989): pp. 539–548.

41. Y. Friedmann, *Prophecy Continuous: Aspects of Ahmadi Religious Thought and Its Medieval Background* (Berkeley and Los Angeles: University of California Press, 1989), Chapter 4. This transformation was the result of the Shāfi'ite jurists' justification of their authority as an extention of that of the Prophet. See E. Landau-Tasseron, "The 'Cyclical Reform': a Study of the *Mujaddid* Tradition," *Studia Islamica*, 70 (1989), pp. 79–117.

42. This second group argued that Khomeini could not be the Lord of Time himself, since the latter would liberate the entire world whereas Khomeini was going to liberate only Iran. See S. A. Arjomand, "Shi'ite Islam and the Revolution in Iran," *Government and Opposition* 16, no. 3 (1981): p. 308.

43. Moḥammadī Rayshahrī, *Tadāvom-e Enqelāb-e Eslāmī-ye Īrān tā Enqelāb-e Jahānī-ye Mandī* (Tehran: Yāser, 1361/1982).

44. *Keyhān*, Shahrivar, 17, 1361/Sept. 8, 1982.

45. Other Shi'ite beliefs also motivated revolutionary action and provided the idiom for its articulation. In mobilizing the Iranian masses for the revolution that was to realize Shi'ite clerical rule on behalf of God and the Hidden Imam, Khomeini and his followers drew heavily on the cult of martyrdom, which constitutes the major component of the Shi'ite theodicy of suffering. The glorification of martyrdom and the assimilation of the revolutionary struggle against the shah to Imam Ḥusayn's uprising against the Umayyad caliph, Yazīd, in the desert of Karbalā in 680, have received ample attention in the coverage of the Iranian revolution by the media. Suffice it to add that Moḥarram was the decisive month for the defeat of the shah, and that the massive protest marches, during which Khomeini was formally declared the Imam of an Islamic government to replace the monarchy, took place on the 'Āshūrā, the day of martyrdom of Imam Ḥusayn. See Arjomand, *Turban for the Crown* p. 134.

     It is interesting to note that the 'Āshūrā is also the day of the reappearance of the Mahdi in many traditions, even though the connection may not have come to the mind of the vast majority of the marchers.

46. Kermānī, *'Alā'em al-Ẓohūr*, p. 100.

47. See J. Baechler, *Revolution* (New York: Harper and Row, 1975); S. N. Eisenstadt, *Revolutions and Transformation of Societies* (New York: Wiley, 1978); J. A. Goldstone, "The Comparative and Historical Study of Revolutions," *Annual Review of Sociology* 8 (1982) pp. 187–207; and S. A. Arjomand, "Iran's Islamic Revolution in Comparative Perspective," *World Politics* 38, no. 3 (1986).

48. Sh. Akhavi, *Religion and Politics in Contemporary Iran* (Albany: State University of New York Press, 1980), pp. 33, 40, 56–58.

49. Eisenstadt, *Revoltions*, pp. 245–246; see also Chapter 1, above.

50. A. Oberschall, *Social Conflict and Social Movement* (Englewood Cliffs, N. J.: Prentice-Hall, 1973), pp. 118–124, 129–132; C. Tilly, *From Mobilization to Revolution* (Reading, Mass.: Addison Wesley, 1978).

51. S. A. Arjomand, "Ideological Revolution in Shi'ism," in *Authority and Politcal Culture in Shi'ism* (Albany: State University of New York Press, 1988).

52. Arjomand, *Turban for the Crown*, Chapter 8.

53. Ibid., p. 214, Table 10.

54. See S. A. Arjomand, "Shi'ite Jurisprudence and Constitution-Making in the Islamic Republic of Iran," in M. Marty and R. S. Appleby, eds., *Fundamentalisms and the State: Remaking Polities, Economies, and Militance* (Chicago: University of Chicago Press, 1992).

55. Cited in Sh. Bakhash, "Islam and Social Justice in Iran," in M. Kramer, ed., *Shi'ism, Resistance and Revolution* (Boulder, Colo. Westview Press, 1987), p. 113.

56. E. A. Tiryakian, "On the significance of De-differentiation," in S. N. Eisenstadt and H. J. Helle, eds., *Macrosociological Theory*, Sage Studies in International Sociology, vol. 33, (London: Sage, 1985.

57. V. Lidz, "Religion and Cybernetic Concepts in the Theory of Action," *Sociological Analysis* 43, no. 4 (1982): 293.

Part III

Normative Contentions and Current Issues

10

Fundamentalism and the Political Mobilization of Women

Martin Riesebrodt

The Problem

One of the most striking images associated with the Iranian revolution and the establishment of an Islamic Republic was that of women veiled in their chadors in mass demonstrations.[1] This public support by women for a social movement and, afterwards, for a government, a major aim of which was to reinforce the traditional segregation between the genders and to impose on women the traditional roles of mothers and housekeepers, puzzled many observers in the West. This occurrence in Iran, an "oriental" country, an Islamic society, would seem to have little relevance for other, especially western, societies. Such a view, however, is misleading.

The Iranian example dramatically reminds us of two general facts. First, the changes in the structure of the family and gender relations are very much part of the central societal problems and conflicts in the twentieth century all over the world. The nationalization and internationalization of markets, the centralization of nation-states led by modernizing elites, and the universal spread of Western mass media and mass culture, to name just three factors of major impact, have shattered the foundations of traditional family structures and gender relations.[2] Second, these conflicts are not conflicts between the sexes but about the structures of gender relations.

Seen from this perspective, it is not at all surprising that the views of women on gender issues are as diverse as are the views of men, and that women therefore actively participate in those conflicts on all sides. In other words, there exists no "natural" position on these issues. And it is not surprising either that fundamentalist movements—with their emphasis on issues of social morals, sexuality, the female body, and the structure of the family—are flourishing not only in Iran and other Islamic countries, like Turkey, Algeria, and Egypt,[3] but also in Western societies. Particularly in the United States differently labeled movements with partly overlapping leadership and constituencies, like Protestant fundamentalism, the "Moral Majority," the "New Christian Right," and the "New Religious Right," all primarily advocate the preservation and/or restoration of the patriarchal family, traditional social morals, and gender relations.[4]

In short, women participating in social movements that support the retraditionalization of gender relations is neither an Iranian, nor an Islamic, nor at all an "exotic" phenomenon, but a potentially universal one that can be found in Western societies as well as in Islamic societies, in Asia and Africa as well as in South and North America.

Of course, not all movements that advocate a retraditionalization of society in general and of gender relations in particular are "fundamentalist" in the sense this term is defined here. The boundaries among fundamentalism, conservatism, and neopatriarchal positions are sometimes fluid and difficult to draw. "Fundamentalism," however, represents a position that is the most radically patriarchal one, and the one most focused on issues of sexuality, gender relations, and the control of the female body. Therefore, from a modern Western point of view, the participation of women in fundamentalist movements of different religious traditions seems to be particularly enigmatic and deserves more attention than it has received so far.[5]

The political mobilization of women by fundamentalism seems to express a twofold paradox, a paradox that is both normative and structural. The normative paradox is that women are mobilized to advocate what, from a modern Western point of view, is their own repression. The structural paradox lies in the fact that fundamentalism attempts to restrict women to the domestic sphere while at the same time organizing them as a public force.

These seeming paradoxes pose three interesting questions. First, is the political mobilization of women by fundamentalism really a paradox? In other words, does this mobilization contradict the ideology and aims of fundamentalist movements? Second, if one does not assume that women in those movements are simply manipulated by men, what are their motivations, experiences, and interests in participating in fundamentalist movements? In other words, what is the social context in which this fundamentalist mobilization of women makes sense to them and is not at all a paradox from their point of view? And third, will the political mobilization of women by fundamentalism end as an irony of history? Or, stated differently, will the mobilization of women in favor of patriarchal structures in the long run promote their emancipation from and rejection of those structures?

Fundamentalism as Radical Religious Traditionalism

Karl Mannheim has defined conservatism as traditionalism become reflexive and Said Arjomand has characterized Shi'ite fundamentalism as "revolutionary traditionalism."[6] Both agree that these types of movements are not just *traditional*, but *traditionalist* in the sense that the existing tradition is reviewed, renewed, and made relevant to the present circumstances. In so doing, the tradition is radicalized as different elements of it become emphasized or accentuated. This reinterpretation of religious tradition has clearly innovative aspects. Old elements are rearranged, new elements are added. In this sense fundamentalism always includes an element of an "invention of tradition."[7] Therefore, fundamentalism is radical religious traditionalism.

Fundamentalism is usually subsumed under the broader category of religious revivalism.[8] But, there are at least two different types of religious revivalism: modernist and fundamentalist, reformist and conservative or reactionary. Despite their opposition both share some features. Both are mobilized by the experience of deep social crisis. Both attempt to overcome this crisis by falling back upon an ideal order of the past, usually that of the founder of the religion. But their pursuit of authenticity takes alternative routes.

The reformers stress the "spirit" of the ancient community and/or claim that the "real meaning" of the religious message has been distorted or at least neglected by established authorities. Reformers want to transform social institutions in order to realize the "liberating spirit" of the ancient religious community and its teachings. The reformist solution to societal crisis is utopian, innovative, and future-oriented. They tend to be optimists regarding human nature and emphasize mutual help, solidarity, and freedom. The reformist ethic is primarily an ethic of conviction.

For fundamentalists authenticity refers not to the "spirit" of the ancient community but to its moral order. They stress the "letter," the rules, the law, and the aspects of authority of the ancient community itself or of a later institutionalized form.[9] In order to overcome the crisis they emphasize obedience to religiously legitimated authorities and claim to restore social institutions in order to realize divine law. They also tend to emphasize punishment and social control. Their approach can be called "mythical," referring to a timeless, unchangeable, fixed eternal truth. The fundamentalist ethic is primarily an ethic of law.[10]

Thus far this definition enables us to distinguish fundamentalism from reformist revivalism. But there are many different types of religious reactions that can be called "fundamentalist" according to this definition. Using this definition alone one could end up comparing the pacifist Amish with the militant Hizbollah, or the celibate Shakers with charismatic television preachers. For a comparative sociological interpretation we need a more precise typology of fundamentalism, based on different attitudes toward the world, and on different forms of social organization.

First, the Weberian distinction between different religious attitudes toward the world might be helpful. Weber differentiated between approval and rejection of the world on the one hand, and among control, adaptation, and withdrawal on the other. Fundamentalists clearly reject the world since their mobilization is caused by the experience of deep crisis. This rejection may lead either to an attitude of world control or to one of withdrawal from the world. Both types can be expressed in a variety of organizational forms.

Withdrawal may take the form of symbolic segregation as a subculture or of spatial separation as a commune. World control may be organized as a religious movement, a social or protest movement, a secret society, or a political party. One must however keep in mind that fundamentalist groups change their attitudes and organizational forms over time. This typological differentiation allows us to isolate those features that are of most interest for our problematic, namely, those politically active fundamentalist movements that seek power not only within religious institutions, but more important, in the general arena of the public sphere.

This typology suggests that the political mobilization of women is restricted to a "fundamentalism of world control," especially when organized as a protest movement or a political party. Therefore, further discussion of fundamentalism and the political mobilization

Figure 10.1 The Typology of Fundamentalism

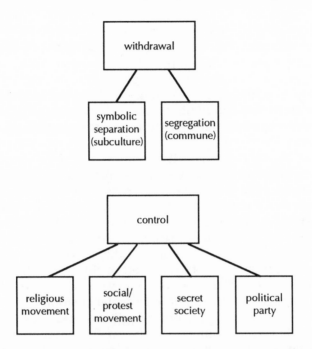

of women will primarily focus on this type of fundamentalism, although we will also pay attention to other types in order to clarify the differences.[11]

We will begin by looking at fundamentalist movements of the same, "world-controlling" type, namely, Protestant fundamentalism in the United States during the 1920s and 1980s, and Shi'ite fundamentalism in Iran before the revolution of 1979. In all these movements, we find a considerable political mobilization of women. Women were involved in the campaigns for Prohibition and against the teaching of Darwinism in public schools in the United States during the early twentieth century, in the "pro-family," anti-abortion, anti-homosexuality, and anti-Equal Rights Amendment crusades since the 1970s, and in the Khomeini movement.[12]

The reasons why women participate in politically active fundamentalist movements are obviously influenced by many factors, which to analyze goes far beyond the scope of this chapter. We will look at four aspects that might shed some light on some of the causes as well as the outcome.

Women in Fundamentalist Ideology:
"Mother-Myth" and "Eve-Myth"

Of course, in order to get a fuller picture of gender relations among fundamentalists one has to analyze not only the theory but also the practice of those relationships. This obviously leads to a more differentiated and fair account, where fundamentalist men might differ from fundamentalist women, middle-class fundamentalists from working-class fundamentalists, urban fundamentalists from small town and rural ones. Within the limits of this chapter this cannot be done.

Therefore, we have to limit our analysis to the question of how women are portrayed in fundamentalist ideology, an ideology shared by male and female fundamentalist leaders and applauded by male and female fundamentalist followers. Accordingly, we will concentrate on this characterization of women in fundamentalist ideology, assuming that it provides a sufficient description of the central features, although certainly not an exhaustive one.

Fundamentalism, be it Protestant or Shi'ite, firmly adheres to the doctrine that God created men and women as different. Biological difference also defines women's social position as subordinate to men. They were created in order to give birth to children and take care of the home. Put differently, the creation of men and women is not seen as the creation of autonomous individuals but as mutually complementary elements of an institution: the patriarchal family.

As Jerry Falwell puts it: "God Almighty created men and women biologically different and with differing needs and roles. He made men and women to complement each other. . . .God has called the father to be the spiritual leader in his family. . . .The husband is to be the decisionmaker. . . .A woman's call to be a wife and mother is the highest calling in the world." He labels the family a "sacred institution."[13] Phyllis Schlafly argues: "Woman and man were made to complement each other. . . .In order for woman and man to complement each other, God made woman look and feel different from man. . . .She complements man physically and emotionally. . . .God planned for this type of interdependence to be cemented with a mutual commitment called marriage.[14]

Shi'ite fundamentalism adheres to a quite similar view of the role of women and the function of the family, as the writings of Khomeini, Motahhari, and the constitution of the Islamic Republic indicate. They too maintain that men and women are created as different, that women should be mothers and housekeepers, that male and female roles within the family are biologically determined and different.[15] A major difference between Protestant and Shi'ite fundamentalism lies in the Shi'ite idea of women's "impurity" as well as in the inferior legal status of women. Here Shi'ite fundamentalism is very much in line with the traditional view of Shia Islam.[16]

Based on this fundamentalist perception of women being created different there remain essentially two options. Either they accept their biological destiny and become agents of God, or they deny this destiny, practice a "perverse" life-style, and become agents of Satan. As agents of God they fulfill their God-given roles as mothers and housekeepers who lift their husbands and preserve the pious home. As agents of Satan they seduce men and corrupt the youth. To express this twofold image of women, perceived as timeless alternative by the fundamentalists, we can distinguish between "mother-myth" and the "Eve-myth."

Female Body and Social Crisis

The experience of crisis that transforms apolitical traditionalists or quietist premillenarians into fundamentalist activists is very much connected with social-moral phenomena. Fundamentalist social criticism overwhelmingly stresses changes within the structure of the family, the social and legal position of women, and sexual morals, especially connected with the public presentation of the female body. When we look at Protestant and Shi'ite fundamentalist ideology we encounter this preoccupation with "moral decay" and other challenges confronting the traditional family. According to fundamentalist ideology one of the most effective weapons of Satan is the female body and its seductive power over men.

In the programmatic book of the Fedayan-i Islam, a terrorist fundamentalist group active in Iran during the 1940s and 1950s,[17] one reads phrases like: "Flames of passion rise from the naked bodies of immoral women and burn humanity into ashes. . . . [T]he unveiling of women has caused the increasing number of broken families and divorces. . . .Women also become less attentive toward their families and husbands and its results are divorce and prostitution."[18]

Khomeini shares this view and sees among the most detrimental phenomena for the Islamic civilization the decay of sexual morals, like "naked" (unveiled) women in the streets.[19] According to the fundamentalists the rapid urban expansion with its increasing social complexity and lack of social control accounts for the anomic situation and promotes the stimulation of passions. "Day and night, men and women face each other in the streets, offices, schools, plants and in other public places and this [sexual] sense is stimulated at all times without control."[20]

The same preoccupation with sexual morals and the female body can be observed in the postrevolutionary practices of the regime. Contrary to prerevolutionary "social" rhetoric little was done to improve the lot of the peasants and the urban poor. The regime abolished, however, immediately after the revolution the "Family Protection Law" of 1967 that guaranteed women an improved legal status. Instead, a law on social morals was proclaimed, in which 107 out of 195 paragraphs deal with the punishment of "sexual crimes," described in graphic detail. Among the first victims of the revolution besides political opponents and religious "heretics" were prostitutes, homosexuals, and adulterers.[21]

This concentration on the "proper" position of women, the control of the female body, and sexuality is not limited to Shi'ite or Islamic fundamentalist movements. The same topics dominate the fundamentalist discourse in the United States, as is indicated by the present campaigns against abortion, homosexuals, pornography, and the Equal Rights Amendment, or the obsession with topics like vice and sexual morals in the publications of the 1920s.

When one looks, for example, at the writings of John Roach Straton, the leading New York fundamentalist during the 1920s, one finds striking parallels with the complaints of Khomeini and the Fedayan-i Islam. Straton published tracts like "The Devil in Modern Babylon," "Slaves of Fashion: The Connection Between Women's Dress and Social Vice," and "The Scarlet Stain of Sexual Impurity." Straton, commenting on a "Carnival-performance," wrote: "The lewd women in that show performed vile 'oriental' dances. . . intended to arouse the lower passions of the young men present."[22]

Fundamentalists also repeatedly emphasized "the power a girl has either to lift men up or pull them down."[23] Straton portrayed the morally corrupt, men-seducing woman in the following way: "The most sinister and menacing figure of our modern life is the cigarette smoking, cocktail drinking, pug dog nursing, half-dressed, painted woman, who frequents the theaters, giggles at the cabarets, gambles in our drawing-rooms or sits around our hotels, with her dress cut 'C' in front and 'V' behind! She is a living invitation to lust, and a walking advertisement of the fact that many of our modern women have lowered their standards of life!"[24] In Shi'ite fundamentalist language this is the description of a "naked woman" and a "prostitute."

For Protestant as well as Shi'ite fundamentalists there follow two imperatives from the satanic power of women. First, one has to close down all institutions centered on the public presentation of the female body, like dance-halls, brothels, and swimming pools. Second, one has to hide and desexualize the female body in public. As we all know, Muslim fundamentalists insist on veiling women to achieve that goal. But Protestant pastor Straton also proposed the introduction of a "decent national costume" for women.[25] Of course, there are differences in the cultural forms and methods used to neutralize female sexuality. In Shi'ism solutions are based on ritualistic segregation,[26] whereas in Protestantism an internalization of ethical principles is stressed.

The counterpart to the satanic Eve is the pious mother. She forms part of the God-given patriarchal family. The basic idea of the relationship between the genders can be summarized in the slogan "different, but equal." Because of biological differences, women have to fulfill their "natural" task as mothers and housekeepers under the leadership of their husbands. Since both sides have to fulfill their "God-given" duties this does not mean a privileged position for either side, but an equality in harmony with their biological destiny. Despite the striking social and cultural differences between Iran and the United States, the functions of the family and, especially, the role of women are described by the fundamentalists in broadly similar categories.

The following statement by the Fedayan-i Islam could be supported by all Protestant fundamentalists: "The best thing for a woman to be is the manager of the house and a mother and wife who will be the producer and the teacher of children at home."[27] The family is seen as a unit based on a sexual division of labor. The special tasks of a woman are to be the wife for her husband, the homemaker for the whole family, and the educator of the children. In this respect women also are indispensable for the preservation of the religious culture of the nation and a pious way of life. This ideal implies that the proper sphere of a woman is the domestic one, the home.

Ironically, when feeling urged to legitimize this gender dualism, Protestant as well as Shi'ite fundamentalists argue that the religious tradition protects and even privileges women. Jerry Falwell, for example, states: "I believe that women deserve more than equal rights." And Ayatollah Khomeini quite similarly argues: "The favour Islam attributes to women is more than what it attributes to men."[28] Both men, of course, spare neither trouble nor expense to preserve these "privileges."

The Political Mobilization of
Fundamentalist Women: A Paradox?

Given the female ideal in fundamentalist ideology the political mobilization of women seems to be a paradox. On the one hand, fundamentalism is rooted in the idea of a God-given difference in the biological and psychological nature of both genders. Consequently, it emphasizes the role of women as mothers and housekeepers, and promotes the segregation between the genders into a male public sphere and a female domestic one. On the other hand, fundamentalism practices the opposite by politically mobilizing women and thereby bringing them out of the domestic into the public sphere. How can this apparent paradox be explained, and how is it legitimized?

We can address these questions by examining the rationale, legitimation, aim, and the social structure of fundamentalist mobilization of women. The reasons for the political mobilization of women rarely are formulated explicitly by the fundamentalists. But the implicit logic seems to be quite clear.

The mobilization of the traditionalist milieu is primarily caused by a process of sociocultural differentiation in the process of rapid urbanization where traditional gender roles, sexual morals, and leisure-time activities are dramatically altered. The rise of a modernist milieu challenges the traditionalists in many respects. The latter loses its culturally dominant, commonly state-approved position. Moreover, cultural reproduction is endangered by the anomic situation in burgeoning cities, by the rise of new life-styles, and by the influence of the general cultural change on the agencies of public education.[29]

When cultural reproduction is endangered and internal erosion is starting, the traditional milieu has three options. The first option is simply to give up and adapt to the modernist life-style. But, if the traditional milieu wants to survive, it can either withdraw from society and form a subculture, or it can challenge the modernist takeover and start a public debate about the principles of social order, the right way of life, and just political, social, and economic institutions. Therefore, a traditionalist milieu that neither wants to adapt nor to withdraw has to become fundamentalist and turn public.

Accordingly, fundamentalists compete in the public realm with the modernist milieu and have to make their alternatives publicly visible. Since fundamentalism is primarily mobilized by issues of proper roles for women and sexual morals this leads necessarily to an inclusion of their female role-models into the public arena and discourse. In this respect the political mobilization of women by fundamentalism is a logical and practical consequence of modern mass politics. But, since it contradicts the original separation of gender-spheres, how is it legitimated and organized?

In order to analyze fundamentalist ideology we need to make a distinction between two levels: social critique and salvation history.[30] To understand the legitimation of the political mobilization of women one has to turn to the salvation history in which the moralistic critique of society is embedded. The crisis perceived by fundamentalists is interpreted as an actualization and dramatization of the eternal struggle between God and Satan, light and darkness, the good and the evil forces. Of course, this struggle is the normal condition of the world before the millennium. But the present situation is exceptional insofar as Satan is taking over. And this has consequences for women, who temporarily have to play a more active role in fighting the satanic forces.

In Shi'ite fundamentalism this can be best illustrated with the change between Fatima and Zainab as role-models for women. In traditional Shi'ism, Fatima, the daughter of Muhammad and wife of 'Alī, serves as the model of a subordinate and obedient woman.[31] Zainab, the daughter of 'Alī and Fatima and the sister of Imam Hussein, is the model of a comrade of men, and a courageous fighter against tyranny.

Whereas in the revolutionary teaching of Ali Shari'ati these two role-models are fused into one, Guity Nashat has shown that in fundamentalist ideology they are kept separate. The model of Fatima is used during stable, ordinary times; the model of Zainab in critical, extraordinary times.[32]

From a fundamentalist point of view, the political mobilization of women is only legitimate in dramatic situations, in order to prevent the evil forces from assuming power and from destroying the godly people and their pious way of life. It is an apocalyptic battle that requires unusual measures. The same apocalyptic scenario dominates the discourse of Protestant fundamentalism during the 1920s as well as during the 1980s. Also here, the ideal role of a woman is that of a mother and housekeeper and only the present crisis legitimates the mobilization of women as a temporary measure.

The aim of the mobilization of women is to defeat the enemy. During the struggle, mobilized women are supposed to actively defend in public the internal structure of the family and the salvation interests of their children. The cooperation between men and women in this struggle also symbolizes the traditional family as an indivisible unit and strengthens its ties. But, at the same time this departure from tradition leads to an at least temporary reinterpretation of the tradition and might even end in a partial redefinition of gender roles. Although the final aim is the reestablishment of a patriarchally structured family, the form in which this structure is expressed might change.

Varieties of Repatriarchalization

Neopatriarchal redefinitions can take different directions depending on the predominant problems of patriarchalism and/or the countermodels they are fighting against in their *Kulturkampf*.

There are at least three different challenges that lead to a (re-)patriarchalization, but in different ways and with different consequences.

The first challenge is the dissolution of the patriarchal family and structure of authority through modernization processes, like secular mass education, spread of mass media and Western culture industry, and effects of urbanization, like social-moral changes. Accordingly, the conflict takes place between the "modernist" milieu and modernizing agencies on the one hand, and the mobilized traditionalist milieu on the other. The negative reference group is the modern "emancipated" woman, the positive reference group the traditionalist one. In this context, political mobilization and an emphasis on the essential structural differences between modern and traditional gender relations are most probable. Therefore, male authority will be stressed.

The second challenge that can lead to a repatriarchalization of gender relations is *machismo*. *Machismo* represents a patriarchalism grown anomic. Here the main aim is a restoration of the patriarchal family by stressing the responsibility of the father for wife and children. The negative reference group is the anomic patriarchal family, the positive reference group the remoralized patriarchal family. Since women (and children) suffer most from these anomic conditions they play a dominant role in the remoralization efforts that usually take the form not of a political but of a religious movement. Women join a religious association and primarily attempt to draw their husband or father of their children into the community. Examples are mass conversions to Pentecostalism in Latin America and black urban Pentecostal churches in the United States.

A third challenge that may lead to a repatriarchalization of gender relations is disappointment of men and women with the new roles and social relations offered by "modern" life-styles. Here, a neopatriarchal redefinition of gender relations that integrates old and new elements is most likely. On the ideological level, female subordination to male authority is acknowledged, but, on the practical level, partnership and mutual responsibility are stressed. This model, although still patriarchal in theory, allows women much more freedom, individuality, and autonomy than does the traditional model. Here, neither the traditional model nor the modern one is totally idealized or rejected. Both are selectively used in order to develop a new vision. Examples are the "social-revolutionary" teachings of Ali Shari'ati in Iran or moderate positions within American evangelicalism and the Religious Right. Given the immense economic, political, social, and, last but not least, cultural differences between the countries, the concrete forms of neopatriarchalism, of course, look quite different.

The distinction between the first and the third reactions can be illustrated by the differences within Shi'ism between the teachings of Khomeini and Shari'ati, whose positions on these issues were often interpreted as being identical. In Khomeini's fundamentalism, the emphasis seems to lie more on a retraditionalization of gender roles and a strengthening of male authority that demands that women return to the Fatima model. Biological differences are emphasized to legitimize the legal and practical subordination of women. Khomeini has a rather traditionalist Shi'ite view of women. He subscribes to all the traditional teachings about the "impurity" of women as well as their inferior ritual and legal status. And he wants to restrict women to the domestic sphere, their public appearance being just a temporary necessity.[33]

Shari'ati, on the other hand, attempts to offer an alternative to the Western model without returning to the traditional one. He sees in Fatima the new ideal woman, who is a self-confident daughter, wife, and mother, at the same time is a heroic fighter against oppression like Zainab.[34] Although his ideal stays within the pattern of the patriarchal family, his teachings are a profound break with tradition in two respects. First, he views women as much more active and individualistic. Women are individuals in their own right who participate in politics. The aspect of subordination, although present, is deemphasized. Second, Shari'ati abolishes restrictions based on the traditional concept of "impurity," which is an even more important break with tradition.[35]

In American Protestantism there are the same two tendencies within the repatriarchalization of gender relations, one more radical emphasizing subordination, one more moderate emphasizing partnership. During the 1920s the authority of the father over the family was apparently more prominent, whereas in more recent times the emphasis seems to have shifted toward partnership. If one compares fundamentalist literature of the 1920s with that of the 1980s the general change in the attitude toward gender relations obviously has had an impact on fundamentalism and its partial transformation into a more moderate evangelical position.[36]

Since we have already outlined the more strict fundamentalist attitude toward gender, we will turn to a somewhat more moderate position represented in the concept of the "New Traditional Woman," as Connaught Marshner, one of the leading female activists of the "New Christian Right," names it.[37] According to Marshner, the new traditional woman is new insofar as she gives up outdated conventions: she is traditional insofar as she emphasizes and lives the traditional values. Conventions are caused by historical circumstances, for example, the education of women or the concrete division of labor within the household. Traditional values are eternal and unchangeable, like the leadership of the husband over the family. Even if the woman would become the chief provider, the husband is still the head of the family.[38]

This neotraditionalist image of women corresponds in many respects with Shari'ati's model. But, put into historical context Shari'ati's Fatima represents a profound break with tradition and implies a creative reinterpretation and transformation of the Shi'ite heritage. Marshner's model, on the other hand, is the legitimation of an already existing practice and thereby a much less dramatic reaffirmation of the patriarchal structure in a new form. Although Shari'ati and Marshner seem to have similar ideals, the meaning and function of either approach are very different given the historical circumstances, social structure, and dominant ideas about women and gender relations in their countries.[39]

The Roles of Women: Traditional Practices and Modern Alternatives

So far, this chapter has not dealt with the question of why women adhere to this traditional ideal and why they support, create, and participate in social movements that center their protest on this topic. To ask this question and to attempt to look for the reasons for such an engagement already challenges an interpretation that explains the political mobilization of women by fundamentalism as male manipulation or by "hegemony," the most recent fashionable attempt to ascribe "false consciousness" to people whose decisions one does not like. Although there are few data available about the concrete motivation for women to participate in a repatriarchalization of social relations, it make sense to assume that women have their reasons. And there exists enough evidence to reject the idea of manipulation.[40]

In parallelism with the three types of problems mentioned above, one can distinguish three types of experiences that motivate women to support (neo-)patriarchal positions. There are women who defend their traditional way of life, those who attempt to remoralize anomic patriarchal structures, and those who convert back to (neo-)patriarchalism after having become disappointed by a modern life-style.

Let us turn first to the women who defend their traditional way of life. In many cases the patriarchal structures might work quite well and have not lost their legitimacy. This legitimacy may also be supported by religious convictions. Undoubtedly many firmly believe in the absolute value of sexual division of labor and patriarchal authority as being legitimated and positively commanded by religion. Another reason might simply be fear of change or a lack of viable alternatives. This kind of traditionalism might be supported by lack of education and skills, and, therefore, by the negative attractiveness of the "modernist" alternative. But this is not necessarily the case.

A further reason for the mobilization of women might be anger and frustration about changes in their traditional way of life enforced by anonymous market forces or bureaucratic agencies that destroy the relative autonomy of local communities and kinship groups. Many lower-class women have to work outside the house for economic reasons, but would prefer to work at home and care for their children. Often they work as domestic servants in the homes of the rich and observe the affluence of people who do not live according to the religious tradition and norms, a classical situation for the problem of theodicy. And their children are particularly exposed to the anomic situation in modern cities. They have little to gain from the modernization of gender relations, but much to lose.

And finally "status" might play a role in the mobilization of women. But, what often is labeled as "status-anxieties" should instead be described as the defense of a way of life that is challenged and devalued by other social groups. Those women express their resentment at being treated with contempt by the modernist milieu and being confronted with pressure to adapt to new role models proposed by modernizing government agencies, educational institutions, commercial advertising, and mass media.

To those defenders of traditionalism belong the majority of women in Protestant fundamentalism in the United States during the early twentieth century as well as many of the lower-class supporters of Khomeini in Iran and other fundamentalist mass movements in the Islamic world.

The second ideal-typical group of women propagating patriarchal gender relations consists of those suffering from anomic patriarchalism, or *machismo*. They have the burden of housekeeping and the education of children without appropriate financial, practical, and emotional support from their husbands or the fathers of their children. They tend to join apolitical religious groups in order to restructure the family and protect their children rather than being attracted by fundamentalist protest movements. To those religious remoralizers of patriarchalism belong particularly the Latin American converts to Pentecostalism.[41]

The third ideal-typical camp of women who support patriarchal positions from a religious point of view are those who convert back to the traditionalist ideal. And there are plausible reasons for this decision, too. One reason might be, of course, religious conversion, the adoption of a religious belief that positively commands a sexual division of labor and patriarchal authority. Another reason might be disappointment about the "modern way of life," like problems with the partner and/or the children, the instability of the modern family, disappointment about the job and professional life, sexual harassment at the workplace, in public transportation, or the like.

When positively valued, the security of the traditional woman's role might offer satisfaction and meaning that the modern role with all its ambiguities does not provide. And the desexualization of the female body in public through "decent" clothing may actually protect women from being harassed.[42] Many of the more recent quite well-educated middle-class converts to evangelicalism and religious conservatism belong to this type.[43] Also the celebrities (singers, dancers, musicians, actors) proudly presented by Protestant as well as Islamic fundamentalists after having overcome a personal crisis by converting back from "modernism" to religious "traditionalism," belong to this category.

All these reasons to defend or to convert back to traditionalist life-styles, ideals, and symbols are, of course, neither mutually exclusive nor do they cover all possible and actual motivations. But they might help us understand why women support fundamentalism and other positions advocating patriarchal ideals. By taking their decisions seriously fundamentalist women offer a critical reevaluation of the discrepancy between the ideals of "modernity" on the one hand, and the actual practices and experiences on the other hand. It seems rather obvious that the mass support of fundamentalism by women is a consequence of social praxis rather than an abstract rejection of "modernity" as a philosophical concept. "Modernity" is not, or at least no longer, judged by what it promises, but by what it delivers. It seems quite obvious that all these different attempts to repatriarchalize gender relations would not be possible without the massive support or even the initiative of women.[44]

The Outcome: An Irony of History?

Hitherto we have dealt with the fundamentalist perspectives on women as well as the ideological context and aim of the fundamentalist mobilization of women. Let us turn now to our final question: What are the consequences of women's political mobilization in fundamentalist movements? Since women are not only mobilized, but are also mobilizers, organizers, and activist leaders the actual outcome of the fundamentalist protest movements cannot be taken for granted or concluded from the fundamentalist ideology.

In ideal-typical exaggeration one can think of three different outcomes. The process could lead to a repatriarchalization of gender relations in the strict fundamentalist sense, emphasizing male authority and reinforcing the separation between a male public and a female domestic sphere. Or, the outcome could be a more moderate version of patriarchalism, what Judith Stacey has called "patriarchy in the last instance,"[45] which stresses partnership rather than authority and redefines the division of labor between men and women. Or, it could result in an "irony of history," where the political mobilization of women by fundamentalism unintendedly leads to a transformation of gender roles and to an emancipation of women from the patriarchal model where the definition of life-spheres based on gender is overcome.

The actual outcome of the political mobilization of women by fundamentalism can neither be deduced from the fact of mobilization nor from the intended result of this mobilization. It is obviously influenced by a variety of factors, many of which we cannot deal with in this context. There seem to exist three decisive factors: the structure of women's participation in the fundamentalist movement itself and the degrees of participation of women in the extradomestic workforce and in higher education.

We can suggest two hypotheses with regard to the outcome of the mobilization of women by fundamentalism, each of which requires more research. First, the more women have their own autonomous and autocephalous institutions within the fundamentalist movements the better the chances are that they will build permanent, stable organizations and train a new generation of female activist leaders. When they lack autonomy and autocephaly it is more probable that their activism will remain a historical episode. Second, the more fundamentalist women participate in higher education and/or in the extradomestic workforce the higher the probability is for a stable institutionalization of the impulse provided by mobilization. This does, of course, not imply that higher education or extradomestic work automatically produces a feminist consciousness. Both factors, however, render an acceptance of strict patriarchal authority much less probable.

Shi'ite Fundamentalism

Let us first turn to the Iranian situation until the revolution and its transformation under the Islamic Republic. Here women are part of a mass movement. Their loyalty belongs to the charismatic leader, but their mobilization is organized through religious associations and their clientelistic networks. Obviously, the public appearance of women in mass demonstrations is a "tremendous departure from the norm."[46] The major question remains: Will this mass mobilization have an impact that will supersede the ideological commitment? A look at the structure of the mobilization suggests that this might not be the case in Iran for the following reasons.

First, the male-dominated structure of mobilization and its orientation toward the charismatic male leader reinforce practically and symbolically the subordination of women to male authority. Second, although the mass mobilization of women could give the impression that they are equal to men, their segregated public appearance proves and reinforces the image of them being "different." Third, there is little or no institutional autonomy and autocephaly of fundamentalist women organizations. Therefore, they lack the continuity, stability, and independence necessary to train a new generation of female activists with farther-reaching aspirations.

At this point it might be helpful to remember the experience of other politically active women. During the Algerian war for independence women were very much part of the resistance movement. But this turned out to be a temporary phenomenon and therefore did not promote changes in the structure of the family and gender relations in the following decades.[47] There is no necessary connection between political mobilization and "emancipation," particularly when the women themselves do not aspire to such an ideal.

There is, however, one decisive difference between Algerian women during the 1950s and Iranian women during the 1970s and 1980s. The participation of Iranian women in the extradomestic workforce as well as in higher education provides many incentives and much more support to transform the impulse of mobilization into an actual redefinition or even overcoming of traditionalism. An interesting reflection of this trend can be observed in the presence of women in the Iranian parliament as well as in some governmental offices.

To sum up, there is not in the structure of the Shi'ite fundamentalist mobilization of women any precondition necessary for a stable institutionalization of women's independence that could lead in the long run to a change in the structural principles of gender relations. Therefore, there is no "irony of history" taking place in the case of Iran as an outgrowth of the political mobilization of women by fundamentalism.

This tendency is clearly supported by the postrevolutionary practice of the regime and by the split between the fundamentalist and social-revolutionary supporters. Khomeini intended the fundamentalist mobilization of women to be a temporary measure to fight the regime of the shah. Most of his "progressive" statements on women before the revolution were purely tactical. After the revolution the pressure on women to defer to men and to withdraw from the public sphere immediately increased. Alternative views of the role of women were discouraged by intimidation and threats of violence.

Compared to the prerevolutionary conditions, the temporary political mobilization of women by Shi'ite fundamentalism has already led to a more radicalized version of the traditional woman's role. Additionally, generations of girls are exposed to a socialization and education based on fundamentalist ideals and many of them will be excluded from modern higher education and professional life.

This does not imply that fundamentalists are opposed to the education of women in general. To the contrary, they are very much in favor of it as long as it is based on the fundamentalist interpretation of Islam and gender segregation is guaranteed. They are aware, as the female mouthpiece of Islamic fundamentalism in Pakistan, Maryam Jameelah, has put it, that "(a)n illiterate and apathetic woman cannot possibly counteract the anti-Islamic influences which are harming her children day and night. Only an intelligent and enthusiastic Muslim womanhood can prove equal to the tasks which confront her now." And Khomeini argues similarly that "Woman is the instructor of society. From the lap of woman human beings emerge. . . . It is woman who, with her correct education, produces humanity, who, with her correct education, cultivates the country."[48]

Even if the exclusion from professional life cannot be a total one, for economic and other reasons, fundamentalism definitely means a step backwards for women with regard to individual autonomy. Furthermore, it will at least slow down the process of erosion of patriarchal authority. This does not at all mean that other models, like the neotraditionalist one of Shari'ati or the modernist Western one, have ceased to exist or will not survive. Both are firmly established and cannot be suppressed in the long run. But it seems obvious that for a certain period of time fewer women are able to practice those alternatives because of social and political pressure. And fewer women might become interested in those alternatives because of their education, internalized values, and aspirations.

If there will be any change in the roles of women and gender relations in Iran it will result from women's participation in higher education and in the extradomestic workforce and from compromises of the regime with more moderate positions than from unintended consequences of the political mobilization of women by the fundamentalist movement itself. However, the provocative fundamentalist claims have already contributed to the development of an Islamic feminism.[49] In this respect one could indeed speak of an "irony of history."

Protestant Fundamentalism and the Religious Right

When we turn to the United States the picture looks quite different compared to Iran. The fundamentalist movement as a whole is by far more pluralistically organized. There is not one charismatic leader comparable to Khomeini, but, of course, there are some people who stand out, like William Riley, Frank Norris, and John Roach Straton during the 1920s and Jerry Falwell and Pat Robertson during the 1980s. And the fundamentalist camp consists of many autonomous groups.

There have also been some major changes within Protestant fundamentalism since the 1920s. First, Protestant fundamentalism has undergone an internal differentiation that reaches from separatist groups to moderate evangelicals. Furthermore, the charismatic groups became widely accepted as belonging to the "Christian Right." And Protestant fundamentalists even cooperate with some groups they had denounced during the 1920s, like Catholics, Jews, and Mormons. Except for the separatists, fundamentalism has become one major element within a conservative ecumenical movement.

In comparison to the role of women within the Shi'ite fundamentalist movement, in the United States women have played a much more prominent role within the movement from the beginning. They are much more part of fundamentalist organizations on different levels. Furthermore, there exist separate women organizations led and run by women, like Phyllis Schlafly's "Eagle Forum" and Anita Bryant's "Save Our Children,Inc."[50] These organizations have autonomy and autocephaly, and are largely independent from male dominance. This autonomy and autocephaly are also part of an evangelical tradition that goes back to the nineteenth century. This organizational independence should result in a change in gender relation by providing the resources as well as the role models.

But there are also trends opposing such a transformation that should not be overlooked. First, these organizations see their primary aim in the fight of feminism and advocate the preservation or reestablishment of the patriarchal structure of authority and morality as obligatory. Second, they also focus their activity primarily on traditional "women-issues," protecting "hearth and home."[51] They are single-issue movements that cooperate with other fundamentalist organizations.

Seen as part of the entire patriarchal movement they reproduce the traditional family model and its sexual division of labor in the public arena. And one should also remember that evangelical or evengelically inspired women movements in American history have always managed to combine public activism with a defense of female domesticity as a norm to be enforced on everybody. If one does not confuse this female activism with emancipation (which should be defined as the overcoming of the obligatory character of gender spheres and patriarchal authority) then one should be aware of the limits of this activism.

What, however, has dramatically changed over the last decades is the participation of women in higher education as well as in the extradomestic workforce. Therefore, a reevaluation of the traditional gender roles has already taken place. To some extent the "new traditional woman" and more recent positions within evangelicalism can be interpreted as a shift in emphasis from authority to partnership.

In the United States the fundamentalist mobilization of women has already produced a neotraditionalist redefinition of the role of women and gender relations. As a consequence it has led to a firm establishment of a traditionalist alternative to the "modern" role of women and a more self-assured propagation of this ideal. Furthermore, the neopatriarchal gender relations have already adapted to modern life-styles. Female subordination, despite its ideological preservation, has in practice already become less important than partnership. Above all, and contrary to Iran, it is lacking support from the legal system.

If we want to speak of an "irony of history" then this phrase applies to the American experience. What has caused this ironic outcome is not the autonomy and autocephaly of institutions run by women alone, however, but the coincidence of this organizational independence with other factors, like the spread of higher education and participation in the extradomestic workforce.

Conclusion

Despite the profound differences between the United States and Iran there are interesting similarities that might indicate a more general trend. In the United States urbanization, industrialization, mass education, and the influence of the mass media did not lead to a general abolishment of patriarchal ideals. Although these processes and the broad participation of women in the workforce apparently promoted a restructuring and reevaluation of gender relations and the family, they did not automatically produce a positive appreciation of this trend in all segments of society. And the case of Iran shows that even in a country with a rather low level of industrialization, and even with the threat of massive violence, an authoritarian, theocratic regime is apparently not able to enforce its traditionalist ideal on all women. The alternatives survive. And the routinization of the revolutionary charisma has already led to a less rigid enforcement of patriarchal moralism and to compromises with other ideals and practices.

The cases of the United States and Iran, therefore, seem to indicate that neither the modernist nor the fundamentalist model can successfully claim a monopoly even under seemingly ideal conditions. Apparently, there are two parallel and partly contradictory historical trends. The first trend consists in an economic and legal rationalization and accordingly desexualization of gender relations, thereby promoting individual autonomy of women as citizens and economic actors. The other trend consists of various attempts to rebiologize gender relations and to strengthen the institution of the family under patriarchal authority, thereby renouncing individual autonomy.

The conflict between these two trends is one between a position emphasizing individual rights and one emphasizing a specific moral order. Or, to put it differently, it is a conflict between the claimed sacrosanctity of the individual and the claimed sacrosanctity of the patriarchal family. Or, to put in different terms again, it is the old conflict between an absolute natural law and a relative natural law, which according to Ernst Troeltsch was at the heart of the conflict between sect and church in the history of Christianity.[52] On the level of social discourse these opposite trends lead to polarization and *Kulturkampf*. On the level of practices they describe the boundaries in which a variety of differently structured gender relations and roles of women are possible.

Furthermore, both cases indicate that the conflict about the proper role of women and the structure of the family is not simply a function of economic development or political struggle for power. It is very much part of a cultural conflict and public discourse about the structure of social relations, about what human beings are and ought to be. Since processes of social and cultural differentiation and individualization are very much at the heart of modernity, as Georg Simmel once correctly diagnosed, the future development will not bring about homogeneity but an increasing variety of ideals and practices. Therefore, the question is not how to avoid diversity and conflict, but how to deal with them.

The recent domination of the public discourse by fundamentalism on the one hand, and radical feminism on the other hand has suggested that there are only two ethical options for the reevaluation of gender relations. Either one supports the "sect" option of absolute natural law and gender-neutral equality, or the "church" option of relative natural law, inborn gender differences, and "God's will" as being expressed in the patriarchal family. But there exists already a third option that is widely practiced but much less prominent in public rhetoric and often not perceived as being equally a moral and ethical choice: the "denominational" option of a culture of pluralism that supports a more pragmatic view of gender relations and gender roles, and accepts a plurality of moral orders.

Such a culture of pluralism is based on the notion of legitimacy as a process in which different models of gender relations with socially and culturally limited claims of validity are negotiated by the people affected. It stresses the participatory character of the procedure by which those models are worked out rather than any predefined content of the models. Instead of imposing one particularistic model on all societies, cultures, and social groups by claiming its universal validity, men and women work out their own models of gender relations with limited claims of validity and associate on the basis of their preferences. This option would also exclude any ascription of social-moral preferences on the basis of cultural or religious tradition, ethnicity, or race.

This "denominational" model seems best suited to take into account the trends of modern societies and cultures toward individualization, pluralization, and globalization. Whereas the "sect" model is based on a radical ethic of ultimate conviction and the "church" model on a rigid ethic of law, the "denominational" model corresponds with an ethic of responsibility that takes into account the forseeable consequences of ethical decisions. Since monopolistic solutions for social-moral problems neither develop automatically nor can they successfully be enforced, as the cases of the United States and Iran have shown, only the pluralistic option seems to combine a maximization of freedom with a minimization of conflict and therefore offers the highest degree of legitimacy.

Notes

1.   See Azar Tabari, "The Enigma of the Veiled Iranian Women," *MERIP Reports*, Feb. 1982, pp. 22–27; Guity Nashat, "Women in the Islamic Republic of Iran," *Iranian Studies* 13 (1980): 165–194.

2.   For the purpose of the following comparison I use the term *traditional* to designate structures of gender relations taken for granted and/or representing dominant cultural ideals. Therefore, the "traditional" family in the United States during the 1920s is identical with the "modern" family as it developed during the nineteenth century in the West.

3.   See Cheryl Bernard and Zalmay Khalilzad, *"The Government of God"—Iran's Islamic Republic* (New York: Columbia University Press, 1984), pp. 95–102; Yvonne Y. Haddad, "Sayyid Qtub: Ideologue of Islamic Revival," in John L. Esposito, ed., *Voices of Resurgent Islam*, (New York: Oxford University Press, 1983); Mervat Hatem, "The Enduring Alliance of Nationalism and Patriarchy in Muslim Personal Status Laws: The Case of Modern Egypt," *Feminist Issues* 6, no. 1 (1986): 19–43; Valerie J. Hoffmann-Ladd, "Polemics on the Modesty and Segregation of Women in Contemporary Egypt, *International Journal of Middle East Studies* 19, no. 1 (1987): 23–50; Marnia Lazreg, "Gender and Politics in Algeria: Unravelling the Religious Paradigm," *Signs* 15, no. 4 (1990): 155–180; Richard P. Mitchell, *The Society of the Muslim Brothers* (London: Oxford University Press, 1969), 223–224,

254–259; Martin Riesebrodt, *Fundamentalismus als patriarchalische Protestbewegung* (Tübingen: J. C. B. Mohr, 1990), pp. 123–213 (English translation *Pious Passion*, University of California Press, 1993); Tabari, "Enigma"; Azar Tabari, "Islam and the Struggle for Emancipation of Iranian Women," in Azar Tabari and Nahid Yeganeh, eds., (London: Zed Press, 1982); Binnaz Toprak, "Politicization of Islam in a Secular State: The National Salvation Party in Turkey," in Said A. Arjomand, *From Nationalism to Revolutionary Islam*, (Albany: State University of New York Press, 1984), pp. 119–133; John A. Williams, "Veiling in Egypt as a Political and Social Phenomenon," in John L. Esposito, ed., *Islam and Development: Religion and Sociopolitical Change* (Syracuse: Syracuse University Press, 1980), pp. 71–85; Rivka Yadlin, "Militant Islam in Egypt: Some Sociocultural Aspects," in Gabriel R. Warburg and Uri M. Kupferschmidt, eds., *Islam, Nationalism, and Redicalism in Egypt and Sudan* (New York: Praeger, 1983), pp. 159–182; Nahid Yeganeh, "Women's Struggle in the Islamic Republic of Iran, in Azar Tabari and Nahid Yeganeh, eds., *In the Shadow of Islam* (London: Zed Press, 1982), pp. 26–74; Nahaid Yeganeh and Nikki Keddie, "Sexuality and Shi'i Social Protest in Iran," in Juan R. J. Cole and Nikki R. Keddie, eds., *Shi'ism and Social Protest* (New Haven: Yale University Press, 1986), pp. 108–136; Sami Zubaida, "The Quest for the Islamic State:' Fundamentalism in Egypt and Iran," in Lionel Caplan, ed., *Studies in Religious Fundamentalism* (Albany: State University of New York Press, 1987), pp. 25–50.

4. See Margaret L. Bendroth, "The Search for 'Women's Role' in American Evangelism, 1930–1980," in George Marsden, ed., *Evangelicalism and Modern America* (Grand Rapids, Michigan: Eerdmans, 1984), pp. 122–134; Jerry Falwell, *Listen America!* (Garden City, N.Y.: Doubleday, 1980); Robert Liebman and Robert Wuthnow, eds., *The New Christian Right* (New York: Aldine, 1983); George Marsden, *Fundamentalism and American Culture* (New York: Oxford University Press, 1980); Riesebrodt, *Fundamentalismus*, pp. 40–122.

5. The fact that this paradox has received so little attention so far, particularly in comparative perspective, accounts for some short-comings of this chapter. Nevertheless, if its structural outline by provoking criticism motivates people to turn their attention to these problems, it will have served its purpose.

6. Karl Mannheim, *Conservatism*, trans. D. Ketteler, V. Meja, and N. Stehr (London: Routledge and Kegan Paul, 1988); Said A. Arjomand, "Traditionalism in Twentieth-Century Iran," in Said A. Arjomand, ed., *From Nationalism to Revolutionary Islam* (Albany: State University of New York Press, 1984), pp. 195–232.

7. Eric Hobsbawm and Terence Ranger, eds., *The Invention of Tradition* (Cambridge: Cambridge University Press, 1983).

8. Riesebrodt, *Fundamentalismus*, pp. 18–24.

9. This distinction parallels a critical statement by the modernist Chicago theologian Shailer Mathews, who criticized the premillenarian funda-

mentalists for "missing the spirit by emphasizing the letter." See
Shailer Mathews, "Will Christ Come Again?" pamphlet, Chicago, 1917,
p. 10.

10. This distinction between modernists and fundamentalists is an ideal-
typical one. This is not to claim that fundamentalists rely exclusively
on an ethic of law or that utopian modernism cannot become authoritarian. This distinction is also based on typical attitudes rather than
on actual outcomes.

11. Of course, other types of fundamentalism as well as conservative and
orthodox forms of religion also based on (neo)patriarchal forms of
gender relations are supported by women in growing numbers. But
women attempt to solve a different problem by joining them, and as
a rule they are not mobilized politically by these groups. Therefore,
the second, structural paradox I have pointed out in the beginning
does not apply to them. See, for example, Lynn Davidman, *Tradition
in a Rootless World* (Berkeley: University of California Press, 1991),
and Debra R. Kaufman, *Rachel's Daughters* (New Brunswick and
London: Rutgers University Press, 1991), with regard to orthodox
Judaism; Elizabeth Brusco, "Colombian Evangelicalism as a Strategic
Form of Women's Collective Action," *Feminist Issues* 6, no. 2 (1986):
3–13; idem, "The Household Basis of Evangelical Religion and the
Reformation of Machismo in Colombia" (Ph.D. diss., City University
of New York, 1986); and David Martin, *Tongues of Fire: The Explosion
of Protestantism in Latin America* (Cambridge, Mass.: Basil Blackwell,
1990), with regard to Latin American Pentecostalism; and Judith
Stacey, *Brave New Families* (New York: Basic Books, 1991) with regard
to American evangelicalism.

12. See among others Joseph Gusfield, *Symbolic Crusade* (Urbana:
University of Illinois Press, 1963); Rebecca Klatch, *Women of the New
Right* (Philadelphia: Temple University Press, 1987); Guity Nashat, ed.,
Women and Revolution in Iran (Boulder, Colo.: Westview Press, 1983).

13. Falwell, *Listen America!* pp. 122, 124, 128, 150; see also James D.
Hunter, *Evangelicalism: The Coming Generation* (Chicago: University
of Chicago Press, 1987), pp. 76–115.

14. Phyllis Schlafly, *The Power of the Christian Woman* (Cincinnati, Ohio:
Standard, 1981), pp. 9, 10, 11; see also Susan D. Rose, *Keeping Them
Out of the Hands of Satan: Evangelical Schooling in America* (New
York: Routledge, 1988), pp. 58–68; Nancy Tatom Ammerman, *Bible
Believers: Fundamentalists in the Modern World* (New Brunswick and
London: Rutgers University Press, 1987), pp. 134–146.

15. See Farah Azari, "Sexuality and Women's Oppression in Iran," in Farah
Azari, ed., *Women of Iran*, (London: Ithaca Press, 1983), pp. 90–156;
Constitution of the Islamic Republic of Iran, trans. and ed. Hamid
Algar (Berkeley: Mizan Press, 1980); William Darrow, "Woman's Place
and the Place of Women in the Iranian Revolution," in Yvonne Haddad
and Ellison Findly, eds., *Women, Religion, and Social Change*, (Albany:

State University of New York Press, 1985); Shireen Mahdavi, "Women and the Shi'i Ulama in Iran," *Middle Eastern Studies* 19 (1983): 23–24; Mina Modares, "Women and Shi'ism in Iran," *m/f* 5/6 (1981): 67–76; Val Moghadam, "Women, Work, and Ideology in the Islamic Republic," *International Journal of Middle East Studies* 20 (1988): 223–228; Nashat, "Women"; Nashat, *Women*; Riesebrodt, *Fundamentalismus*, pp. 154–157, 172; Eliz Sanasarian, "Political Activism and Islamic Identity in Iran," in Lynne B. Iglitzin and Ruth Ross, eds., *Women in the World*, (Santa Barbara: ABC-Clio, 1986), pp. 214–218. Basically the same position is taken in Sunni fundamentalism by representatives such as Maudoodi and Jameelah (see Maryam Jameelah, *Islam and the Muslim Woman Today* [Sant Nagar, Lahore: Mohammad Yusuf Khan, 1976]).

16. Ruhollah Khomeini, *A Clarification of Questions*, trans. J. Borujerdi (Boulder, Colo.: Westview Press, 1984); see particularly problems 434–507 on menstruation.

17. Adele Ferdows, "Religion in Iranian Nationalism" (Ph.D. diss. Indiana University, 1967).

18. Fedayan-I Islam, "Rahnema-Yi Haqa'iq," translated as "The Book of Ideology by the Fadyan Islam" by Adele Ferdows. Printed as appendix to ibid. pp. 9–11.

19. Ruhollah Khomeini, *Islam and Revolution*, ed. Hamid Algar (Berkeley: Mizan Press, 1980), pp. 31, 33, 58, 170–171, 222.

20. Fedayan-I Islam, "Rahnema-yi Haqa'iq," p. 9.

21. Azari, "Sexuality," pp. 135–136; Monika Schuckar, *Der Kampf gegen die Sünde. Frauenbild und Moralpolitik in der Islamischen Republik Iran* (Gießen: Reihe Internationalismus-Informationen Nr. 10, 1983).

22. John Roach Straton, *The Menace of Immorality in Church and State* (New York: George H. Doran, 1920), p. 57.

23. *The King's Business* (Bible Institute of Los Angeles, 1923), pp. 233, 317.

24. Straton, *Menace*, p. 49.

25. Ibid., pp. 49–50.

26. See Shahin Gerami, "The Privatization of Woman's Role in the Islamic Republic of Iran, in Gustavo Benavides and M. W. Daly, eds., *Religion and Political Power* (Albany: State University of New York Press, 1989), pp. 99–118; Shahla Haeri, *Law of Desire* (Syracuse: Syracuse University Press, 1989), pp. 75–102; Jan Hjärpe, "The Attitude of Islamic Fundamentalism Towards the Question of Women in Islam," in Bo Utas, ed., *Women in Islamic Societies* (Atlantic Highlands: Humanities Press, 1983), pp. 12–25.

27. Fedayan-I Islam, "Rahnema-Yi Haqa'iq," p. 12. Cf. Falwell, *Listen America!* p. 124; Schlafly, *Power.*

28. Falwell, *Listen America!*, pp. 150–151; speech by Khomeini cited in Tabari and Yeganeh, eds., *Shadow of Islam*, p. 99.

29. Riesebrodt, *Fundamentalismus* pp. 231–235.

30. Ibid., pp. 29–31.

31. Moojan Momen, *An Introduction to Shi'i Islam* (New Haven: Yale University Press, 1985), pp. 235–236; Nashat, *Women*, p. 211; Esko Naskali, "Women of the Prophet's Family as They Feature in Popular Bazaar Literature," in Utas, ed., *Women*, pp. 245–249; Gustav E. Thaiss, "Religious Symbolism and Social Change: The Drama of Husain," (Ph.D. diss., Washington University, 1973), pp. 45–48, 378–379.

32. Nashat, *Women*, pp. 211–212.

33. Khomeini, *Clarification*.

34. Ali Shariati, *Fatima Is Fatima*, trans. L. Bakhtiar (Tehran: Shariati Foundation, 1981); Adele Ferdows, "Women and the Islamic Republic," *International Journal of Middle East Studies* 15 (1983): 283–298; Nashat, "Women", p. 212.

35. Ferdows points out correctly the ambivalence in Shari'ati's concept of women ("Women"; "Shariati and Khomeini on Women,' in Nikki R. Keddie and Eric Hooglund, eds., *The Iranian Revolution and the Islamic Republic*, [Syracuse: Syracuse University Press, 1986]). But instead of seeing in it a new development, she identifies his position with that of Khomeini and Motahhari.

36. See, for example, Hunter, *Evangelicalism*, pp. 76–115.

37. Connaught C. Marshner, *The New Traditional Woman* (Washington, D.C.: Free Congress Research and Education Foundation, 1982). Within evangelical Christianity there are much more extreme positions than Marshner's, emphasizing either stronger patriarchal authority or female equality.

38. Klatch, *Women*, pp. 145–146.

39. Here the necessity of a historical and cultural contextualization of any definition of feminism becomes obvious. See Karen Offen, "Defining Feminism: A Comparative Historical Approach," *Signs* 14, no. 1 (1988): 119–157.

40. See, for example, Mary E. Hegland, "'Traditonal' Iranian Women: How They Cope," *Middle East Journal* 36, no. 4 (1982): 483–501. In Latin American Pentecostalism it is the women who "manipulate" the men; see Martin, *Tongues*, p. 181; Brusco, "Colombian Evangelicalism."

41. Brusco, "Colombian Evangelicalism"; idem., "Household Basis of Evangelical Religion" Salvatore Cucchiari, "Between Shame and Sanctification: Patriarchy and Its Transformation in Sicilian Pentecostalism," *American Ethnologist* 17, no. 4 (1990): 687–707; Lesley Gill, "'Like a Veil to Cover Them': Women and the Pentecostal Movement in La Paz," *American Ethnologist* 17, no. 4 (1990): 708–721; Martin, *Tongues*.

42. See, for example Williams, "Veiling," p. 82.

43. Susan D. Rose, "Women Warriors: The Negotiation of Gender in a Charismatic Community," *Sociological Analysis* 48, no. 3 (1987): 245–258; Rose, *Evangelical Schooling*; Judith Stacey, "Sexism by a Subtler Name? Postindustrial Condition and Postfeminist Conscious-

ness in the Silicon Valley," *Socialist Review* 96 (1987): 7–28; Judith Stacey and Elizabeth Gerard, ' "We Are Not Doormats': The Influence of Feminism on Contemporary Evangelicals in the United States," in Faye Ginsburg and Anna Lowenhaupt Tsing, eds., *Uncertain Terms: Negotiating Gender in American Culture*, (Boston: Beacon Press, 1990).

44. In this respect the parallel to the Ku Klux Klan during the 1920s is obvious. See Kathleen M. Blee, *Women of the Klan: Racism and Gender in the 1920s* (Berkeley: University of California Press, 1991).

45. Stacey, *Families*, p. 133.

46. Guity Nashat, "Women in the Ideology of the Islamic Republic," in Guity Nashat, ed., *Women and Revolution in Iran*, (Boulder, Colo.: Westview Press, 1983) p. 212. In this article, Nashat describes very carefully and illuminatingly how the fundamentalists control the discourse in order to bring women "back on track."

47. The rise of fundamentalism in Algeria is another proof.

48. Jameelah, *Islam*, p. 15; speech by Khomeini cited in Azar Tabari and Nahid Yeganeh, eds., *In the Shadow of Islam*, (London: Zed Press, 1982) p. 101.

49. Fatima Mernissi's feminist reinterpretation of the Koran is only one among numerous attempts to challenge the predominance of conservative and fundamentalist interpreters. See Fatima Mernissi, *The Veil and the Male Elite*, trans. M. J. Lakeland (Reading, Mass.: Addison Wesley, 1989).

50. Klatch, *Women*, pp. 119–153.

51. Alan Crawford, *Thunder on the Right* (New York: Pantheon Books, 1980), pp. 144–164.

52. See Ernst Troeltsch, *The Social Teaching of the Christian Churches*, trans. O. Wyon (New York: Macmillan), pp. 328–349. Troeltsch also makes the interesting observation that the Protestant sects in America incorporated many "churchly" elements by relying on Paul rather than on the preaching of Jesus, particularly the Sermon on the Mount. A similar development seems to be true with regard to Iranian Shi'ism, which also integrated "churchly" and "sectarian" elements.

11

An American Paradox: The Place of Religion in an Ambiguous Polity

Steven M. Tipton

A reinvigorated debate over the place of religion in American public life has been bubbling away for a decade now, mainly in social philosophy and constitutional law. But it has important sociological implications, and it makes crucial sociological assumptions. This chapter touches on both in the course of staking out a third position in this debate between "philosophical liberals" and their "communitarian" critics.

Civic and Liberal Freedoms

What stymies most current efforts to chart the place of religion in a free, self-governing society like America's is the inescapably problematic, peculiar, and essential ambiguity of the American polity, both as a cultural locale and a constellation of institutional arrangements. Given this premise, the paradox of religion's situation in our public life and its constitutional expression can be grasped if not resolved.

In *Habits of the Heart* the authors distinguished the meaning of freedom within the context of the civic republican and biblical moral traditions from its meaning in the traditions of utilitarian and expressive individualism.[1] This accords with what we might simply term "civic freedom" in the positive sense of our freedom as a people *to* govern ourselves together; and "liberal freedom" In the negative sense of our freedom as individuals *from* others' interference.[2] Note how this distinction underlies bifocal construal of religious freedom as the Constitution defines it. The First Amendment states, "Congress shall make no law respecting an establishment of religion or prohibiting the free exercise thereof." The amendment's first clause prohibits a religious establishment or state church. The second clause protects "the free exercise of religion." Seen from the traditional standpoint of "civic freedom," the exercise of religion is the controlling idea, which nonestablishment serves. The establishment of any particular confessional religion or church is prohibited because it would infringe on the free exercise and positive institutionalization of religion generally in what was already a confessionally diverse nation 200 years ago.

Such infringement would not simply coerce some citizens to support a confession not their own. It would exclude these citizens from full political membership and public participation based on religious differences. Further, disestablishing and "deconfessionalizing" religion does not simply serve to protect churches from state interference, and the state from wars of religion. It enables all citizens to conceive the common purposes of their lives together in relation to "God's purposes and Nature's laws," to use terms set by the Declaration of Independence. In this universal light it allows them to judge these common purposes, to argue them coherently, and to live them out more or less persuasively. Thus religion lies at the moral center of public life, even as the institutional bodies of church and state remain distinct, each governed by its own members.

If the free exercise of religion is conceived primarily in terms of "liberal freedom," by contrast, the logic of the two clauses is inverted. Disestablishment controls the free exercise of religion, and subsumes it into the concept of "the separation of church and state," a phrase without constitutional standing but with great intuitive power in this second cultural context. Religious freedom then commonly comes to be construed as the individual's right to worship any god or none at all, and religion becomes a private matter of no inherent concern to political society. Disestablishment and deconfessionalization imply privatization and, by confusion with principles of religious toleration, they justify efforts to bracket religion outside of public life.

Now, these difficulties of constitutional interpretation stem from something more than institutionally disembodied cultural conflict or confusion between two conceptions of freedom as a cardinal political virtue. They reflect a fundamental American ambiguity: Are we a republic in recognizable relation to classical or Calvinist republics, and dependent for our integrity upon a sense of civic virtue and the mores of republican citizenship? Or are we a liberal constitutional state, governed through the coordination of individuals' conflicting interests and equal rights? The American answer, in short, is that we have sought to be both—to enjoy civic and liberal freedoms alike—to retain the moral integrity and binding public spirit of a republic in the political structure of a liberal constitutional state, with its stress on voluntarism and personal sovereignty.[3] In so doing we have lived with profound tensions. Overriding concern for self-interest is the very definition of the corruption of republican virtue, which must check free choice even as it guides free conscience through a sense of mutual responsibility and duty.[4] Yet from the beginning American society has been a mixture of republican and liberal political ideals and arrangements, not a pure type of either one.

With this ambiguity in mind, consider the unambiguous context in which philosophical liberalism has come to see religious groups mainly as a divisive problem for "modern democratic states," as philosopher John Rawls posits, since these groups feature "controversial" conceptions of the common good, institutional strategies for realizing them, and conflicting ethics for evaluating them, which are all irresolvable in a morally pluralistic society.[5] So Rawls seeks rational agreement on moral rules in the form of contractual principles of "justice as fairness" that can be justified without favoring any one of the conceptions of good that divide Americans. But such justification itself turns out to presuppose a particular conception of the person as prior to, rather than constituted by moral commitments.[6] For Rawls, "free and equal" persons take part in society as "a fair system of cooperation." They act "rationally to pursue a conception of one's own rational advantage, or good."[7]

Since, as a matter of social and historical fact, there is not just one conception of the person implicit in American culture, we can note the formulation of Rawls' claim at this point in order to clarify the sociological premises that underpin philosophical arguments of the sort he advances: "Recall that a Kantian view, in addressing the public culture of a democratic society, hopes to bring to awareness a conception of the person and of social cooperation conjectured to be implicit in that culture, or at least congenial to its deepest tendencies when properly expressed and presented."[8]

A version of Rawls' mutually disinterested, procedurally consistent, risk-averse selves primarily committed to maximizing their own individual rights and liberties is indeed a conception of selfhood implicit in American society's public culture. That does not mean this is the only such conception, and Rawls is not claiming it is. But neither does it mean that this is the predominant conception; or, more subtly, as Rawls *is* claiming, that such individuals constitute the conception of selfhood congenial to the *deepest* tendencies of our democratic society's public culture, while other conceptions by implication express and fit its shallower tendencies. This last formulation reveals that such liberal arguments rest not only on a particular conception of the good constitutive of the sort of person who will bracket "controversial" moral and religious convictions in reasoning toward procedural principles of justice. Such arguments also rest on a particular conception of the public culture of American society and the institutional arrangement of the American polity as consisting in essence of a liberal constitutional state to the exclusion of a republic.

Rawls' own efforts to clarify justice as fairness as a political, not metaphysical, concept begin by specifying that it is "a political conception of justice for a constitutional democracy," by which he means "such a society's main political, social, and economic instititions, and how they fit together into one unified system of social cooperation."[9] Such conceptions of American society as a constitutional democracy are at once too narrowly focused and too broadly generalized. To understand why, we can begin with the countervailing insight that "One's participation in politics and law is and must be based on one's most basic convictions about human good," as Michael Perry puts it.[10] Such convictions are essential to constitute persons and ground political deliberation and choice. But, in fact, such convictions not only ground our public participation, but also arise from it. They are defined and learned in terms of the multiple moral traditions within our culture. They are learned through our practical experience within the multiple spheres of social life to which these moral traditions ring true—in the family, school, and religious communities, for example, as well as politics and law.

Thus democratic politics itself requires the moral commitments and practices of the varied moral communities that together make up our pluralistic culture and link the normative spirit of politics and religion even as the institutional bodies of church and state remain distinct. Seen as an "overlapping consensus" these commitments support rather than subvert democratic politics.[11] But part of the fundamental bias of modern liberal philosophical and sociological theorists of religion and politics—and their communitarian critics—is their common reliance on oversimplified consensus models of culture and community to grasp the nature of moral unity within social diversity.

In fact, contrary to philosophical liberals and their communitarian critics alike, what holds us together as a polity and a people is not some comprehensive cultural agreement conceived as a value-consensus, or as a value-free arrangement of rules and rights to coordinate our disparate interests and ideals across seamless subcultural communities. Rather, we are held together by the coherence of our moral disagreement and argument within an ongoing cultural conversation that embraces multiple moral traditions, languages, practices, and social settings.[12] Through this process come into being the "semicovenants," the "conditional absolutes," and the situationally shared and varied "ought-tos," as historian of religion Martin Marty calls them, which critically rework and balance our social order across institutional spheres.[13] This argument does not go on simply among moral communities, each organically fused together around shared values and myths it socializes into its members. The moral argument of public life goes on within each one of us and among us all, because we all share a common culture woven of contrasting moral traditions that themselves embody continuities of conflict over how we ought to live together. And all of us lead lives that span the different social institutions and practices to which traditions ring more or less true, including a polity that is at once a religious republic and a liberal constitutional state.

Philosophical liberals' accounts of religion in American public life along the lines of Rawls are skewed by lack of religious insight, in sum, but also by a glaring political oversight and an oversimplified consensus model of culture. Specifying American society to be "a liberal constitutional democracy" whose basic structure fits its main political, social, and economic institutions together into "one unified system of social cooperation," as Rawls does, frames too narrowly focused and too grandly overgeneralized a view to make moral sense of our polity.[14] As a result, it misses the reciprocal fact that, in addition to being a divisive problem, religion in American society has also been part of its mediative answer to problems posed by philosophical liberalism itself, in its moral and political tension with our republicanism.

Civil Religion and Public Theology

Religion mediates this tension, first, by establishing a locus of moral sovereignty above the sovereignty of the state.[15] The Declaration of Independence points to the sovereignty of God over the collective political society itself when it refers in paragraph 1 to "the laws of Nature and of Nature's God" which stand above and judge the laws of men and women. Notwithstanding the subtle eighteenth-century relation of biblical to natural religion, the self-evident truths "that all Men are created equal, that they are endowed by their Creator with certain inalienable Rights" reveal a distinctly (although not entirely) biblical God who is much more than a first principle of nature, who has purposes in history, including American liberty. This is a God who creates individual human beings and actively endows them with rights no government can abrogate or create by its own legislative act. Nor can it even recognize such rights by its own constitutive social contract unless this contract is also a covenant in accord with the natural and ultimate order of existence.

It is significant that solemn public reference to a God who stands above the nation and whose ends are moral standards to judge the nation's conduct and justify its existence becomes a permanent feature of American political life ever after. It is also significant that these religious and civic ideals are thinly if securely institutionalized, without explicit legal support or sanction in the Constitution or the liberal side of our cultural heritage that it expresses.[16]

The religious and ethical needs of a genuine republic to symbolize the ultimate order of existence in which its civic virtues and values make moral sense could hardly be met by a formal "civil religion," a partly "Enlightenment religion," so thinly institutionalized *within* American government.[17] Instead these republican needs have been met in good part by predominantly biblical religious communities institutionalized *outside* any formal political structures, and by the broad range of "public theology" they have fostered. The range of public theology, as Martin Marty has called it in contrast to civil religion, reaches from the Great Awakening through abolitionism, the social gospel, and the civil rights movement to the present.[18] If such examples of public theology sound suspiciously like a liberal Protestant litany in their selectivity, we might also recall the Gospel of Wealth, Manifest Destiny, Temperance, and Christian anticommunism, to name a few more. And we should go on to heed the varieties of public theology at present, including its evangelical, fundamentalist, Christian-realist, feminist, and liberationist currents. This reminds us that public theology in

America has always unfolded as an argument and dialogue, not as a single sermon or a sociological canon, a theocratic monologue or a sectarian cacophony.

That is not to downplay the intensified cultural conflict now evident within our public theology. But it is to affirm that this moral struggle does not compel us to seek to "get religion out of politics," or to establish some brave new symbolic universalism in American public life.[19] To do so would invert the Constitution's controlling provision to protect the free exercise of religion. While invoking the principle of church-state separation, such an effort in practice could well amount to establishing philosophical liberalism itself as a state creed of latter-day Enlightenment fundamentalism.

As a matter of sociological fact, the lines of our present cultural conflict do not divide religious believers and nonbelievers, the churched and the unchurched, so significantly as they divide "cultural conservatives and liberals" across the churches and down the middle of the "moderate" Protestant denominations, American Catholicism, and the spectrum of Orthodox-to-Reform Judaism.[20] As a matter of cultural interpretation, expert efforts have been made to sociologize away the dense moral substance of this conflict by reducing it to the symbolic politics of Bible-believers versus secular humanists, or the ideal and material interests of locals versus cosmopolitans, the old business class versus the new knowledge class, and antimodern moral absolutists versus modernized moral relativists. Despite these efforts, we do not yet fully grasp the larger moral meaning and cultural pattern of this conflict, nor do we appreciate its long-term promise for our public life. Rather than a dichotomization of civil religion or an uncivil war of theocrats and apostates with a remnant of old-fashioned, wishy-washy religious liberals caught, as always, in the middle with nothing but their good intentions, in truth we are all living in the midst of a fertile if painful broadening of public theology's ambit among the educated, urbanized middle class. It is this moral argument over how we ought to order our lives together which traditionally conservative Protestants, Catholics, and Jews have now entered in sufficient numbers and with sufficient eloquence as well as clout to make their voices heard.

If we are willing to keep wrestling with one another, listening to one another, and trying to practice what we preach in order to persuade one another by example and critical, conciliar dialogue alike, then this broadened public theology will deepen and enrich the moral argument of our public life as a whole. It has already done so, in fact. It has enriched public argument over the fundamental construal of our religious and civic traditions to be true to the present and its problems. This is especially crucial for those problems, such as abortion, the family, peace, and the poor, which have no neat solutions within the one-dimensional moral universe of individual interests and rights, elaborated through national self-determination into the overriding geopolitical interests of individual nation-states.

Democratic republics, as opposed to liberal constitutional states, not only need to affirm moral ends beyond the rights and liberties of individuals. They need to accept responsibility for the moral and civic education of their citizens, on whose good character they depend. In this second respect religion has crucially mediated tensions between our liberal and republican political impulses.[21] The liberal state by its own account and our firsthand experience is eminently unqualified to inculcate moral virtue in its independent citizens. At the same time, federalism in America has allowed local and state governments to function as moral educators in many respects, especially in the public schools for most of our history. But the most important schools for republican virtue in America have been the churches, as Tocqueville pointed out when he concluded that religion is the first of our political institutions.[22]

Tocqueville saw religion restraining the self-interested elements of American liberalism and turning them toward public-spirited forms of citizenship that allowed republican institutions to survive.[23] John Adams, during his first year as vice-president under the new liberal constitutional regime, drew similar conclusions: "We have no government armed with power capable of contending with human passions unbridled by morality and religion. Our constitution," he wrote, "was made only for a moral and a religious people. It is wholly inadequate to the government of any other."[24] For all the brilliance of Tocqueville's institutional analysis, his cultural functionalism assumes too simple a picture of moral consensus for modern America, if not for his own era. Today philosophical liberals and their communitarian critics alike are using oversimplified models of a comprehensive value-consensus or a value-neutral arrangement of contractual rules and rights, allied with similarly streamlined conceptions of "legitimation" to define the functional relation of religion to political authority. These ideas skew our vision of the public church and its culturally active, argumentative role in the polity, by contrast to its institutional separation from the state. They also obscure an enduring criterion of our polity's moral health: whether the uneasy but essential compromise that John Adams summed up between republicanism and liberal constitutionalism in American public life remains vigorously well-balanced today.

Political thinkers from Aristotle to Montesquieu have seen republics always tending to degenerate and require reform; for republics depend on the mores, customs, and the overall way of life of a people, which embrace their religion and economy, not just the regulatory structure of their state and laws. The substance and integrity of traditionally religious and republican forms of moral insight and argument are necessary to rebalance, not replace, the interests, rights, and contracts of liberal individualism in American public discourse. This public need entails a commitment to the interdependent forms of community that inspire such insight and the ways of life that enact it. This public need also pertains to our understanding of the modern welfare state itself, not just to specific problems it faces.

The Polity as a Moral Cummunity

In sharp contrast to the half-century of civic and religious debate that surrounded the rise of the American welfare state, it has undergone great expansion and then slowdown if not reversal since 1960 with little real *moral* argument on its overall growth and limits, and, more important, on its overarching purpose, order, and justice. With the dramatic exception of civil rights issues, political consideration of its recent growth has been concerned chiefly with judging the legitimacy of claims to social provision by numerous groups of "clients" according to the dynamics of group-interest pluralism. Its still more recent slowdown has taken place on much the same grounds, with the state's mainly middle-class clients welcoming "tax relief" in the face of eroded real income and bolstered spending on defense, debt service, and S and L bailouts.

It is an ironic picture, as Theda Skoopol notes, of farmers sustained since the New Deal by public works and price supports who now "oppose government spending, welfare, and bureaucracy and merely want interest subsidies for farmers." They are joined by blue-collar union members and middle-class suburbanites long helped by public programs from the Wagner Act to home mortgage subsidies. "The unionists want particular jobs in particular industries saved through federal bail-outs, but oppose 'welfare hand-outs,' and the middle-class suburbanites want college loans preserved but oppose 'bureaucratic quotas' enforcing affirmative action for blacks. And so forth." Now that "federal spending does not appear to guarantee a healthy economy and a steadily growing pie of benefits and opportunities from which every interest group can have more with no hard public choices," concludes Theda Skocpol, we must face the need for effective political coalitions to span class, race, and urban-rural interests and set up "authoritative governmental centers" to engage in national economic planning and action.[25]

But under these conditions, in which asserted rights often conflict and aggregated interests always unbalance the public budget's bottom line, we must also face the need to deepen our moral insight and broaden the argument into our reasons and institutions for common provision. Perhaps we can agree with Michael Walzer's affirmation that "the welfare state expresses a certain civil spirit, a sense of mutuality, a commitment to justice. . . . Communal provision is required for the whole range of social goods that make up what we think of as our way of life. Not my way of life or yours, but ours, the life we couldn't have if we didn't plan for it and pay for it together."[26]

Yet even if we can so agree, we cannot plan and pay for the social goods that make up "our" way of life unless we learn from and argue with one another about the different moral goods that constitute the diverse ways of life we share in practice. The meanings of mutuality, civil spirit, and justice are not uniformly self-evident to all of us in each institutional sphere or in their proper interrelation. This is not just because our interests conflict, and our perceptions vary with our social location. It is also because we construe these ideas within different moral traditions, and the different ways we read and interrelate these traditions vary with our cultural location. We will not be willing to plan and pay for our essential social goods, unless we can elicit from one another and criticize the thick moral goods and exemplary stories from contrasting cultural traditions that enable us to envision our polity, and our society, as a moral community. As long as it remains a morally neutral association of communities with their own "values and life-styles," we will be moved to take a public part in the social order only when it is *our* rights that are being threatened or *our* ox that is being gored.

Who Is Left Out?

Quantitative evidence indicates that structural changes in our political and economic institutions over the past two decades have made public participation even less likely among the undereducated lower middle class and the underpaid working poor—let alone among the jobless and homeless poor, who are disproportionately women, children, and persons of color.[27]

Such facts should make us skeptical of calls for greater public participation that extend beyond the educated middle class, as Herbert Gans chided *Habits of the Heart*.[28] This holds true even when this participation is depicted as the means to achieve greater economic justice. We should be skeptical, that is, unless we recognize how education, work, and economic security themselves function as constitutive conditions of such public participation.

So we should indeed ask which governing symbols and modes of moral discourse best express and justify a good society, and inspire us to work for it. But we should also ask which institutional conditions are needed to cultivate genuinely dialectical, representative civic discourse and the sort of persons who can practice it. Such moral conversation requires a circle of persons small enough and possessed of enough shared time and learning to permit an equal and alternative balance of participation in turning a topic round and round.[29] Thoughtful and decisive civic conversation in a mass society, if it is to extend beyond small elites, requires broad economic participation and social equality. It requires sufficiently high economic production, bureaucratic efficiency, and wide distribution of their benefits to free the time and focus the attention of women and men of every race and economic class for the shared reflection, learning, and cultural fluency that confer the public power to speak and the moral authority to be heeded. Because shared public languages and arguments about how to live together are what unite us as a people, not identical interests or shared values, we need to develop a more civic conception of community itself, instead of the homogeneously romanticized, white clapboard idea of it that now prevails.[30] We need communal as well as political institutions that serve to encourage debate about our moral differences and confusions about how to live together, instead of striving simply to celebrate our common convictions and broker our opposing interests. We need to encourage such debate, instead of trying to foreclose it for the sake of collective self-interest in a slice of the nation's economic pie or the comfortable fellow-feeling of a neighborhood community, congregation, or family. This means we need to revive a more educative, less state-bound conception of politics itself, grounded in dialectical argument instead of administrative procedures or legislative interest-brokering.

It also means we need to revive a more covenantal and catechetical conception of religion, rooted in the sacramental soul of shared worship yet committed to critical, conciliar public dialogue and opposed to theocratic lobbying. Instead of overprivatized pastoral care for the many and underpublicized political activism for the few in the denominational equivalent of a cultural free market, the church as a school for virtue, like good schools themselves, offers the polity a model for civic life more like a forum than a marketplace, an administrative bureaucracy, or, for that matter, "a bully pulpit." The church as the community of all God's creatures offers the larger society no prospect of an orthodox paradise on earth, a sectarian voting bloc, or a cheerful congregational fellowship writ large. Like republican self-government, in truth, it offers us the sometimes uplifting, sometimes tragically troubling, often uncomfortable practices of a moral community where we cannot escape or exclude the strangers we are to engage in argument as well as love.

Notes

1. See Robert Bellah, Richard Madsen, William Sullivan, Ann Swidler, and Steven Tipton, *Habits of the Heart* (Berkeley: University of California Press, 1985), pp. 29–34.
2. Charles Taylor, "Religion in a Free Society," unpublished paper presented at the Williamsburg Charter Foundation Symposium on the First Amendment Religious Liberty Clauses and American Public Life, 1988, Charlottesville, Va.), pp. 1–2.
3. Here and below, argument and often wording follow Robert N. Bellah, "Religion and the Legitimation of the American Republic," in Robert N. Bellah and Phillip Hammond, eds., *Varieties of Civil Religion* (New York: Harper and Row, 1980), pp. 7–10.
4. Ibid. See also Michael J. Sandel, "Religious Liberty: Freedom of Conscience or Freedom of Choice?" unpublished paper, presented at the Williamsburg Charter Foundation Symposium, 1988.
5. John Rawls, "Kantian Constructivism in Moral Theory," *Journal of Philosophy* 77 (1980): 536, 542. See also Rawls, "Justice as Fairness: Political Not Metaphysical," *Philosophy and Public Affairs* 14, no. 3 (1985): 223, 225, 226, 230.
6. See Michael J. Perry, "Religious Dimensions of the American Political Process, unpublished paper presented at the Conference on Religious Dimensions of American Constitutionalism, Emory University Law School, 1988, p. 13; also his *Morality, Politics, and Law* (New York: Oxford University Press, 1988). Critics of Rawls on this controversial point include Michael J. Sandel, *Liberalism and the Limits of Justice* (Cambridge: Cambridge University Press, 1982), pp. 1–11, 12, 55, 58–59, 172–173; Sandel, "The Procedural Republic and the Unencumbered Self," *Political Theory* 12 (1984); and Samuel Scheffler, "Moral Scepticism and Ideals of the Person," *Monist* 62 (1979): 288, 295.
7. Rawls, "Political Not Metaphysical," p. 233.
8. Rawls, "Kantian Constructivism," p. 569; quoted in Perry, "Religious Dimensions," p. 44, n. 19.

9. Rawls, "Political Not Metaphysical," pp. 223, 224–225.
10. Perry, "Religious Dimensions," pp. 31–32.
11. Rawls, "Political Not Metaphysical," pp. 223, 225–226. Cf. Perry, "Religious Dimensions," p. 23.
12. Steven Tipton, "Moral Languages and the Good Society," *Soundings* 69, nos. 1–2 (1986): 167–171.
13. Martin Marty, "Religion and American Constitutionalism," unpublished paper, presented at the Conference on Religious Dimensions of American Constitutionalism, Emory University Law School, 1988.
14. Rawls, "Political Not Metaphysical," pp. 224–225.
15. Bellah, "Religion and Legitimation," pp. 11–12. See also Taylor, "Free Society," p. 8.
16. Ibid.
17. Bellah, "Religion and Legitimation," p. 14.
18. Martin E. Marty, *The Public Church: Mainline, Evangelical, Catholic* (New York: Crossroad, 1981), p. 16.
19. Taylor, "Free Society," p. 14.
20. Robert Wuthnow, *The Restructuring of American Religion* (Princeton: Princeton University Press, 1988), Chapters 7–9. See also Wade Clark Roof and William McKinney, *American Mainline Religion* (New Brunswick: Rutgers University Press, 1987), Chapter 3.
21. Bellah, "Religion and Legitimation," pp. 16–17.
22. Alexis de Tocqueville, *Democracy in America*, ed. J. P. Mayer (Garden City, N.Y.: Doubleday Anchor Books, 1969), p. 292.
23. Bellah, "Religion and Legitimation," pp. 16–17.
24. John Adams, quoted in John R. Howe, Jr., ed., *The Changing Political Thought of John Adams* (Princeton: Princeton University Press, 1966), p. 185.
25. Theda Skoopol, "The Legacies of New Deal Liberalism," unpublished paper, 1982.
26. Michael Walzer, "The Community," *The New Republic* 186, no. 13 (1982): 11–12.
27. See, for example, Ronald Jepperson and David Kamens, "The Expanding State and the U.S. 'Civic Culture': The Changing Character of Political Participation and Legitimation in the Post-War U.S. Polity," unpublished paper, presented at the annual meeting of the American Political Science Association, 1985.
28. Herbert J. Gans, *Middle American Individualism* (New York: Free Press, 1988), pp. 103–120.
29. Ralph B. Potter, "Qualms of a Believer," in Charles Reynolds and Ralph Norman, eds., *Community in America: The Challenge of Habits of the Heart* (Berkeley: University of California Press, 1988), pp. 125–126.
30. Christopher Lasch, "The Communitarian Critique of Liberalism," in Reynolds and Norman, ed., *Community in America*, pp. 173–184.

Index

287